Ranma 1/2

VOL. 2

VIZ Media Edition

STORY & ART BY

RUMIKO TAKAHASHI

Ranma 1/2

VOL. 2
VIZ Media Edition (2nd Edition)

Story and Art by
RUMIKO TAKAHASHI

English Adaptation/Gerard Jones and Matt Thorn
Touch-Up Art & Lettering/Wayne Truman
Cover Design/Hidemi Sahara
Graphics & Design/Sean Lee
Editors (1st Edition)/Satoru Fujii and Trish Ledoux
Editor (VIZ Media Edition)/Julie Davis

VP, Production/Alvin Lu
VP, Publishing Licensing/Rika Inouye
VP, Sales & Product Marketing/Gonzalo Ferreyra
VP, Creative/Linda Espinosa
Publisher/Hyoe Narita

Printed in Canada

Published by VIZ Media, LLC
P.O. Box 77010
San Francisco, CA 94107

1st Edition published 1993

VIZ Media Edition (2nd Edition)
10
First printing, April 2003
Tenth printing, March 2009

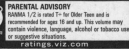

PARENTAL ADVISORY
RANMA 1/2 is rated T+ for Older Teen and is
recommended for ages 16 and up. This volume may
contain violence, language, alcohol or tobacco use,
or suggestive situations.
ratings.viz.com

www.viz.com

store.viz.com

CONTENTS

STORY THUS FAR

Soun Tendo is the owner and proprietor of a martial arts school. He has three lovely young daughters—Akane, Nabiki, and Kasumi. According to an agreement Soun made years ago with his old friend Genma Saotome, one of these three must become the fiancée of Genma's teenage son, Ranma. Youngest daughter Akane—who says she hates boys—is quickly nominated for bridal duty by her sisters.

Unfortunately, Ranma and his father have suffered a strange accident. While training in China, both plunged into one of many "accursed" springs at the legendary martial arts training ground of Jusenkyo. These springs transform the unlucky dunkee into whoever—or whatever—drowned there hundreds of years ago.

From now on, a splash of cold water turns Ranma's father into a giant panda, and Ranma becomes a beautiful, busty young woman. Hot water reverses the effect...but only until next time.

To make matters worse, although their parents are still determined to see Ranma and Akane marry and carry on the training hall, both seem to have a strange talent for accumulating suitors. Will the two ever work out their differences, get rid of all these extra people, or just call the whole thing off? And will Ranma ever get rid of his curse?

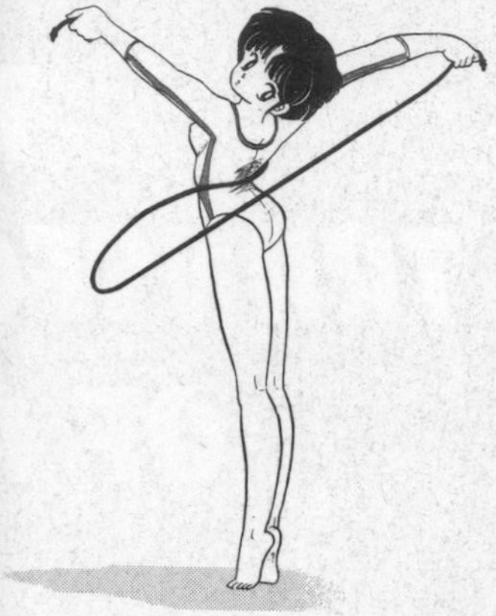

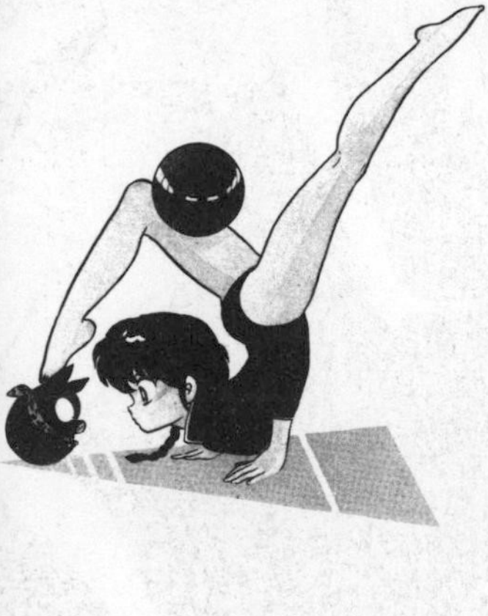

Part 1

THE TRANSFORMATION OF RYOGA

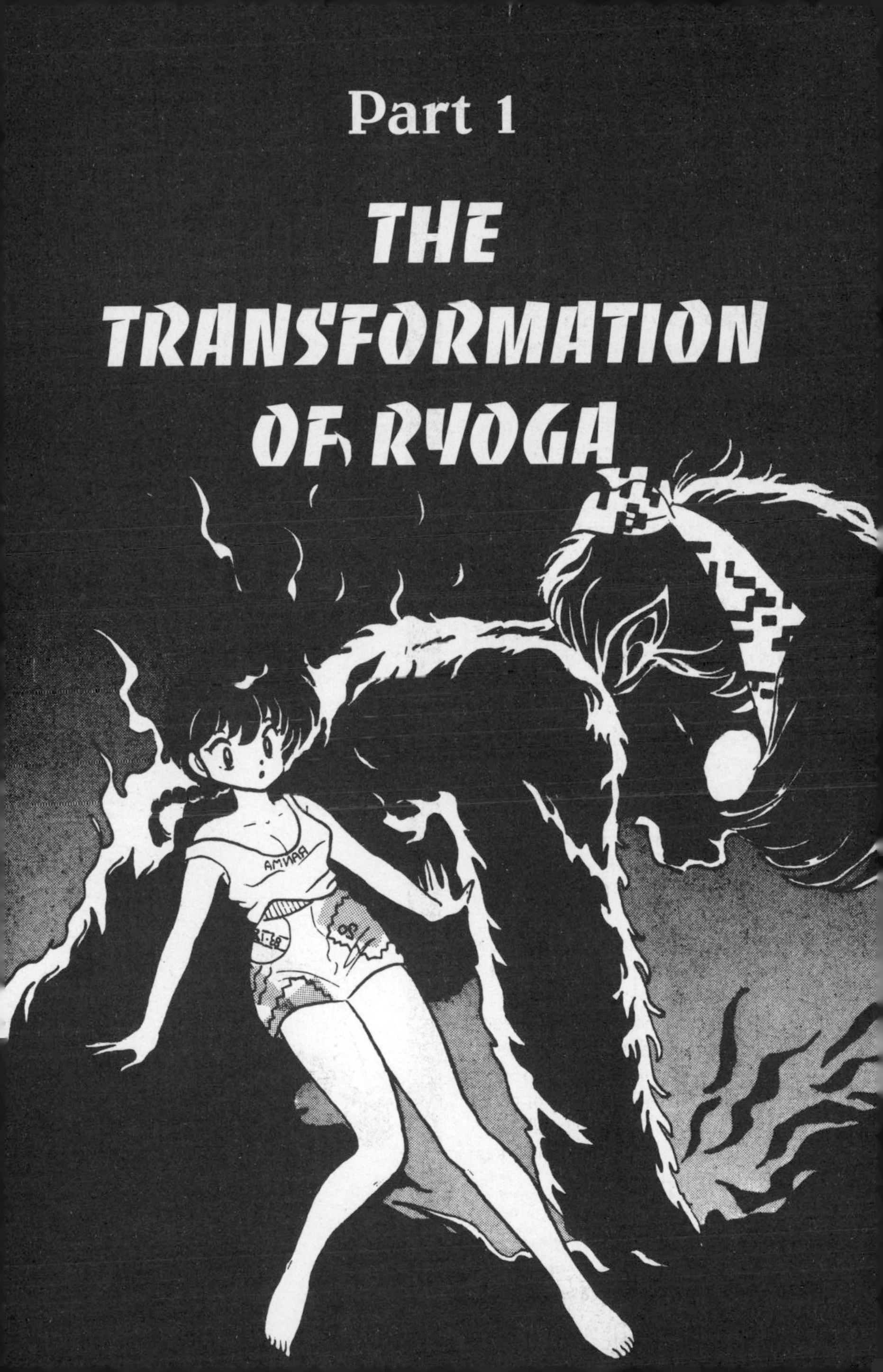

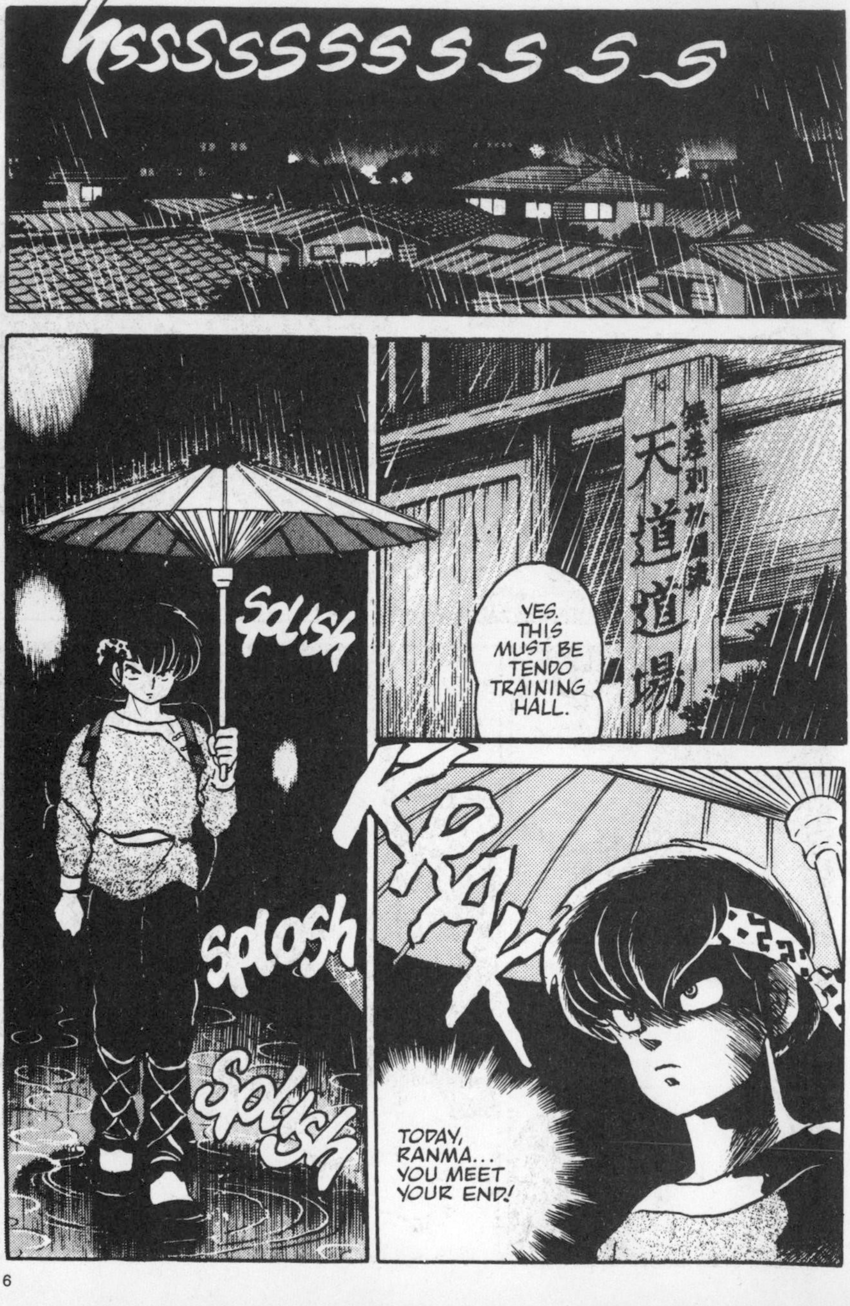
hsssssssssss
splish
splosh
splash
無差別格闘流
天道道場
YES. THIS MUST BE TENDO TRAINING HALL.
KRAK
TODAY, RANMA... YOU MEET YOUR END!

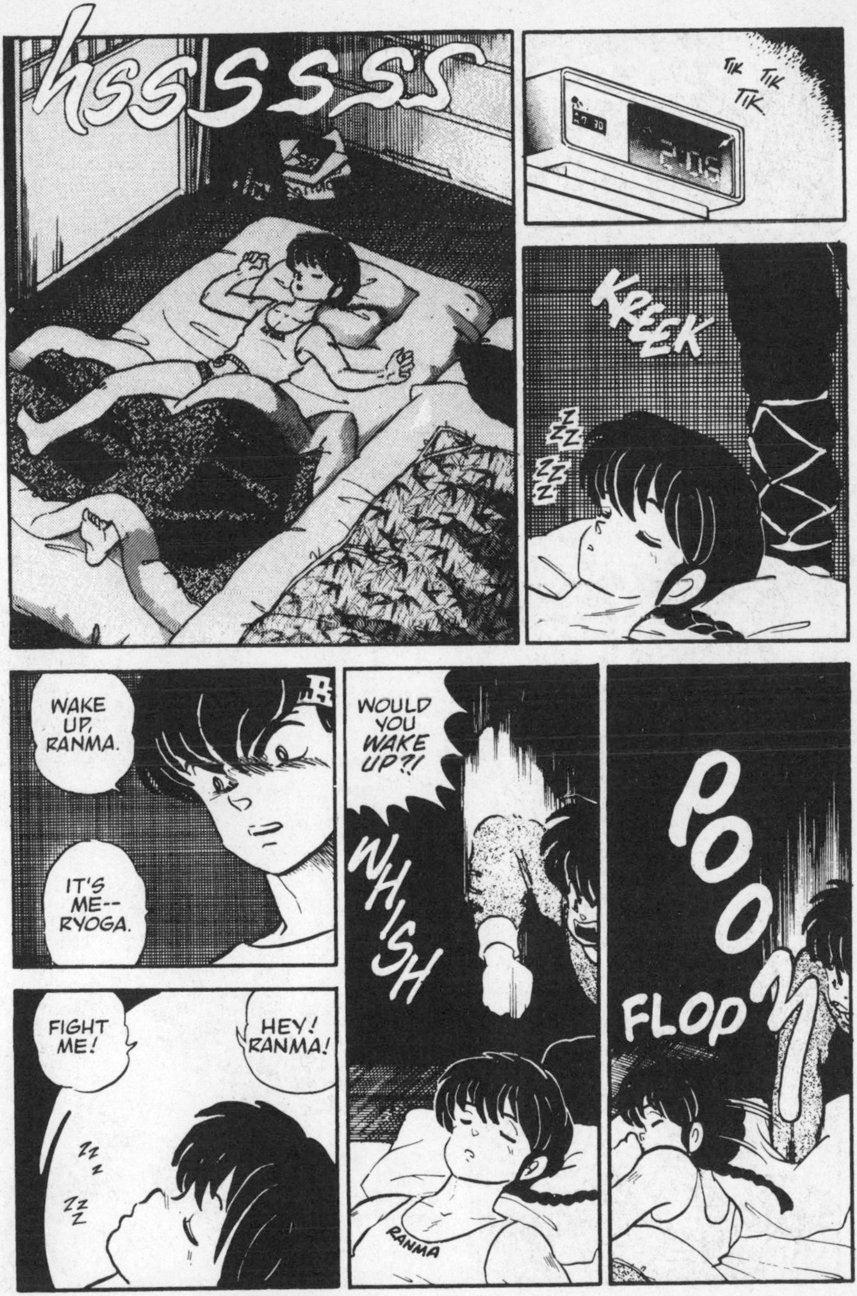
hssssss
TIK TIK TIK
KREEK
Z Z Z
Z Z Z
WAKE UP, RANMA.
IT'S ME-- RYOGA.
WOULD YOU WAKE UP?!
WHISH
POOOM
FLOP
FIGHT ME!
HEY! RANMA!
Z Z Z
Z Z Z
RANMA

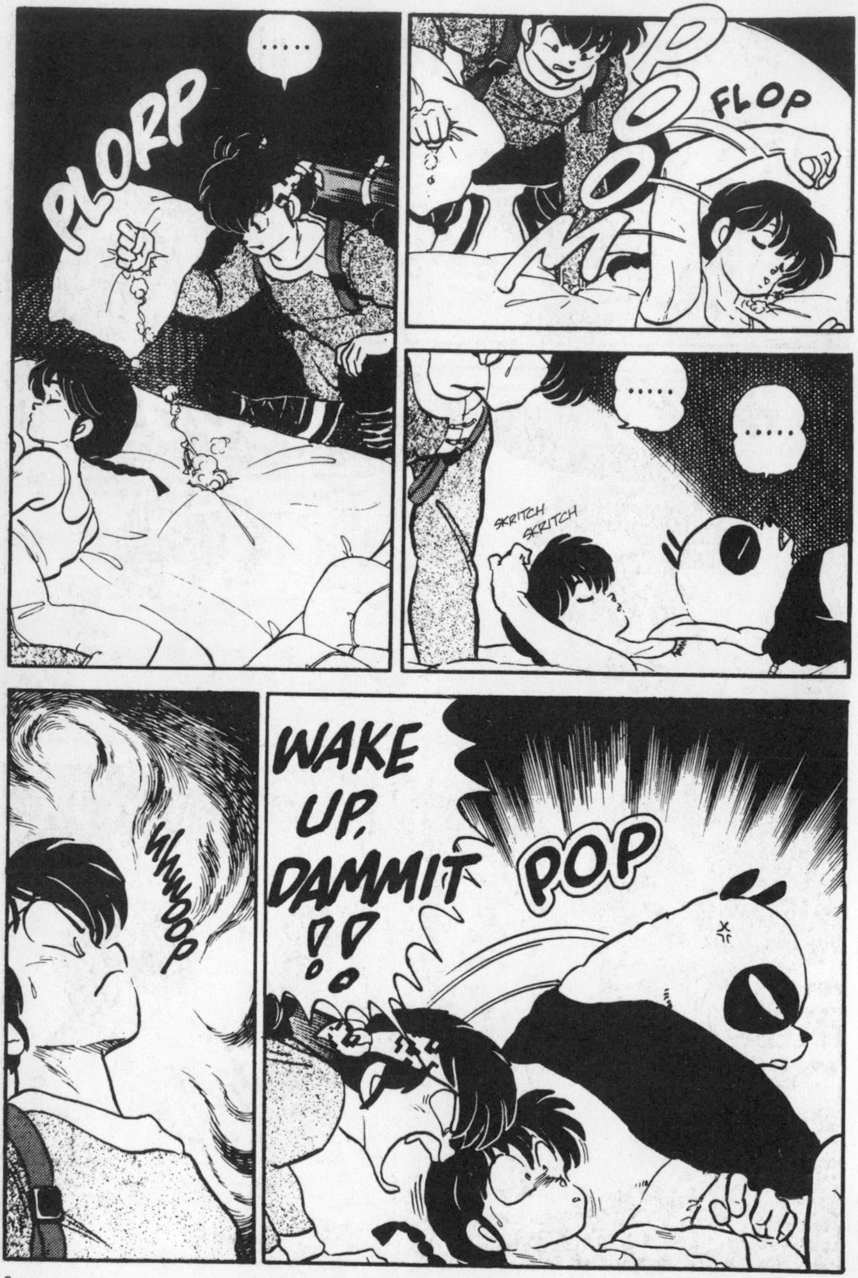
......
PLORP
POOOM
FLOP
......
......
SKRITCH
SKRITCH
WHOOP
WAKE UP, DAMMIT!!
POP

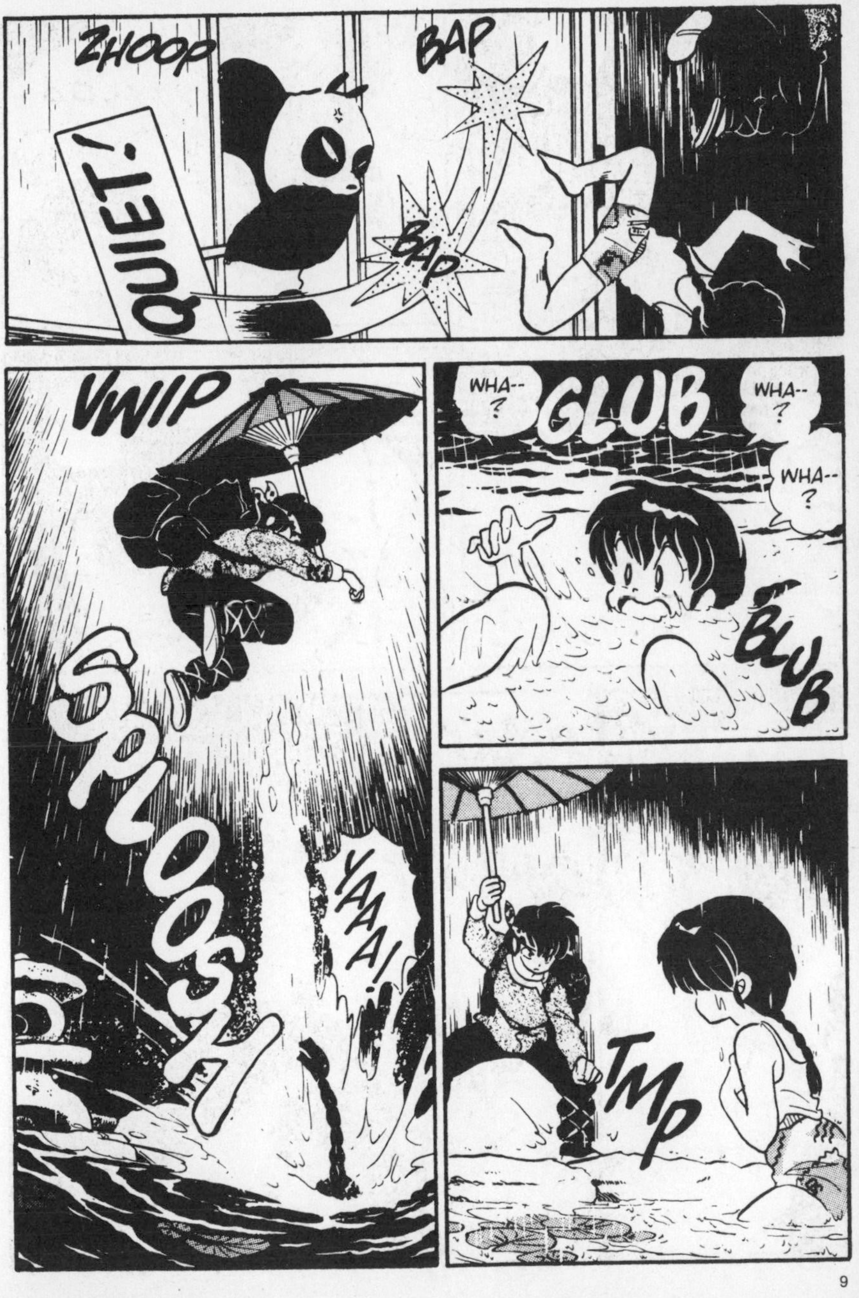
ZHOOP
QUIET!
BAP
BAP
VWIP
SPLOOSH!
YAAAA!
WHA-- ?
GLUB
WHA-- ?
WHA-- ?
BLUB
TMP

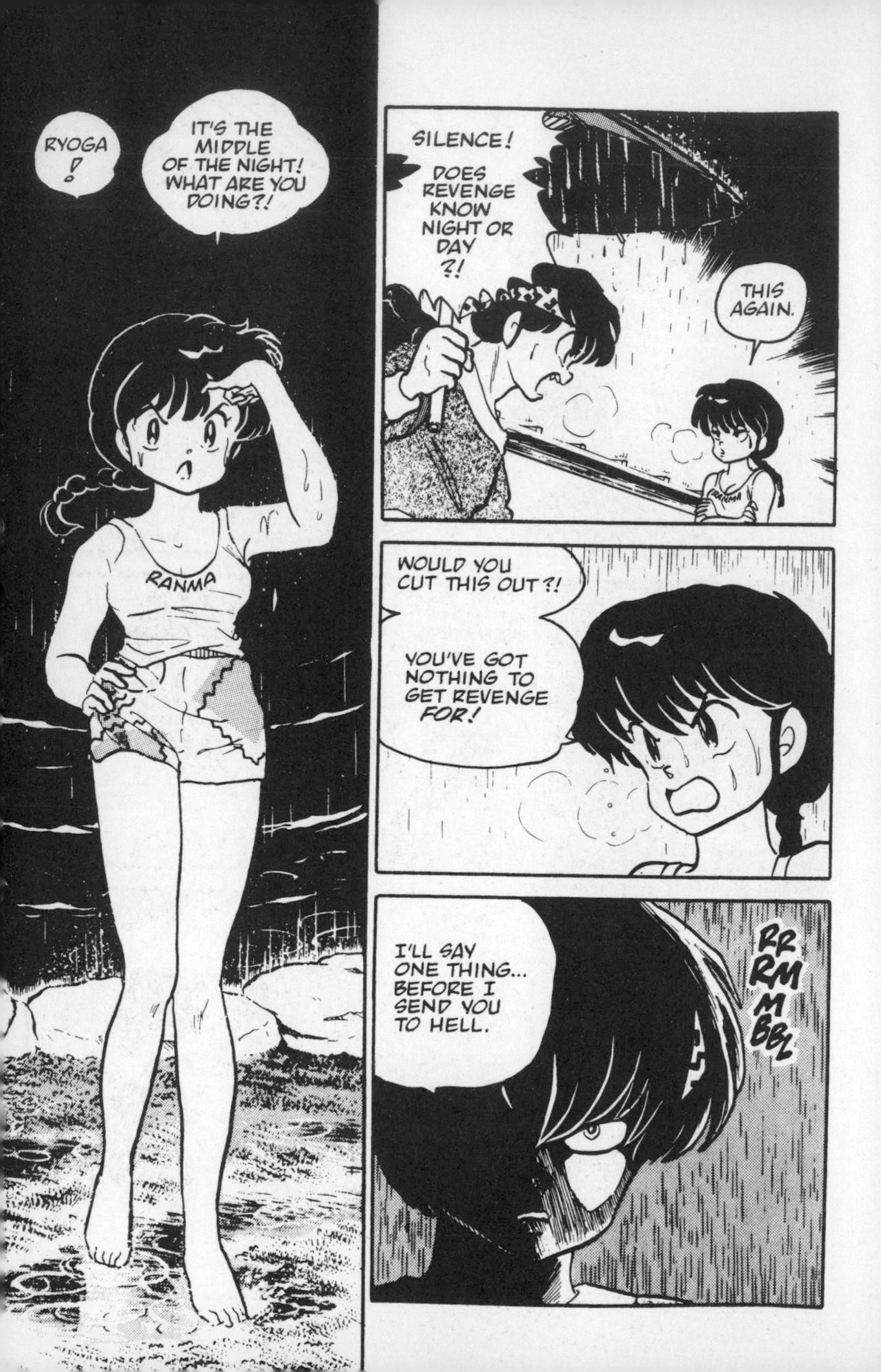
RYOGA!
IT'S THE MIDDLE OF THE NIGHT! WHAT ARE YOU DOING?!
RANMA
SILENCE!
DOES REVENGE KNOW NIGHT OR DAY?!
THIS AGAIN.
RANMA
WOULD YOU CUT THIS OUT?!
YOU'VE GOT NOTHING TO GET REVENGE FOR!
I'LL SAY ONE THING... BEFORE I SEND YOU TO HELL.
RRRMMBBL

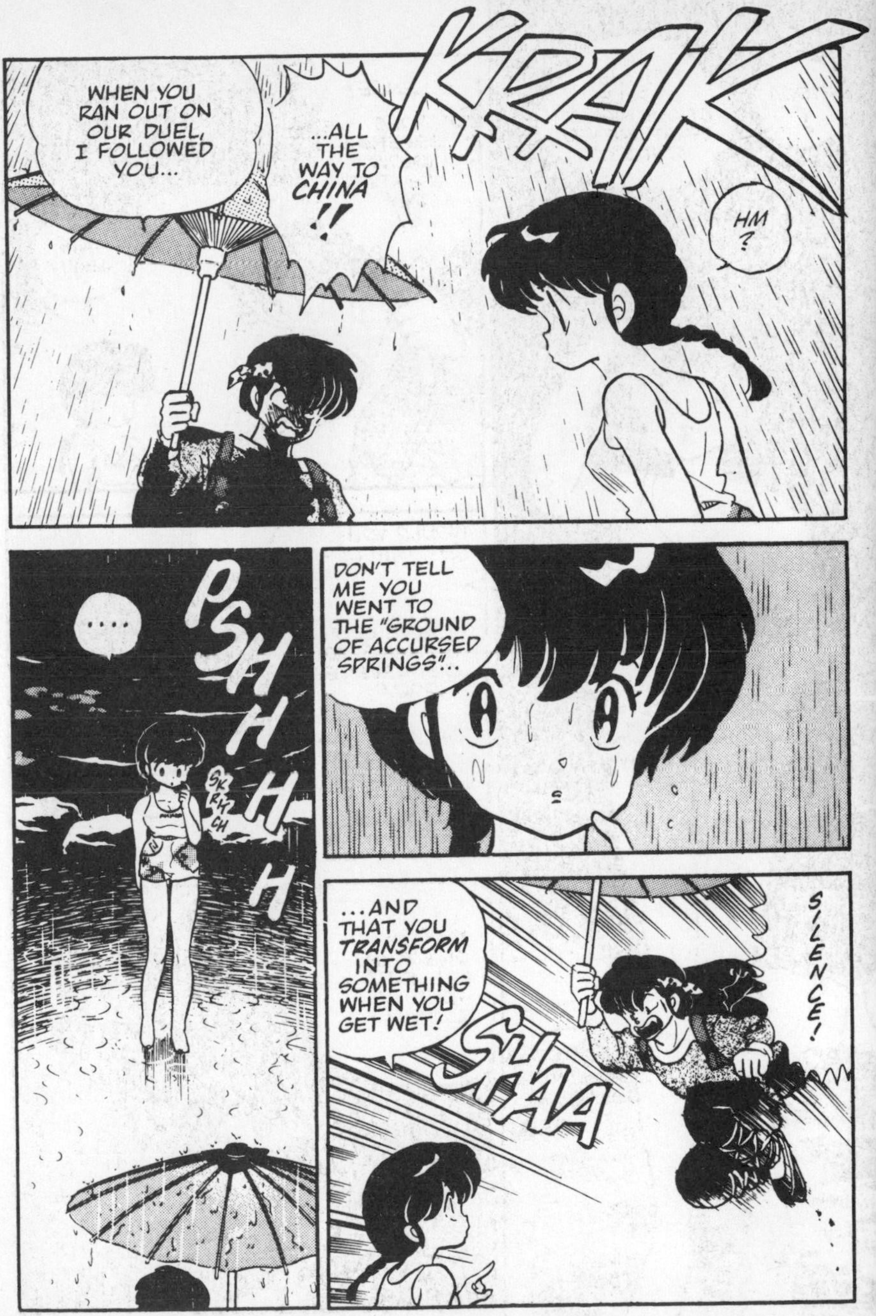
WHEN YOU RAN OUT ON OUR DUEL, I FOLLOWED YOU...
...ALL THE WAY TO CHINA !!
KRAK
HM ?
....
PSHHHHH
SKRTCH
DON'T TELL ME YOU WENT TO THE "GROUND OF ACCURSED SPRINGS"...
...AND THAT YOU TRANSFORM INTO SOMETHING WHEN YOU GET WET!
SHAA
SILENCE!

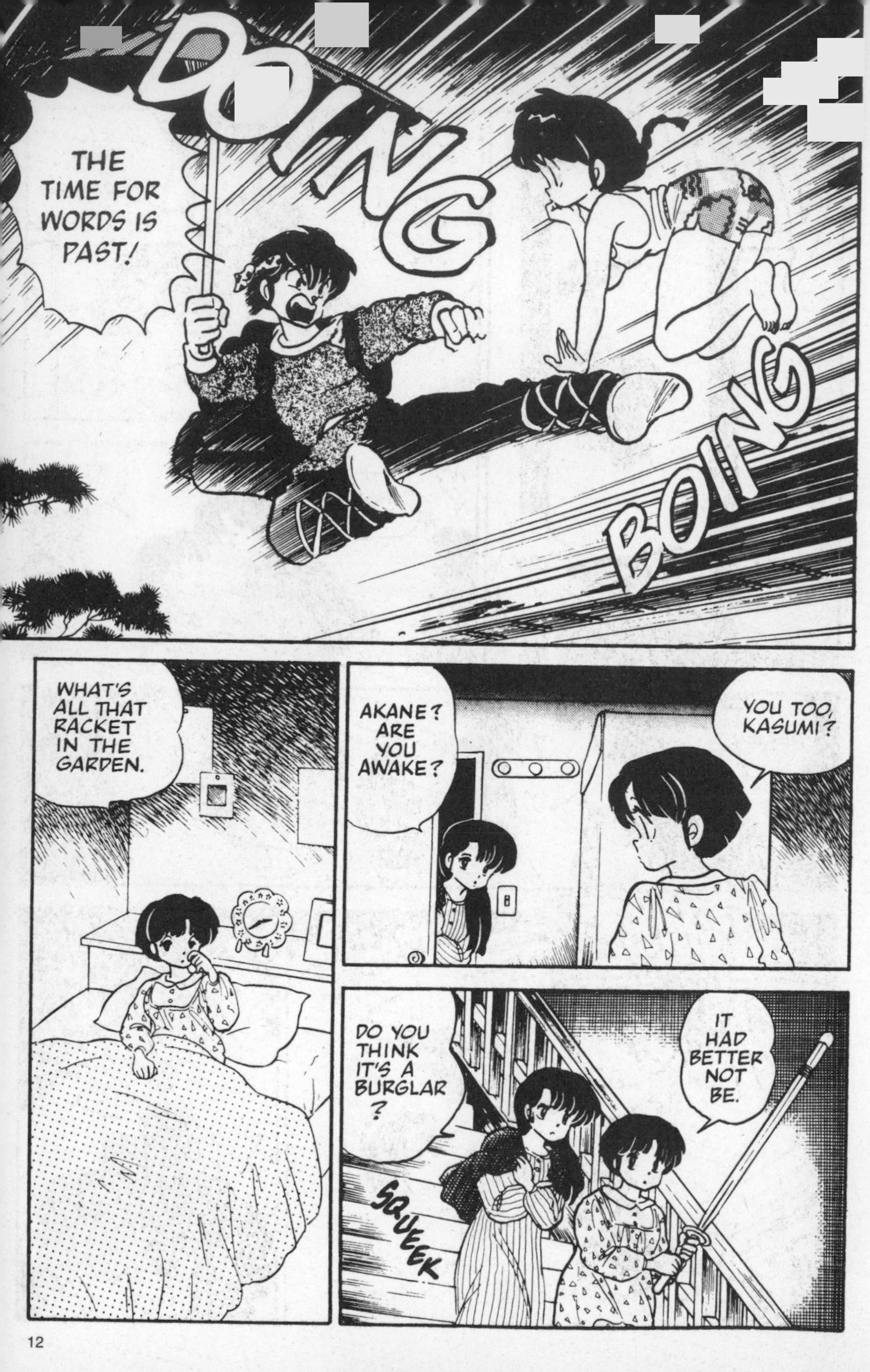
DOING
THE TIME FOR WORDS IS PAST!
BOING
WHAT'S ALL THAT RACKET IN THE GARDEN.
AKANE? ARE YOU AWAKE?
YOU TOO, KASUMI?
DO YOU THINK IT'S A BURGLAR?
IT HAD BETTER NOT BE.
SQUEEK

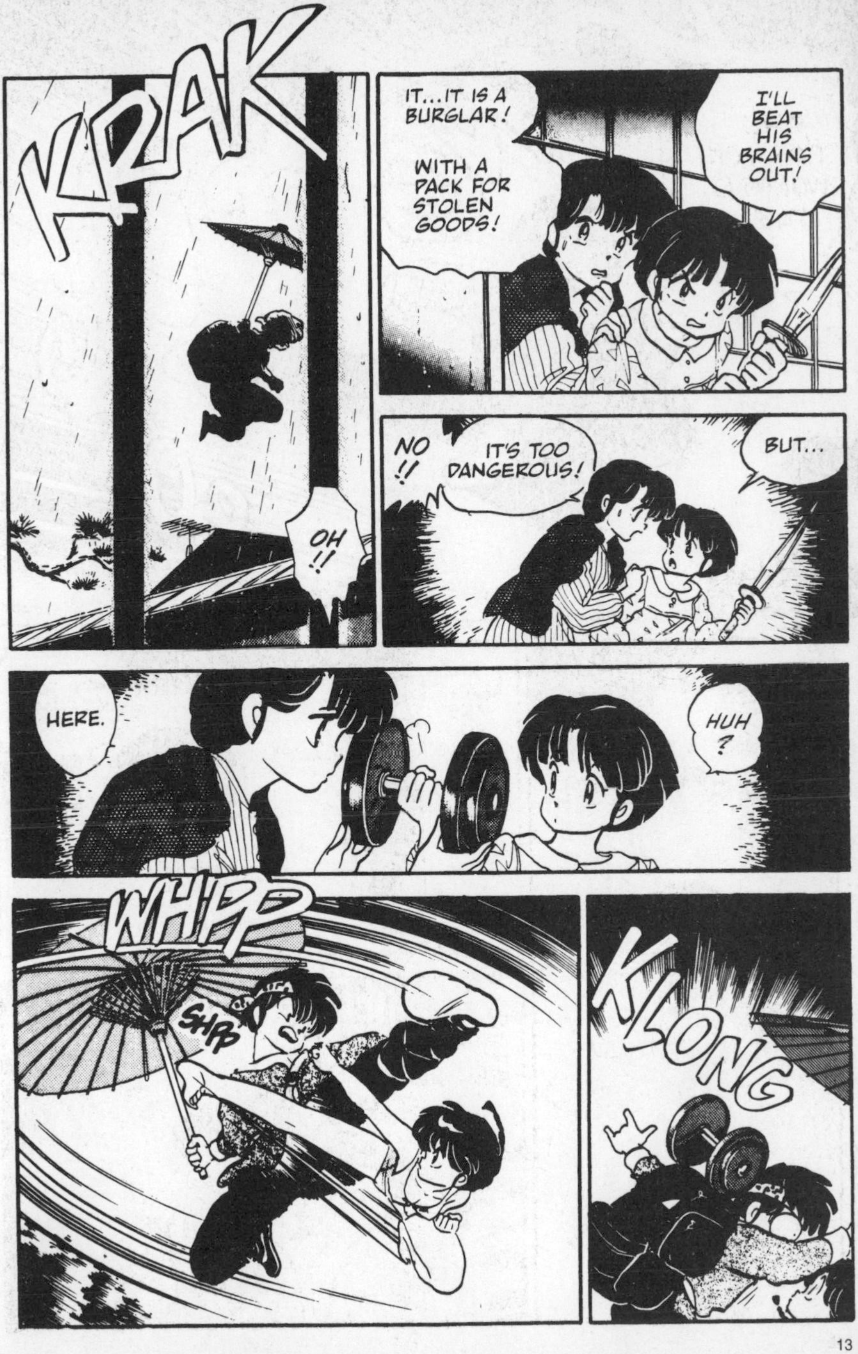
KRAK
OH !!
IT...IT IS A BURGLAR!
WITH A PACK FOR STOLEN GOODS!
I'LL BEAT HIS BRAINS OUT!
NO !!
IT'S TOO DANGEROUS!
BUT...
HERE.
HUH ?
WHPP
SHPP
KLONG

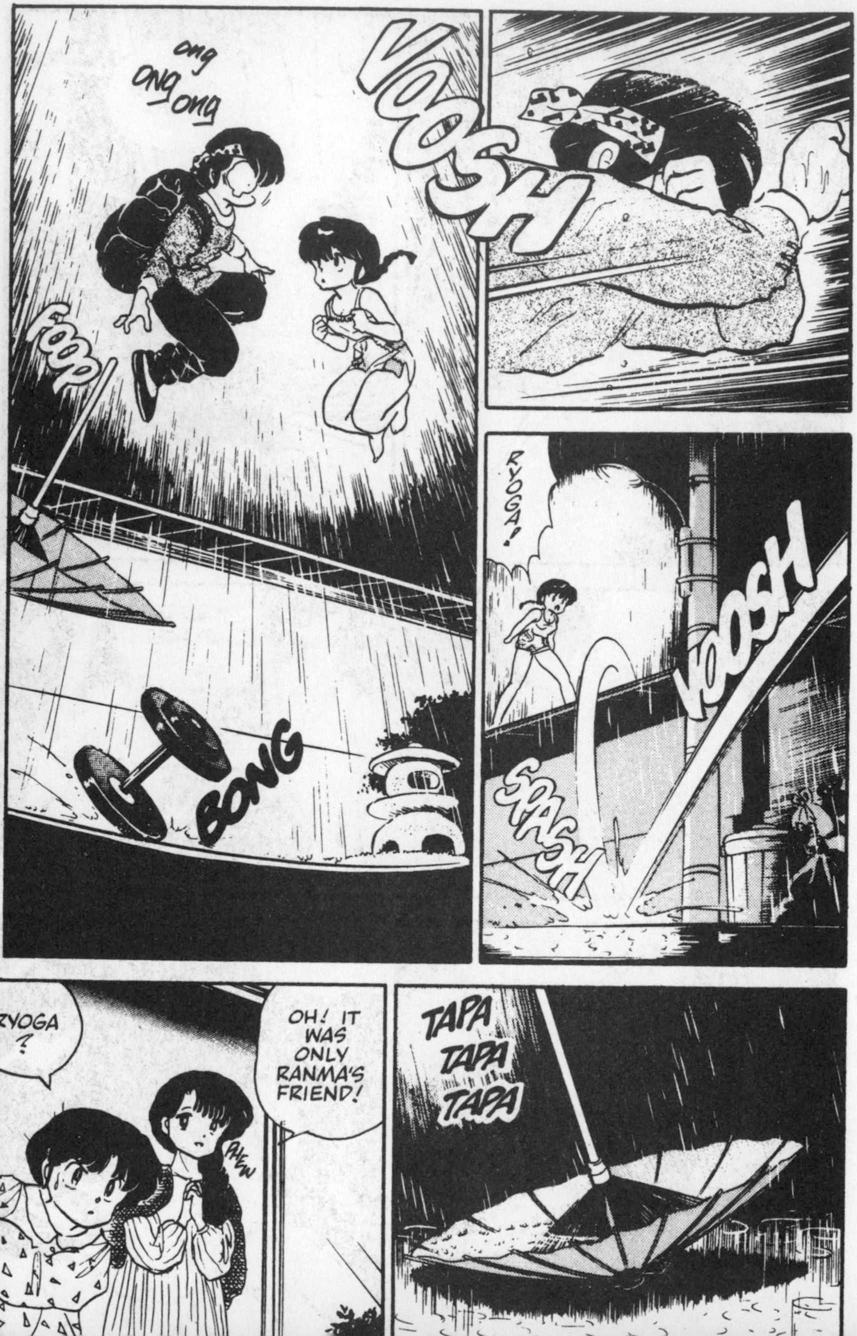
ong
ong ong
VOOSH
FOOP
BONG
RYOGA!
VOOSH
SPASH
RYOGA ?
OH! IT WAS ONLY RANMA'S FRIEND!
PHEW
TAPA TAPA TAPA

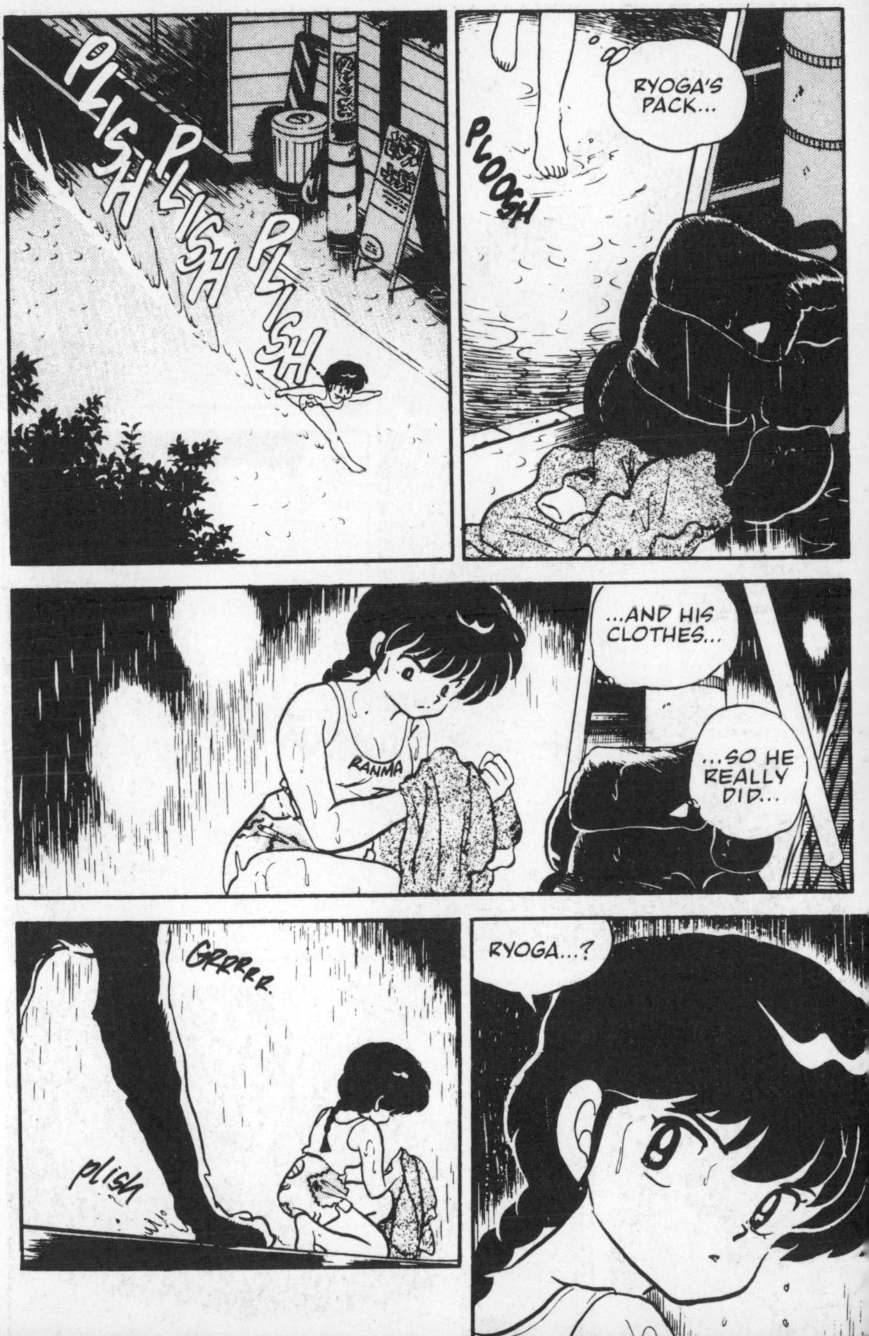
PLISH
PLISH
PLISH
PLISH
RYOGA'S PACK...
PLOOSH
...AND HIS CLOTHES...
...SO HE REALLY DID...
GRRRRR
plish
RYOGA...?

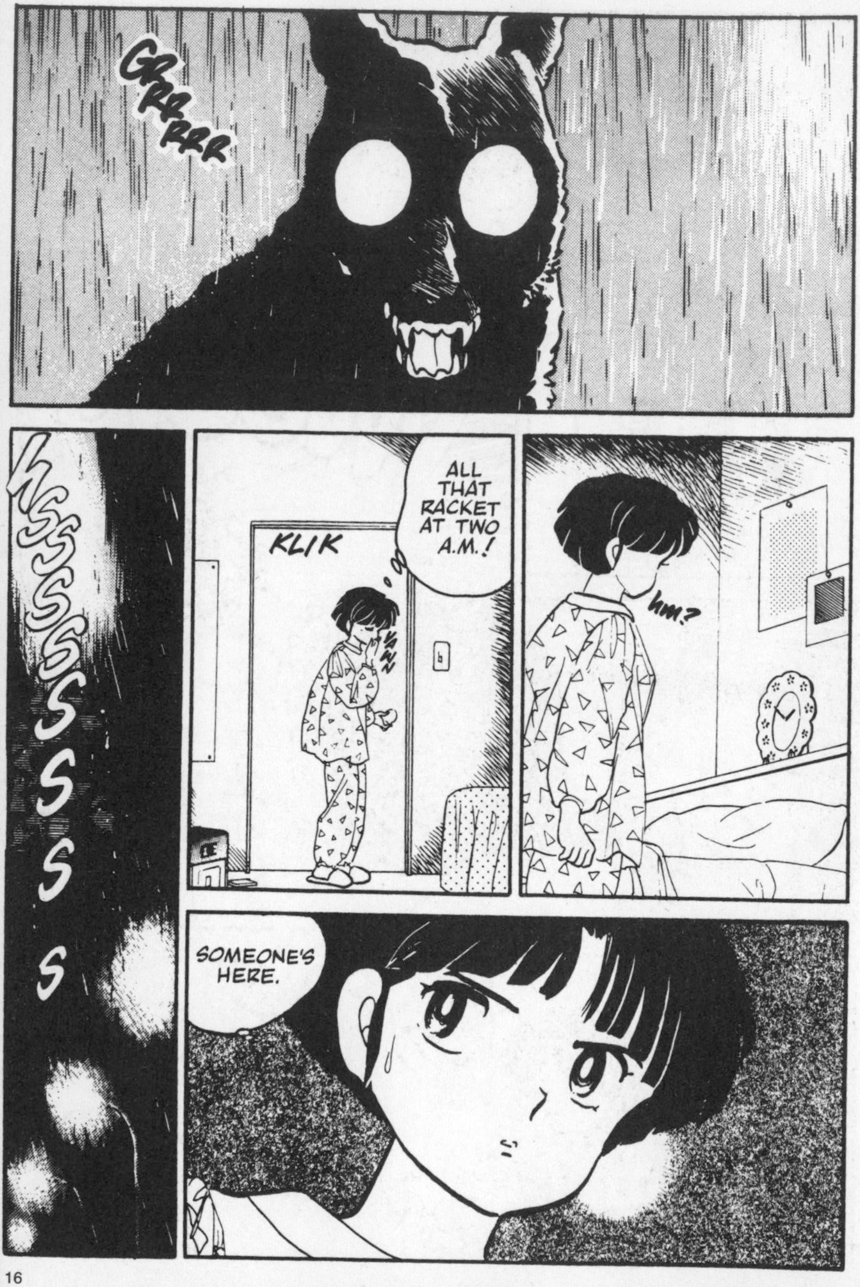
GRRRRRR
HSSSSSSSSS
KLIK
ALL THAT RACKET AT TWO A.M.!
YAWN
HM?
SOMEONE'S HERE.

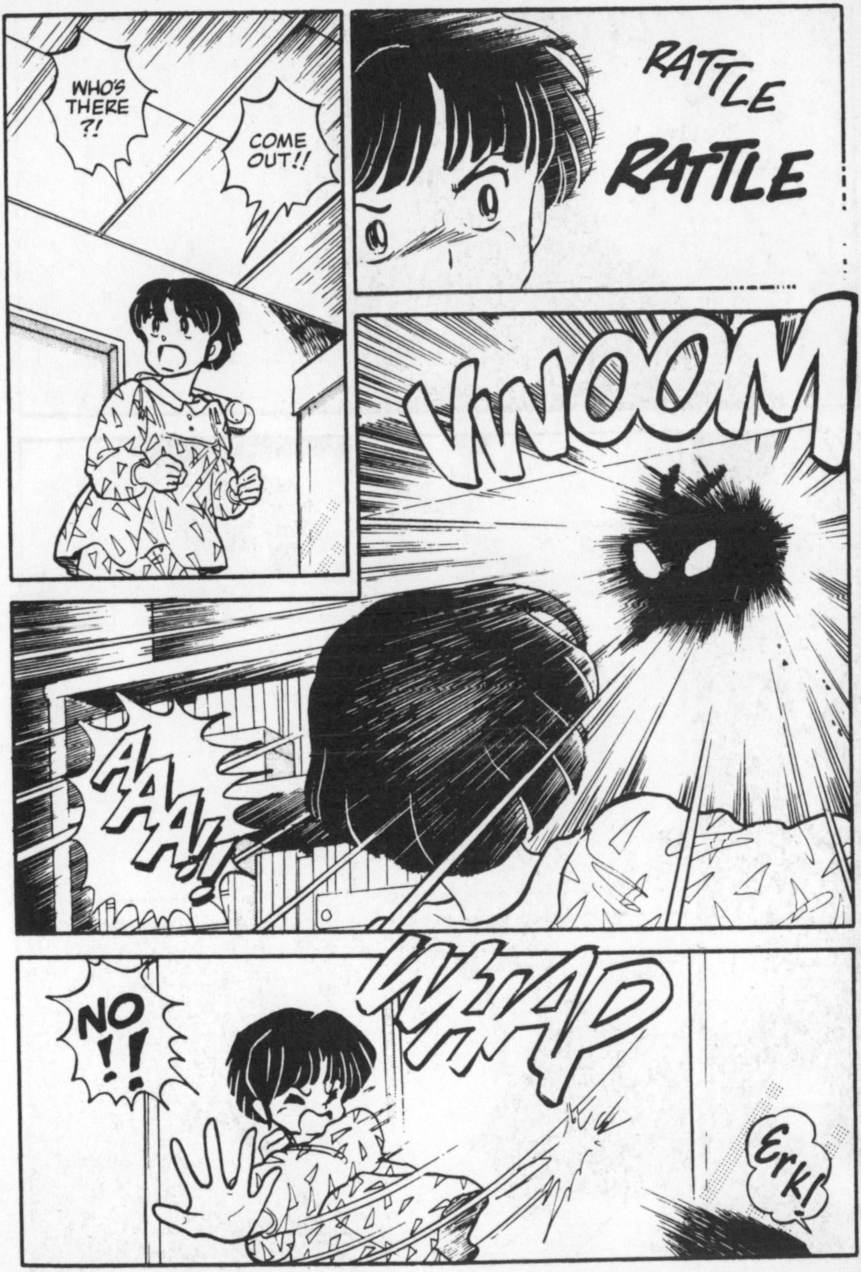
WHO'S THERE ?!
COME OUT!!
RATTLE
RATTLE
VWOOM
AAA!!
NO !!
WHAP
Erk!

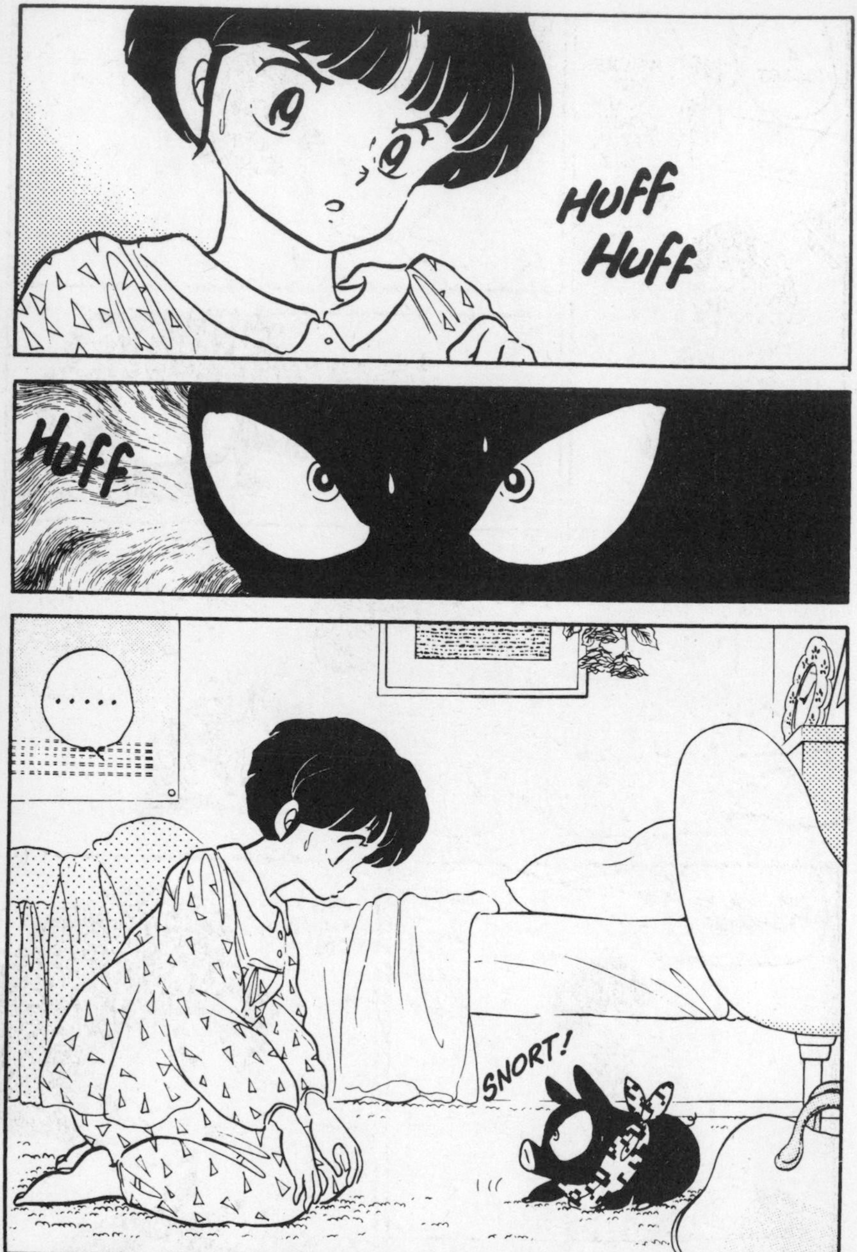
HUFF
HUFF
HUFF
.....
SNORT!

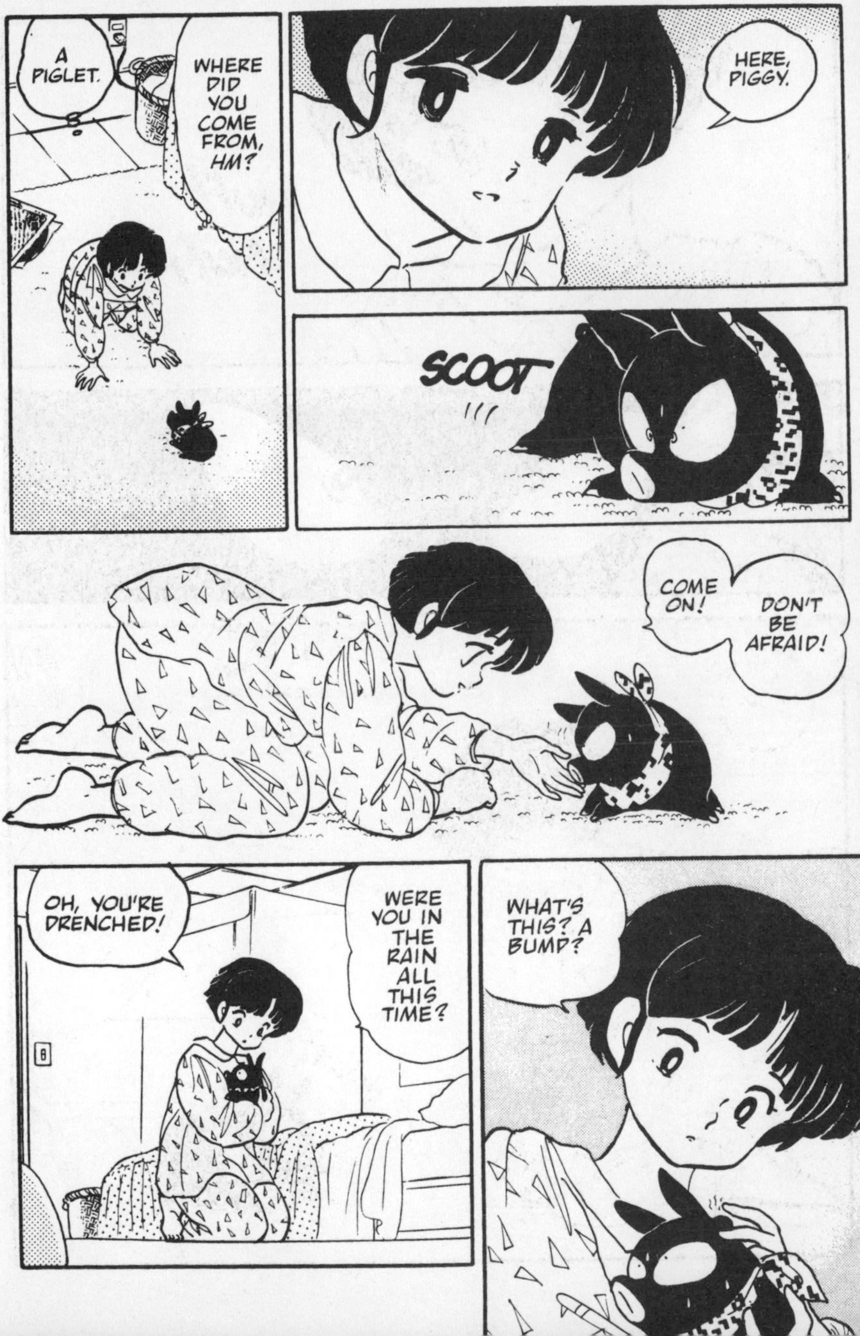
A PIGLET.
WHERE DID YOU COME FROM, HM?
HERE, PIGGY.
SCOOT
COME ON!
DON'T BE AFRAID!
OH, YOU'RE DRENCHED!
WERE YOU IN THE RAIN ALL THIS TIME?
WHAT'S THIS? A BUMP?

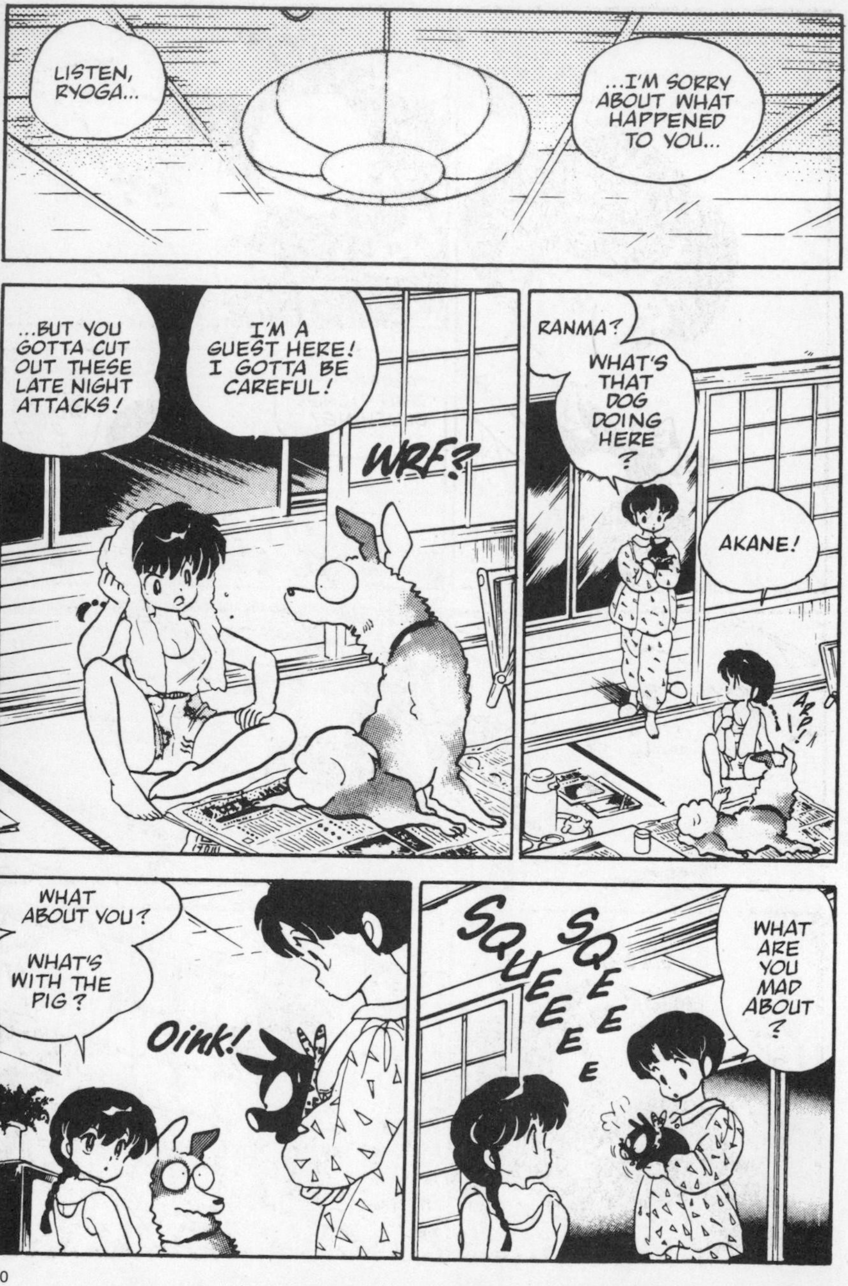
LISTEN, RYOGA...
...I'M SORRY ABOUT WHAT HAPPENED TO YOU...
...BUT YOU GOTTA CUT OUT THESE LATE NIGHT ATTACKS!
I'M A GUEST HERE! I GOTTA BE CAREFUL!
WRF?
RANMA?
WHAT'S THAT DOG DOING HERE?
AKANE!
ARP!
WHAT ABOUT YOU?
WHAT'S WITH THE PIG?
Oink!
SQUEEEE
SQEEEE
WHAT ARE YOU MAD ABOUT?

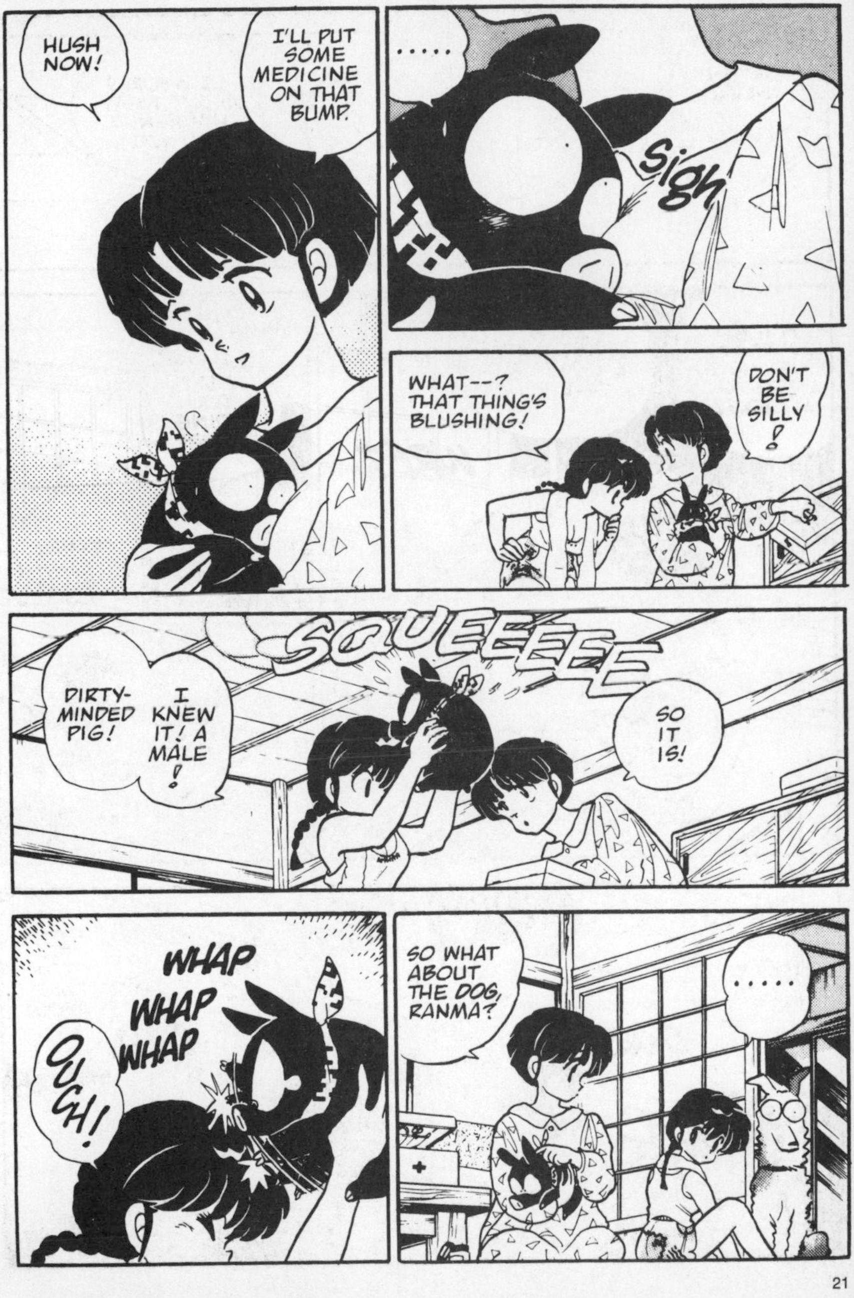
HUSH NOW!
I'LL PUT SOME MEDICINE ON THAT BUMP.
.....
Sigh
WHAT--? THAT THING'S BLUSHING!
DON'T BE SILLY!
SQUEEEEEE
DIRTY-MINDED PIG!
I KNEW IT! A MALE!
SO IT IS!
WHAP
WHAP
WHAP
OUCH!
SO WHAT ABOUT THE DOG, RANMA?
.....

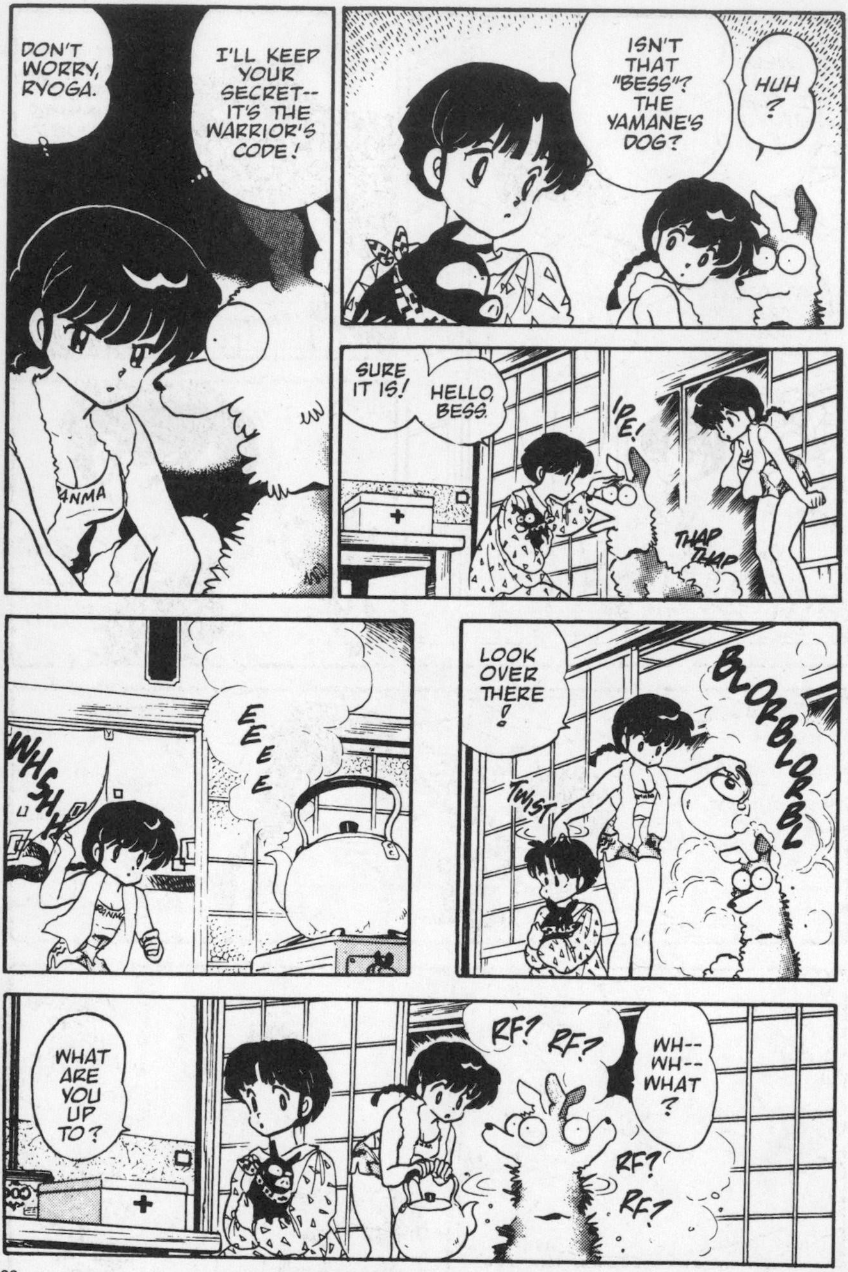
DON'T WORRY, RYOGA.
I'LL KEEP YOUR SECRET-- IT'S THE WARRIOR'S CODE!
ISN'T THAT "BESS"? THE YAMANE'S DOG?
HUH?
SURE IT IS!
HELLO, BESS.
IPE!
THAP THAP
WHSHH
EEEE
LOOK OVER THERE!
TWIST
BLORBLORBL
WHAT ARE YOU UP TO?
RF? RF?
WH-- WH-- WHAT?
RF? RF?

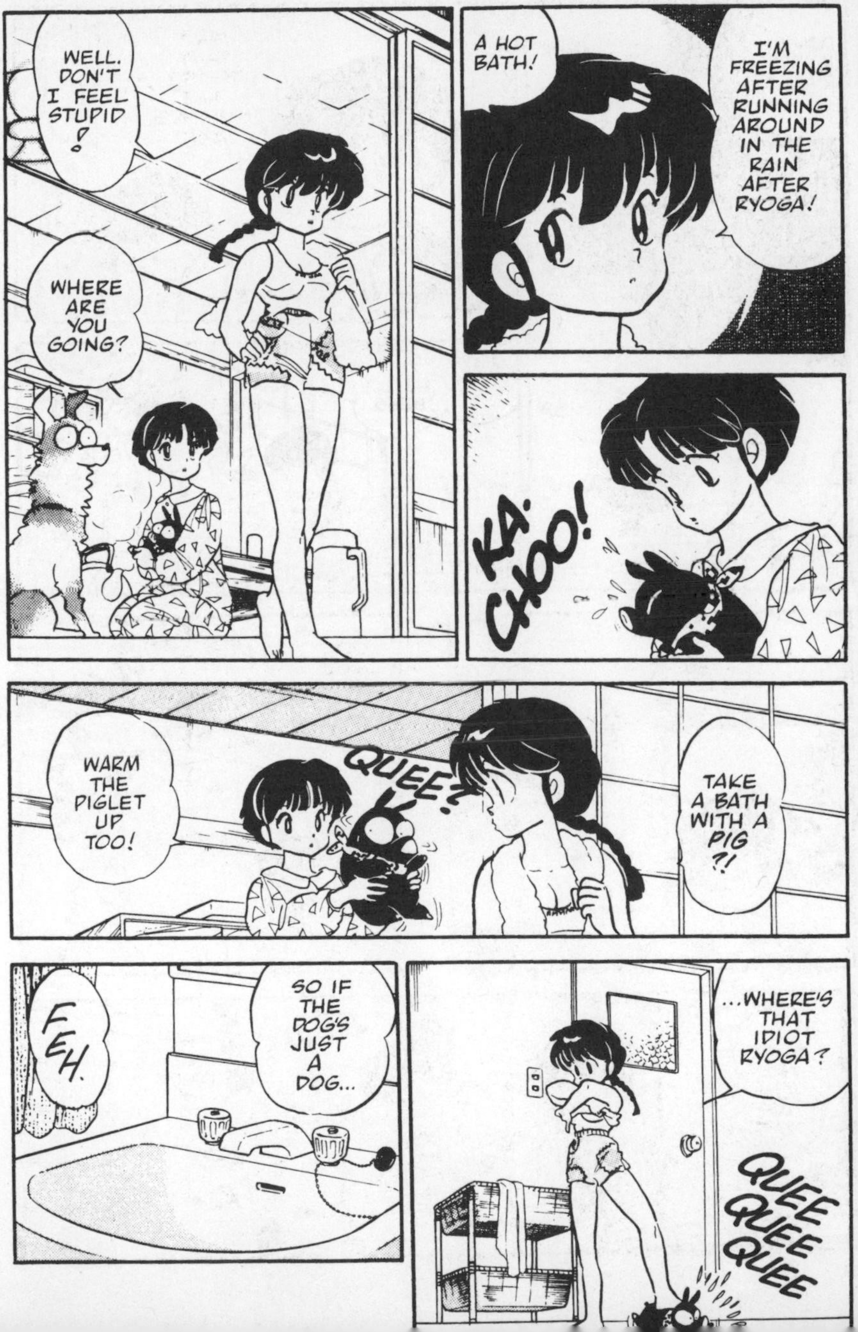
WELL. DON'T I FEEL STUPID!
WHERE ARE YOU GOING?
A HOT BATH!
I'M FREEZING AFTER RUNNING AROUND IN THE RAIN AFTER RYOGA!
KA-CHOO!
WARM THE PIGLET UP TOO!
QUEE?
TAKE A BATH WITH A PIG?!
FEH.
SO IF THE DOG'S JUST A DOG...
...WHERE'S THAT IDIOT RYOGA?
QUEE QUEE QUEE

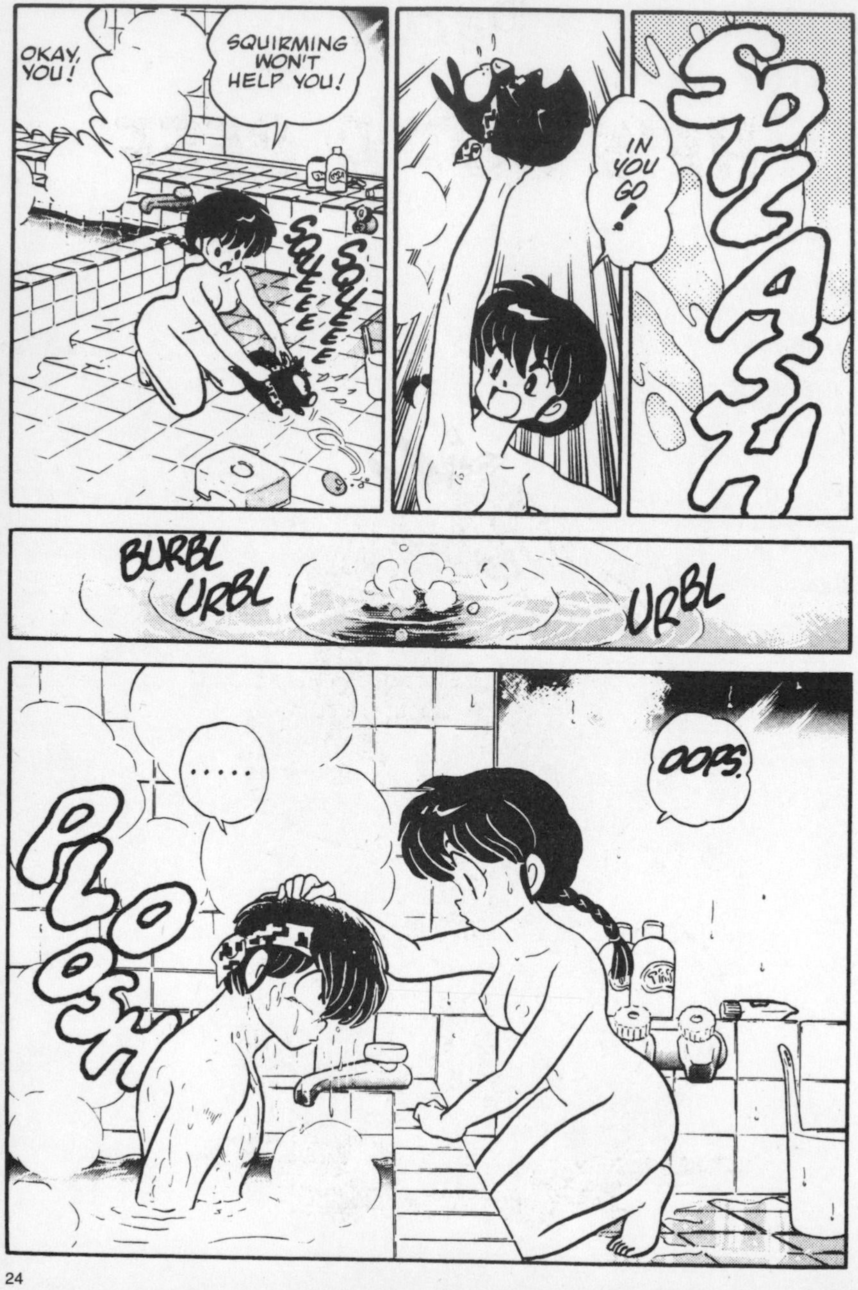
OKAY, YOU!
SQUIRMING WON'T HELP YOU!
SQUEEEEE
SQUEEEEE
IN YOU GO!
SPLASH
BURBL
URBL
URBL
.....
OOPS.
PLOOSH

Part 2
HE'S GOT A BEEF

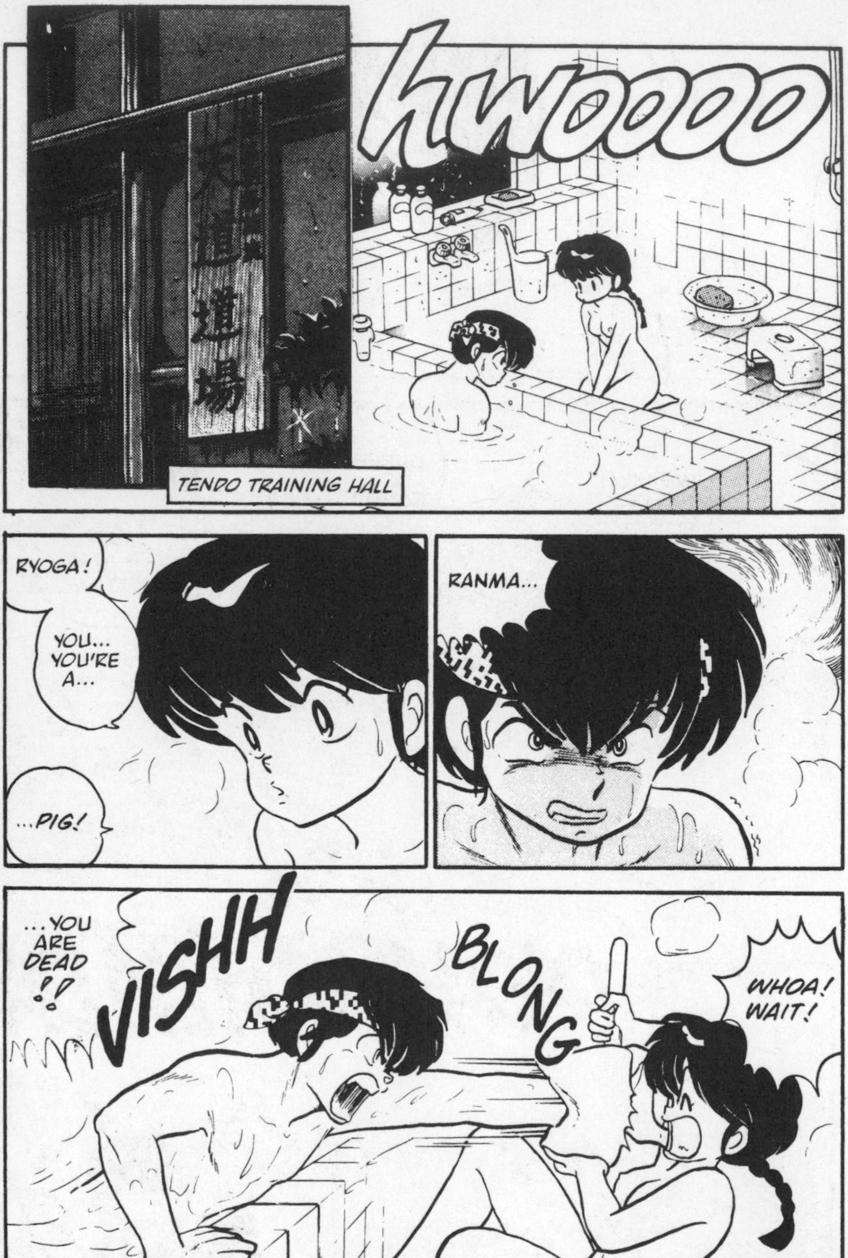
HWOOOO
TENDO TRAINING HALL
RYOGA!
YOU... YOU'RE A...
...PIG!
RANMA...
...YOU ARE DEAD!!
VISHH
BLONG
WHOA! WAIT!

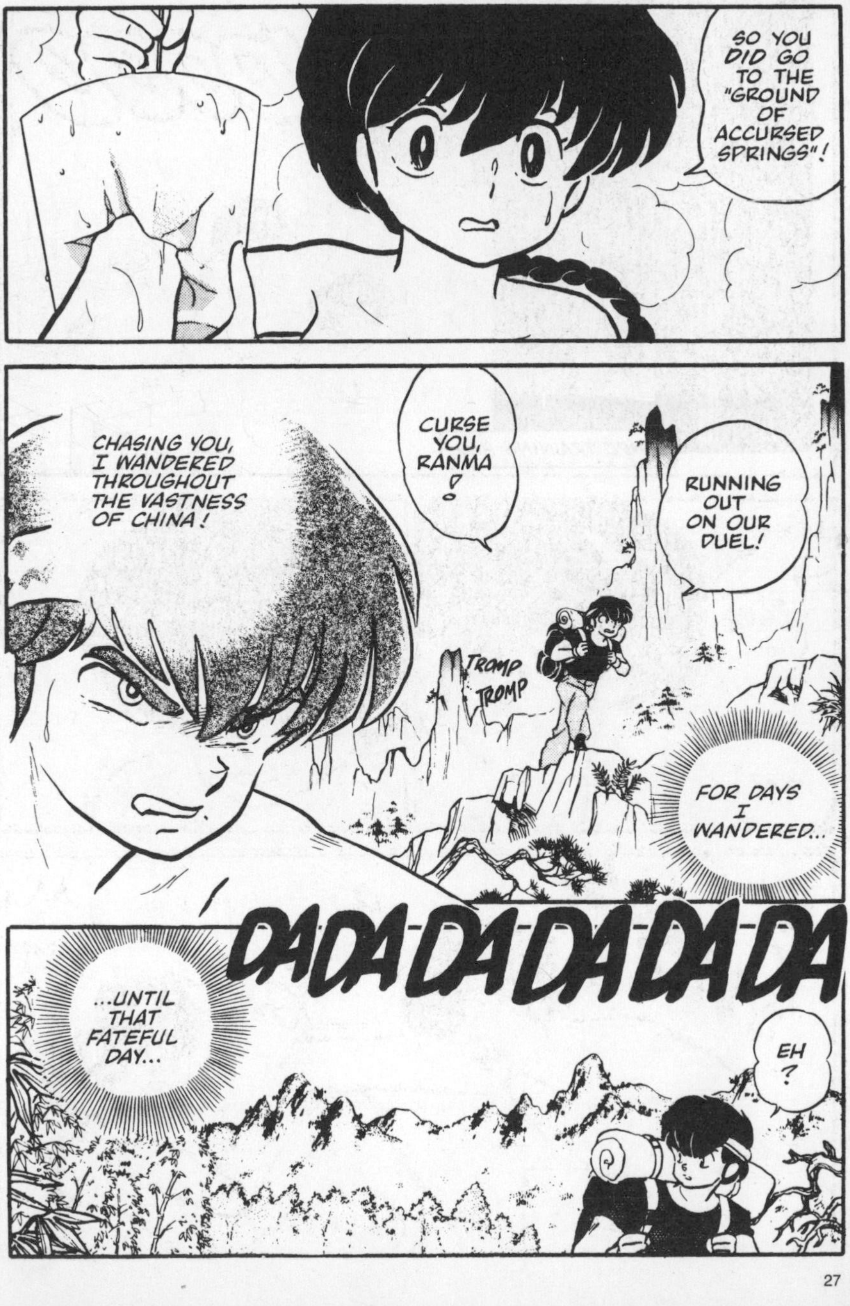
SO YOU DID GO TO THE "GROUND OF ACCURSED SPRINGS"!
CHASING YOU, I WANDERED THROUGHOUT THE VASTNESS OF CHINA!
CURSE YOU, RANMA!
RUNNING OUT ON OUR DUEL!
TROMP TROMP
FOR DAYS I WANDERED...
DADADADADADADA
...UNTIL THAT FATEFUL DAY...
EH?

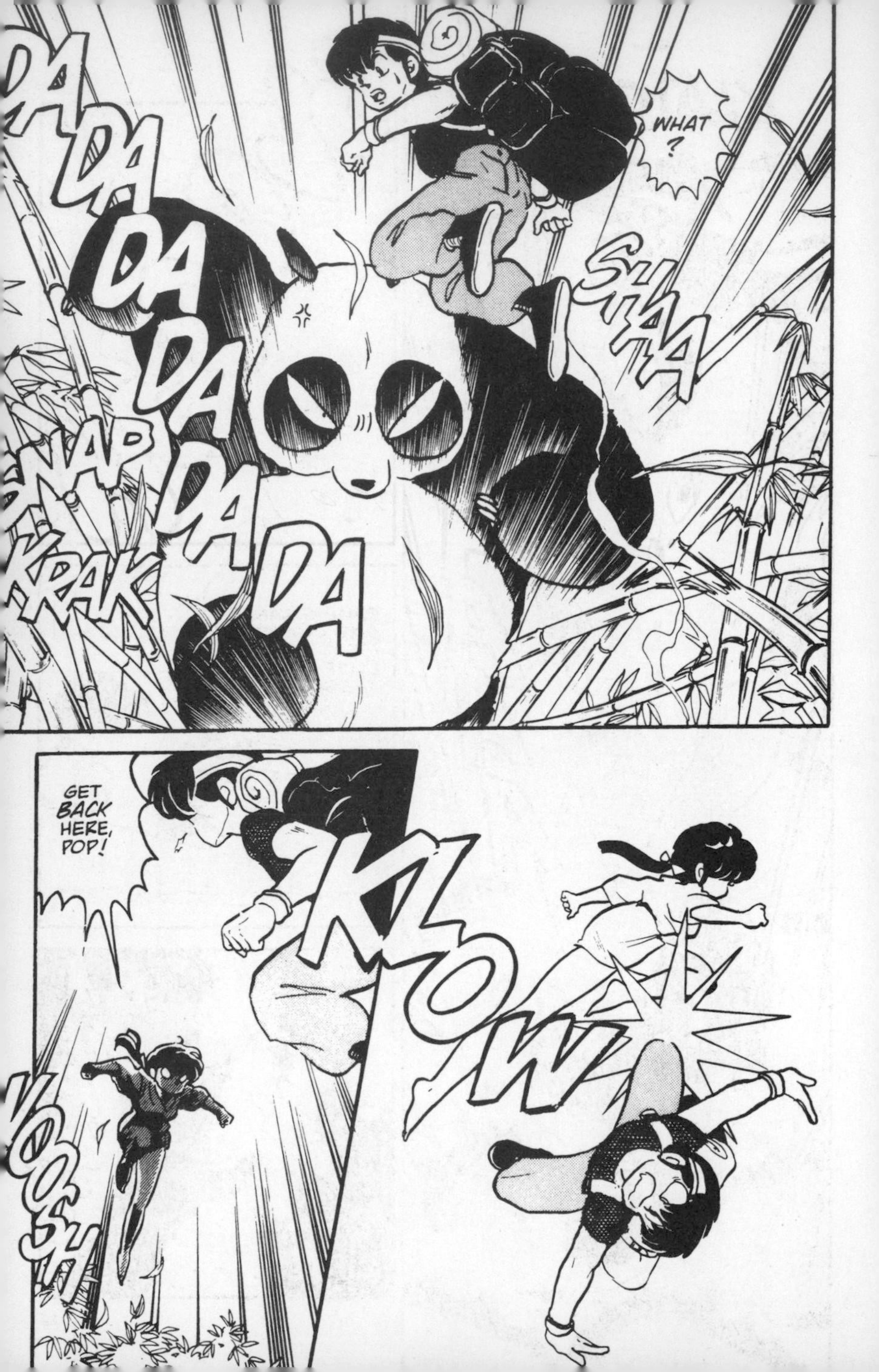
DA DA DA DA DA DA
SNAP
KRAK
WHAT?
SHAA
GET BACK HERE, POP!
KWOW
WOOSH

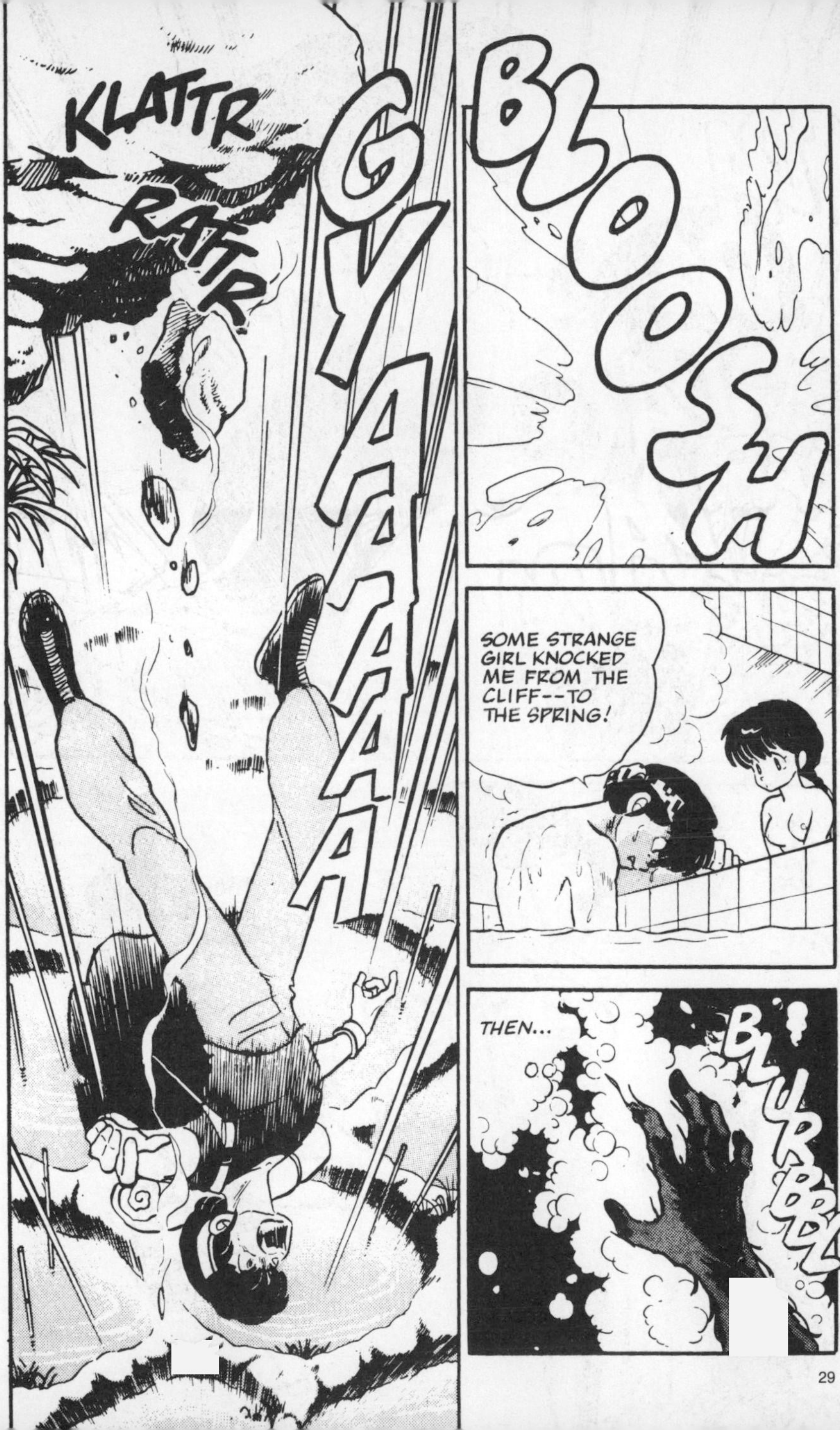
KLATTR
RATTR
GYAAAAA
BLOOSH
SOME STRANGE GIRL KNOCKED ME FROM THE CLIFF--TO THE SPRING!
THEN...
BLURBBL

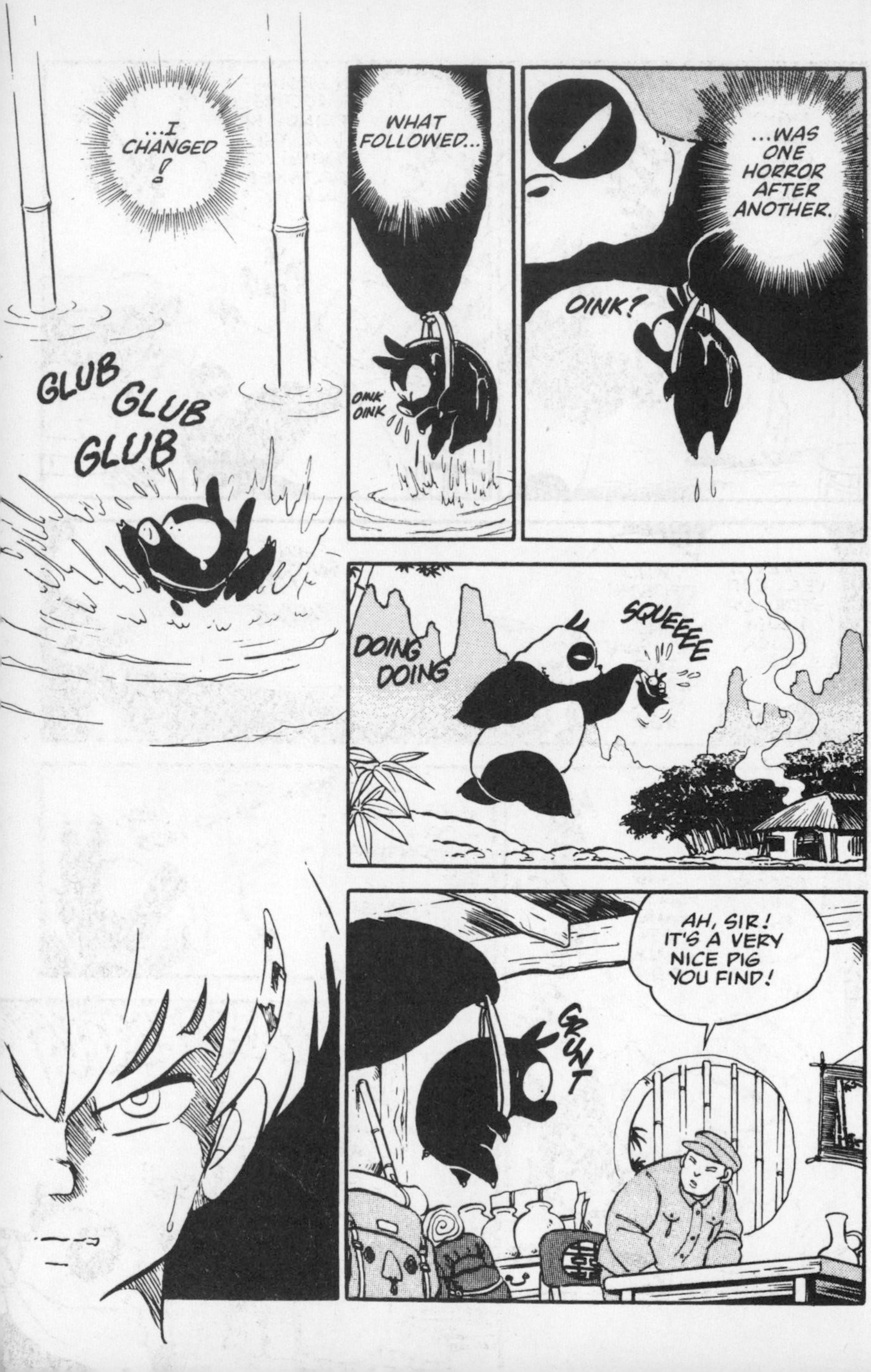
...I CHANGED!
GLUB GLUB GLUB
WHAT FOLLOWED...
OINK OINK
...WAS ONE HORROR AFTER ANOTHER.
OINK?
DOING DOING
SQUEEEEE
AH, SIR! IT'S A VERY NICE PIG YOU FIND!
GRUNT

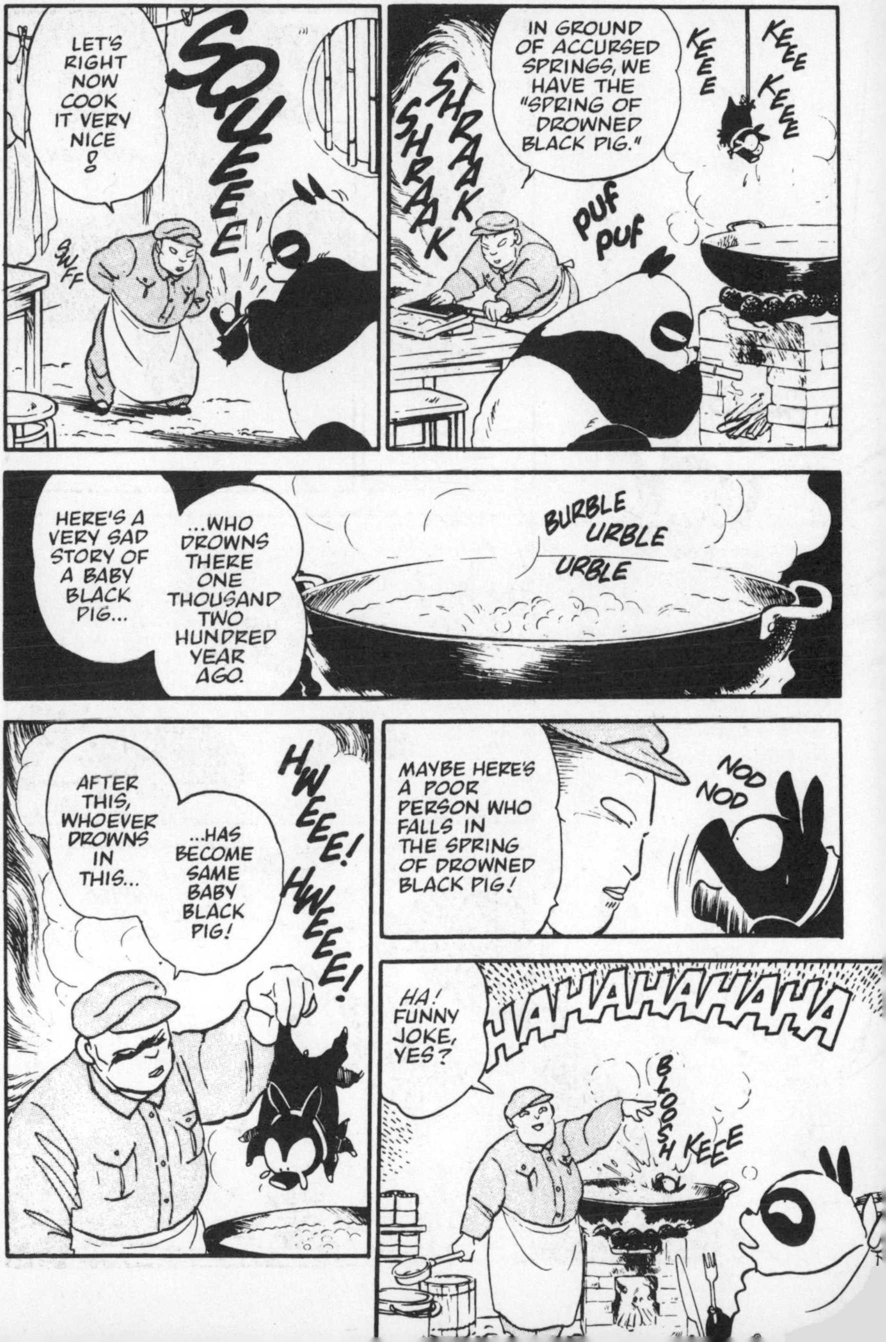
LET'S RIGHT NOW COOK IT VERY NICE!
SQUEEEEE
SWFF
IN GROUND OF ACCURSED SPRINGS, WE HAVE THE "SPRING OF DROWNED BLACK PIG."
SHRAAK SHRAAK
KEEE
KEEE KEEE
PUF PUF
HERE'S A VERY SAD STORY OF A BABY BLACK PIG...
...WHO DROWNS THERE ONE THOUSAND TWO HUNDRED YEAR AGO.
BURBLE URBLE URBLE
AFTER THIS, WHOEVER DROWNS IN THIS...
...HAS BECOME SAME BABY BLACK PIG!
HWEEEE! HWEEEE!
MAYBE HERE'S A POOR PERSON WHO FALLS IN THE SPRING OF DROWNED BLACK PIG!
NOD NOD
HA! FUNNY JOKE, YES?
HAHAHAHAHAHA
BLOOSH
KEEE

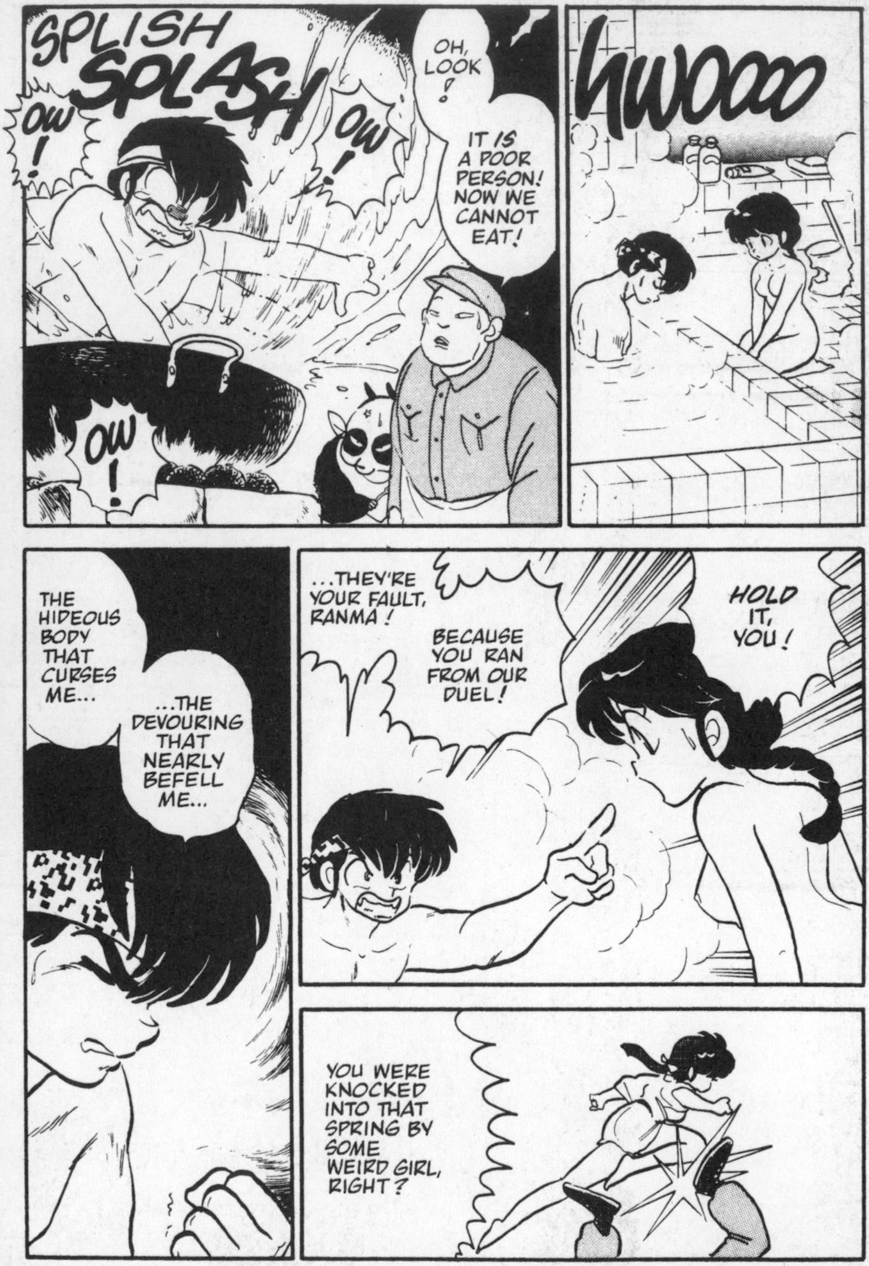
SPLISH SPLASH
OW!
OW!
OW!
OH, LOOK!
IT IS A POOR PERSON! NOW WE CANNOT EAT!
HWOOOO
THE HIDEOUS BODY THAT CURSES ME...
...THE DEVOURING THAT NEARLY BEFELL ME...
...THEY'RE YOUR FAULT, RANMA!
BECAUSE YOU RAN FROM OUR DUEL!
HOLD IT, YOU!
YOU WERE KNOCKED INTO THAT SPRING BY SOME WEIRD GIRL, RIGHT?

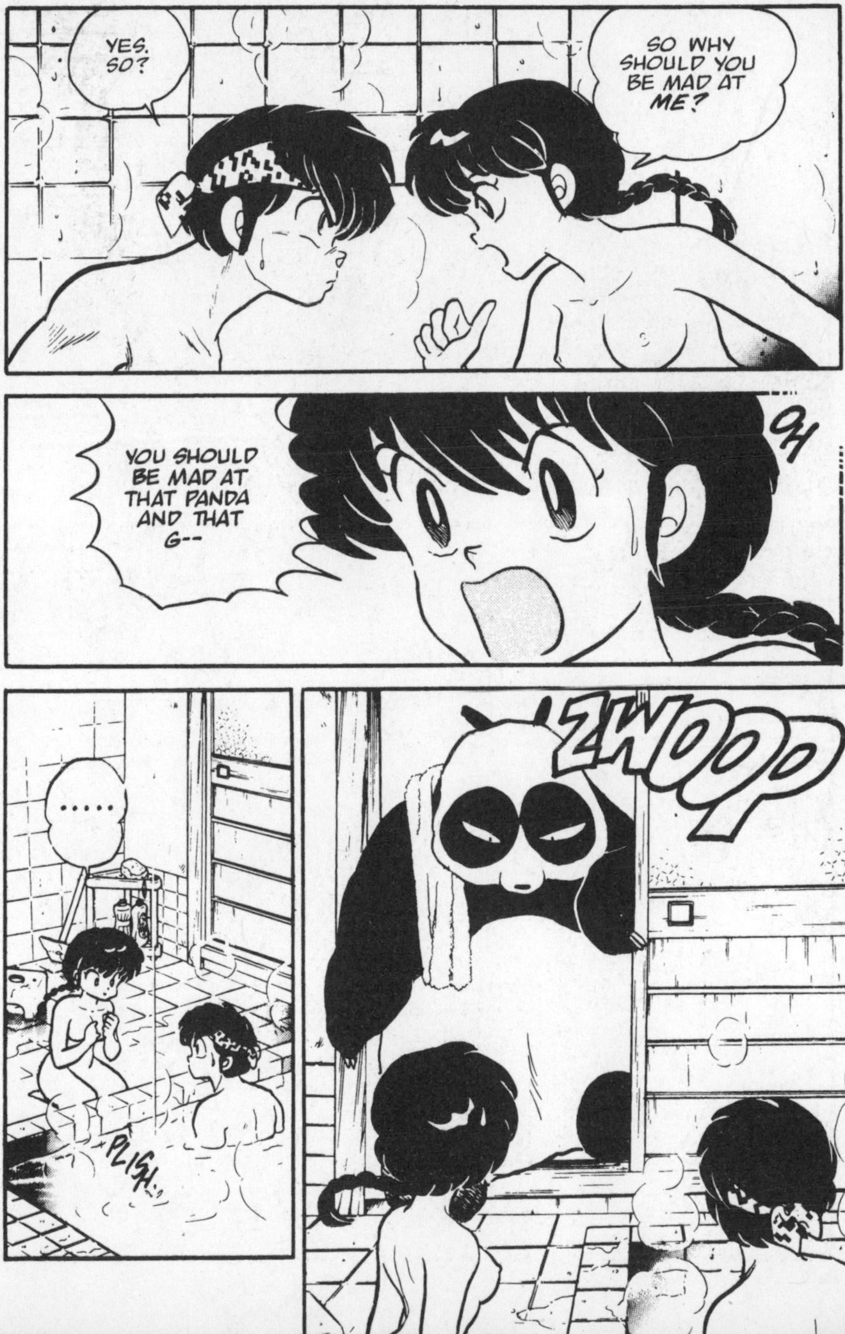
YES. SO?
SO WHY SHOULD YOU BE MAD AT ME?
YOU SHOULD BE MAD AT THAT PANDA AND THAT G--
OH
......
PLISH..
ZWOOP

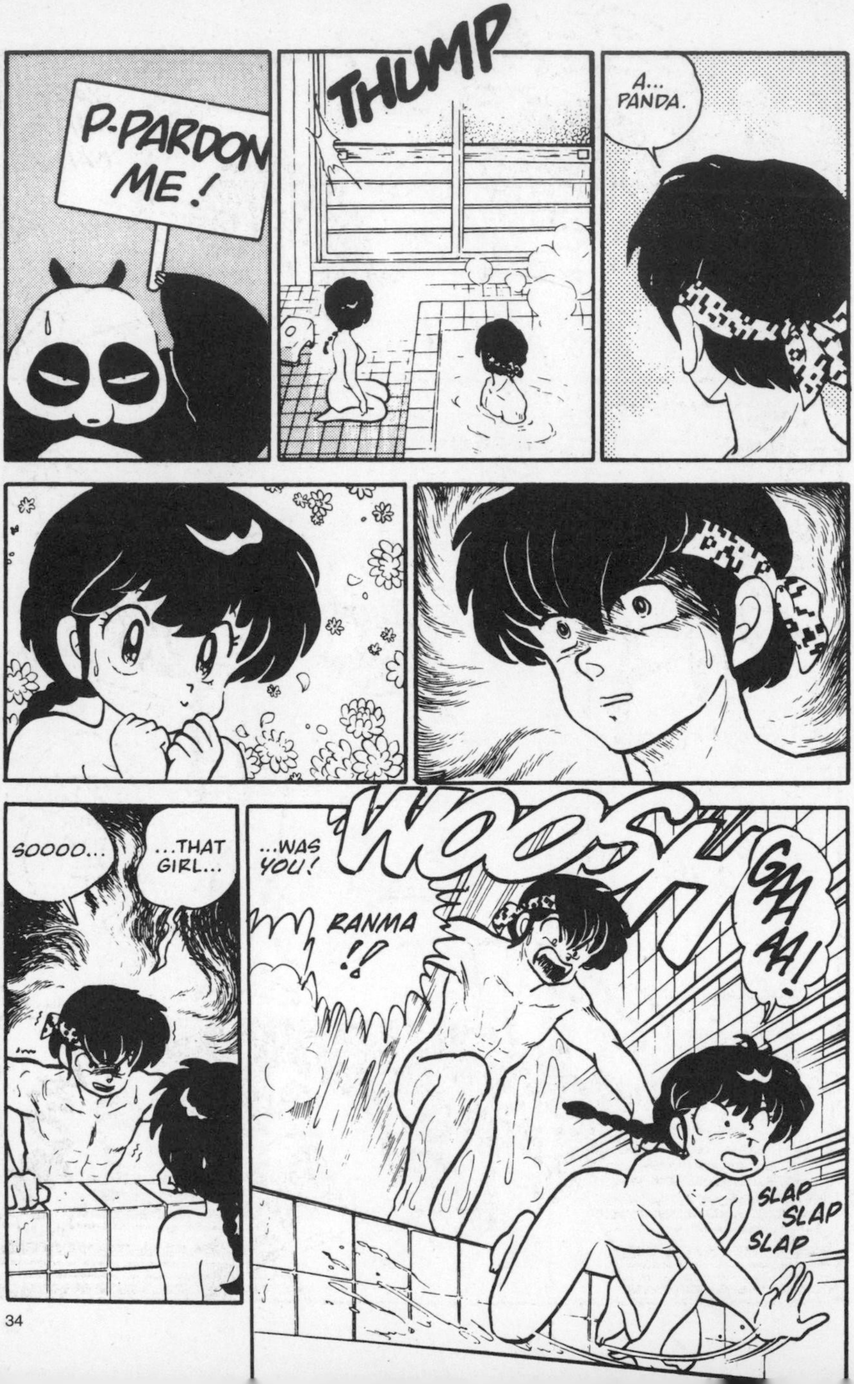
P-PARDON ME!
THUMP
A... PANDA.
SOOOO...
...THAT GIRL...
...WAS YOU!
WOOSH
RANMA !!
GAAAAA!
SLAP SLAP SLAP

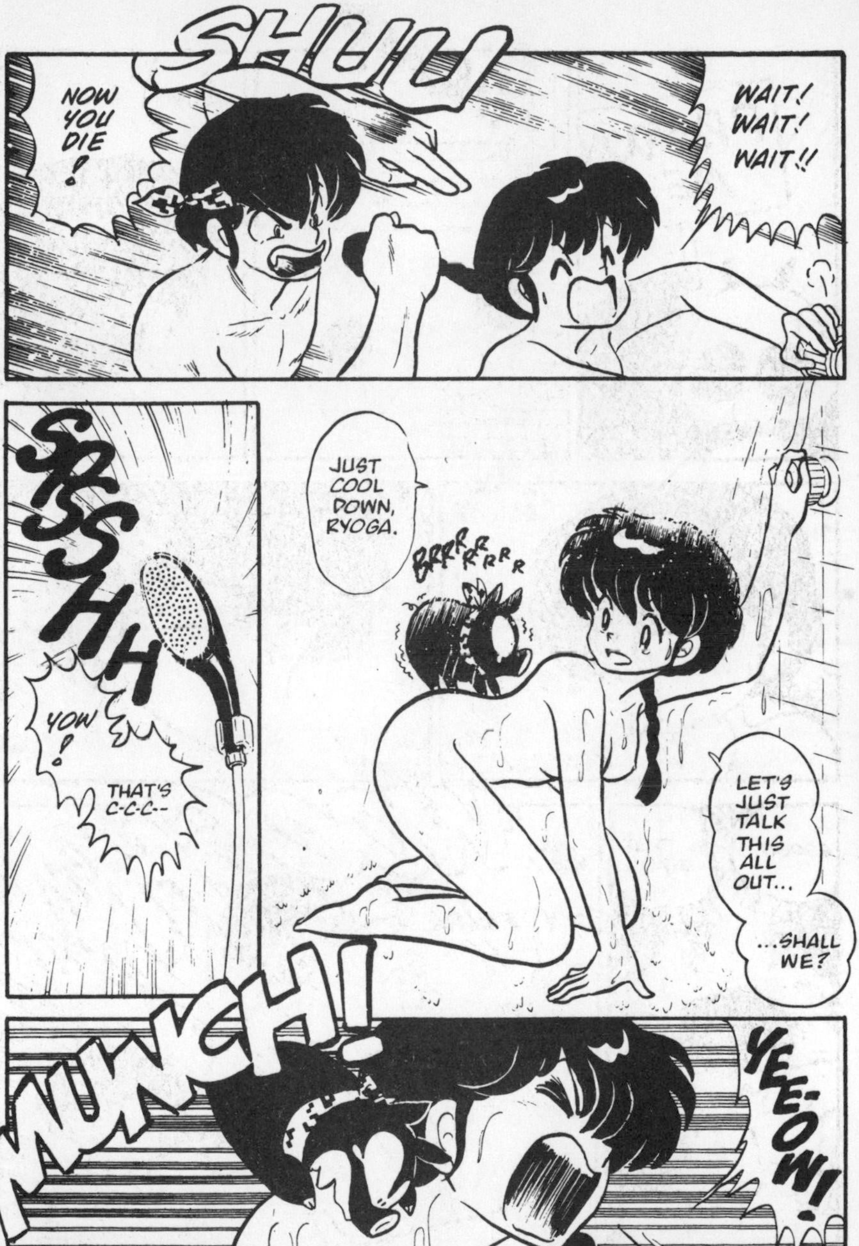
SHUU
NOW YOU DIE!
WAIT! WAIT! WAIT!!
SPSSHH
YOW!
THAT'S C-C-C--
JUST COOL DOWN, RYOGA.
BRRRRRRRRR
LET'S JUST TALK THIS ALL OUT...
...SHALL WE?
MUNCH!!
YEE-OW!

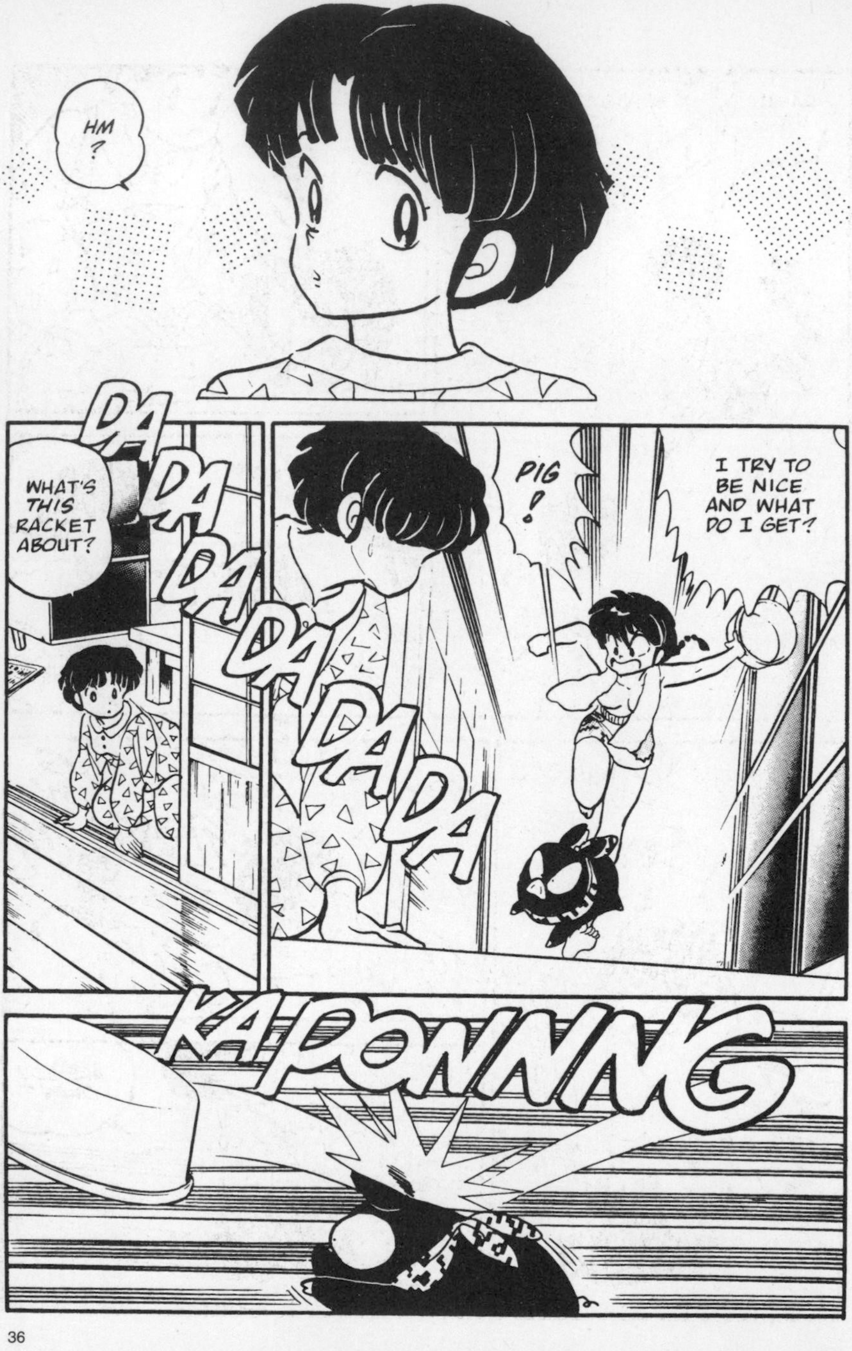
HM ?
DA DA DA DA DA DA DA
WHAT'S THIS RACKET ABOUT?
PIG !
I TRY TO BE NICE AND WHAT DO I GET?
KAPONNNG

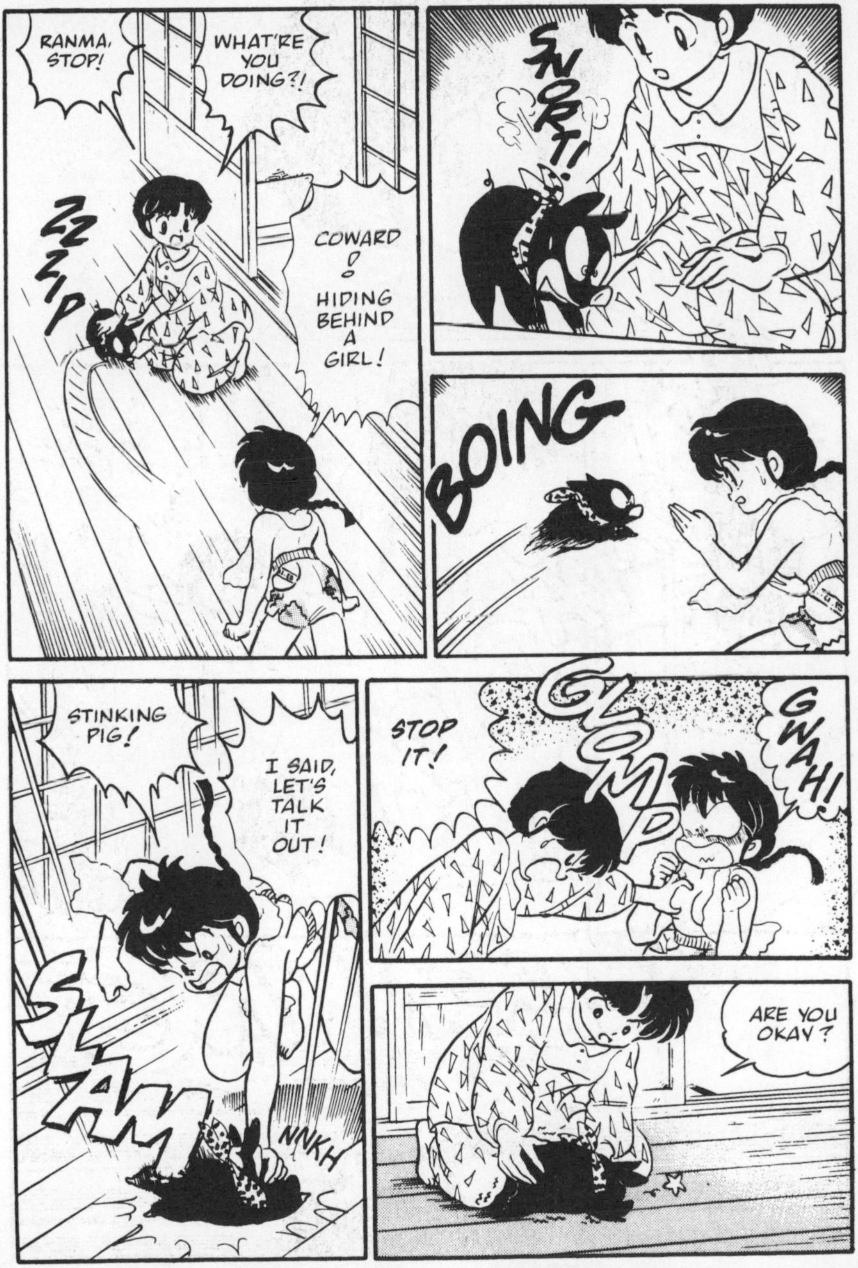
RANMA, STOP!
WHAT'RE YOU DOING?!
ZZZIP
COWARD! HIDING BEHIND A GIRL!
SNORT!
BOING
STINKING PIG!
I SAID, LET'S TALK IT OUT!
SLAM
NNKH
STOP IT!
GLOMP
GWAH!
ARE YOU OKAY?

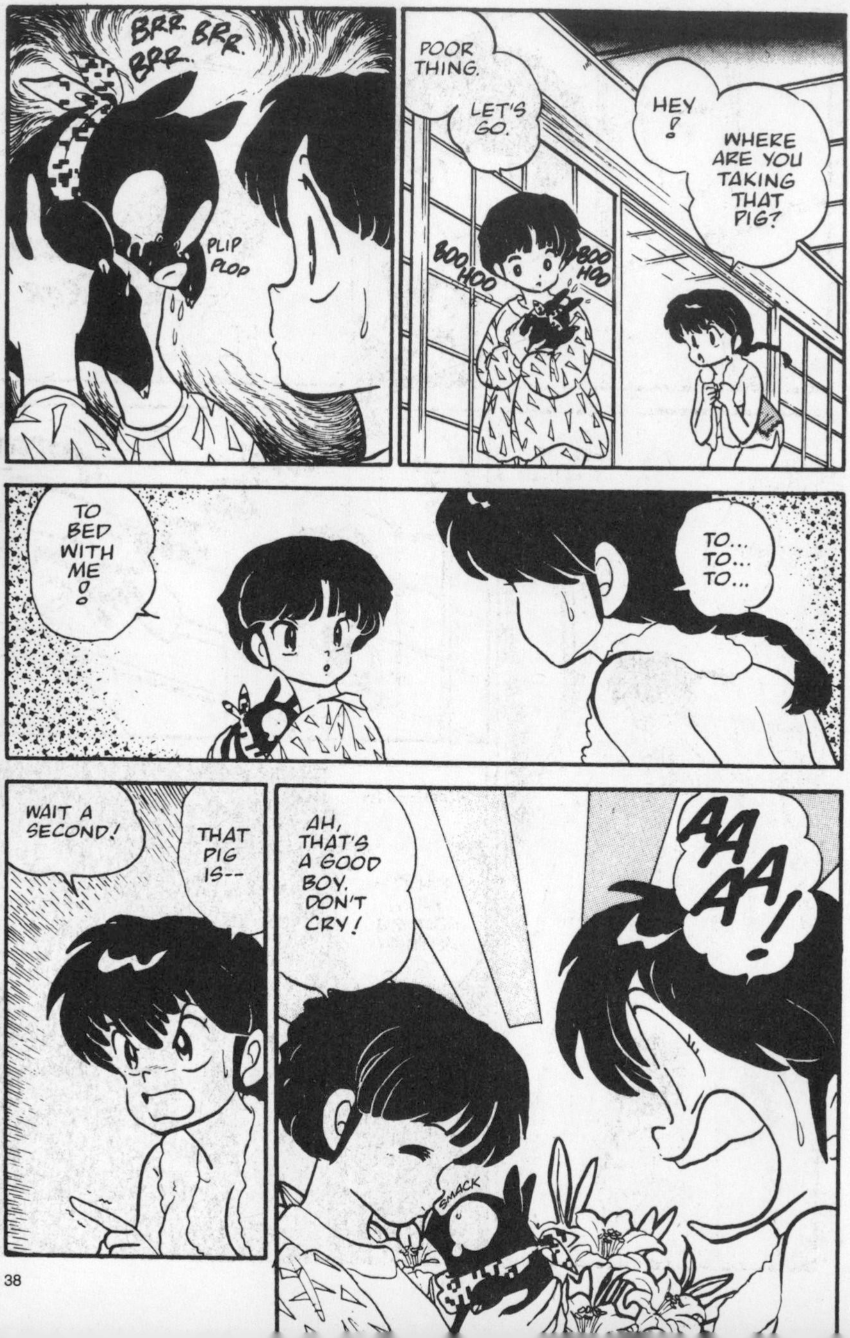
BRR. BRR. BRR.
PLIP PLOP
POOR THING.
LET'S GO.
BOO HOO
BOO HOO
HEY!
WHERE ARE YOU TAKING THAT PIG?
TO BED WITH ME!!
TO... TO... TO...
WAIT A SECOND!
THAT PIG IS--
AH, THAT'S A GOOD BOY. DON'T CRY!
AAAA!
SMACK

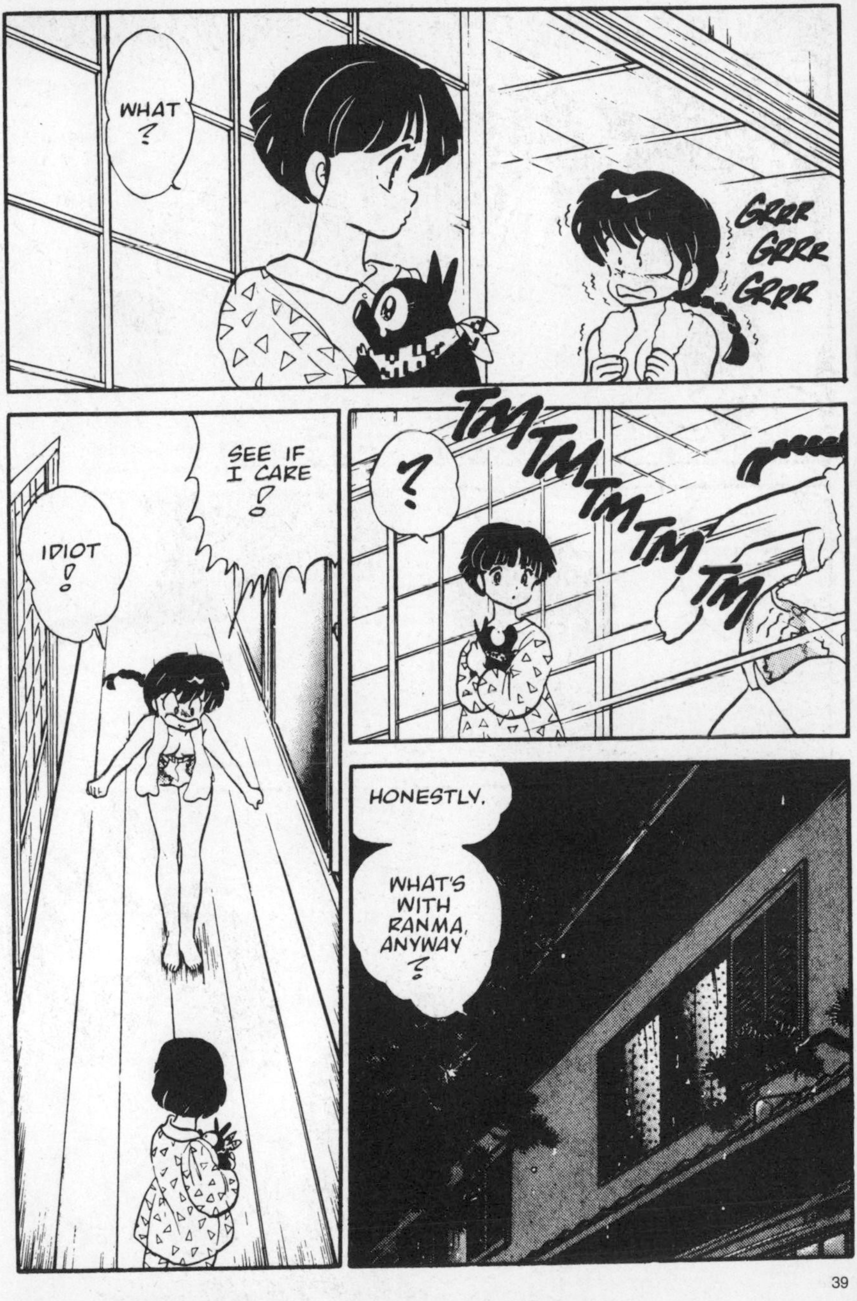

WHAT ?
GRRR GRRR GRRR
SEE IF I CARE !
IDIOT !
?
TM TM TM TM TM TM
HONESTLY.
WHAT'S WITH RANMA, ANYWAY ?

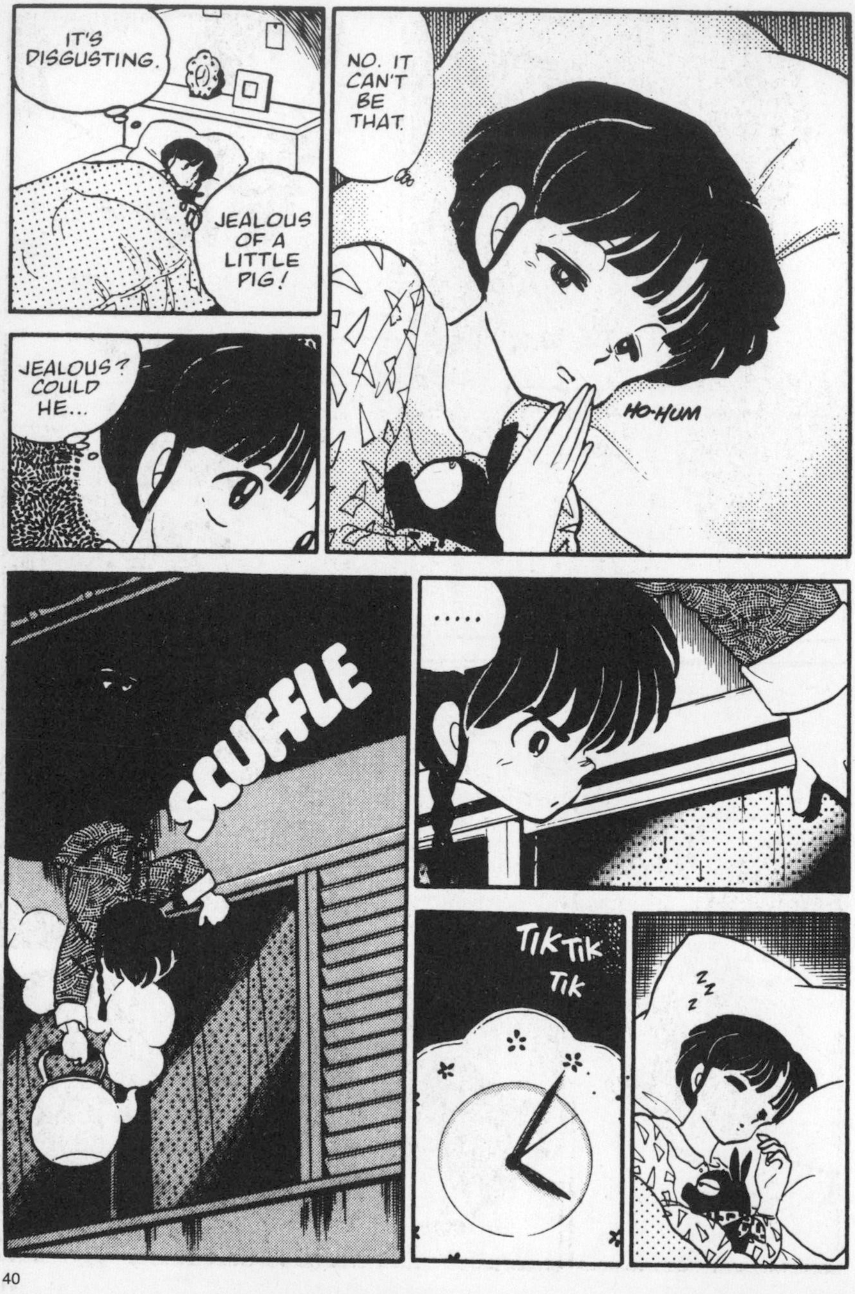
IT'S DISGUSTING.
JEALOUS OF A LITTLE PIG!
NO. IT CAN'T BE THAT.
JEALOUS? COULD HE...
HO-HUM
SCUFFLE
......
TIK TIK TIK
Z Z Z

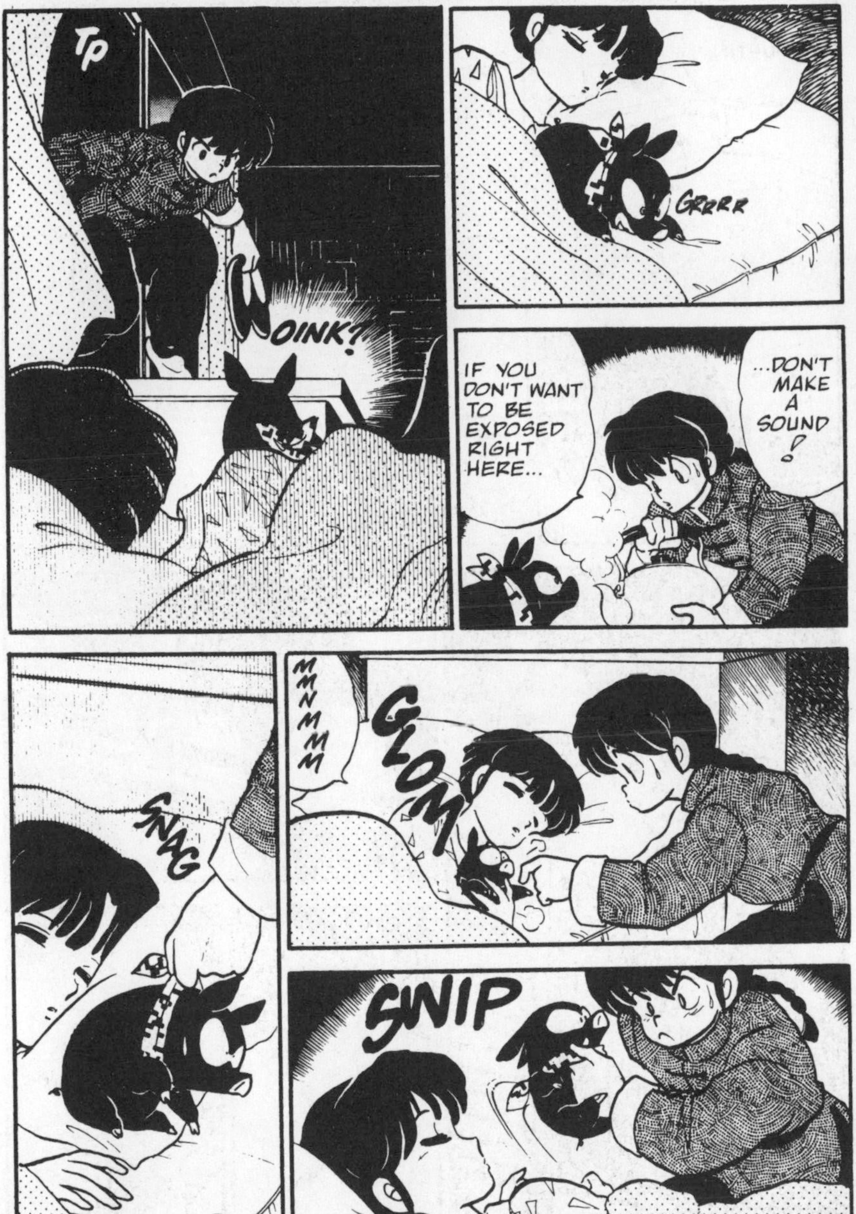
Tp
OINK?
GRRRR
IF YOU DON'T WANT TO BE EXPOSED RIGHT HERE...
...DON'T MAKE A SOUND!
SNAG
MMNMMMM
GLOM
SNIP

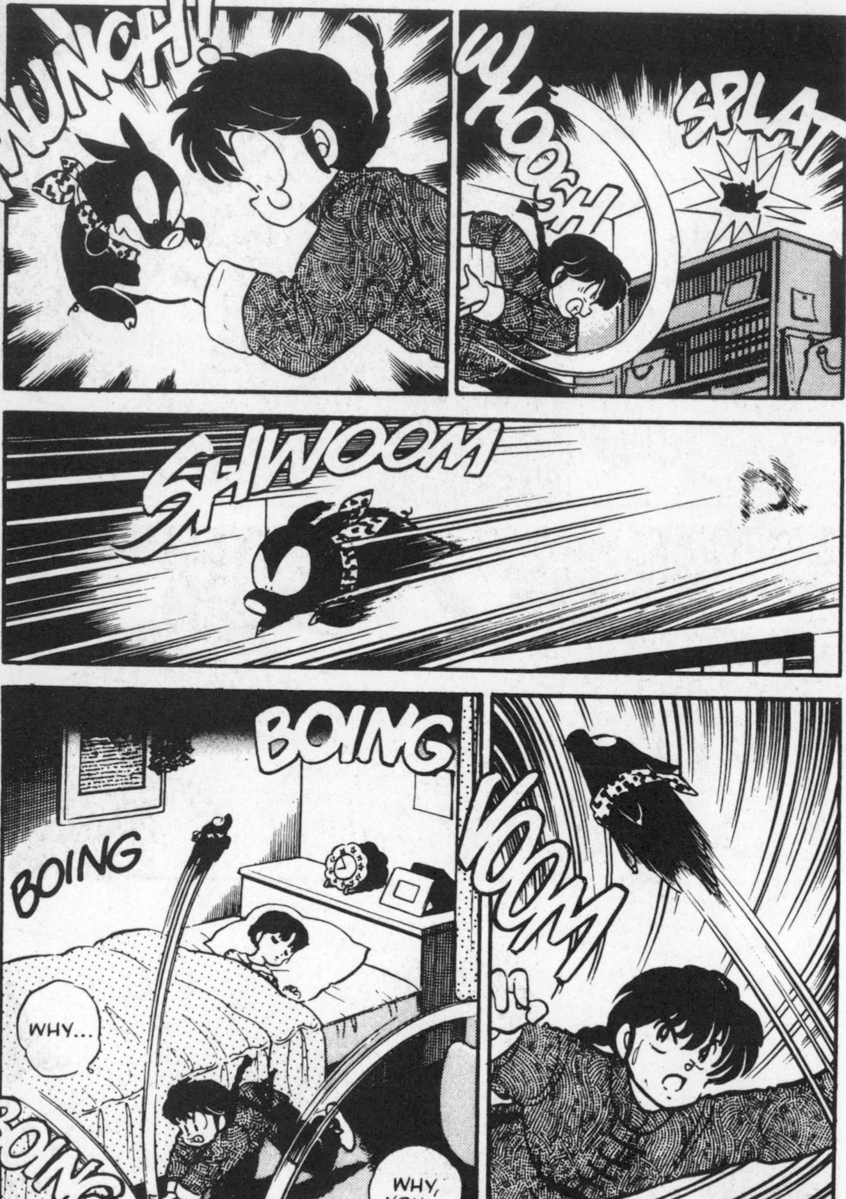
MUNCH!!
WHOOSH
SPLAT
SHWOOM
BOING
BOING
WHY...
BOING
WHY, YOU...
VOOM

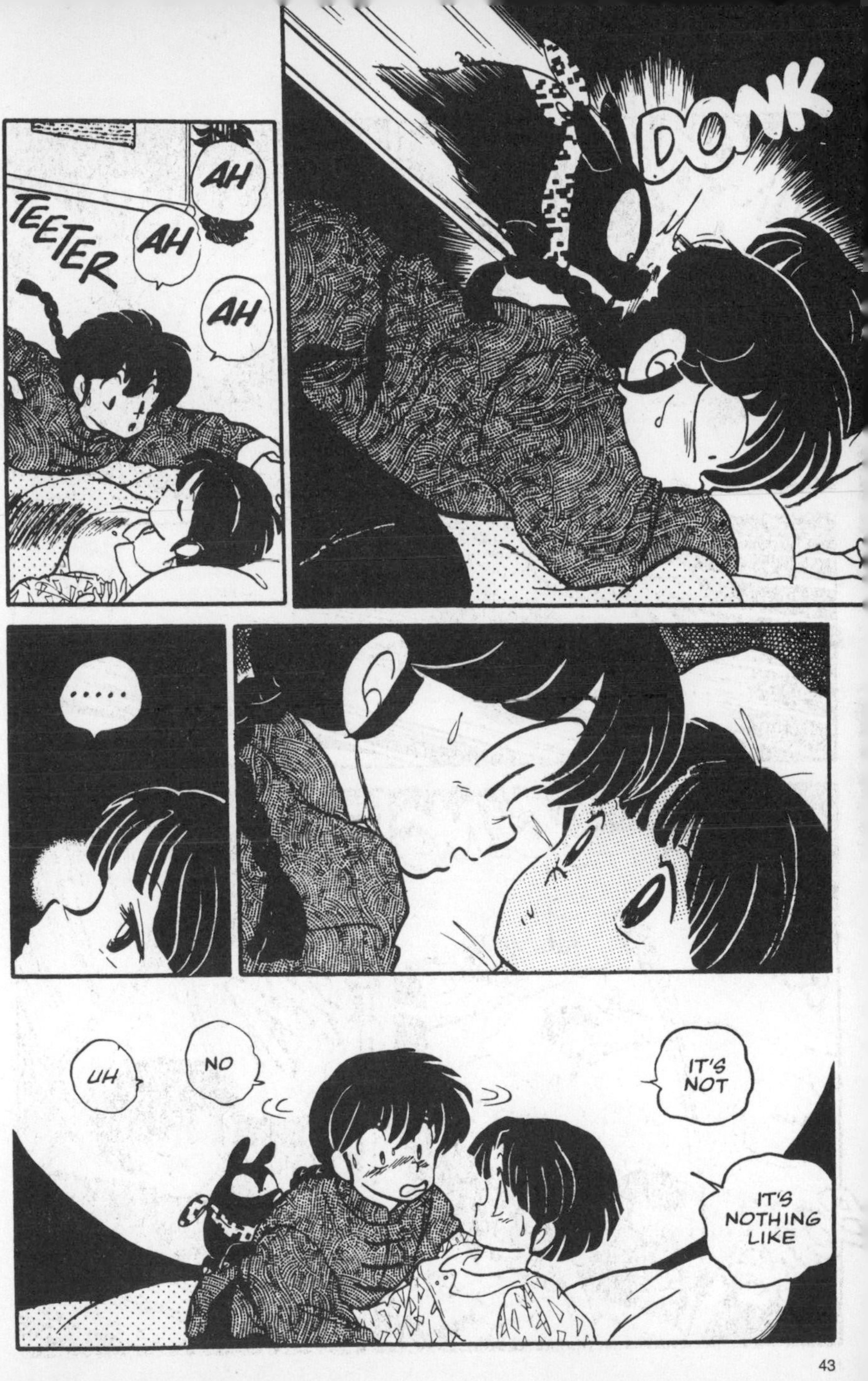

AH
AH
AH
TEETER
DONK
.....
UH
NO
IT'S NOT
IT'S NOTHING LIKE

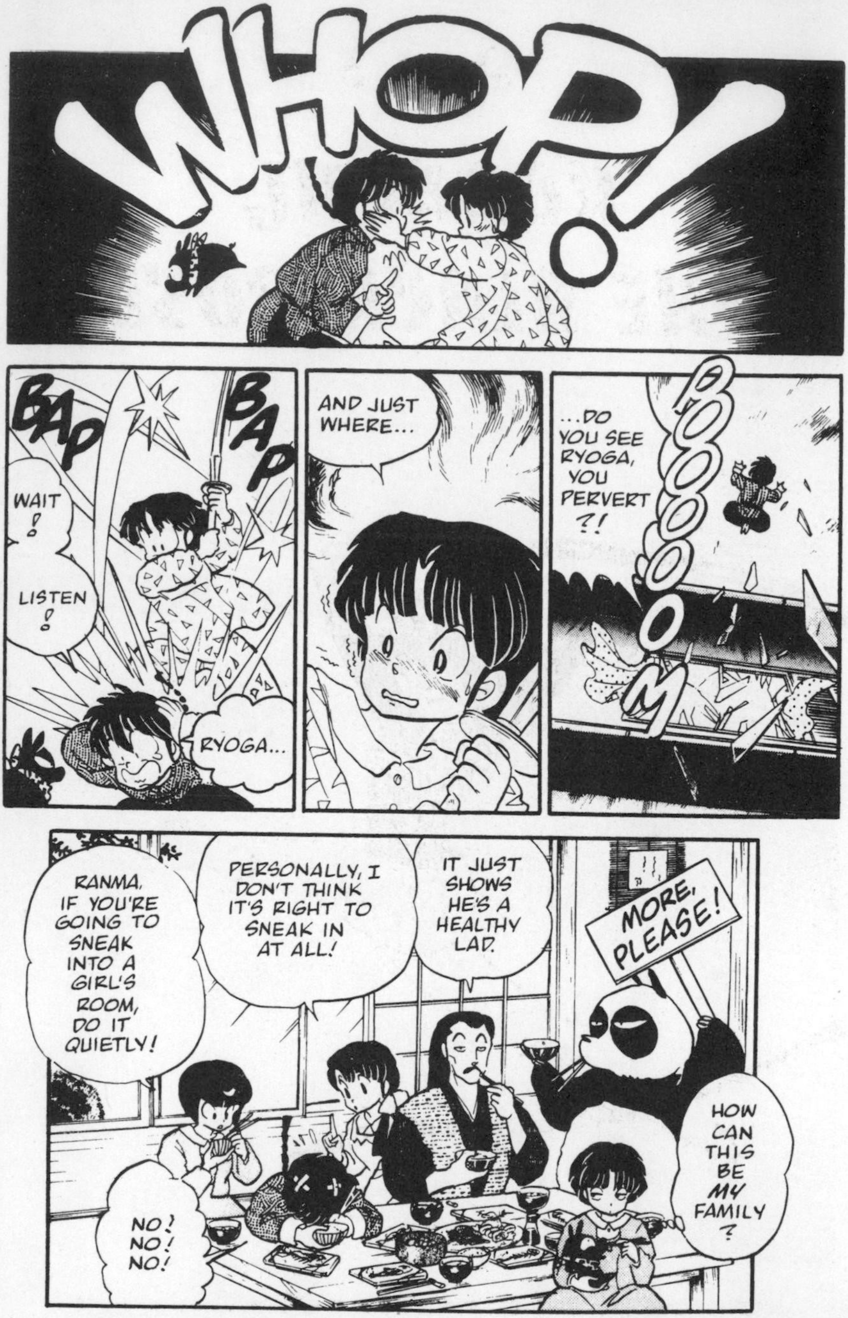
WHOP!
BAP
BAP
WAIT!
LISTEN!
RYOGA...
AND JUST WHERE...
...DO YOU SEE RYOGA, YOU PERVERT?!
BOOOOOOOOM
RANMA, IF YOU'RE GOING TO SNEAK INTO A GIRL'S ROOM, DO IT QUIETLY!
PERSONALLY, I DON'T THINK IT'S RIGHT TO SNEAK IN AT ALL!
IT JUST SHOWS HE'S A HEALTHY LAD.
MORE, PLEASE!
NO! NO! NO!
HOW CAN THIS BE MY FAMILY?

Part 3

KODACHI, THE BLACK ROSE

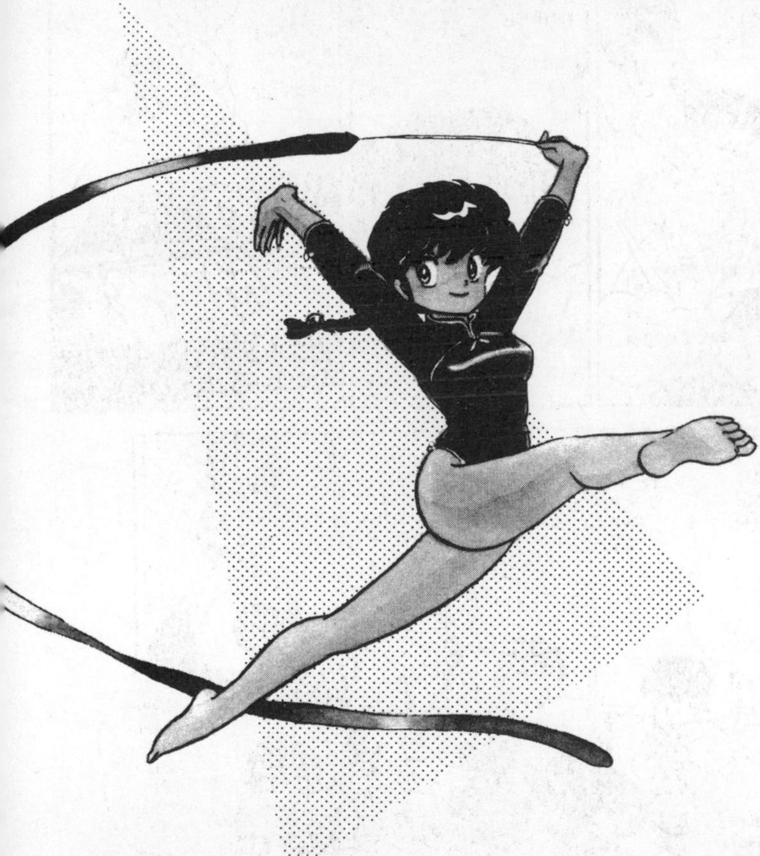

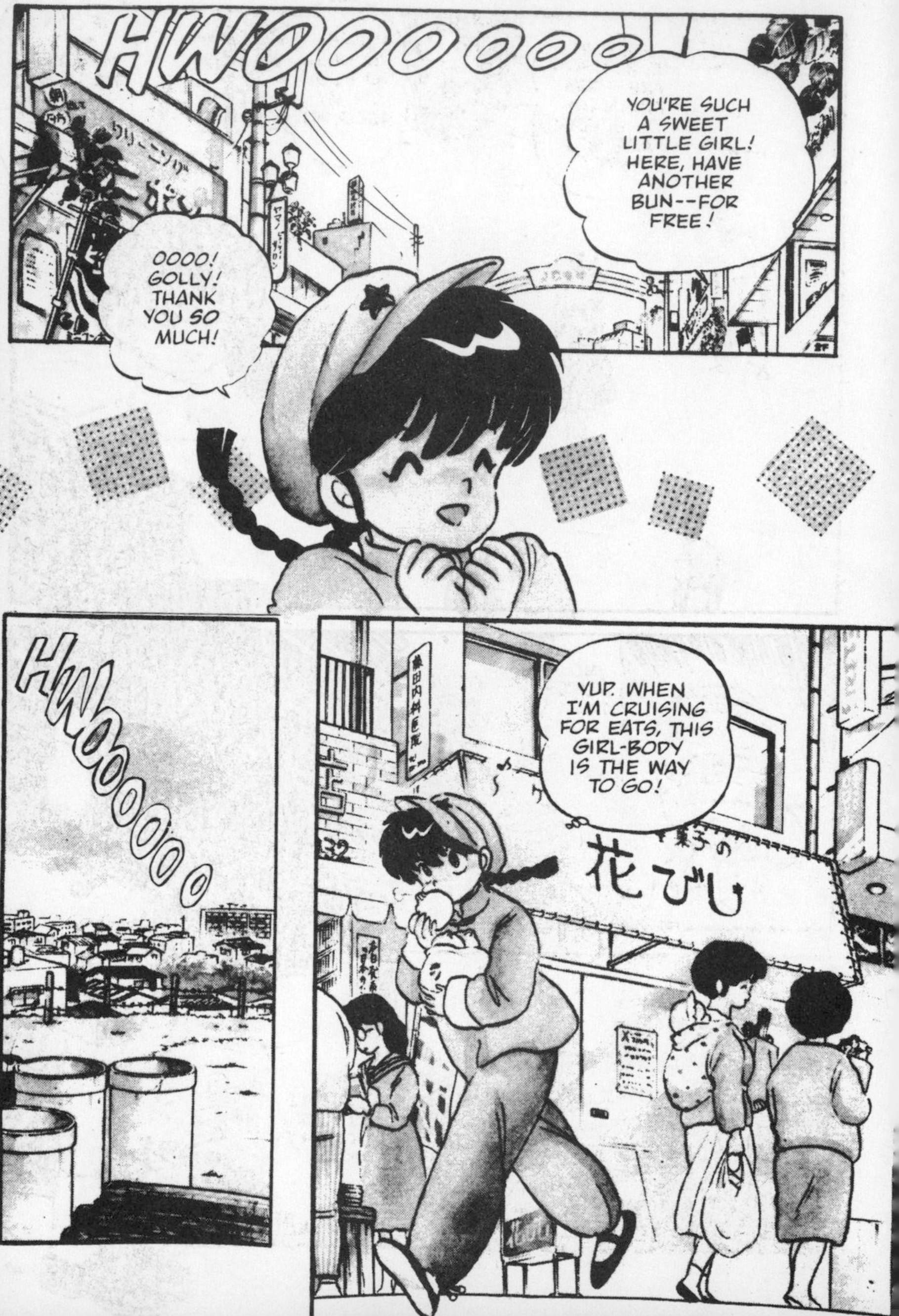
HWOOOOOOO
YOU'RE SUCH A SWEET LITTLE GIRL! HERE, HAVE ANOTHER BUN--FOR FREE!
OOOO! GOLLY! THANK YOU SO MUCH!
HWOOOOOOO
YUP. WHEN I'M CRUISING FOR EATS, THIS GIRL-BODY IS THE WAY TO GO!
花びし

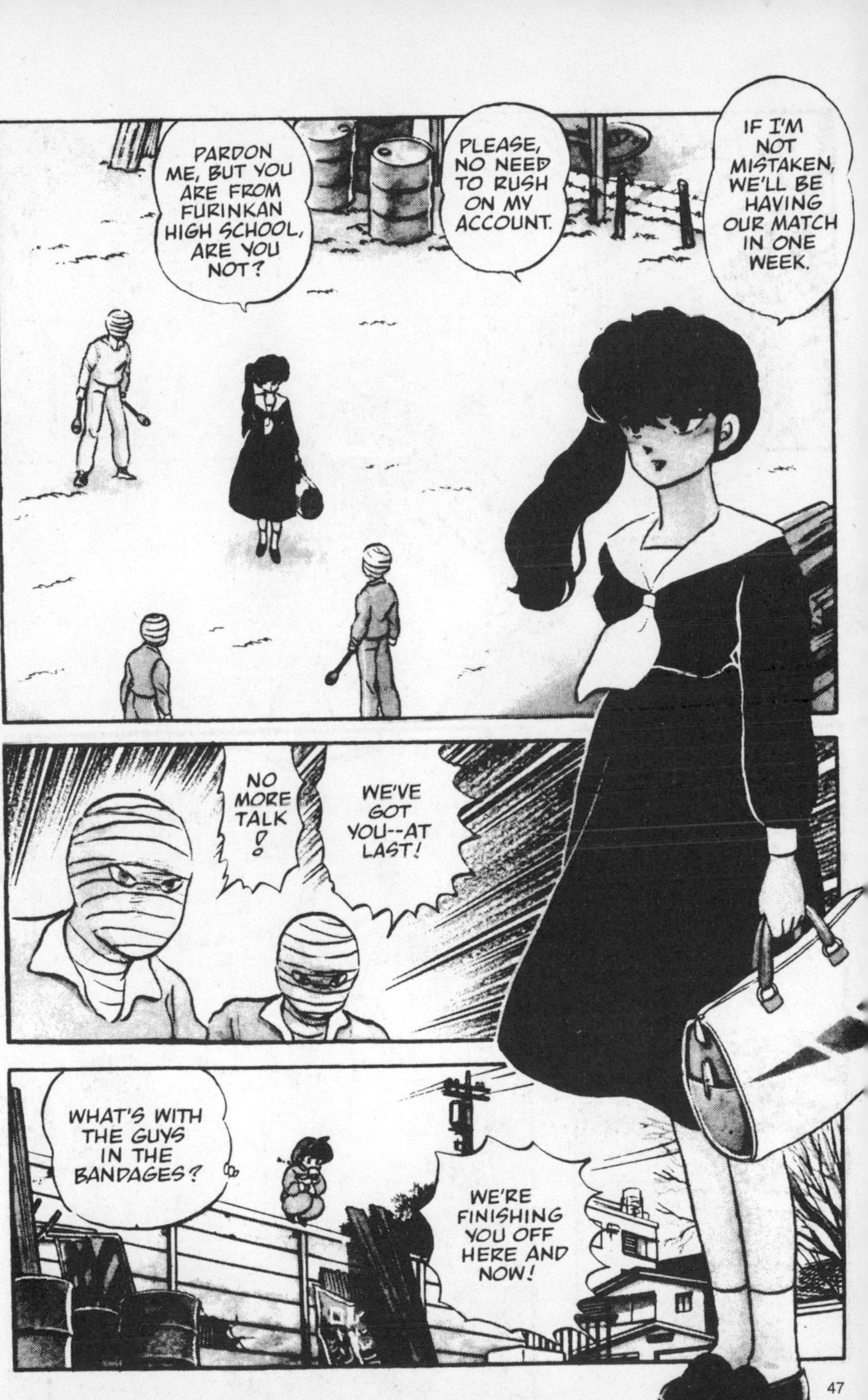
PARDON ME, BUT YOU ARE FROM FURINKAN HIGH SCHOOL, ARE YOU NOT?
PLEASE, NO NEED TO RUSH ON MY ACCOUNT.
IF I'M NOT MISTAKEN, WE'LL BE HAVING OUR MATCH IN ONE WEEK.
NO MORE TALK!
WE'VE GOT YOU--AT LAST!
WHAT'S WITH THE GUYS IN THE BANDAGES?
WE'RE FINISHING YOU OFF HERE AND NOW!

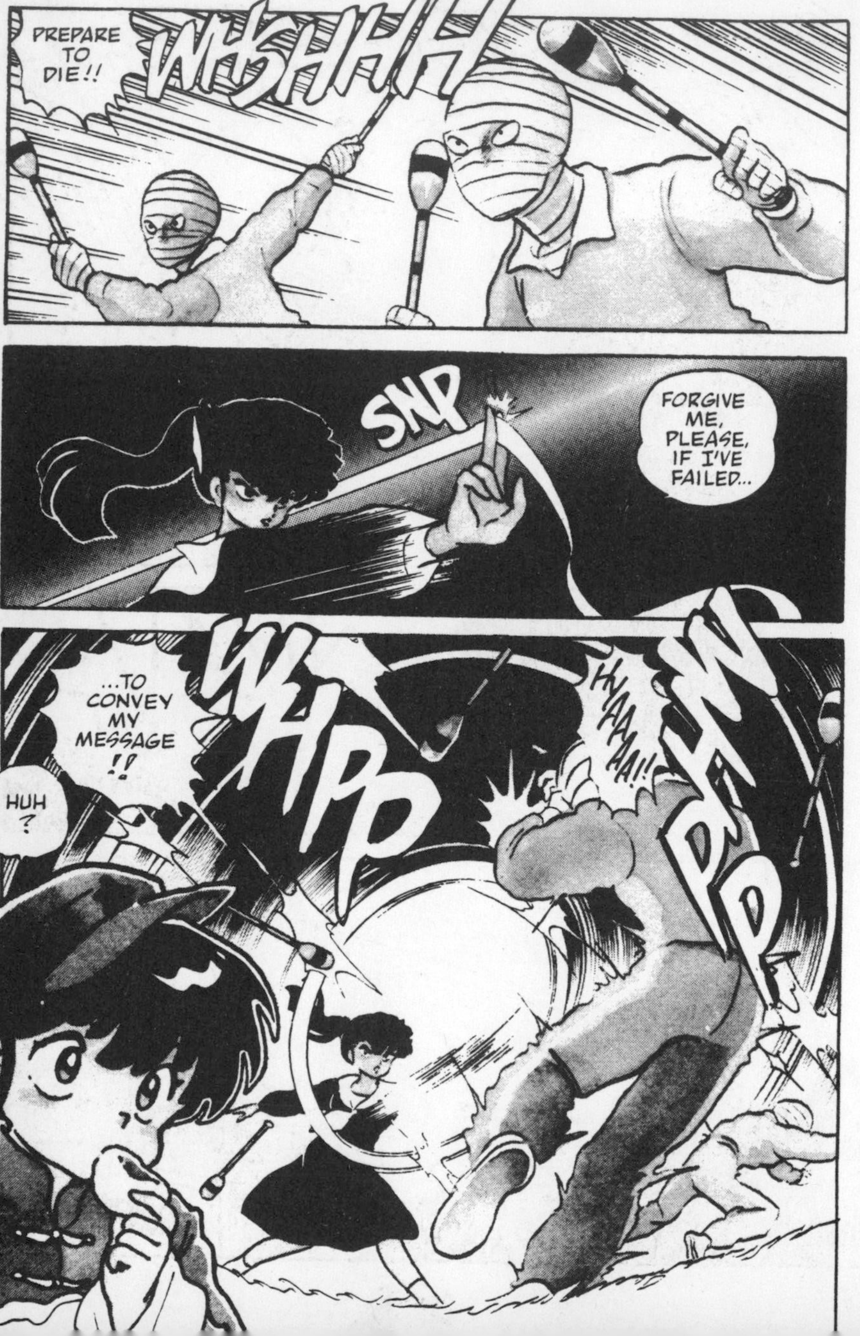
PREPARE TO DIE!!
WHSHHH
SNP
FORGIVE ME, PLEASE, IF I'VE FAILED...
...TO CONVEY MY MESSAGE!!
HUH?
WHPP
HYAAAAA!!
WHPP

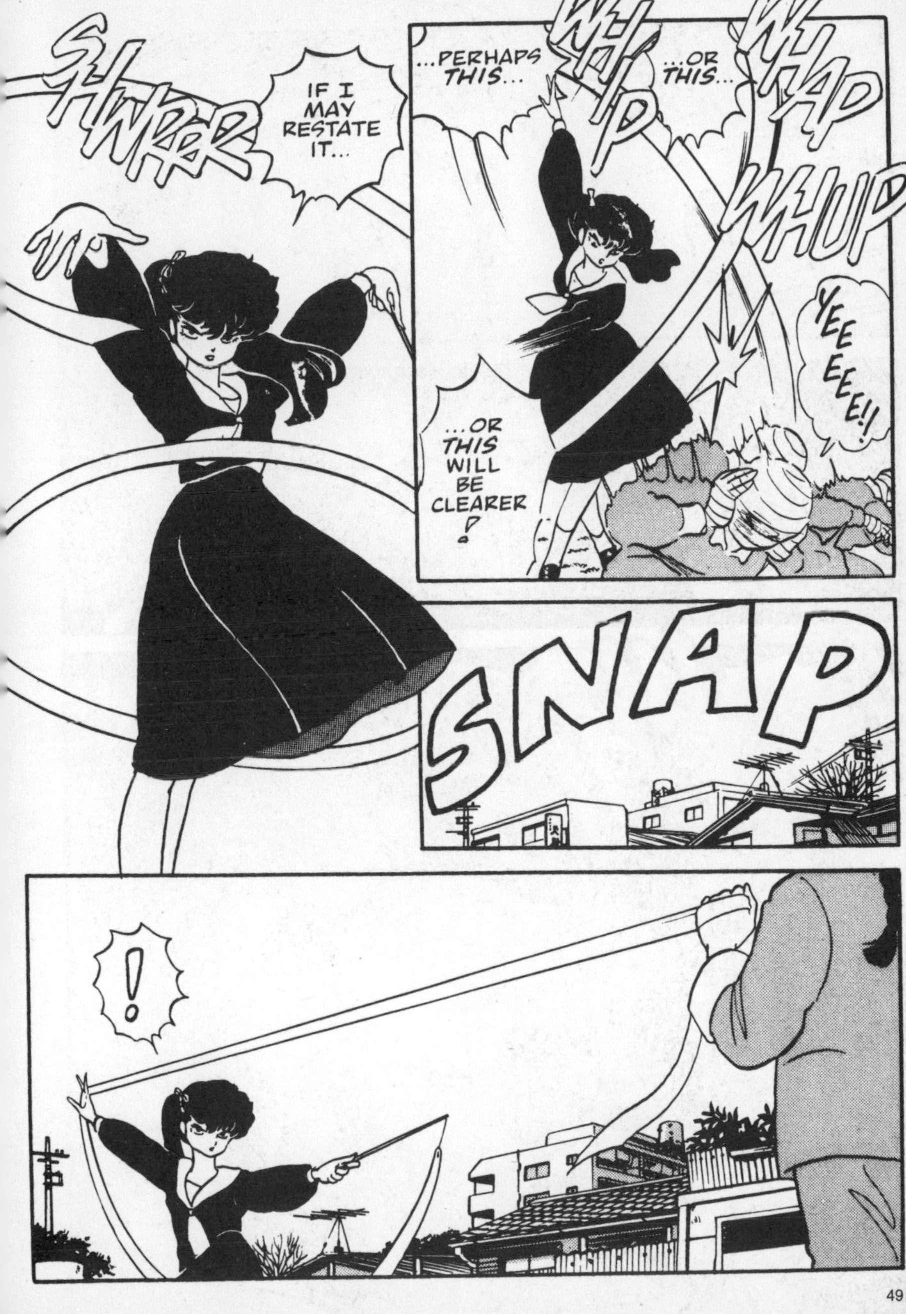
SHWEEEE
IF I MAY RESTATE IT...
...PERHAPS THIS...
WHIP
...OR THIS...
WHAP
WHUP
...OR THIS WILL BE CLEARER!
YEEEEEE!!
SNAP
!

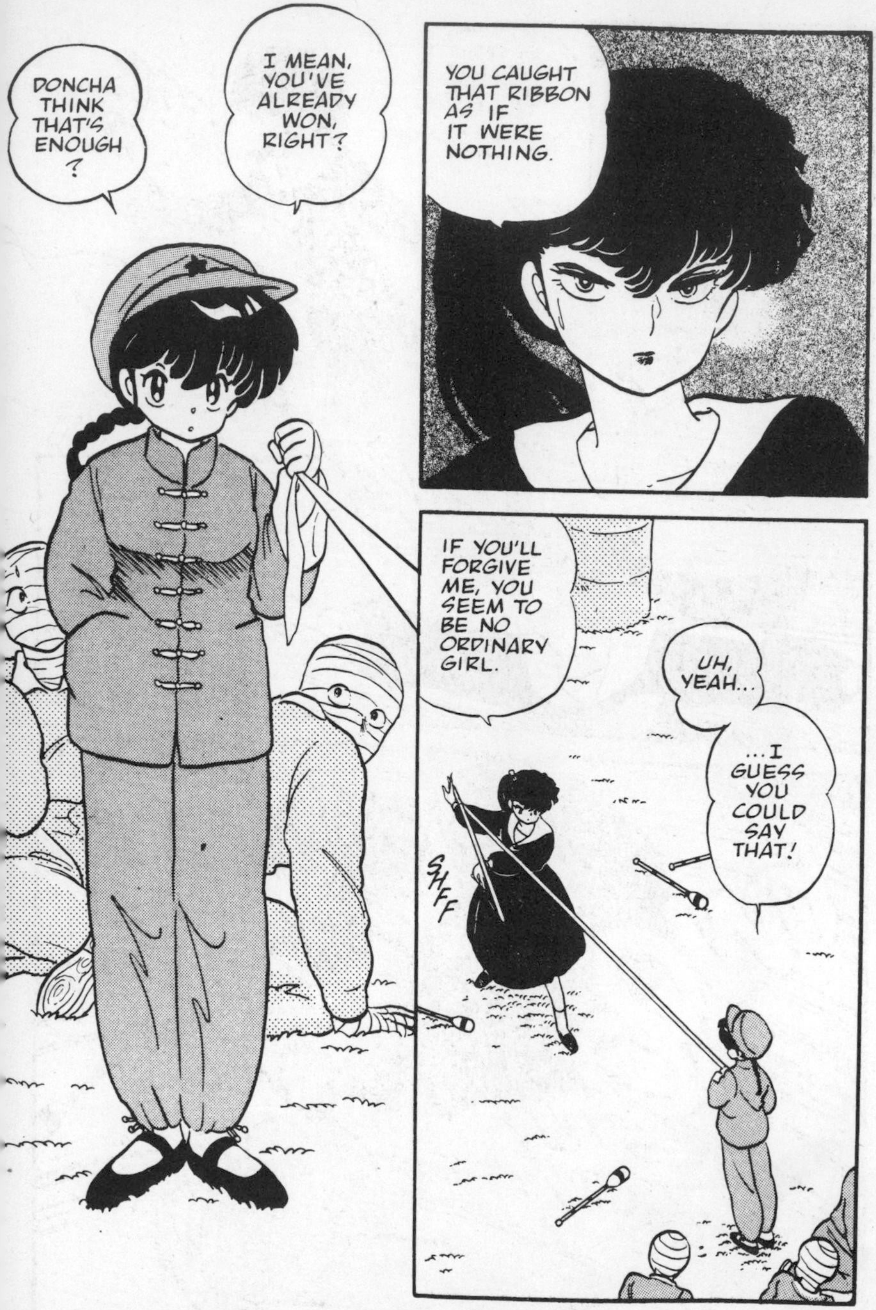

DONCHA THINK THAT'S ENOUGH?
I MEAN, YOU'VE ALREADY WON, RIGHT?
YOU CAUGHT THAT RIBBON AS IF IT WERE NOTHING.
IF YOU'LL FORGIVE ME, YOU SEEM TO BE NO ORDINARY GIRL.
SHFF
UH, YEAH...
...I GUESS YOU COULD SAY THAT!

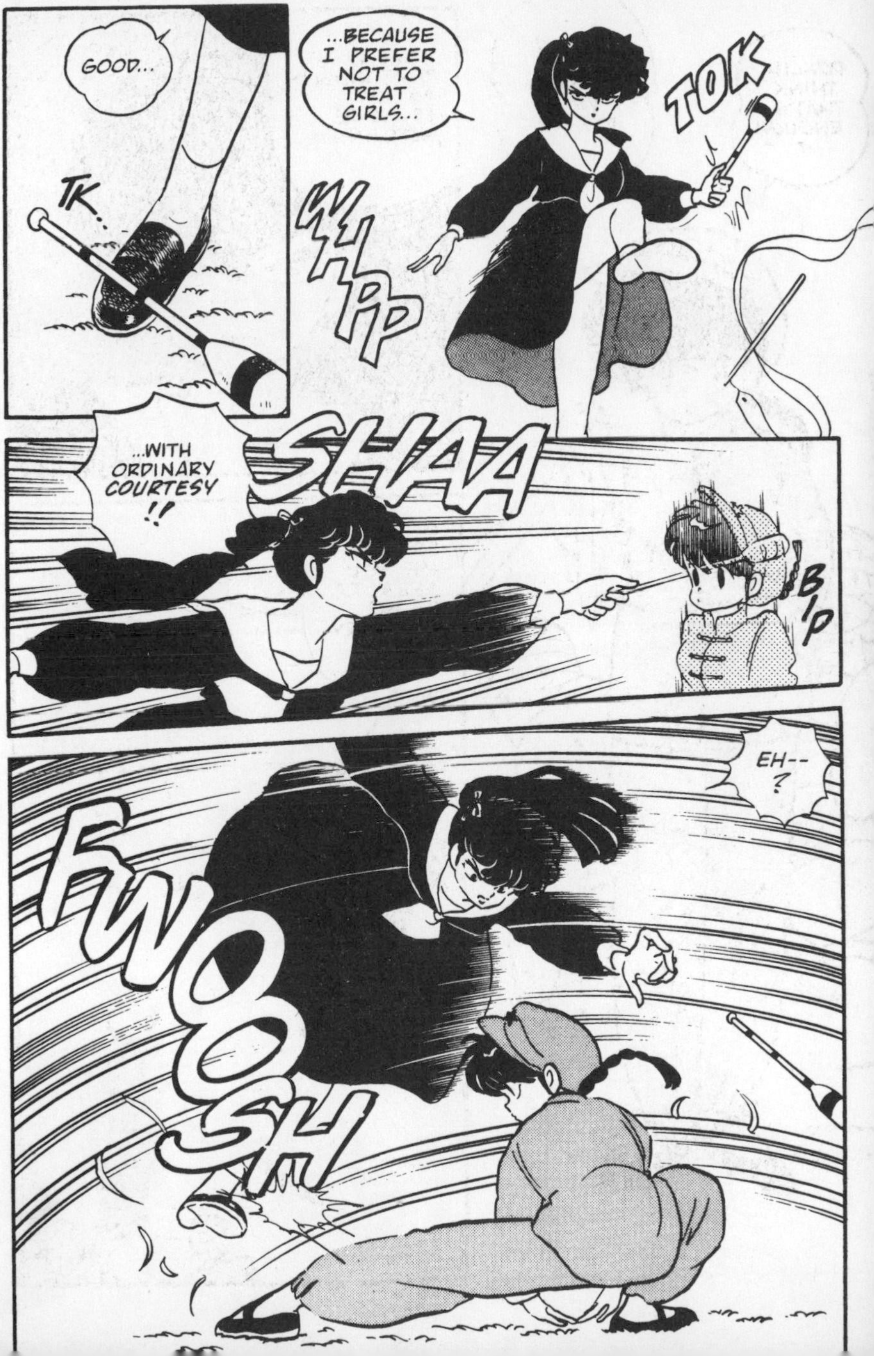
GOOD...
TK...
...BECAUSE I PREFER NOT TO TREAT GIRLS...
TOK
WHIPP
...WITH ORDINARY COURTESY!!
SHAA
BIP
EH--?
FWOOSH

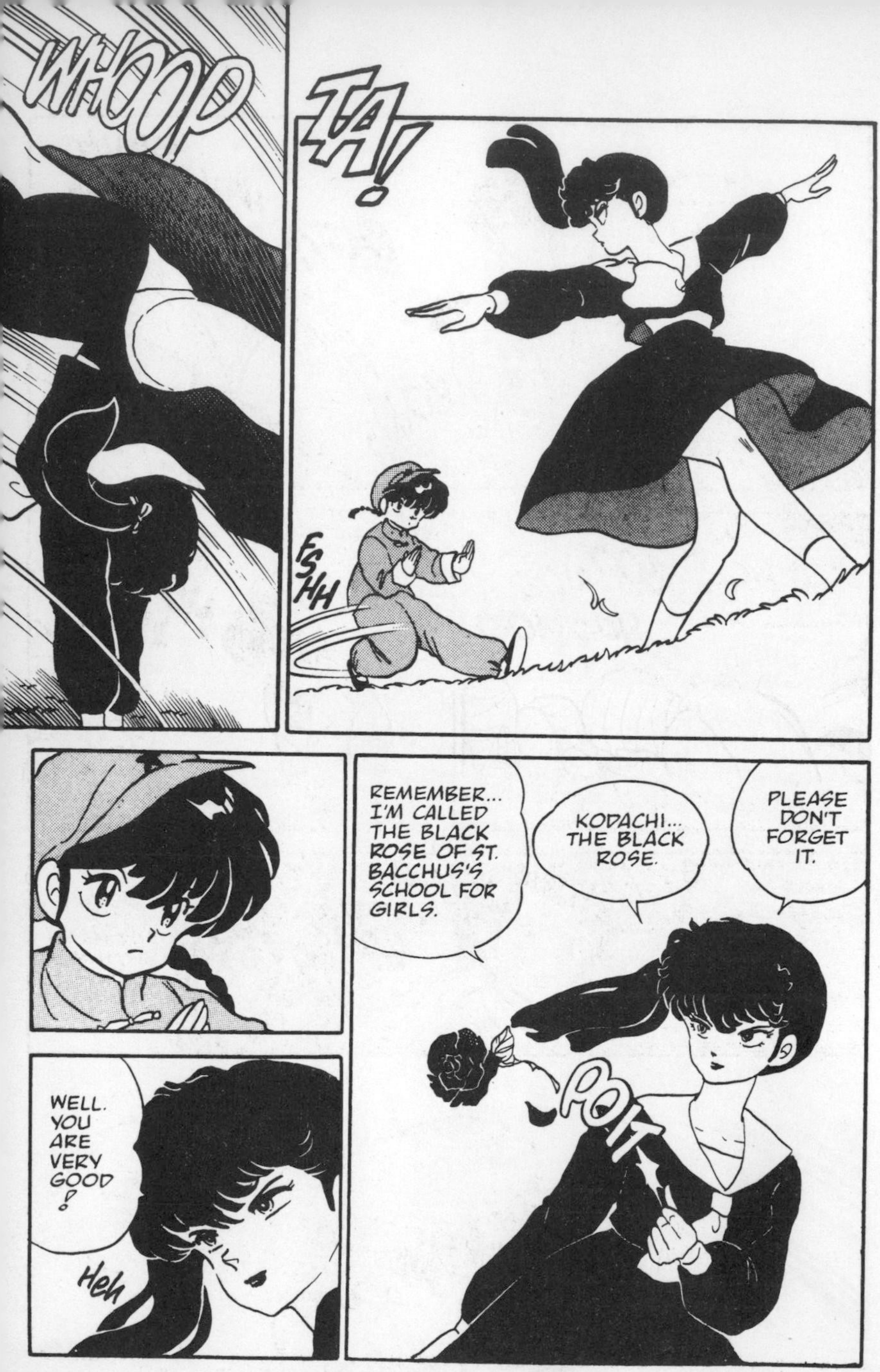
WHOOP
TA!
FSHH
WELL. YOU ARE VERY GOOD!
Heh
REMEMBER... I'M CALLED THE BLACK ROSE OF ST. BACCHUS'S SCHOOL FOR GIRLS.
KODACHI... THE BLACK ROSE.
PLEASE DON'T FORGET IT.
POIT

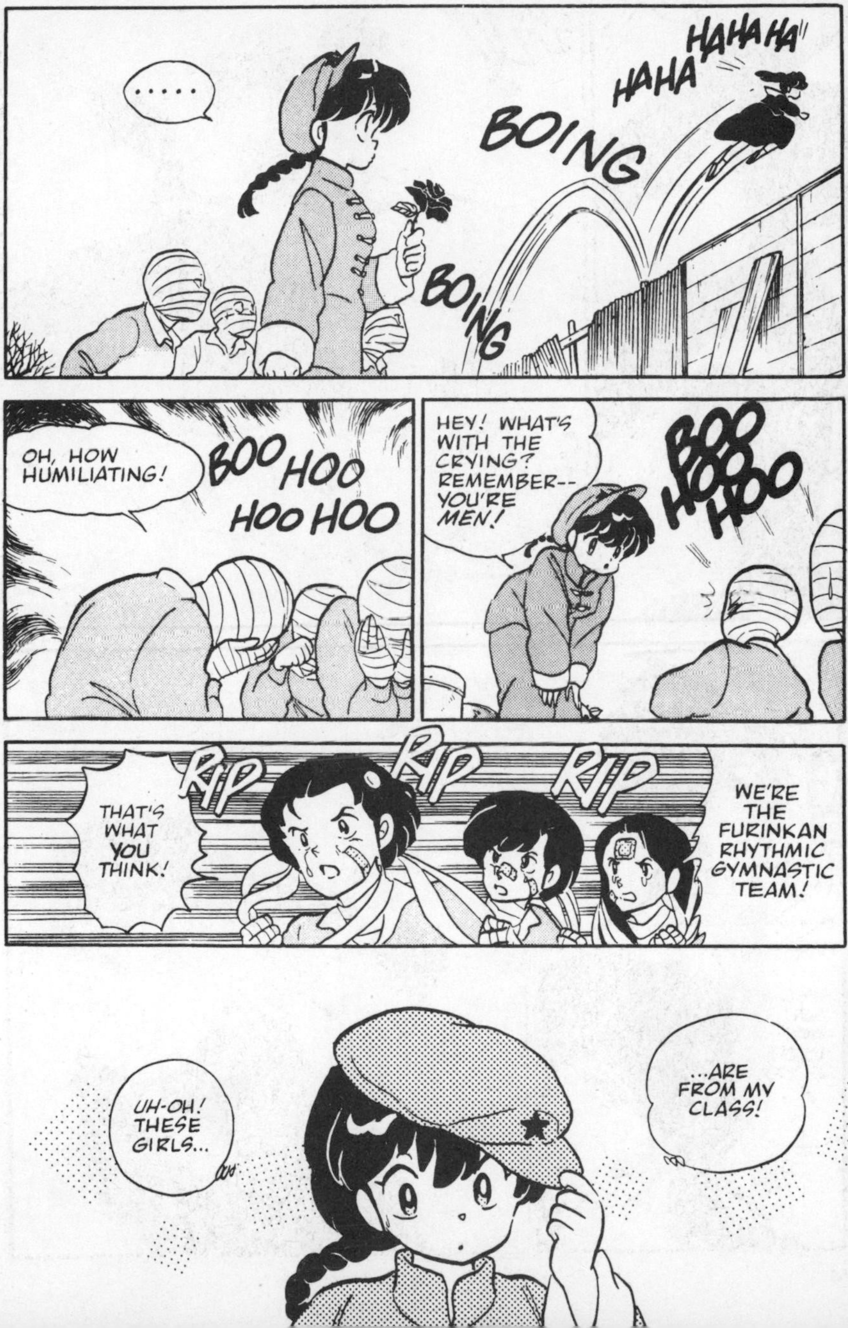
.....
BOING
BOING
HAHA
HAHAHA
OH, HOW HUMILIATING!
BOO HOO HOO HOO
HEY! WHAT'S WITH THE CRYING? REMEMBER-- YOU'RE MEN!
BOO HOO HOO
THAT'S WHAT YOU THINK!
RIP
RIP
RIP
WE'RE THE FURINKAN RHYTHMIC GYMNASTIC TEAM!
UH-OH! THESE GIRLS...
...ARE FROM MY CLASS!

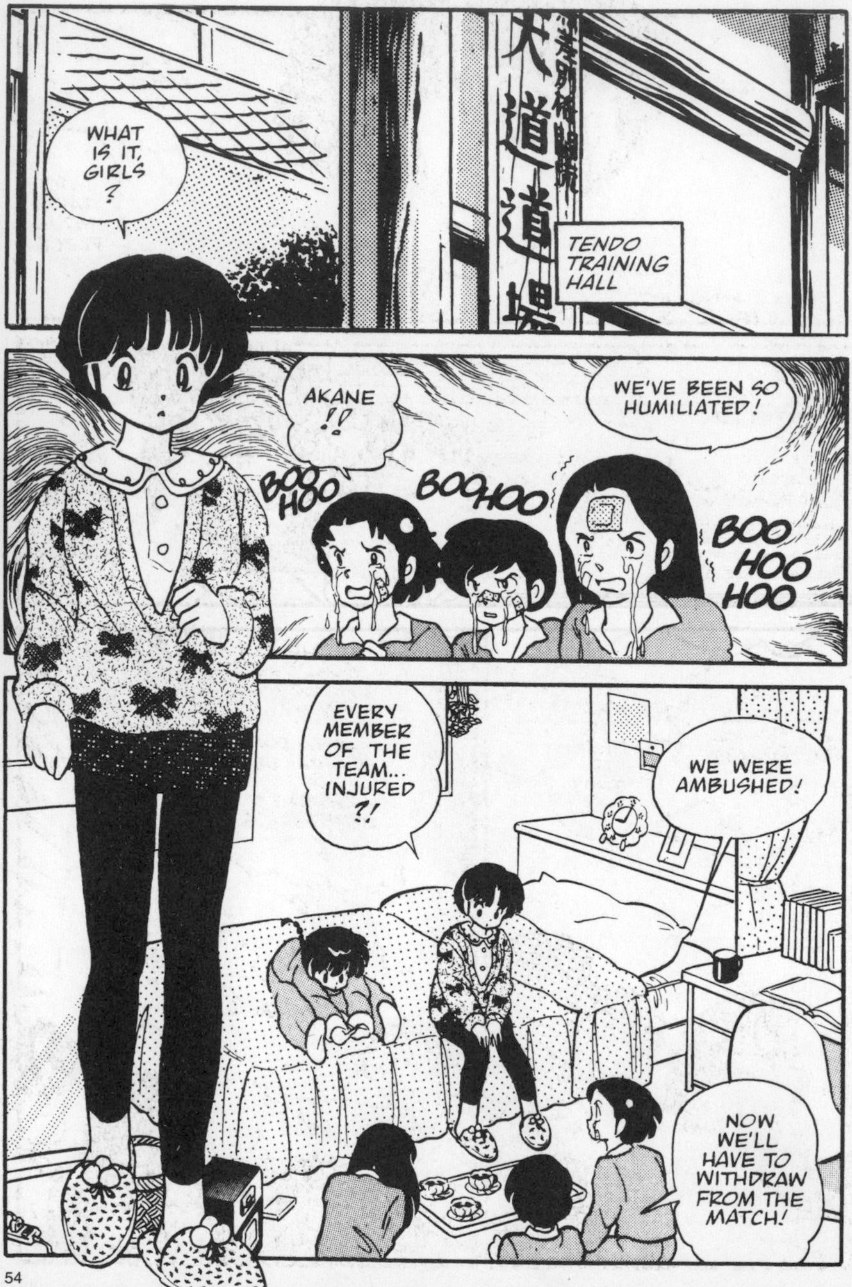
WHAT IS IT, GIRLS?
大道道場
TENDO TRAINING HALL
AKANE!!
WE'VE BEEN SO HUMILIATED!
BOO HOO
BOOHOO
BOO HOO HOO
EVERY MEMBER OF THE TEAM... INJURED?!
WE WERE AMBUSHED!
NOW WE'LL HAVE TO WITHDRAW FROM THE MATCH!

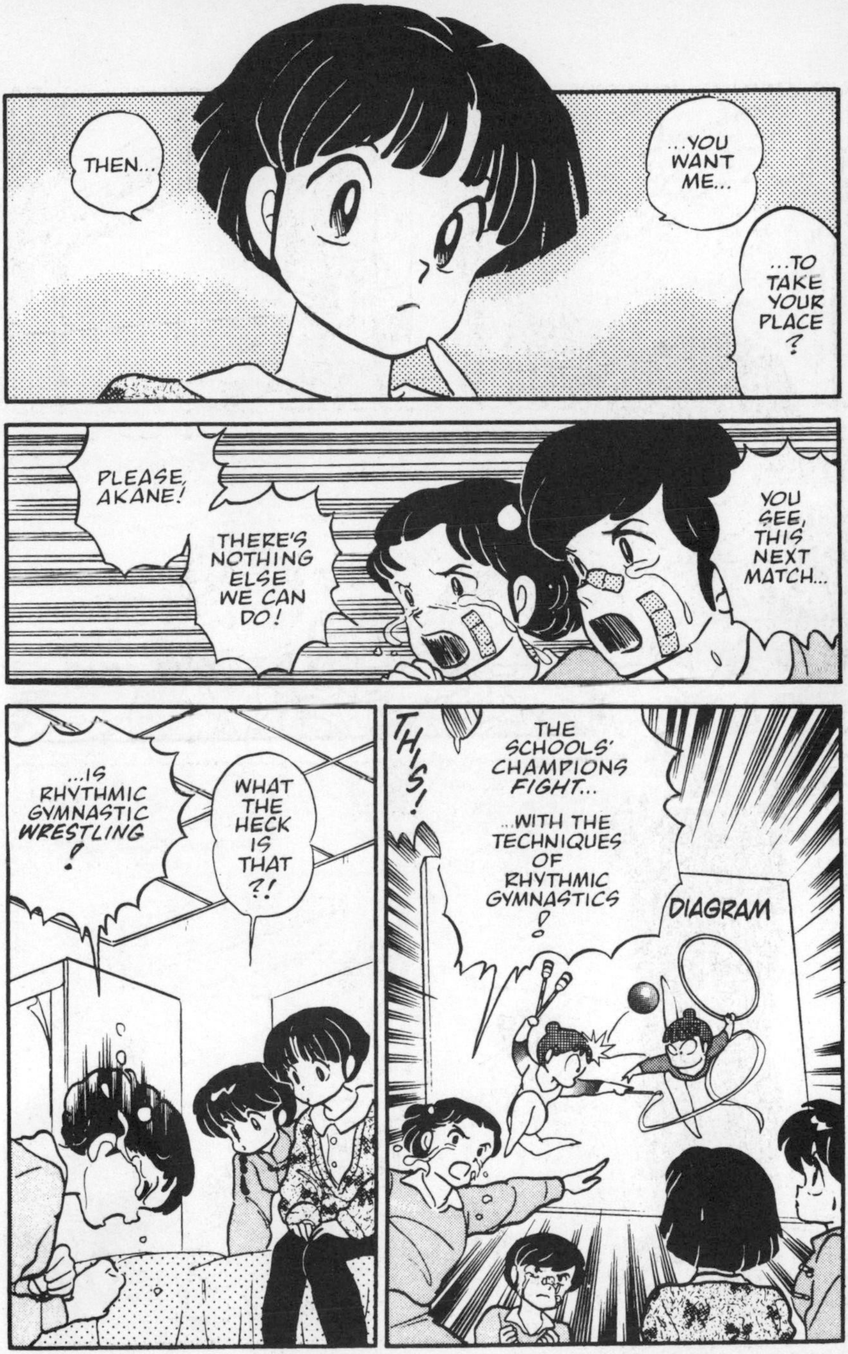
THEN...
...YOU WANT ME...
...TO TAKE YOUR PLACE?
PLEASE, AKANE!
THERE'S NOTHING ELSE WE CAN DO!
YOU SEE, THIS NEXT MATCH...
...IS RHYTHMIC GYMNASTIC WRESTLING!
WHAT THE HECK IS THAT?!
THIS!
THE SCHOOLS' CHAMPIONS FIGHT...
...WITH THE TECHNIQUES OF RHYTHMIC GYMNASTICS!
DIAGRAM

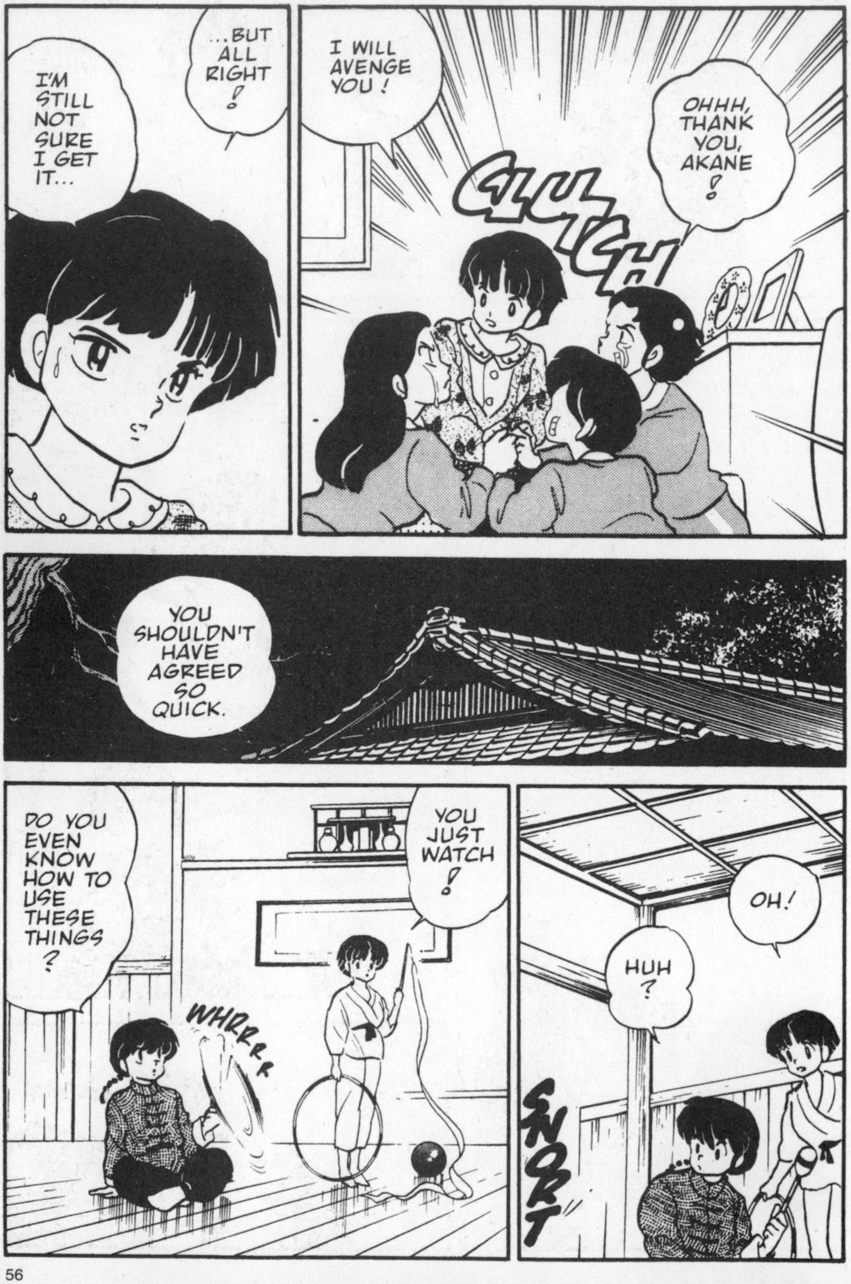

I'M STILL NOT SURE I GET IT...
...BUT ALL RIGHT!
I WILL AVENGE YOU!
CLUTCH
OHHH, THANK YOU, AKANE!
YOU SHOULDN'T HAVE AGREED SO QUICK.
DO YOU EVEN KNOW HOW TO USE THESE THINGS?
WHRRRR
YOU JUST WATCH!
OH!
HUH?
SNORT

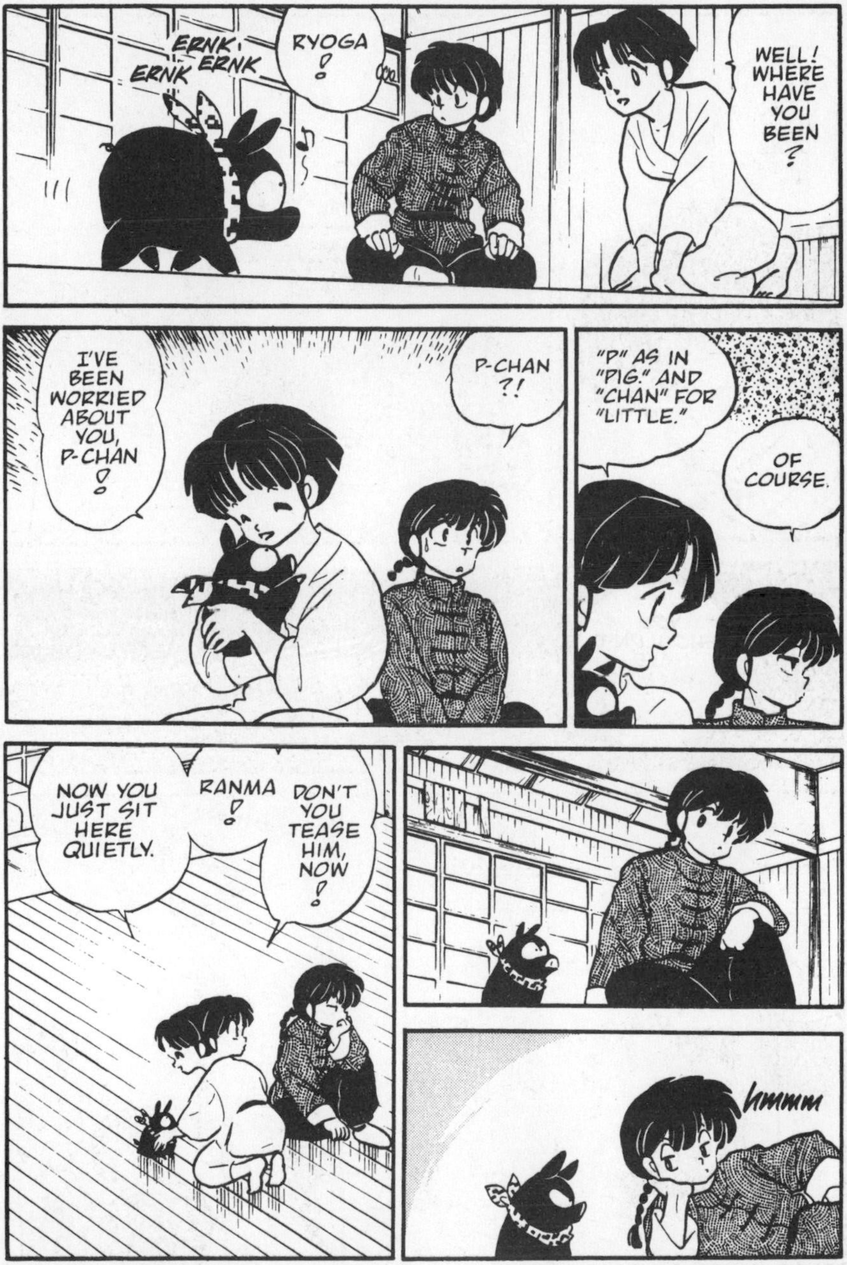
ERNK ERNK ERNK
RYOGA!
WELL! WHERE HAVE YOU BEEN?
I'VE BEEN WORRIED ABOUT YOU, P-CHAN!
P-CHAN?!
"P" AS IN "PIG." AND "CHAN" FOR "LITTLE."
OF COURSE.
NOW YOU JUST SIT HERE QUIETLY.
RANMA! DON'T YOU TEASE HIM, NOW!
HMMMM

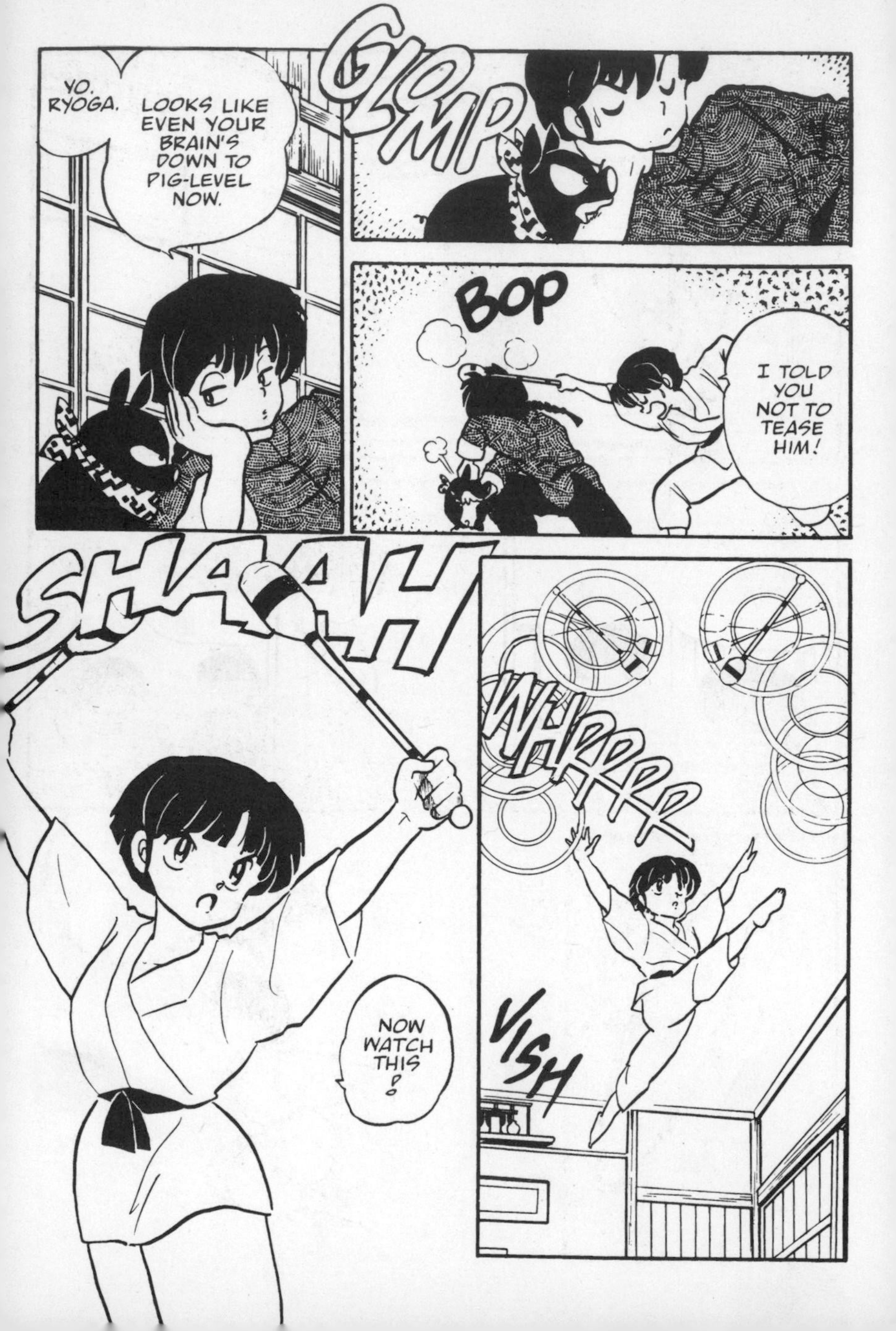
YO. RYOGA.
LOOKS LIKE EVEN YOUR BRAIN'S DOWN TO PIG-LEVEL NOW.
GLOMP
BOP
I TOLD YOU NOT TO TEASE HIM!
SHAAH
NOW WATCH THIS!
WHRRRR
VISH

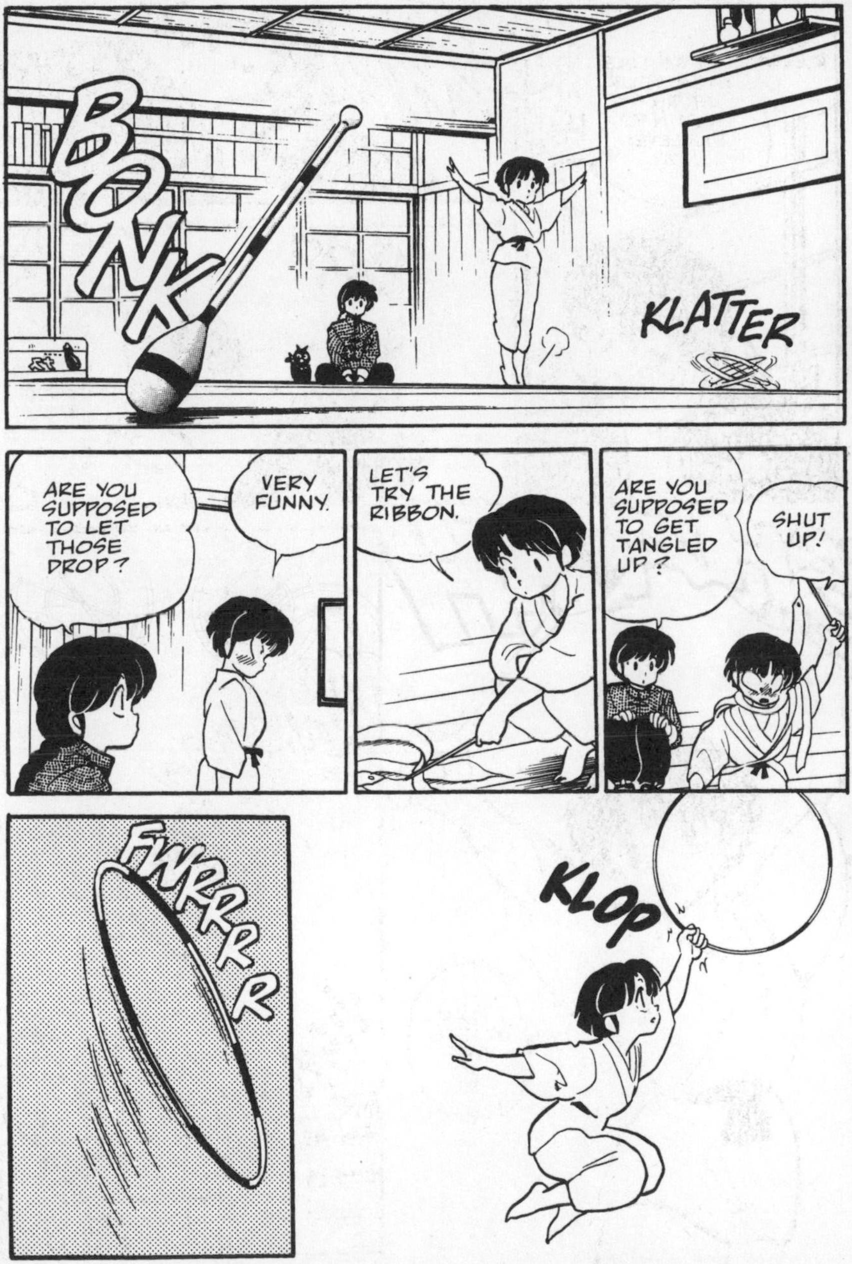
BONK
KLATTER
ARE YOU SUPPOSED TO LET THOSE DROP?
VERY FUNNY.
LET'S TRY THE RIBBON.
ARE YOU SUPPOSED TO GET TANGLED UP?
SHUT UP!
FWRRRR R
KLOP

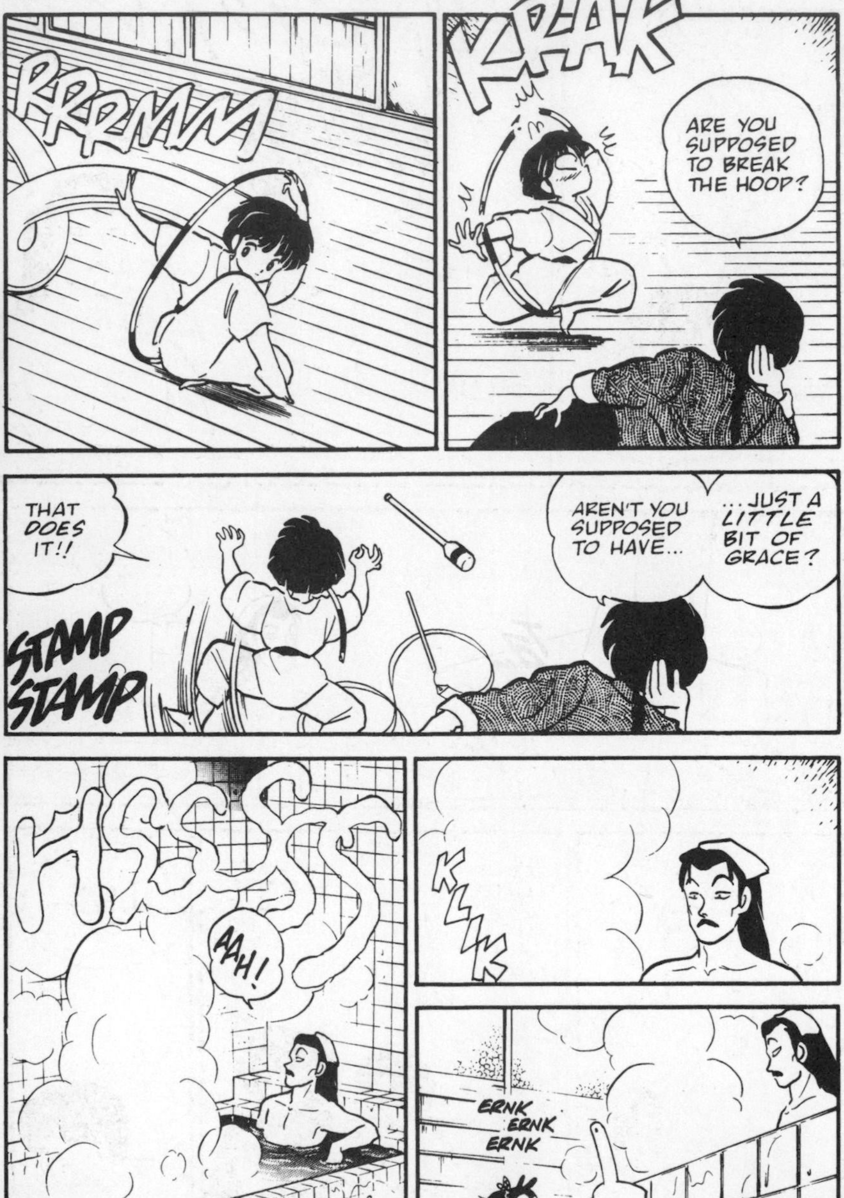
RRRMMM
KRAK
ARE YOU SUPPOSED TO BREAK THE HOOP?
THAT DOES IT!!
STAMP STAMP
AREN'T YOU SUPPOSED TO HAVE...
...JUST A LITTLE BIT OF GRACE?
HISSSS
AAH!
KLIK
ERNK ERNK ERNK

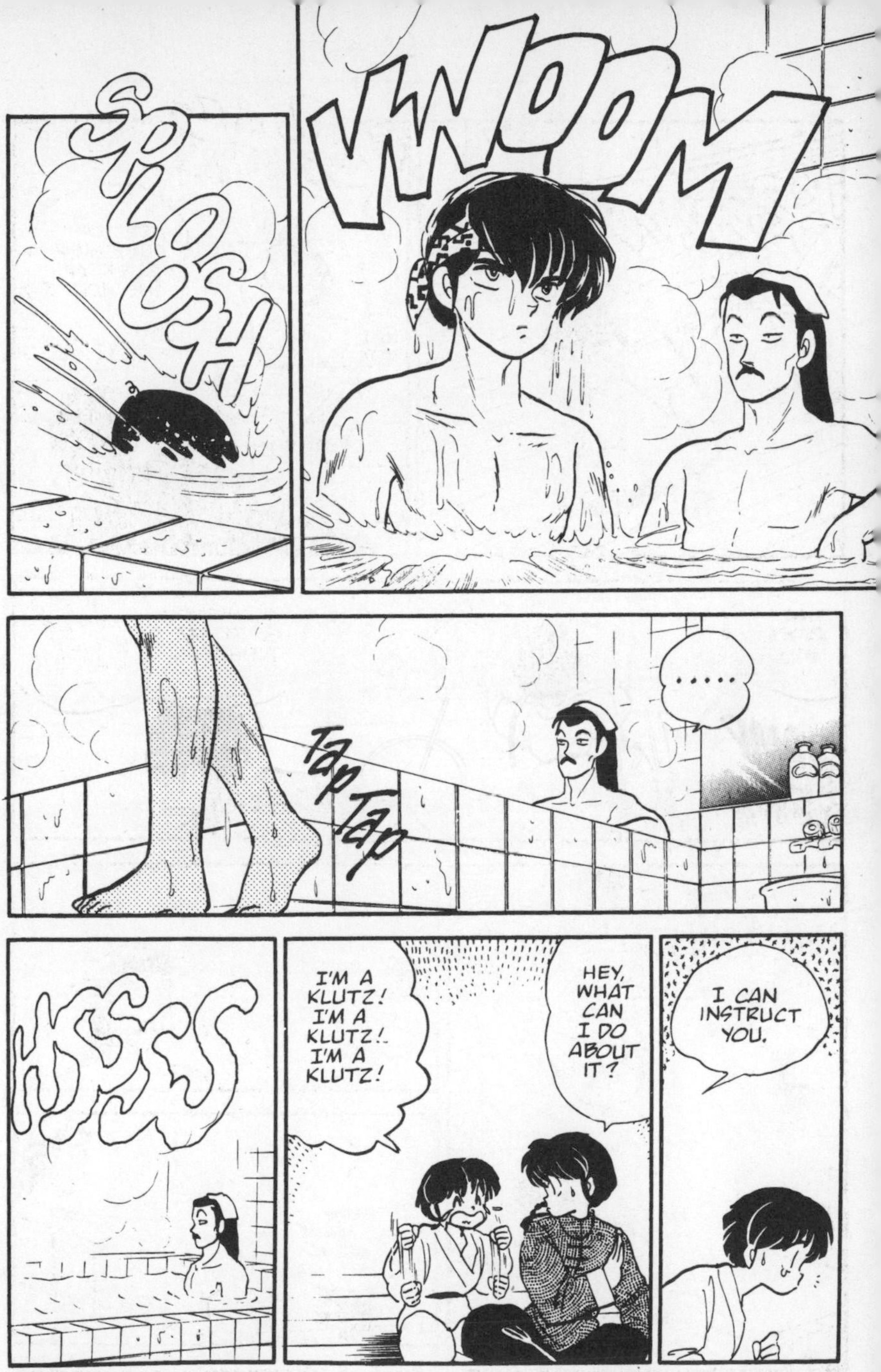
SPLOOSH
VWOOM
.....
TAP TAP
HSSSS
I'M A KLUTZ! I'M A KLUTZ! I'M A KLUTZ!
HEY, WHAT CAN I DO ABOUT IT?
I CAN INSTRUCT YOU.

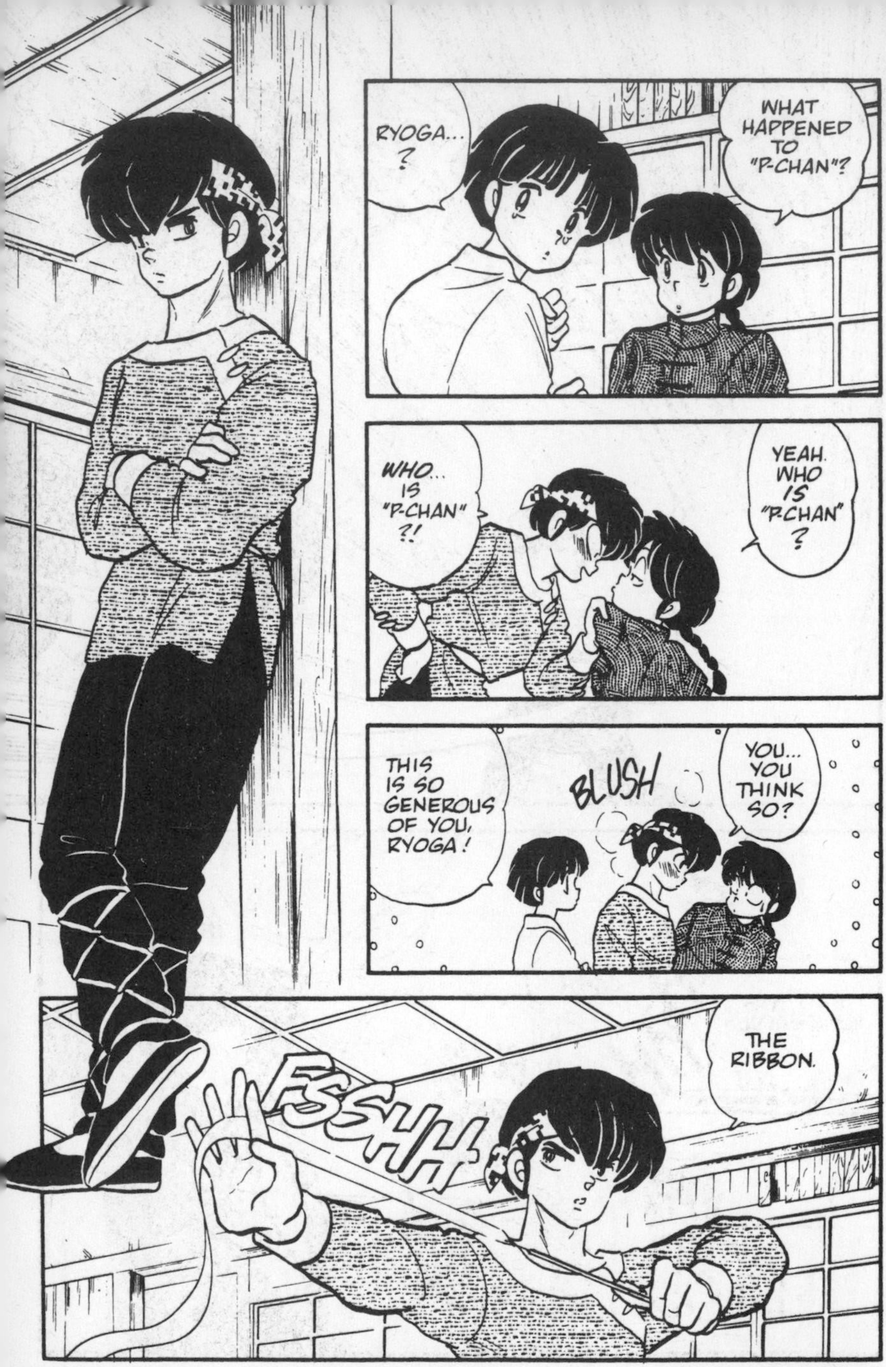
RYOGA... ?
WHAT HAPPENED TO "P-CHAN"?
WHO... IS "P-CHAN" ?!
YEAH. WHO IS "P-CHAN" ?
THIS IS SO GENEROUS OF YOU, RYOGA!
BLUSH
YOU... YOU THINK SO?
FSSHH
THE RIBBON.

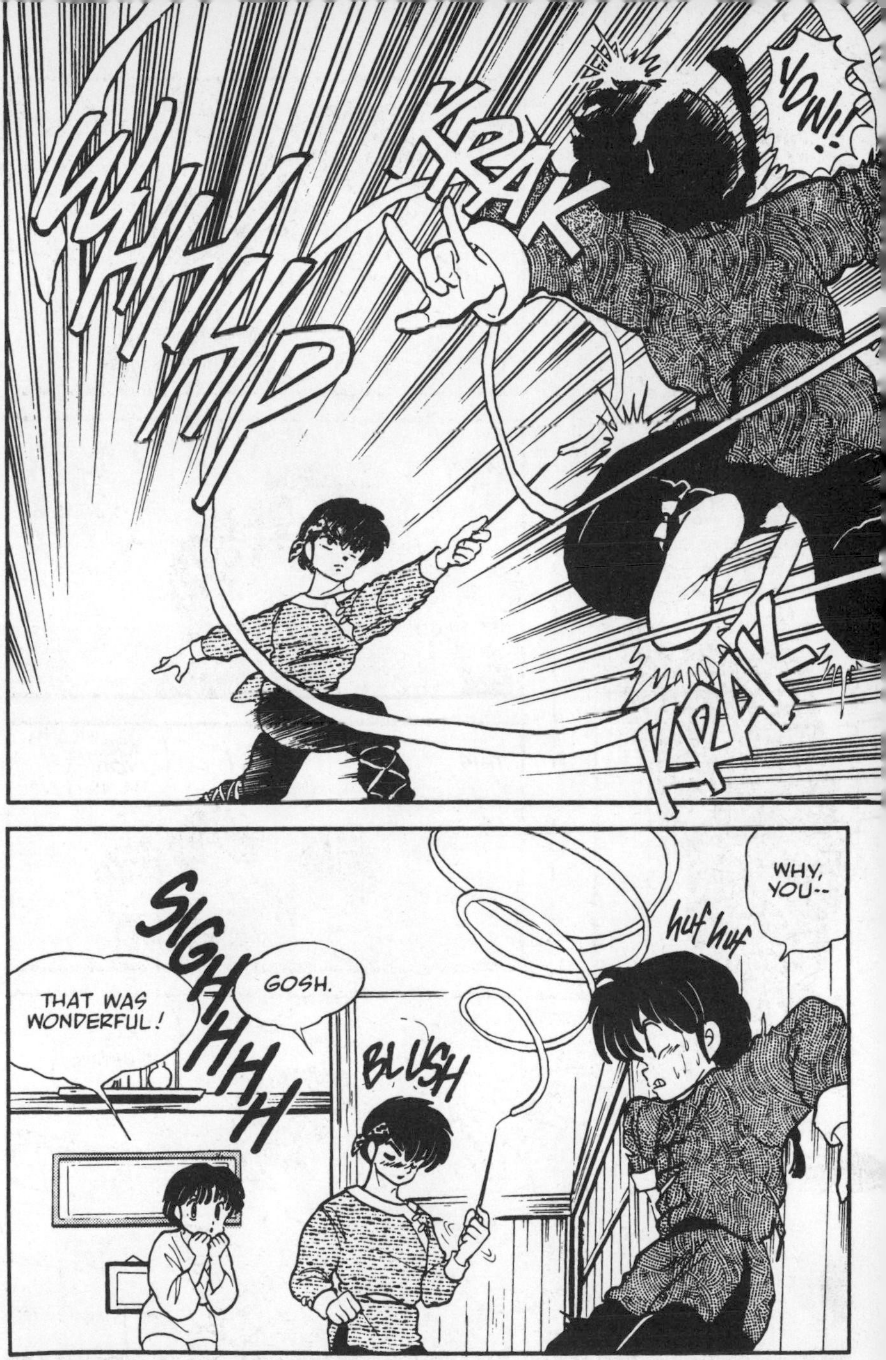
WHHIP
KRAK
YOW!!
KRAK
THAT WAS WONDERFUL!
SIGHHHH
GOSH.
BLUSH
huf huf
WHY, YOU--

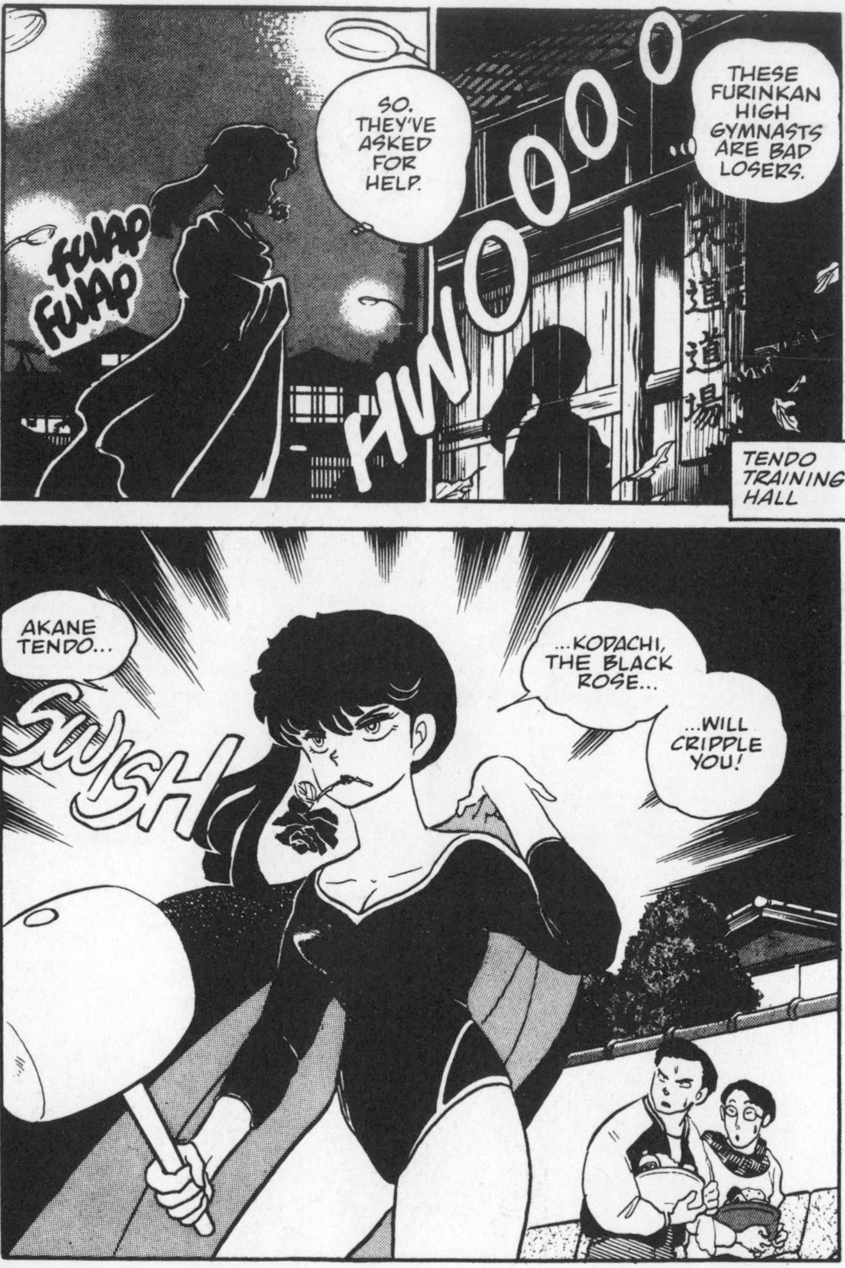
SO. THEY'VE ASKED FOR HELP.
FWAP FWAP
HWOOOOOO
THESE FURINKAN HIGH GYMNASTS ARE BAD LOSERS.
TENDO TRAINING HALL
AKANE TENDO...
SWISH
...KODACHI, THE BLACK ROSE...
...WILL CRIPPLE YOU!

Part 4

THE LOVE OF
THE BLACK ROSE

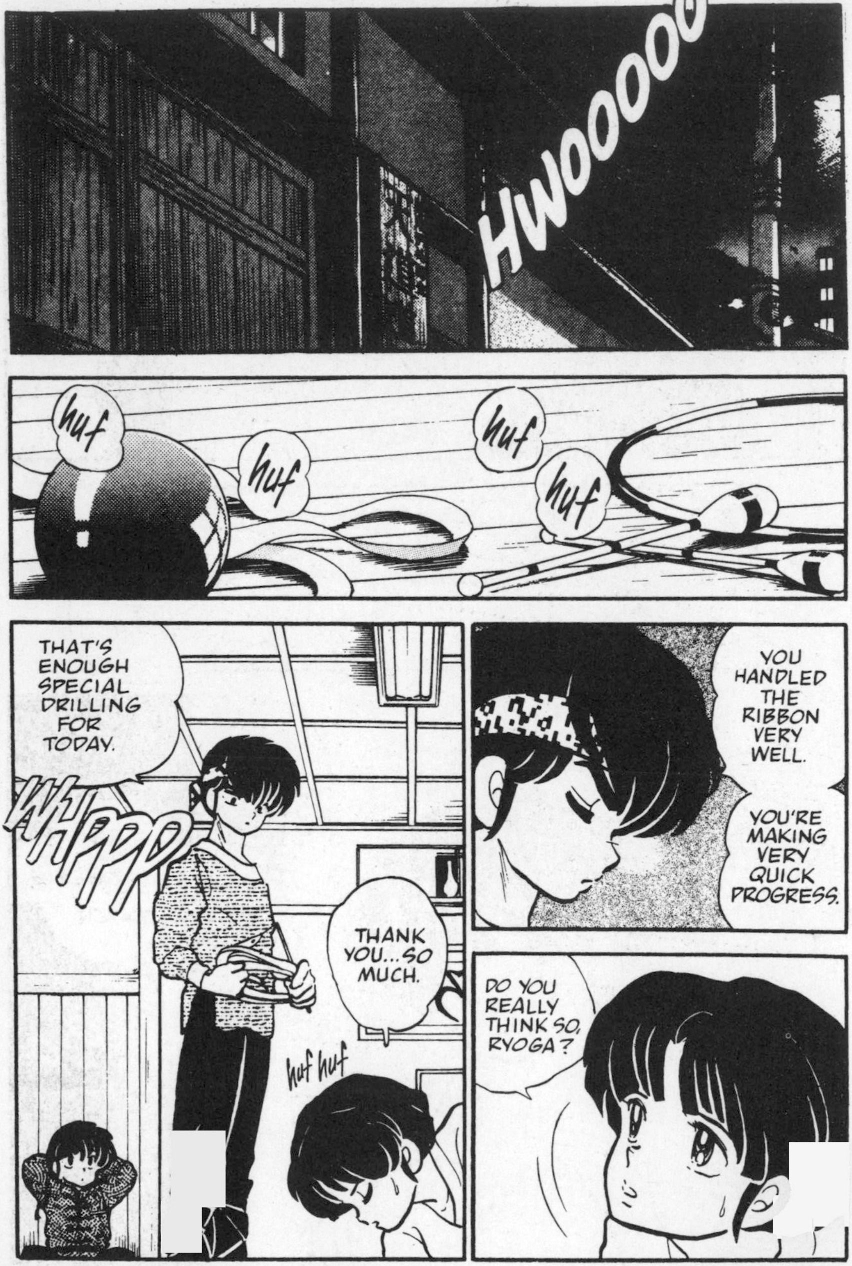
HWOOOOO
huf
huf
huf
huf
THAT'S ENOUGH SPECIAL DRILLING FOR TODAY.
WHPPP
THANK YOU... SO MUCH.
huf huf
YOU HANDLED THE RIBBON VERY WELL.
YOU'RE MAKING VERY QUICK PROGRESS.
DO YOU REALLY THINK SO, RYOGA?

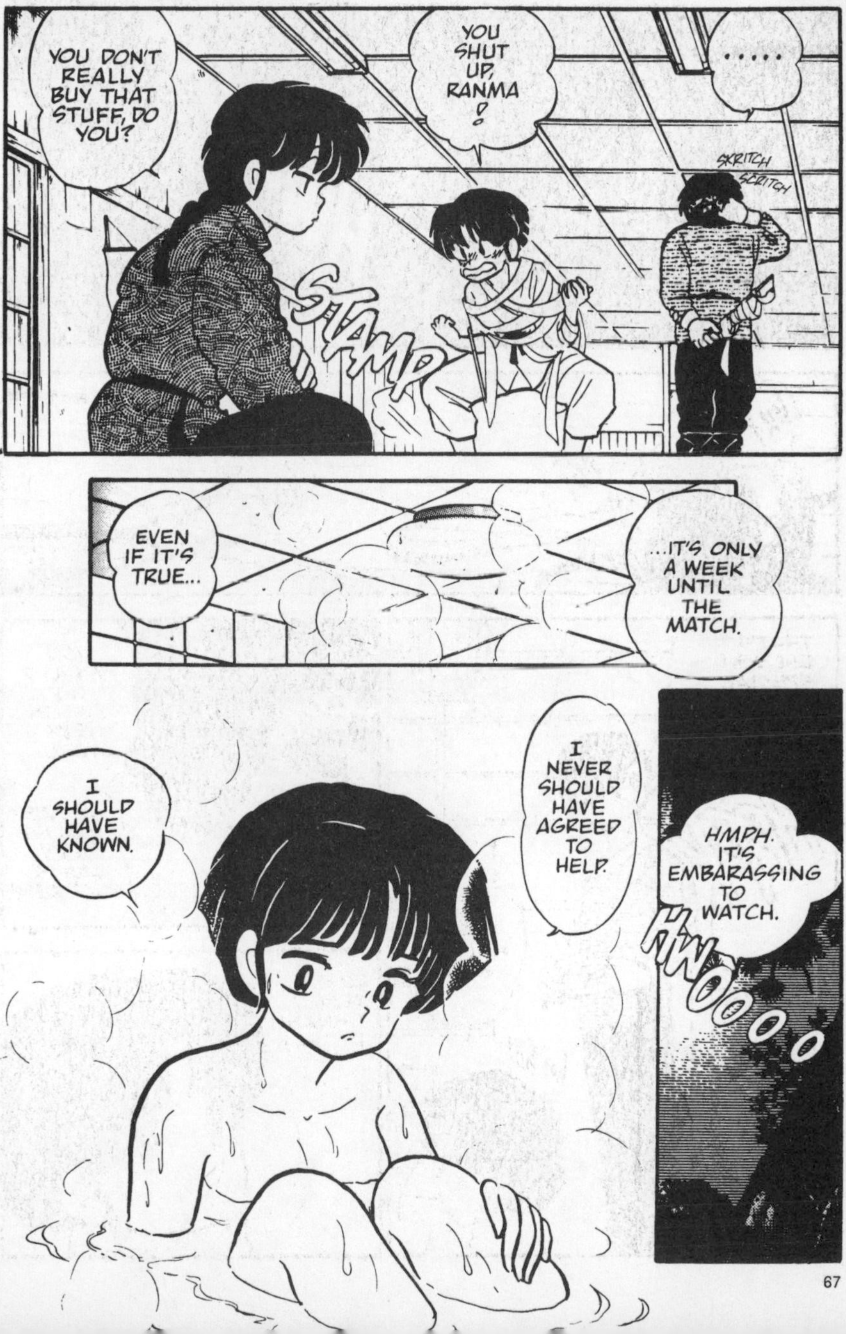
YOU DON'T REALLY BUY THAT STUFF, DO YOU?
YOU SHUT UP, RANMA!
.....
SKRITCH SKRITCH
STAMP
EVEN IF IT'S TRUE...
...IT'S ONLY A WEEK UNTIL THE MATCH.
I SHOULD HAVE KNOWN.
I NEVER SHOULD HAVE AGREED TO HELP.
HMPH. IT'S EMBARASSING TO WATCH.
HWOOOOO

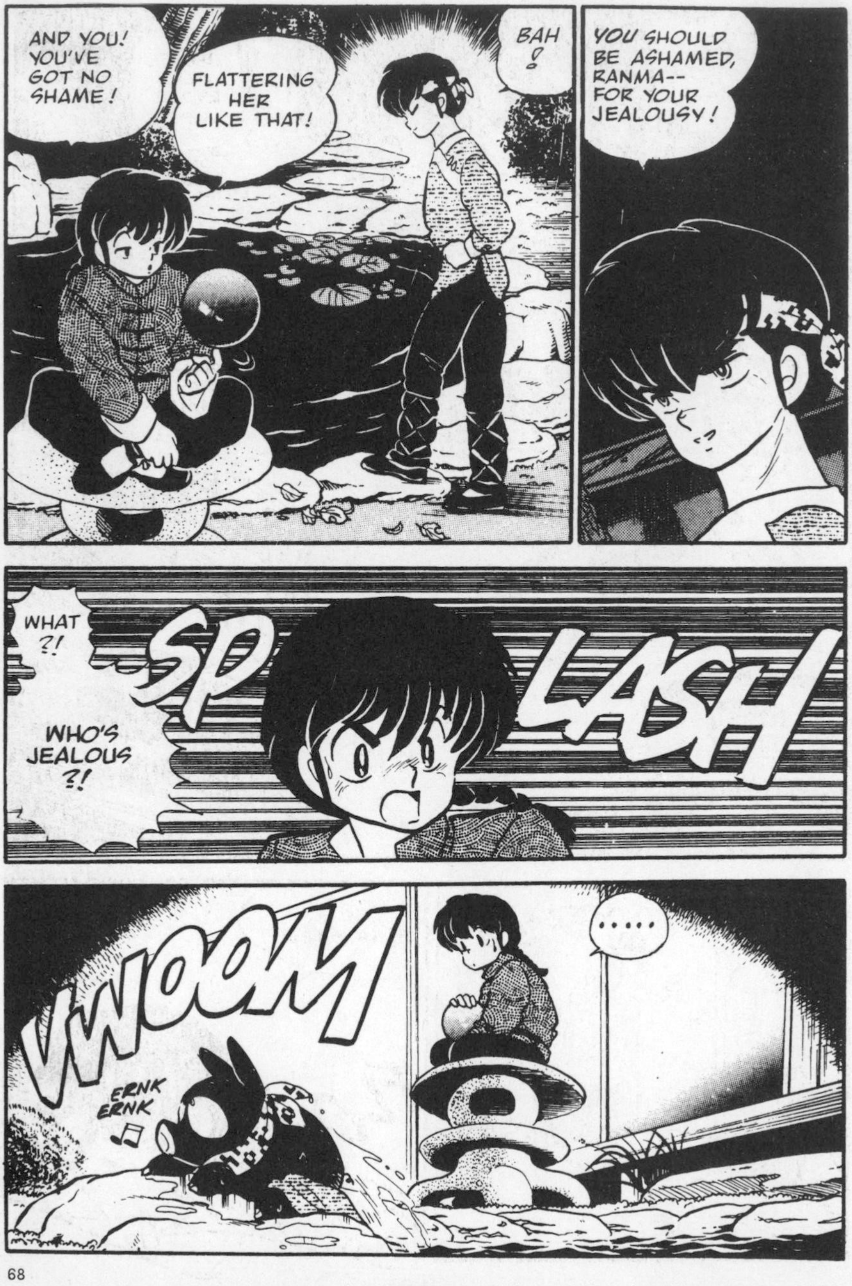
AND YOU! YOU'VE GOT NO SHAME!
FLATTERING HER LIKE THAT!
BAH!
YOU SHOULD BE ASHAMED, RANMA-- FOR YOUR JEALOUSY!
WHAT ?!
SPLASH
WHO'S JEALOUS ?!
WOOM
ERNK ERNK ♫
.....

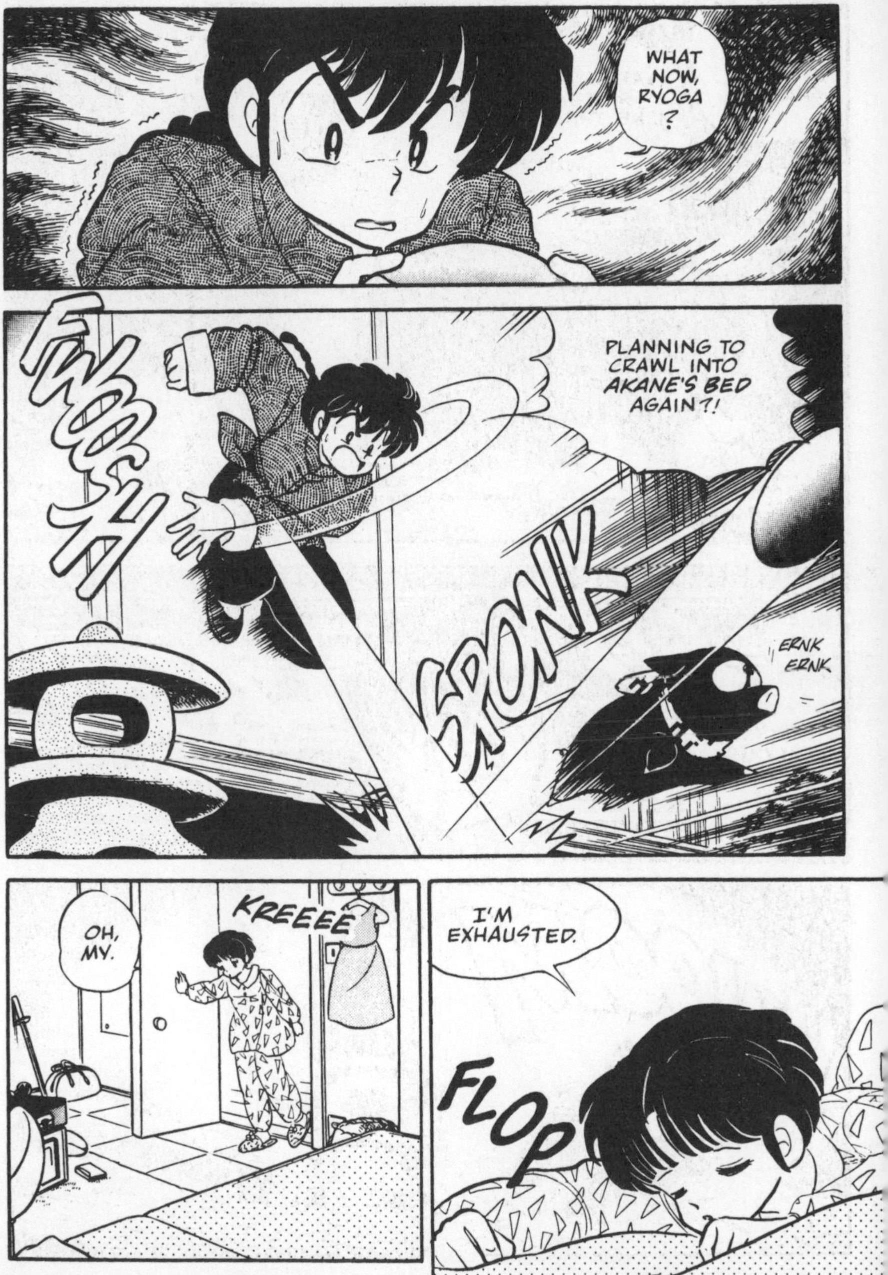
WHAT NOW, RYOGA?
FWOOSH
PLANNING TO CRAWL INTO AKANE'S BED AGAIN?!
SPONK
ERNK ERNK
OH, MY.
KREEEE
I'M EXHAUSTED.
FLOP

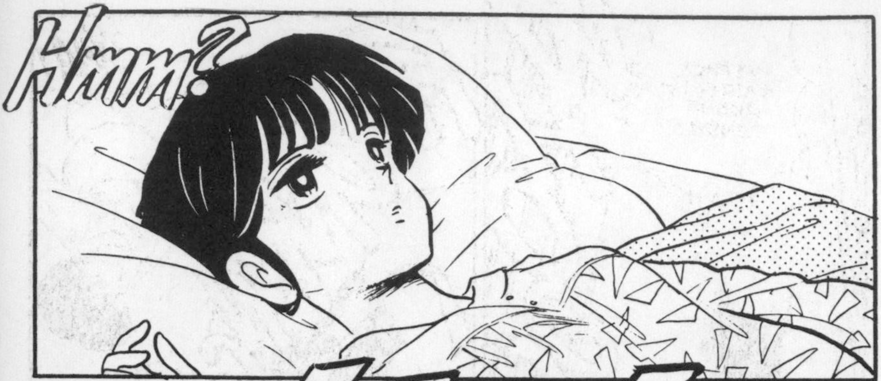
Hmm?
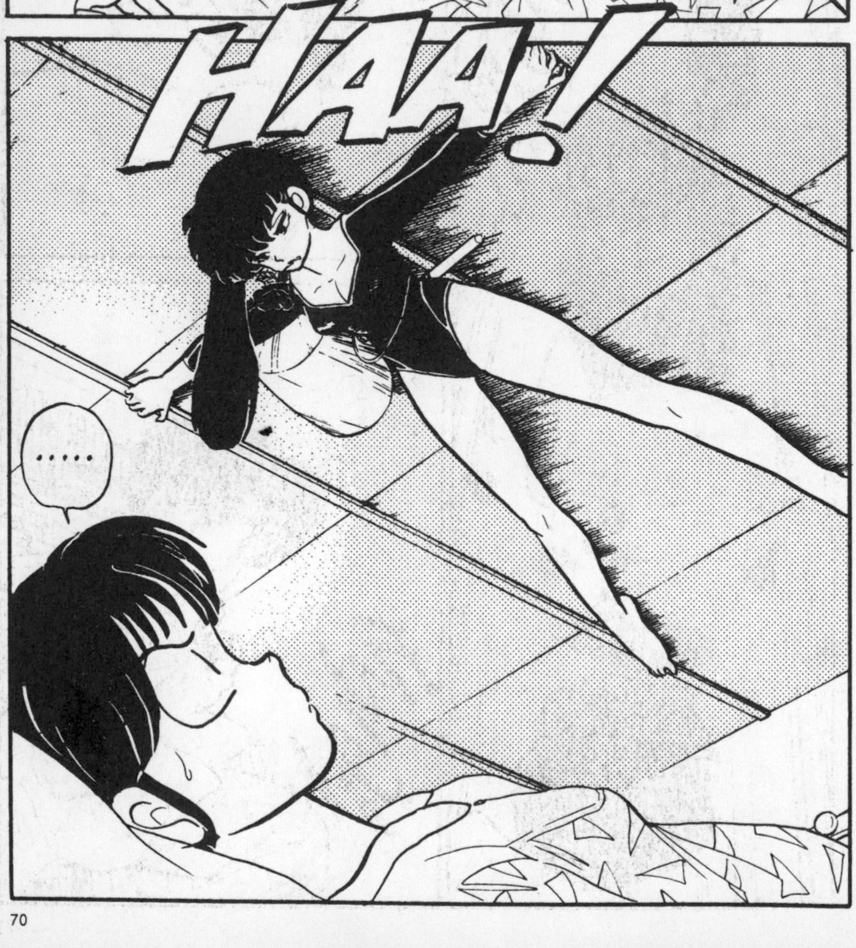
HAA!
......

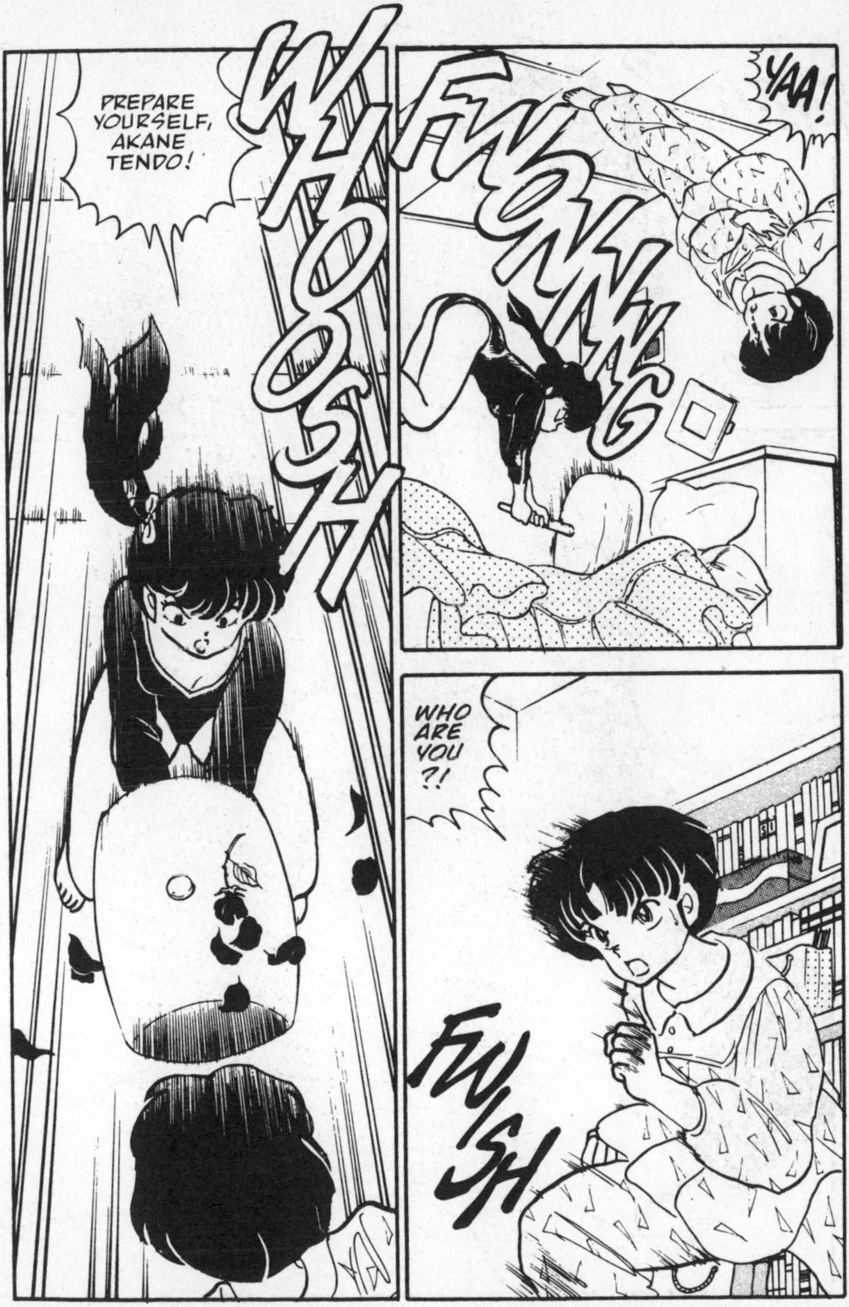
PREPARE YOURSELF, AKANE TENDO!
WHOOSH
WHUNNNG
YAA!
WHO ARE YOU?!
FWISH

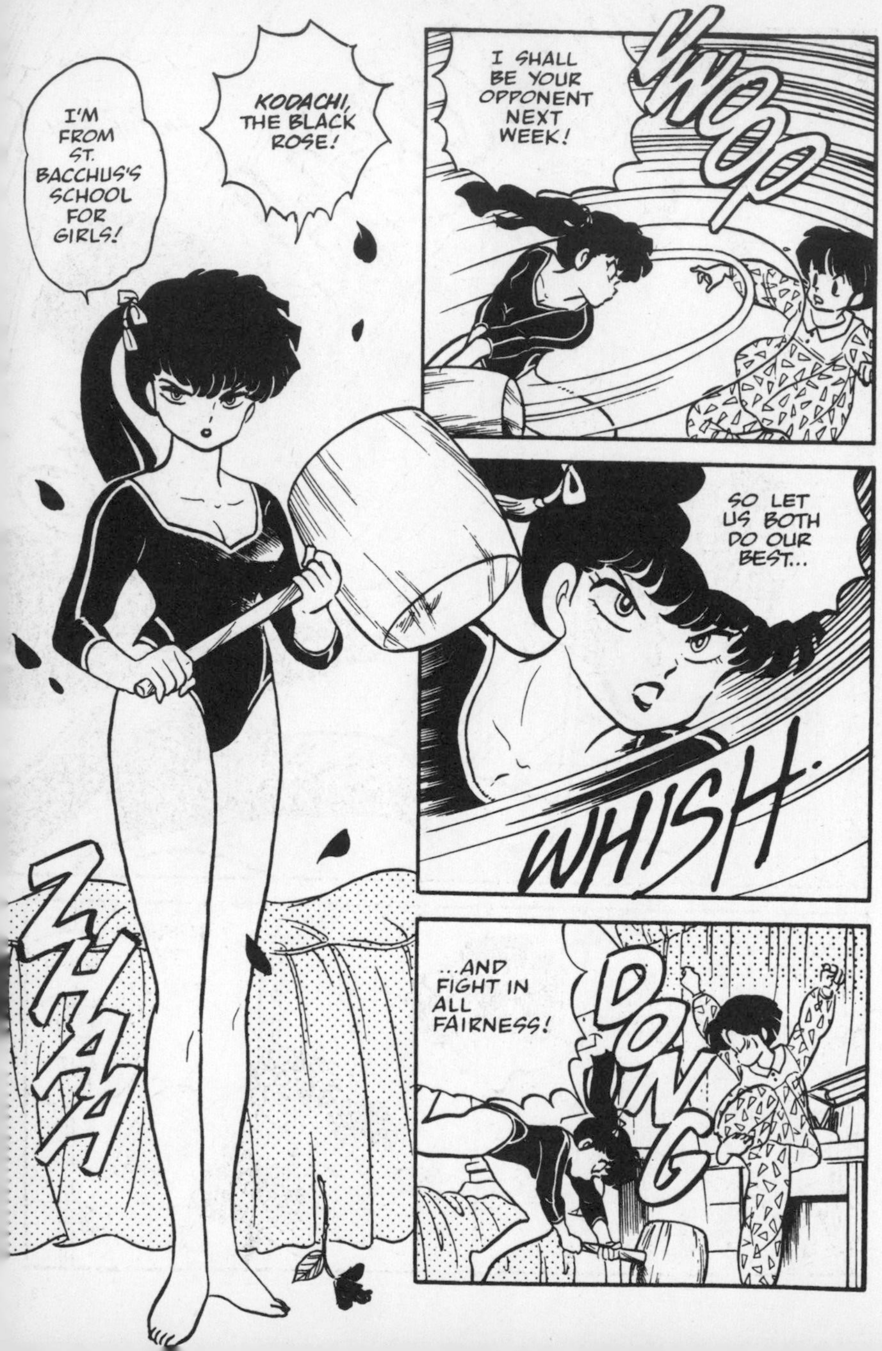
I'M FROM ST. BACCHUS'S SCHOOL FOR GIRLS!
KODACHI, THE BLACK ROSE!
ZHAA
I SHALL BE YOUR OPPONENT NEXT WEEK!
WOOP
SO LET US BOTH DO OUR BEST...
WHISH.
...AND FIGHT IN ALL FAIRNESS!
DONG

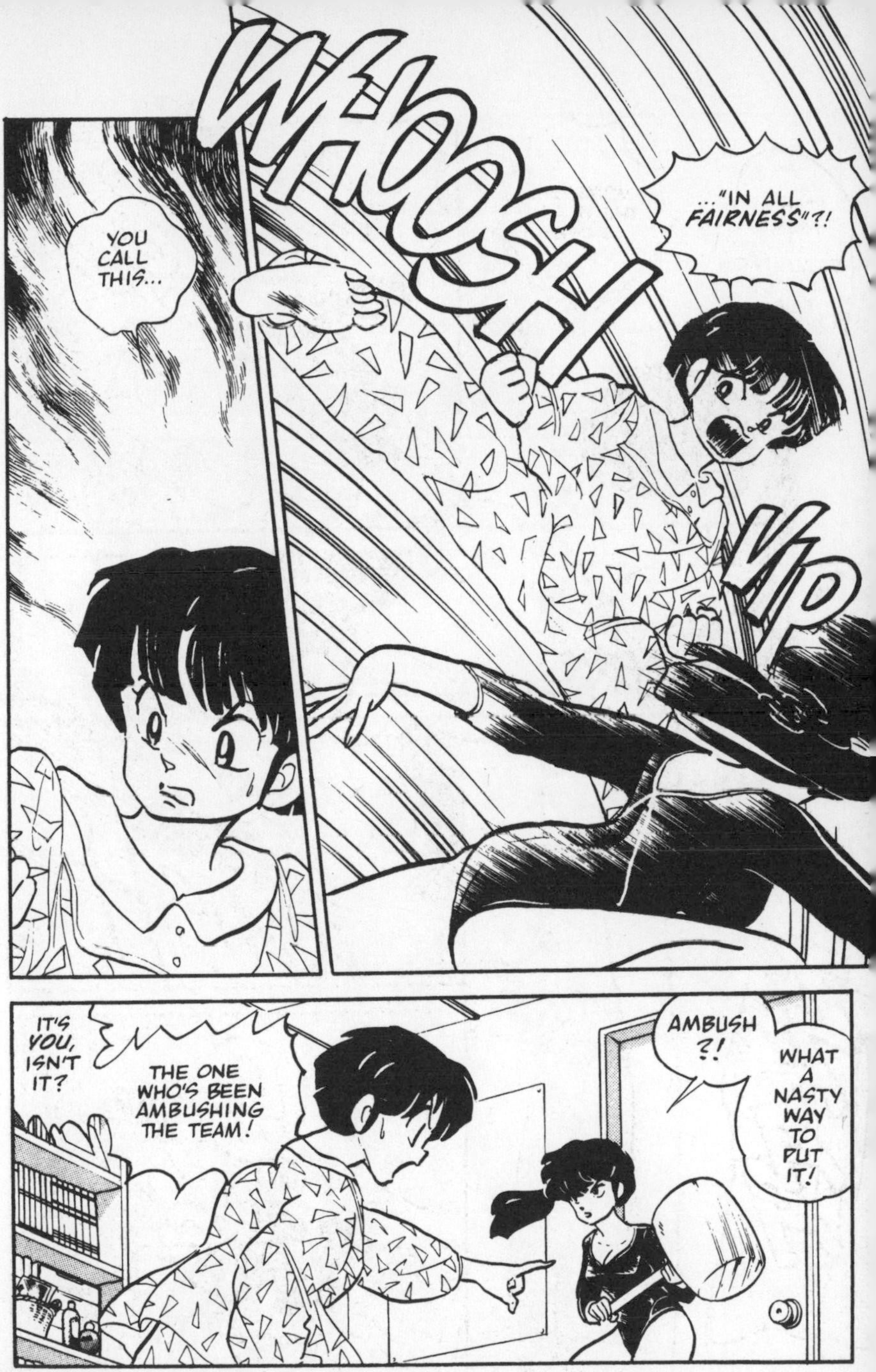
WHOOSH
YOU CALL THIS...
..."IN ALL FAIRNESS"?!
VIP
IT'S YOU, ISN'T IT?
THE ONE WHO'S BEEN AMBUSHING THE TEAM!
AMBUSH?!
WHAT A NASTY WAY TO PUT IT!

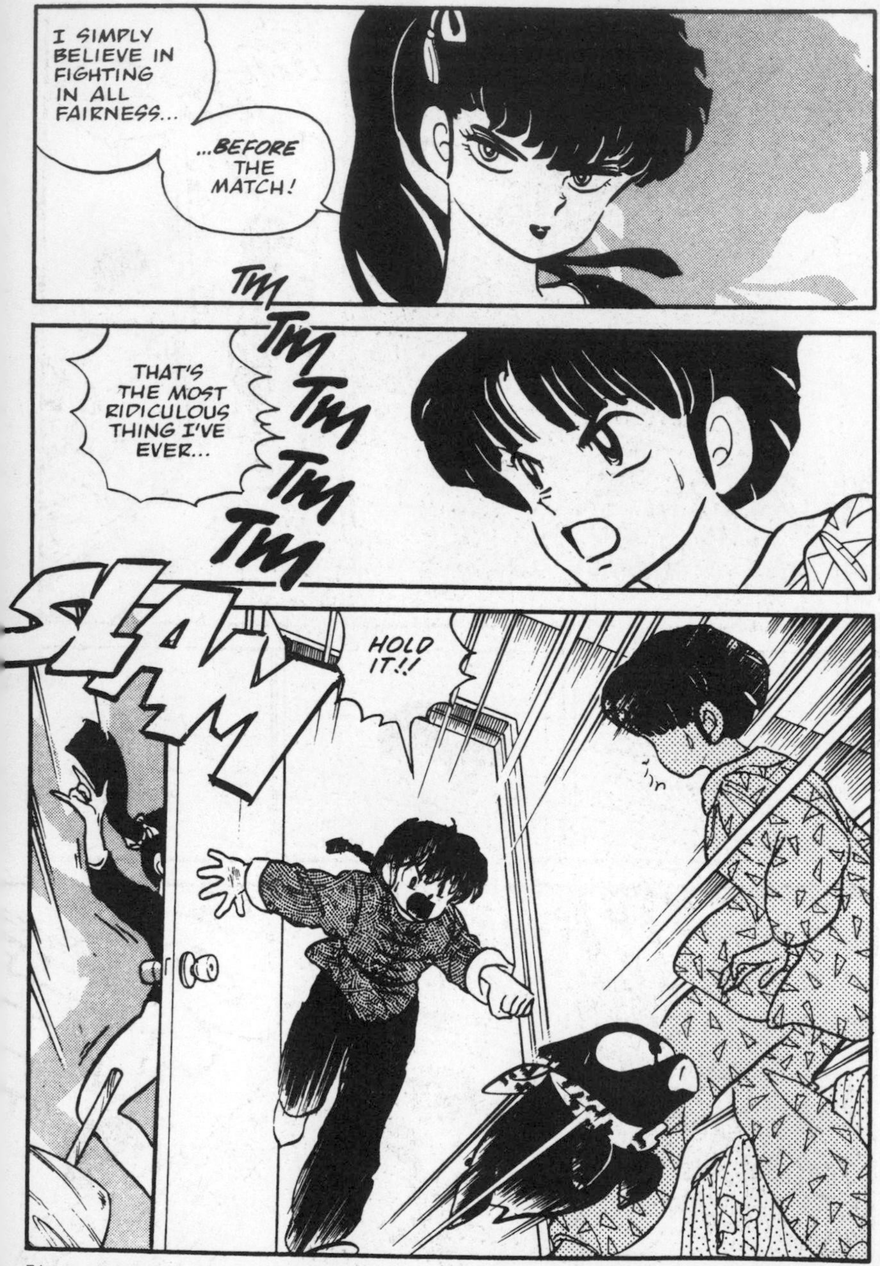
I SIMPLY BELIEVE IN FIGHTING IN ALL FAIRNESS...
...BEFORE THE MATCH!
TM TM TM TM TM TM
THAT'S THE MOST RIDICULOUS THING I'VE EVER...
SLAM
HOLD IT!!

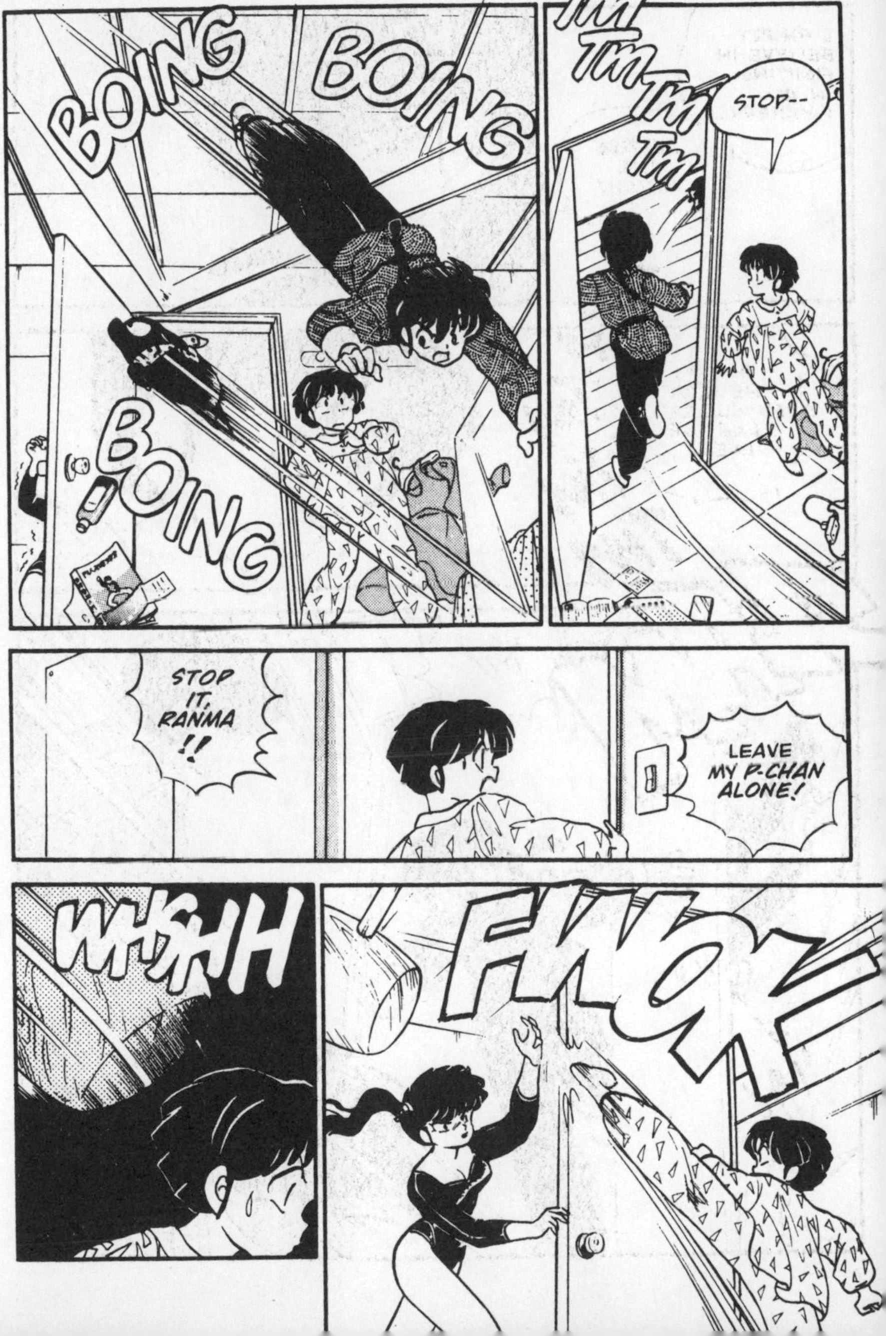
BOING
BOING
BOING
Tm Tm Tm Tm
STOP--
STOP IT, RANMA!!
LEAVE MY P-CHAN ALONE!
WHSHH
FWOK

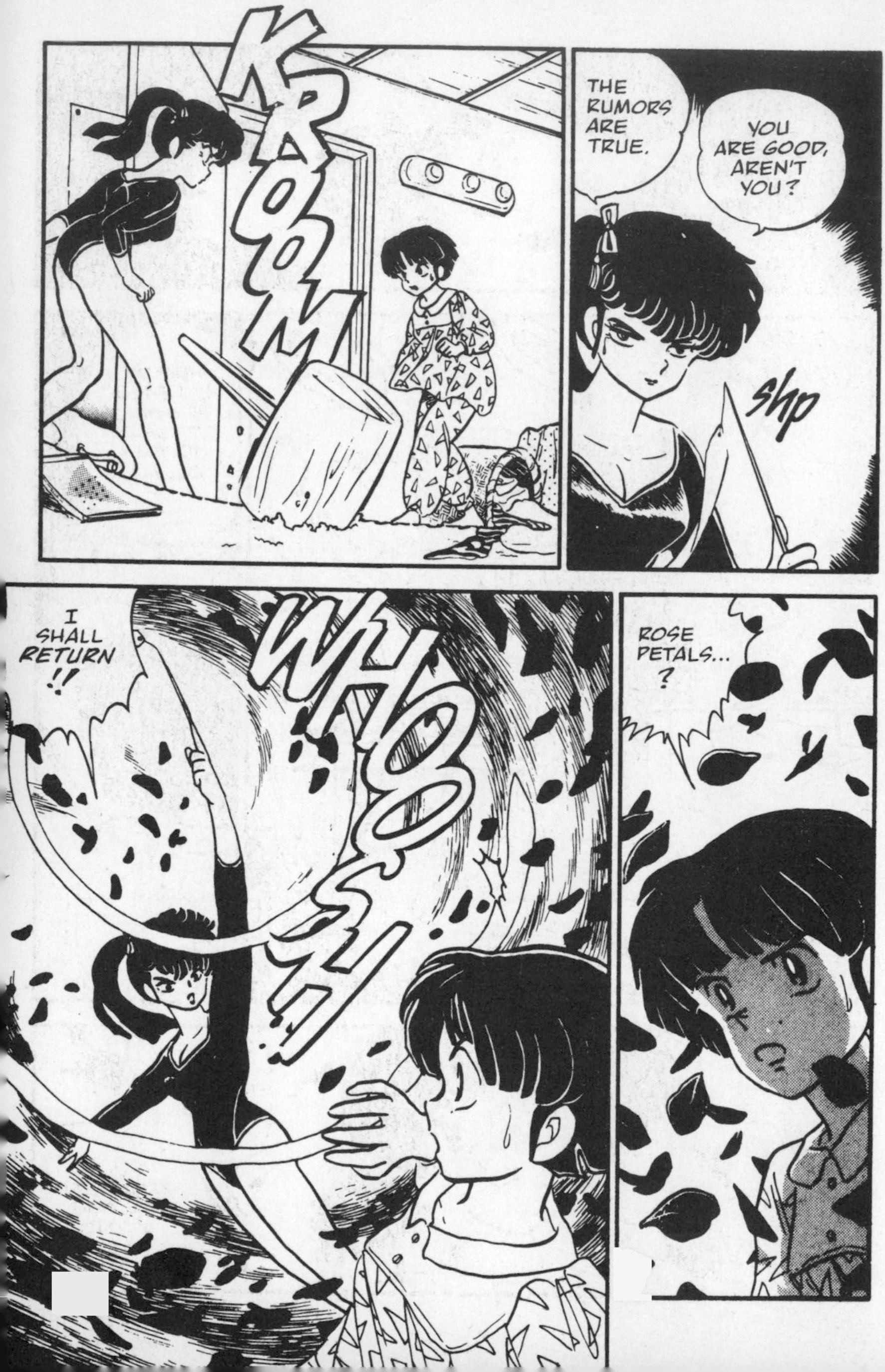
KROOM
THE RUMORS ARE TRUE.
YOU ARE GOOD, AREN'T YOU?
shp
I SHALL RETURN!!
WHOOSH
ROSE PETALS...?

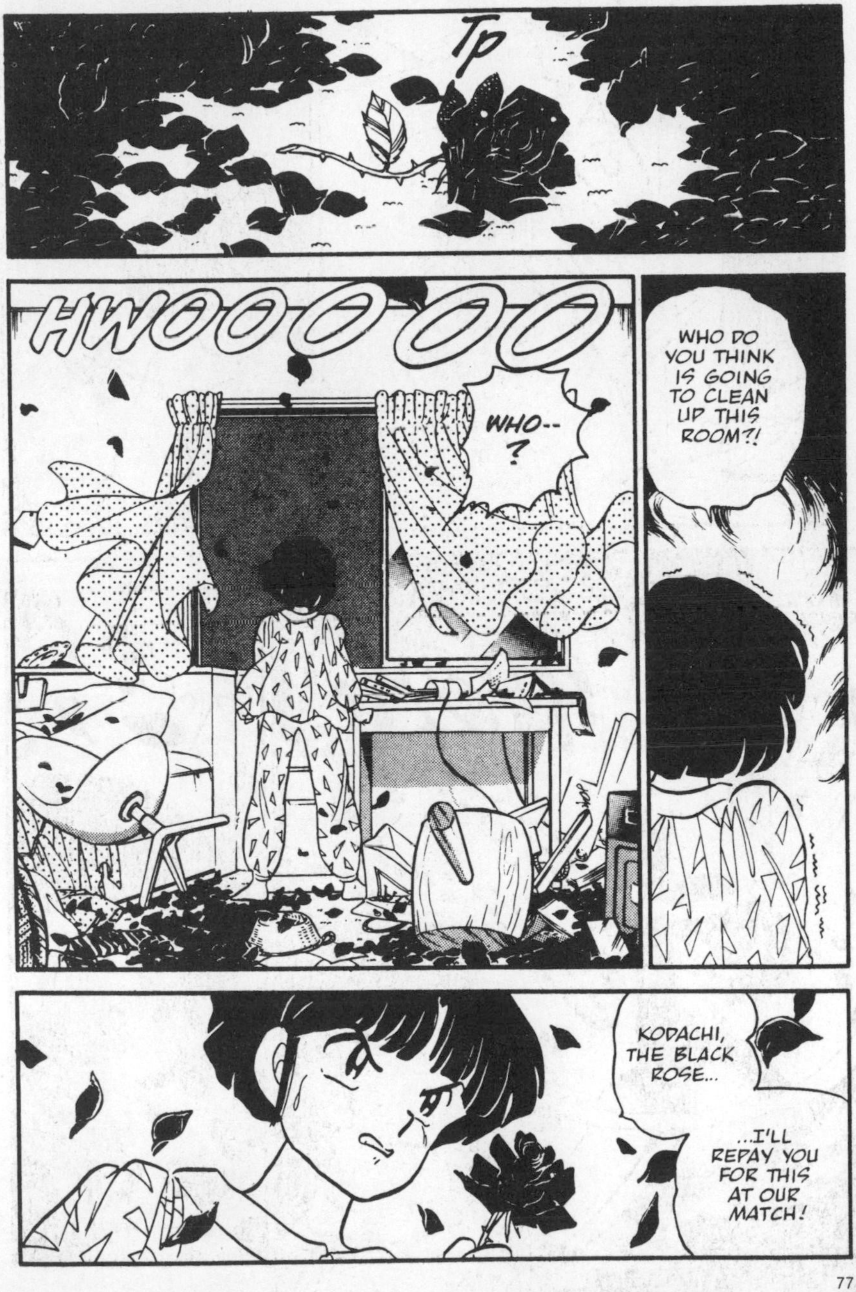
Tp
HWOOOOO
WHO--?
WHO DO YOU THINK IS GOING TO CLEAN UP THIS ROOM?!
KODACHI, THE BLACK ROSE...
...I'LL REPAY YOU FOR THIS AT OUR MATCH!

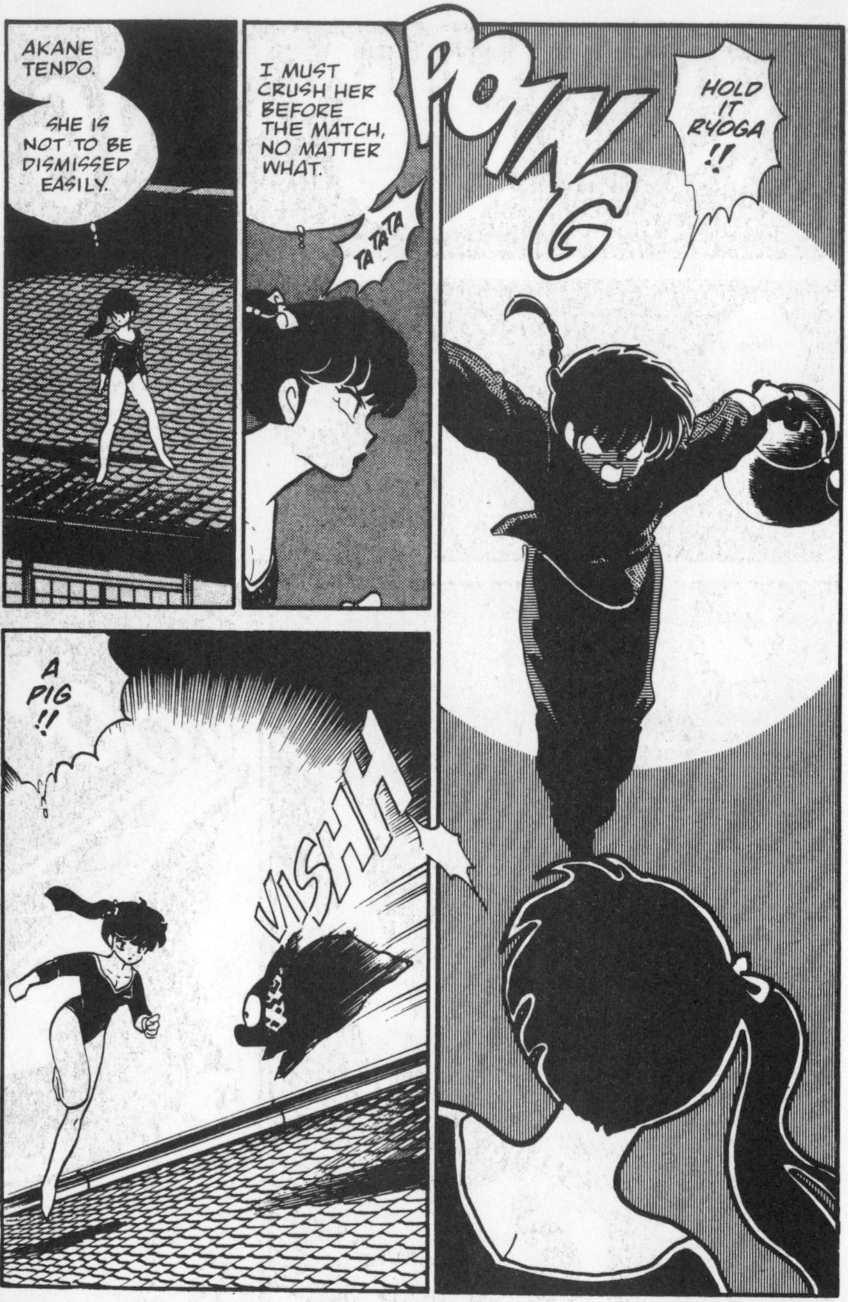
AKANE TENDO.
SHE IS NOT TO BE DISMISSED EASILY.
I MUST CRUSH HER BEFORE THE MATCH, NO MATTER WHAT.
TA TA TA
A PIG !!
VISHH
POING
HOLD IT RYOGA !!

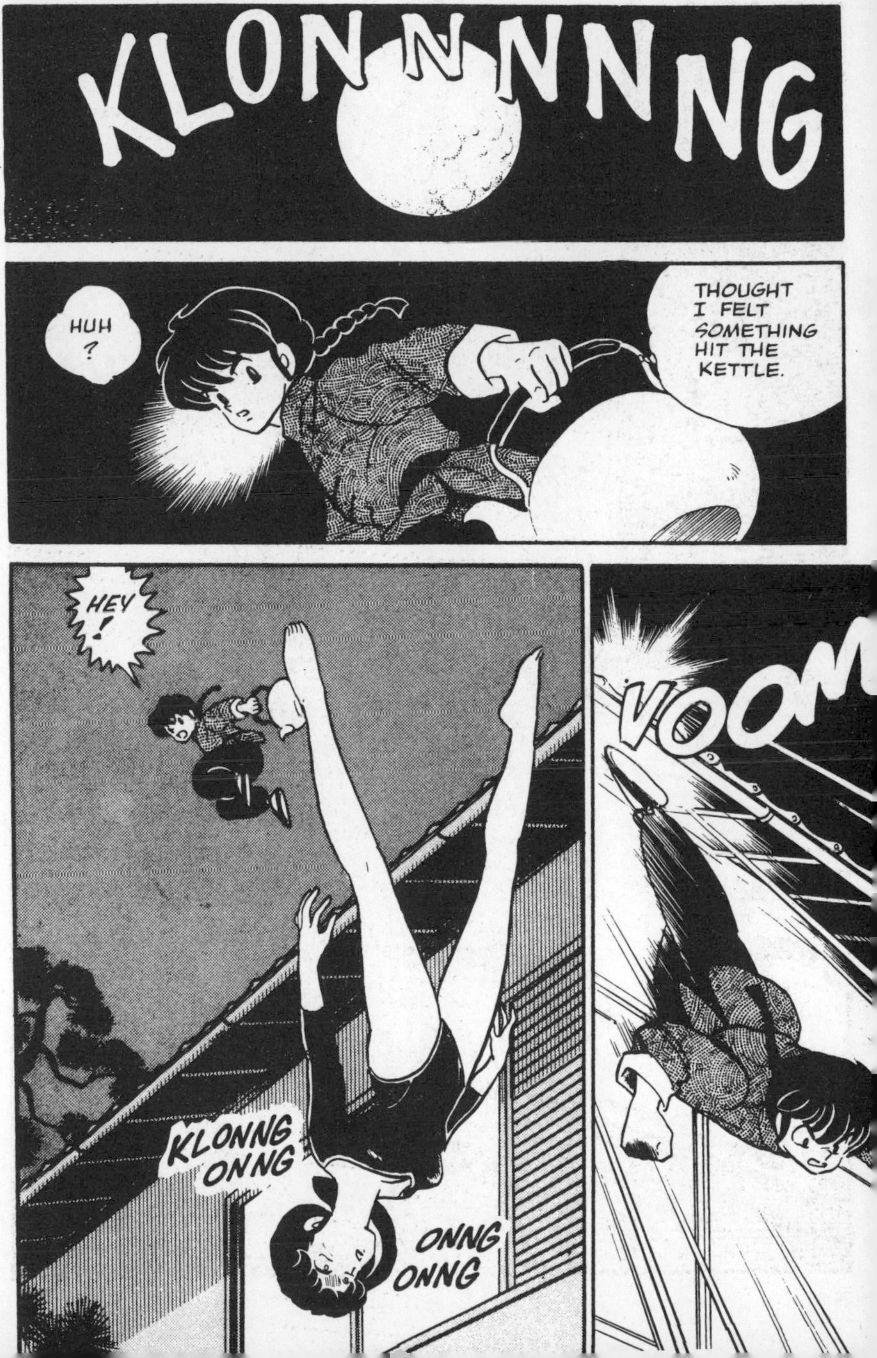
KLONNNNNG
HUH?
THOUGHT I FELT SOMETHING HIT THE KETTLE.
HEY!
KLONNG ONNG
ONNG ONNG
VOOM

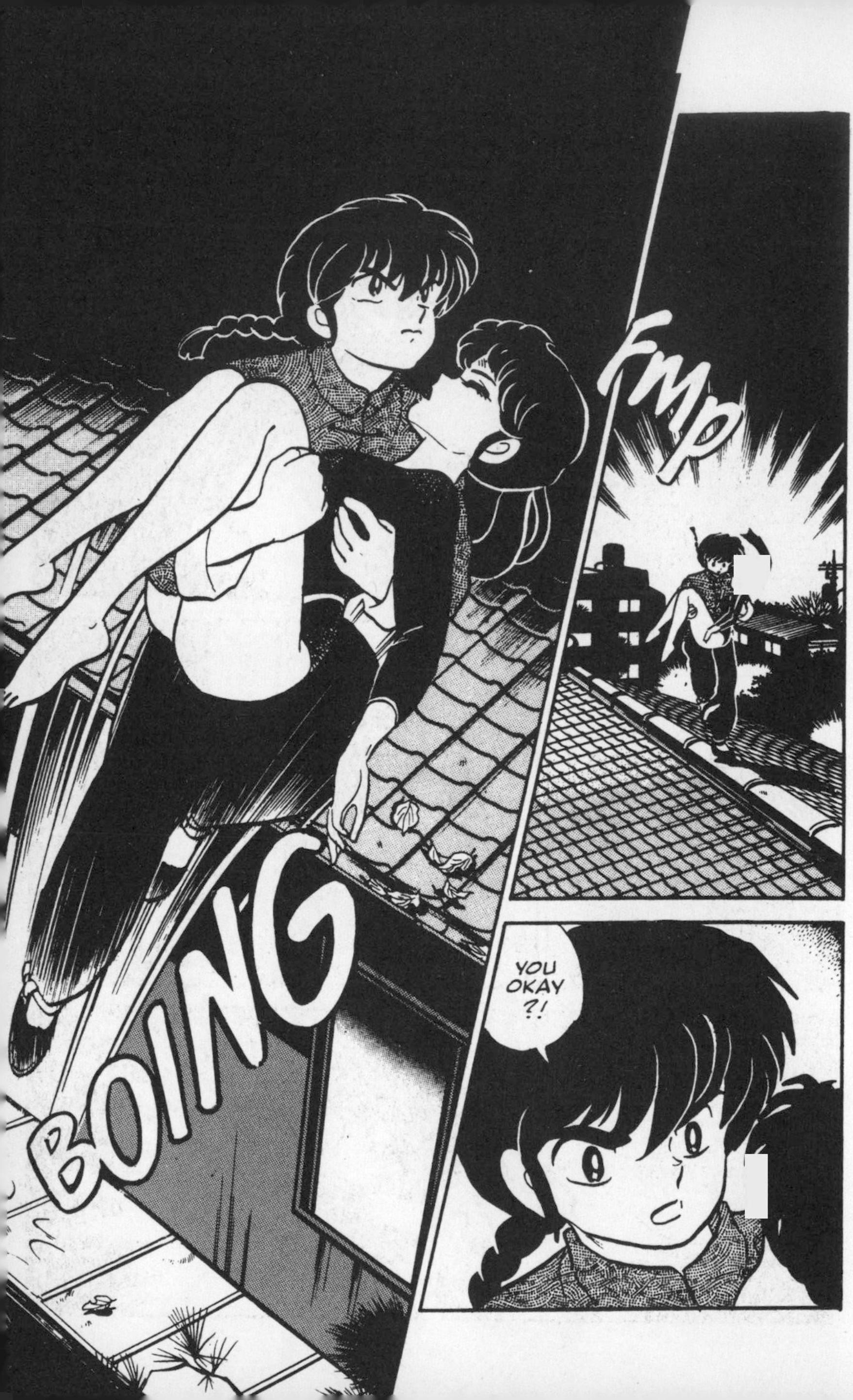
BOING
fmp
YOU OKAY ?!

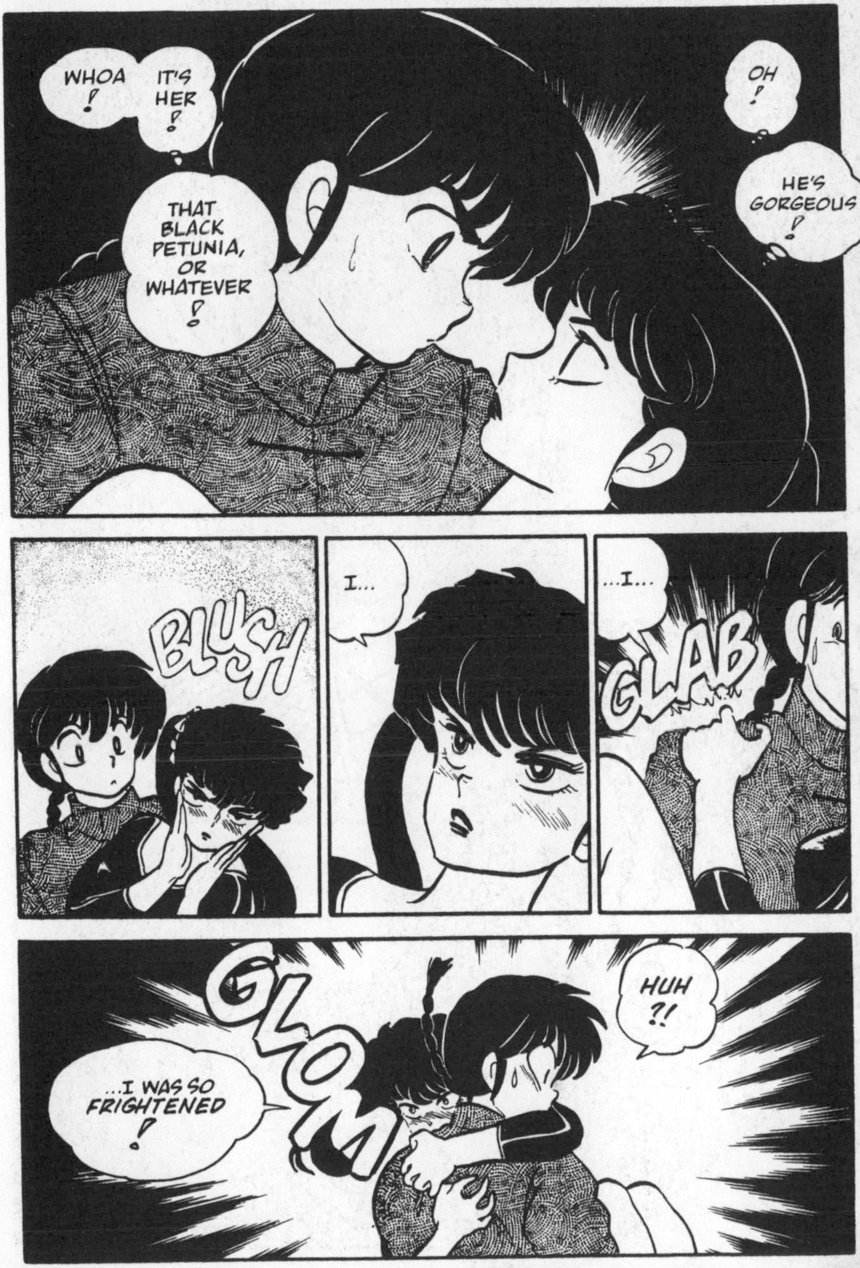
WHOA!
IT'S HER!
THAT BLACK PETUNIA, OR WHATEVER!
OH!
HE'S GORGEOUS!
BLUSH
I...
...I...
GLAB
GLOM
HUH?!
...I WAS SO FRIGHTENED!

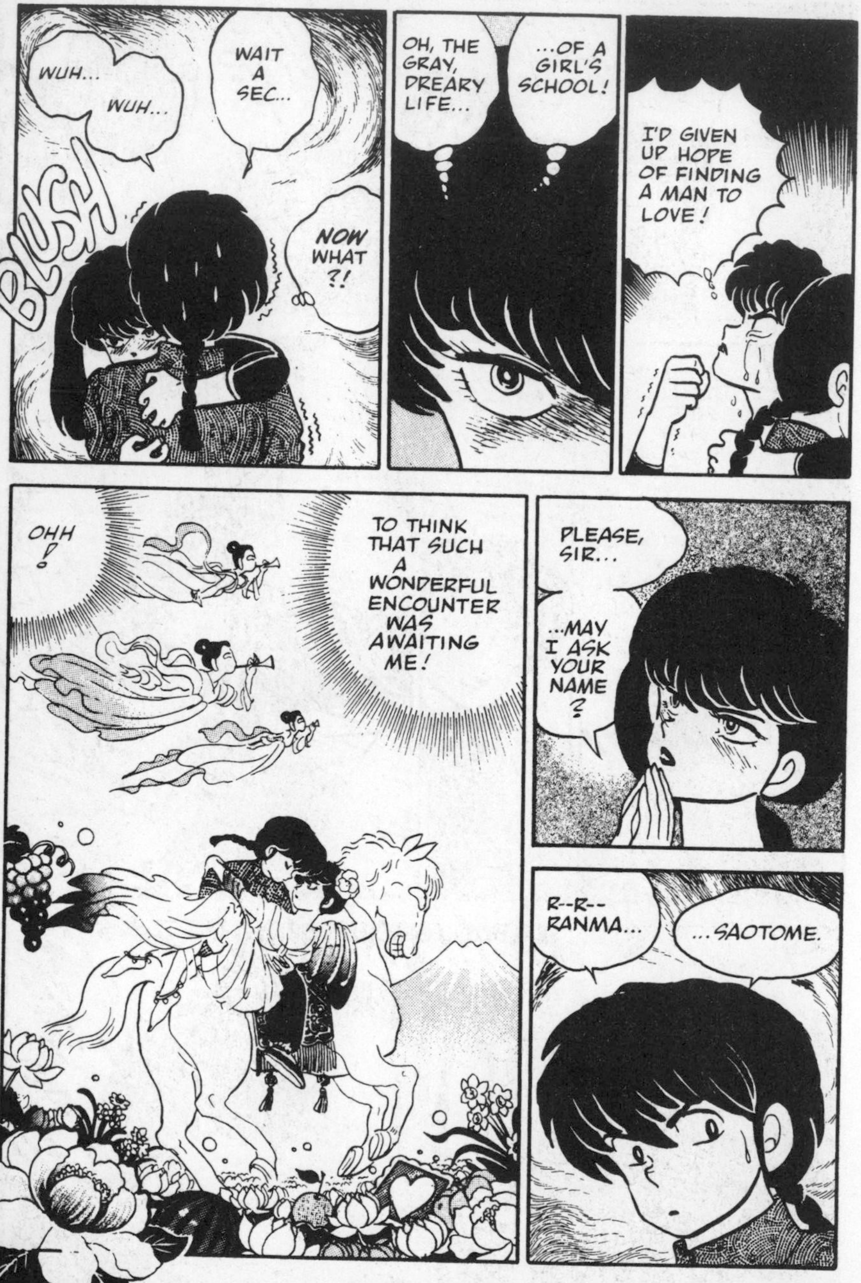
WUH... WUH...
WAIT A SEC...
BLUSH
NOW WHAT ?!
OH, THE GRAY, DREARY LIFE...
...OF A GIRL'S SCHOOL!
I'D GIVEN UP HOPE OF FINDING A MAN TO LOVE!
OHH!
TO THINK THAT SUCH A WONDERFUL ENCOUNTER WAS AWAITING ME!
PLEASE, SIR...
...MAY I ASK YOUR NAME ?
R--R-- RANMA...
...SAOTOME.

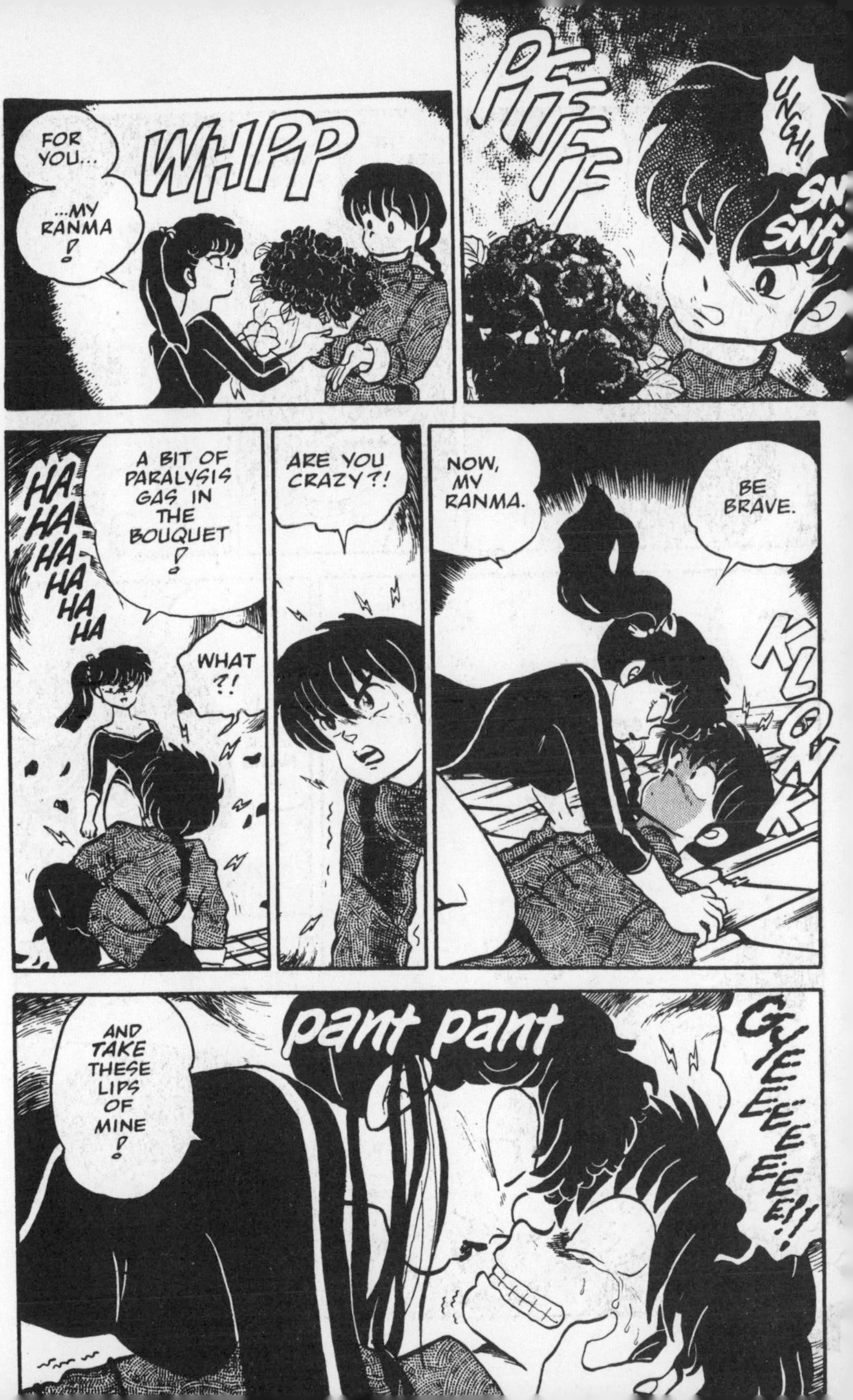
FOR YOU...
...MY RANMA!
WHPP
PFFFF
UNGH!
HA HA HA HA HA HA
A BIT OF PARALYSIS GAS IN THE BOUQUET!
WHAT?!
ARE YOU CRAZY?!
NOW, MY RANMA.
BE BRAVE.
KLONK
AND TAKE THESE LIPS OF MINE!
pant pant
GYEEEEEEE!!

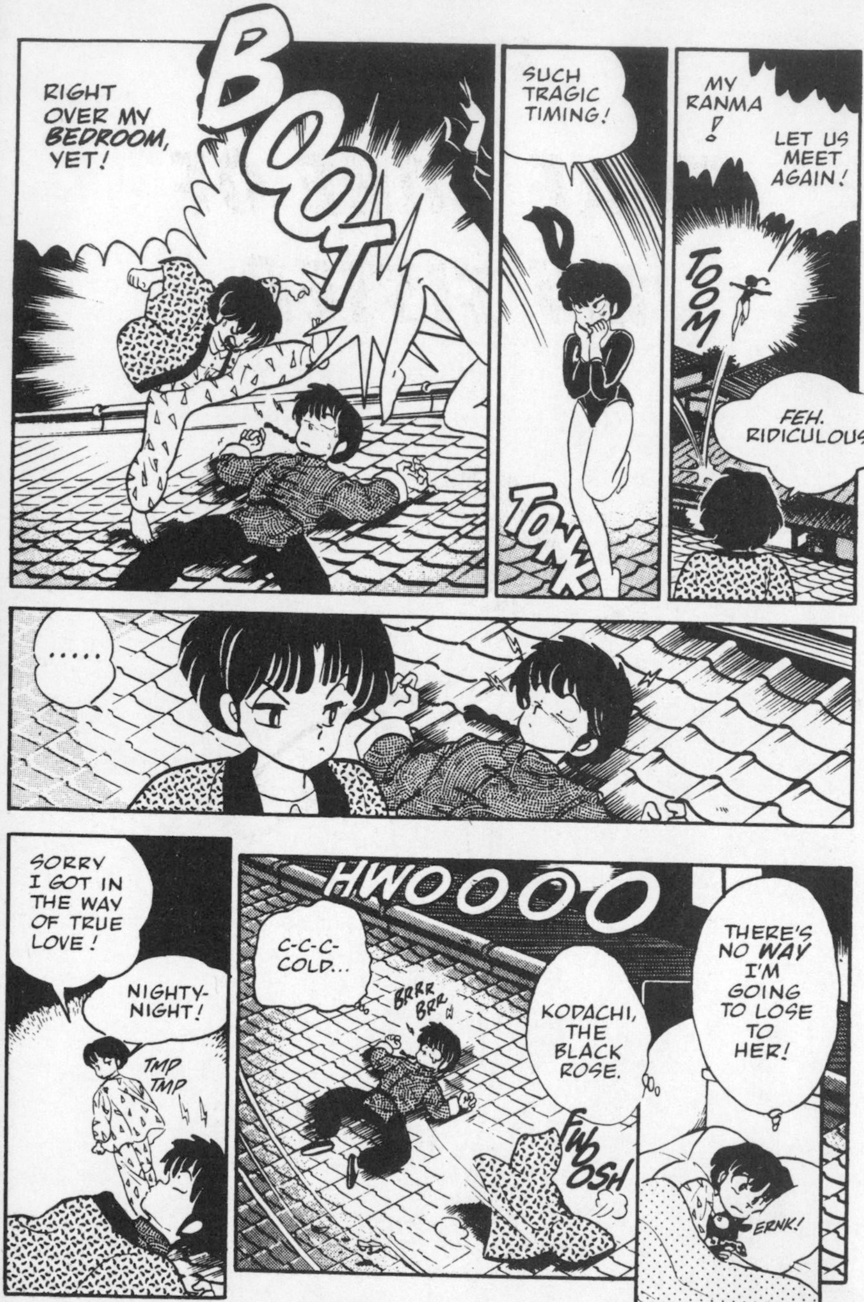
RIGHT OVER MY BEDROOM, YET!
BOOT
SUCH TRAGIC TIMING!
TONK
MY RANMA!
LET US MEET AGAIN!
TOOM
FEH. RIDICULOUS.
.....
SORRY I GOT IN THE WAY OF TRUE LOVE!
NIGHTY-NIGHT!
TMP TMP
HWOOOOO
C-C-C-COLD...
BRRR BRR
KODACHI, THE BLACK ROSE.
FWOOSH
THERE'S NO WAY I'M GOING TO LOSE TO HER!
ERNK!

Part 5

TAKE CARE OF
MY SISTER

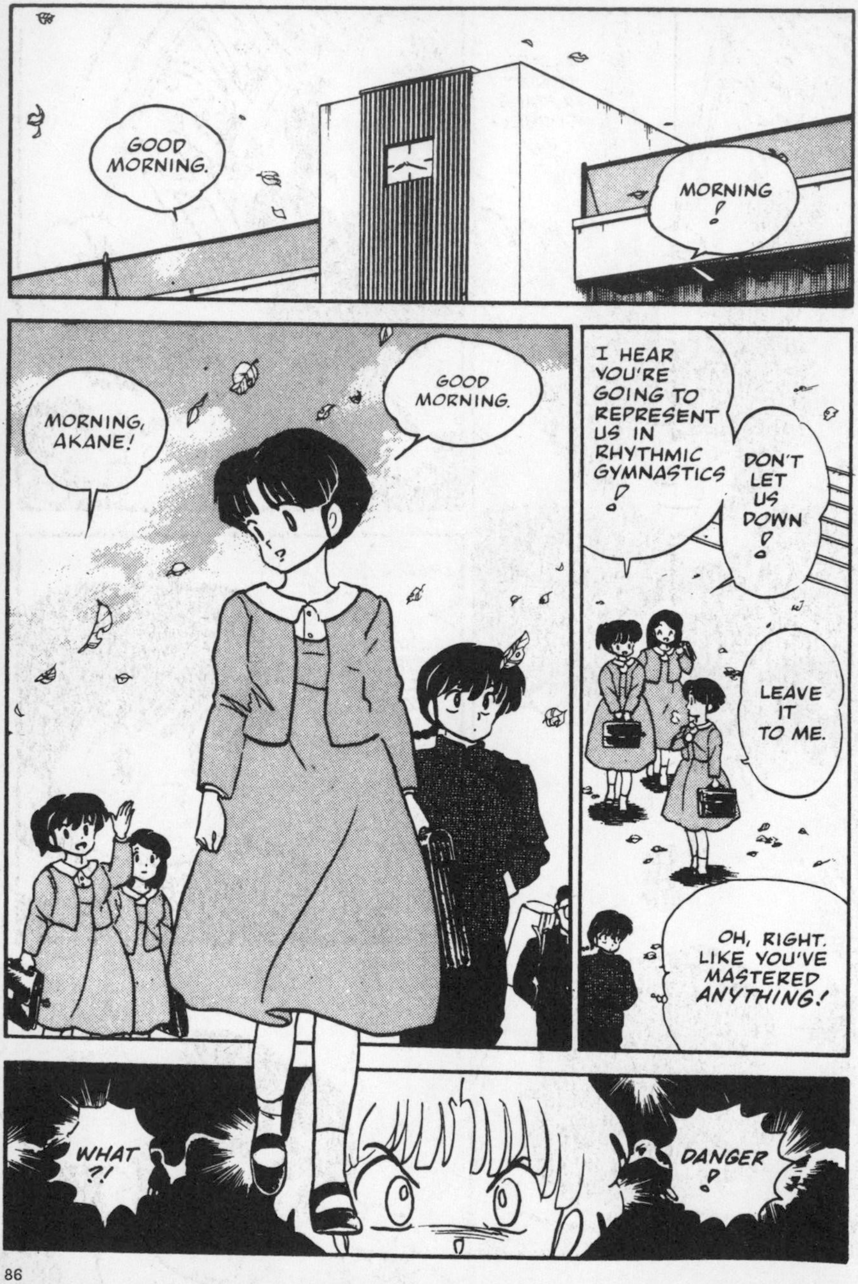
GOOD MORNING.
MORNING!
MORNING, AKANE!
GOOD MORNING.
I HEAR YOU'RE GOING TO REPRESENT US IN RHYTHMIC GYMNASTICS!
DON'T LET US DOWN!
LEAVE IT TO ME.
OH, RIGHT. LIKE YOU'VE MASTERED ANYTHING!
WHAT?!
DANGER!

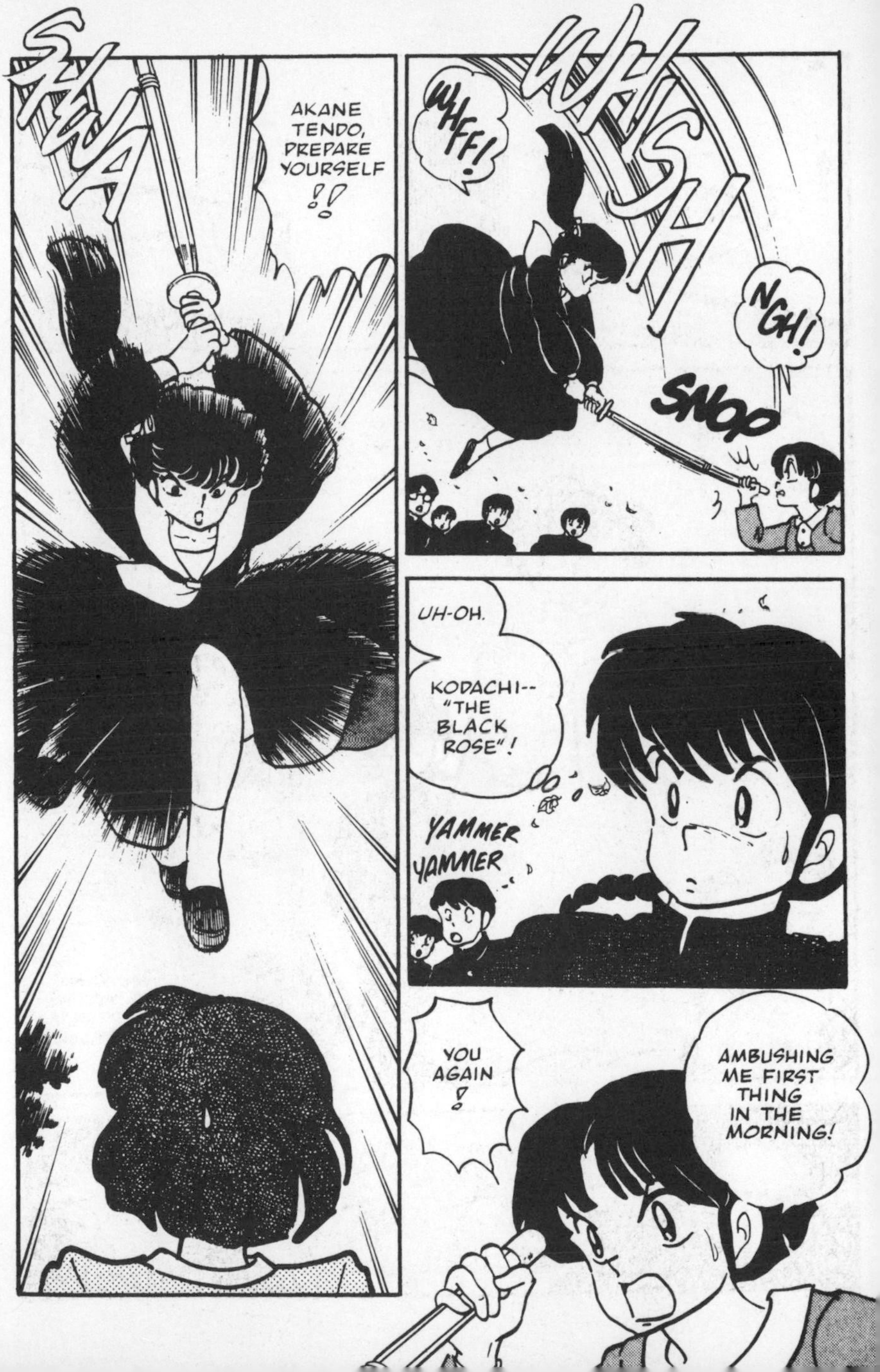
SHWA
AKANE TENDO, PREPARE YOURSELF !!
WHFF!
WHISH
NGH!
SNOP
UH-OH.
KODACHI-- "THE BLACK ROSE"!
YAMMER YAMMER
YOU AGAIN !
AMBUSHING ME FIRST THING IN THE MORNING!

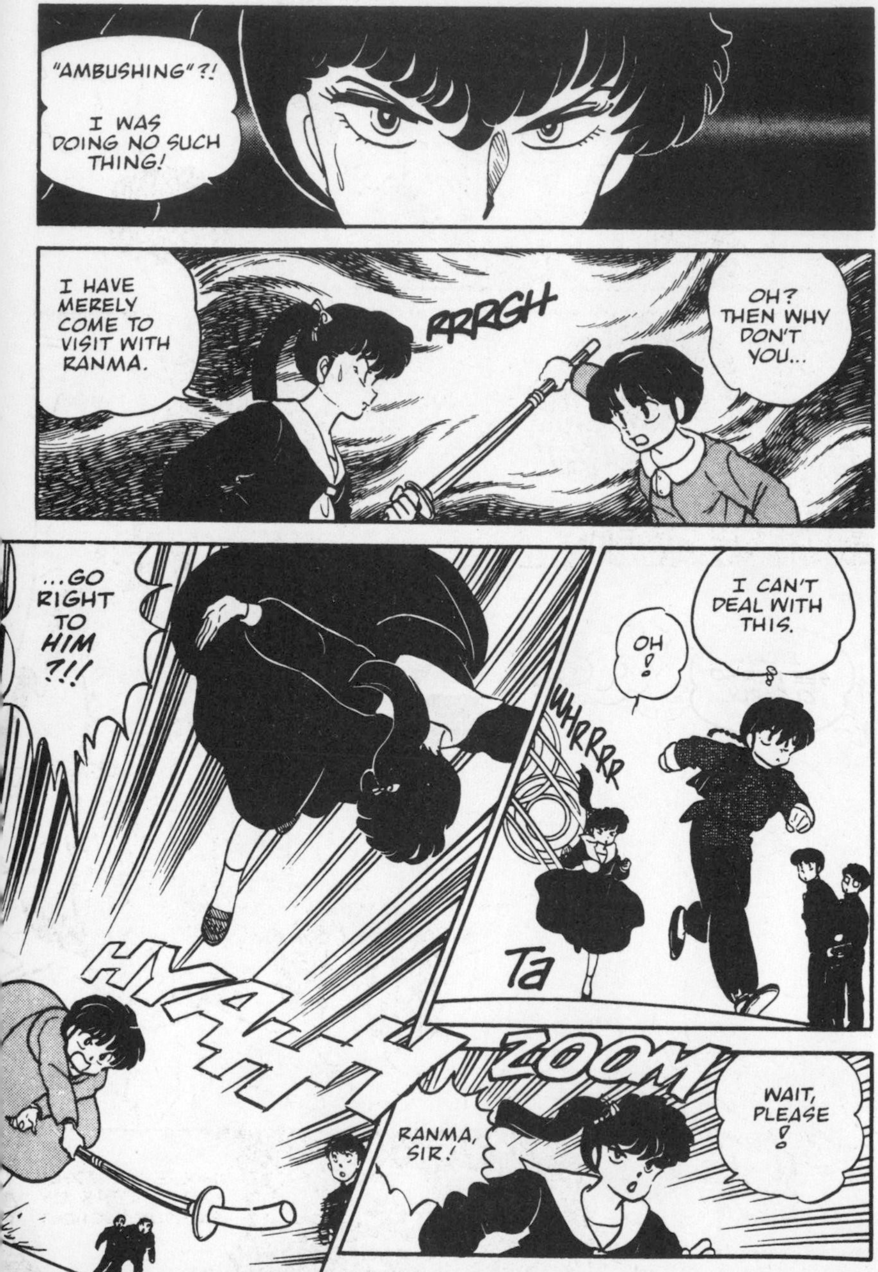
"AMBUSHING"?!
I WAS DOING NO SUCH THING!
I HAVE MERELY COME TO VISIT WITH RANMA.
RRRGH
OH? THEN WHY DON'T YOU...
...GO RIGHT TO HIM ?!!
HYA
I CAN'T DEAL WITH THIS.
OH!
WHRRRR
Ta
ZOOM
RANMA, SIR!
WAIT, PLEASE!

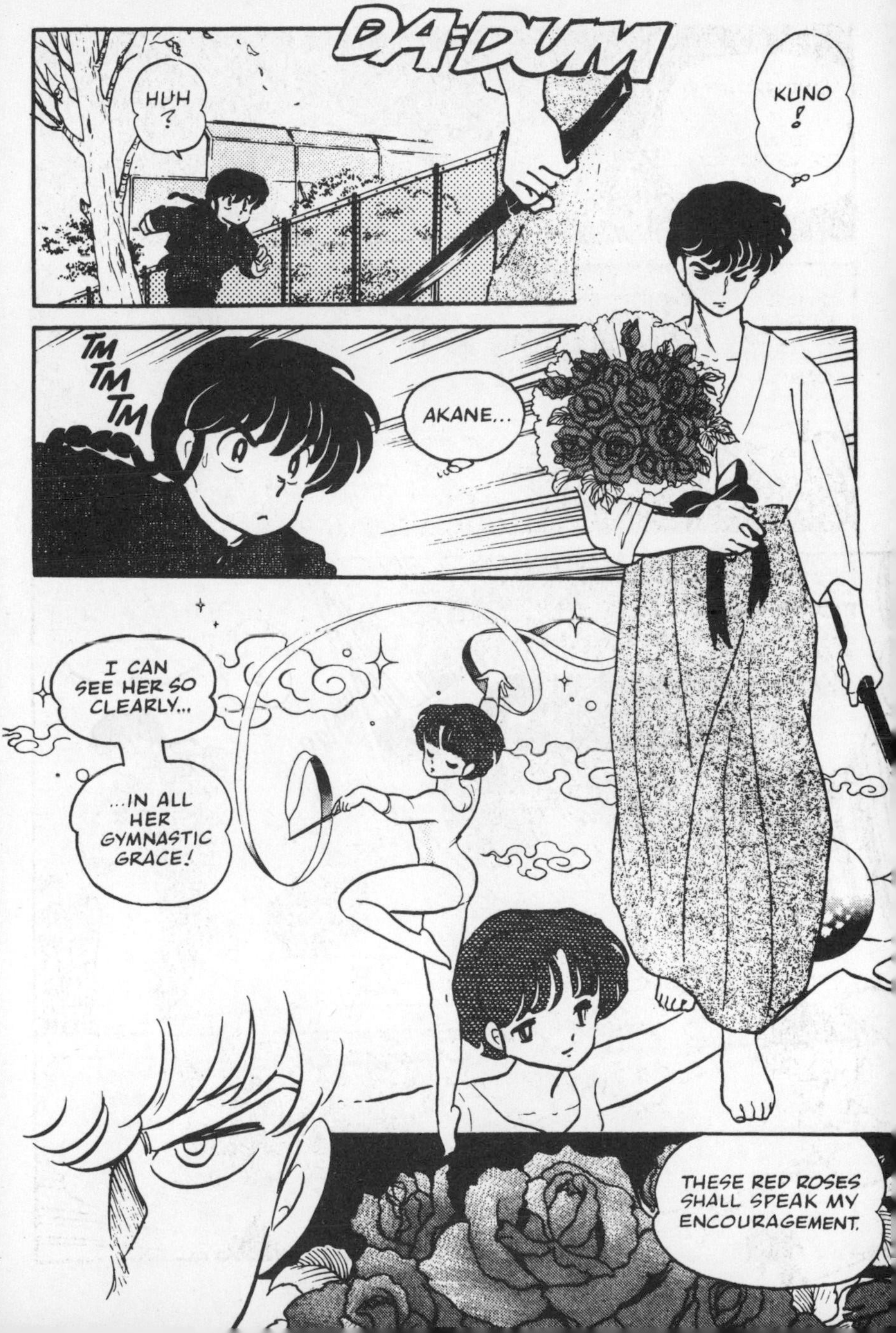
DA-DUM
HUH?
KUNO!
TM TM TM
AKANE...
I CAN SEE HER SO CLEARLY...
...IN ALL HER GYMNASTIC GRACE!
THESE RED ROSES SHALL SPEAK MY ENCOURAGEMENT.

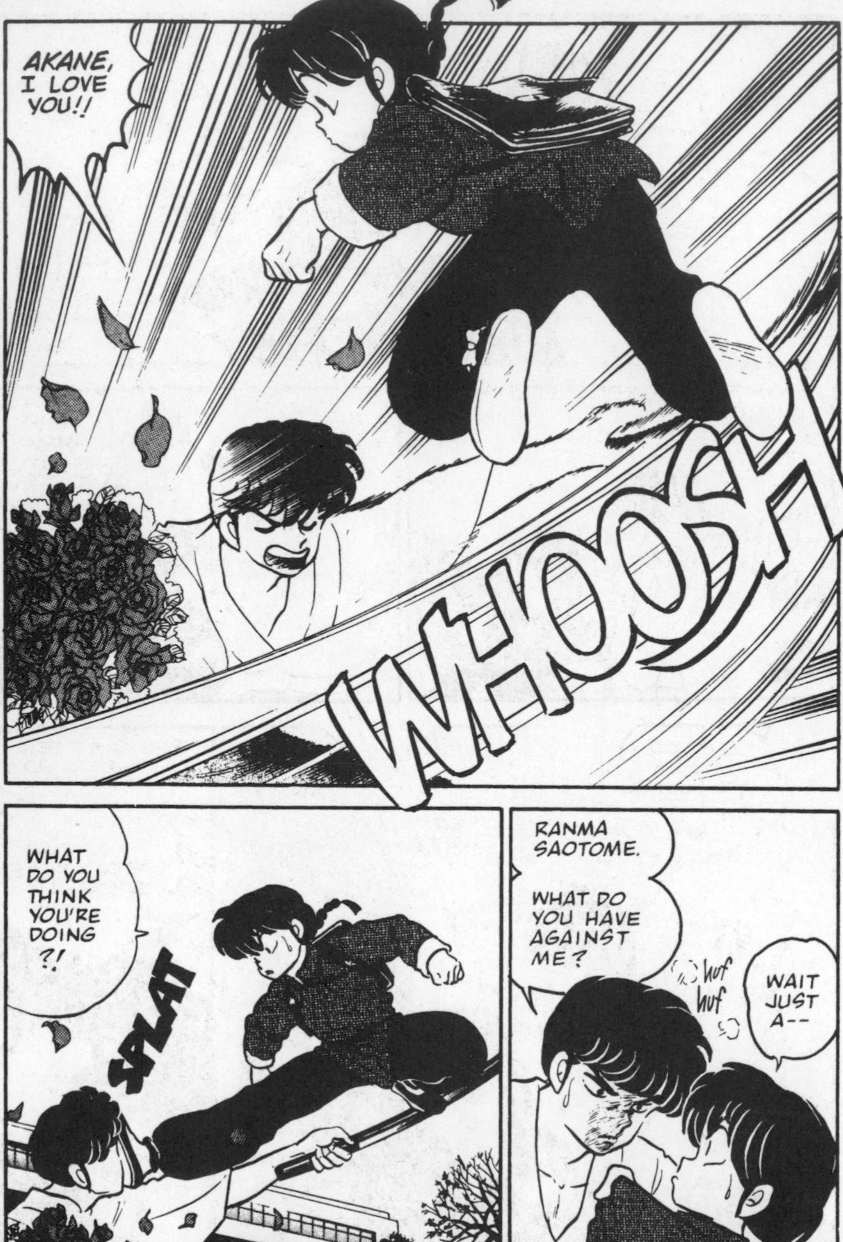
AKANE, I LOVE YOU!!
WHOOSH
WHAT DO YOU THINK YOU'RE DOING ?!
SPLAT
RANMA SAOTOME.
WHAT DO YOU HAVE AGAINST ME?
huf huf
WAIT JUST A--

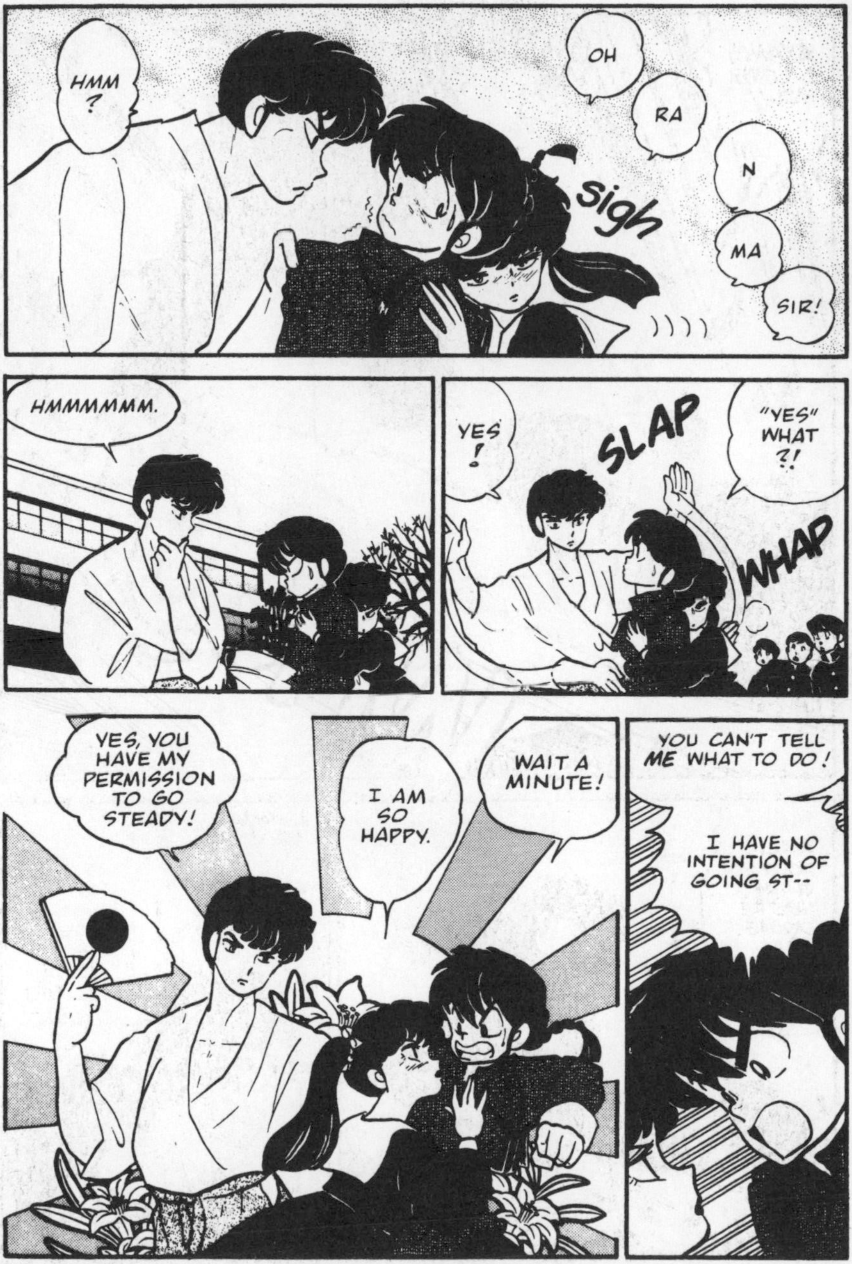
HMM ?
OH
RA
N
MA
SIR!
sigh
HMMMMMM.
YES !
SLAP
"YES" WHAT ?!
WHAP
YES, YOU HAVE MY PERMISSION TO GO STEADY!
I AM SO HAPPY.
WAIT A MINUTE!
YOU CAN'T TELL ME WHAT TO DO !
I HAVE NO INTENTION OF GOING ST--

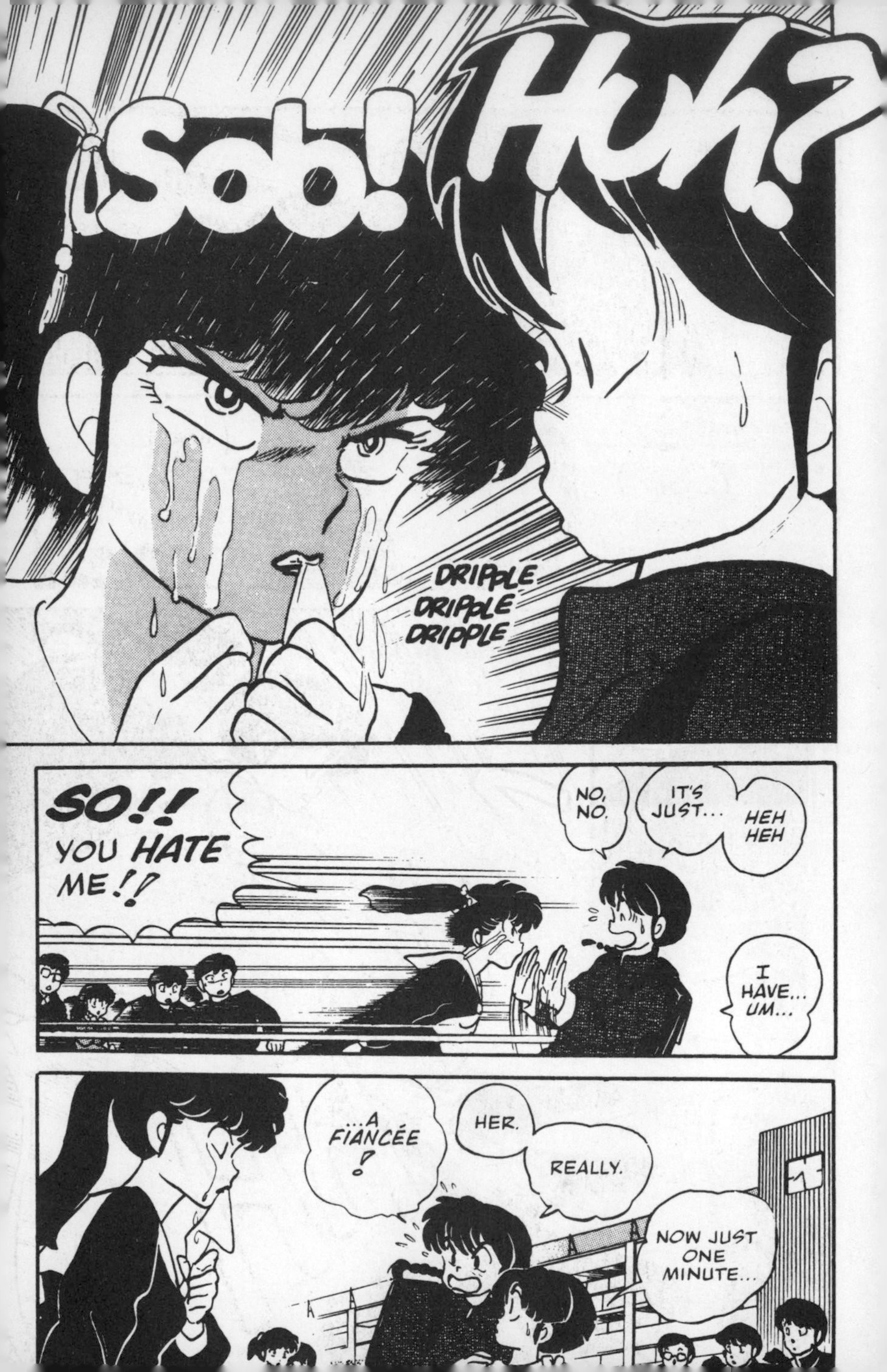
Sob!
Huh?
DRIPPLE DRIPPLE DRIPPLE
SO!! YOU HATE ME!!
NO, NO.
IT'S JUST...
HEH HEH
I HAVE... UM...
...A FIANCÉE!
HER.
REALLY.
NOW JUST ONE MINUTE...

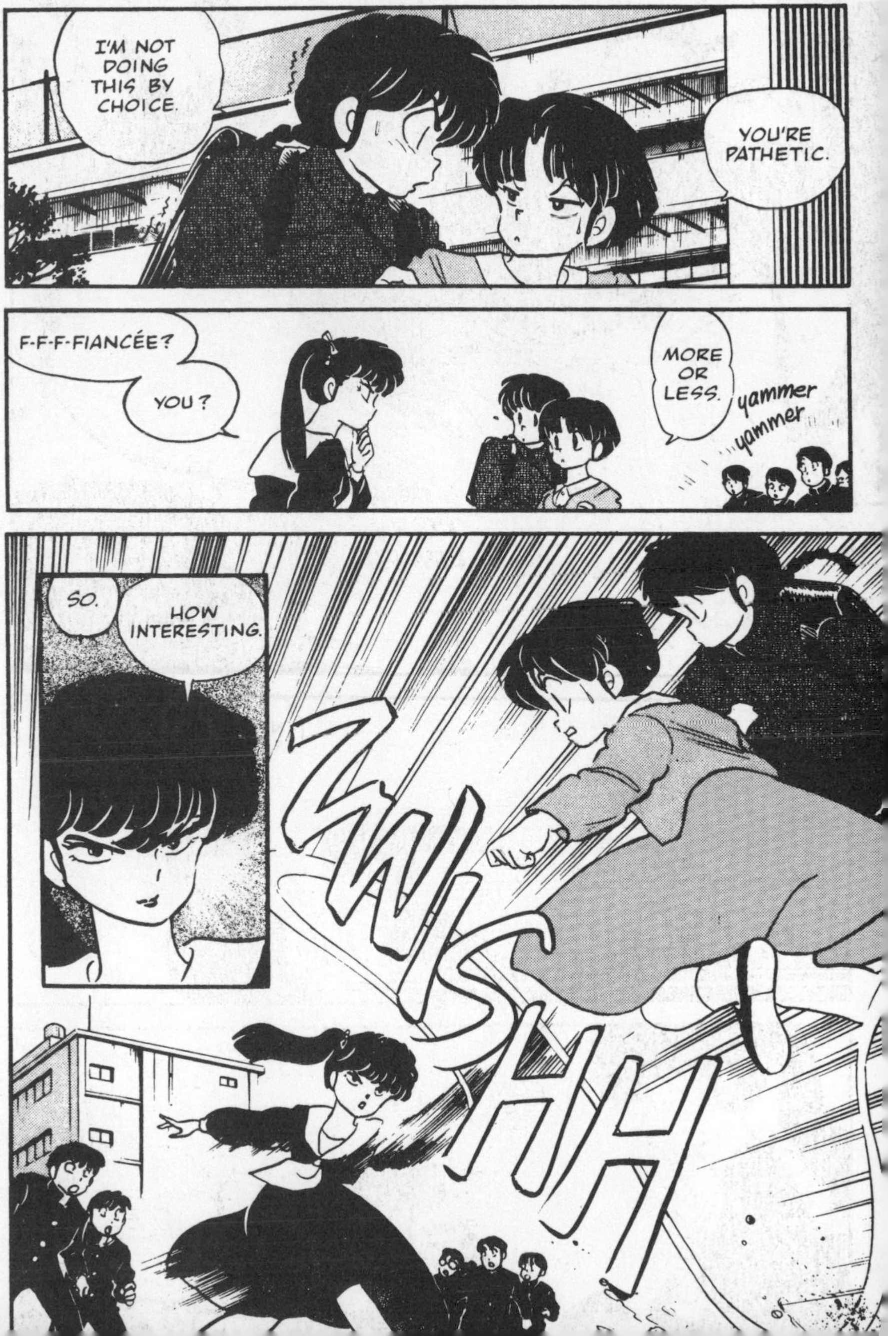
I'M NOT DOING THIS BY CHOICE.
YOU'RE PATHETIC.
F-F-F-FIANCÉE?
YOU?
MORE OR LESS.
yammer yammer
SO.
HOW INTERESTING.
SWISHH

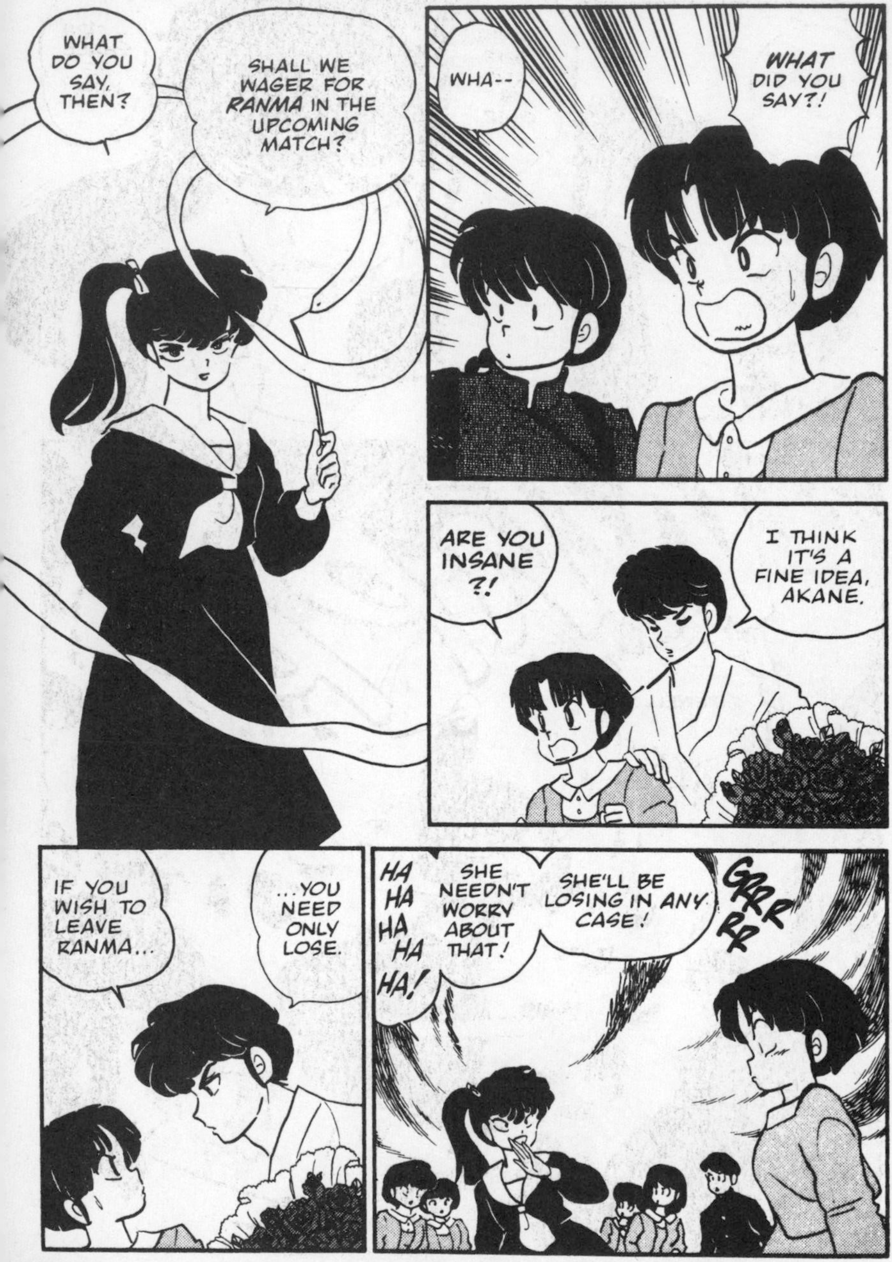
WHAT DO YOU SAY, THEN?
SHALL WE WAGER FOR RANMA IN THE UPCOMING MATCH?
WHA--
WHAT DID YOU SAY?!
ARE YOU INSANE ?!
I THINK IT'S A FINE IDEA, AKANE.
IF YOU WISH TO LEAVE RANMA...
...YOU NEED ONLY LOSE.
HA HA HA HA HA!
SHE NEEDN'T WORRY ABOUT THAT!
SHE'LL BE LOSING IN ANY CASE!
GRRRRR

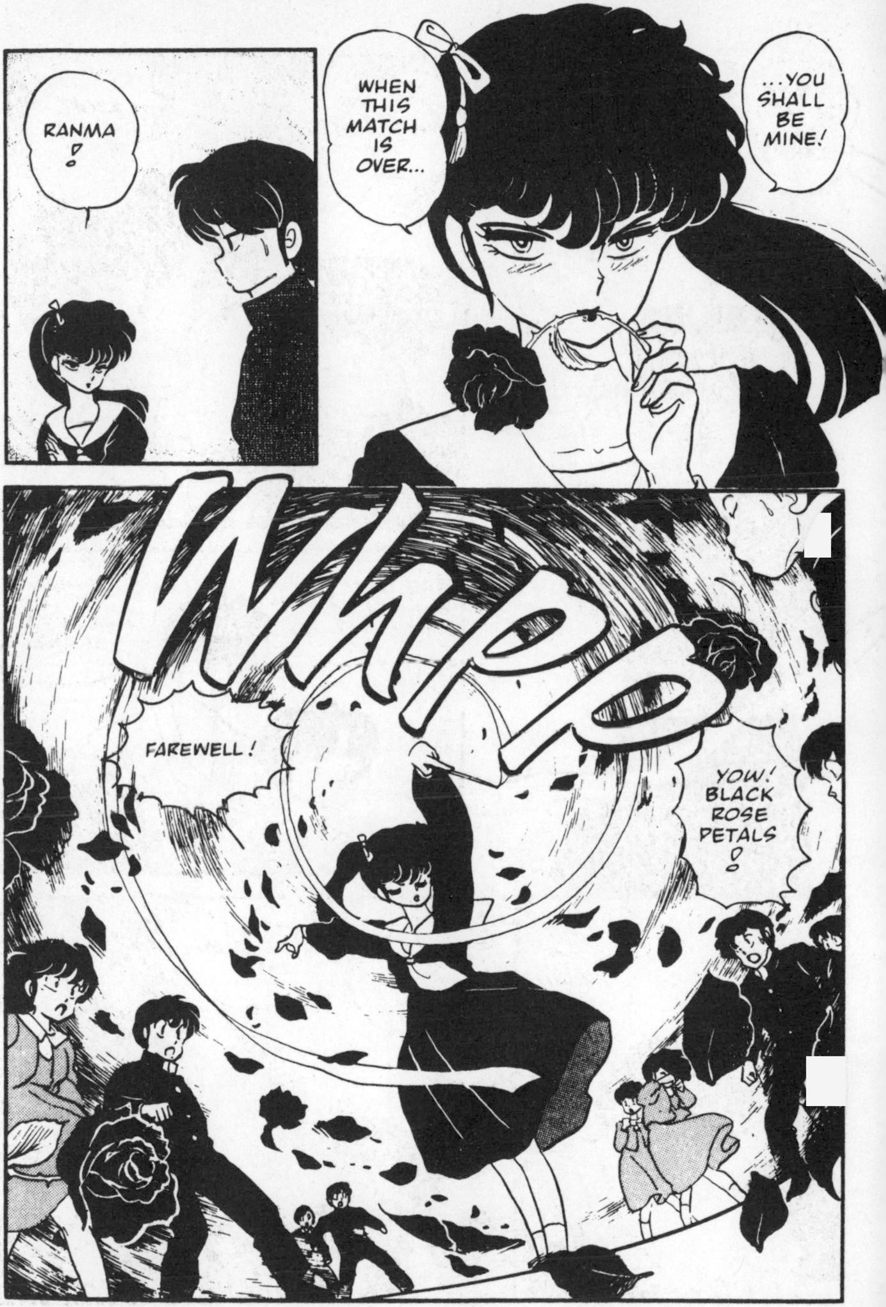
RANMA?
WHEN THIS MATCH IS OVER...
...YOU SHALL BE MINE!
WHIPP
FAREWELL!
YOW! BLACK ROSE PETALS?

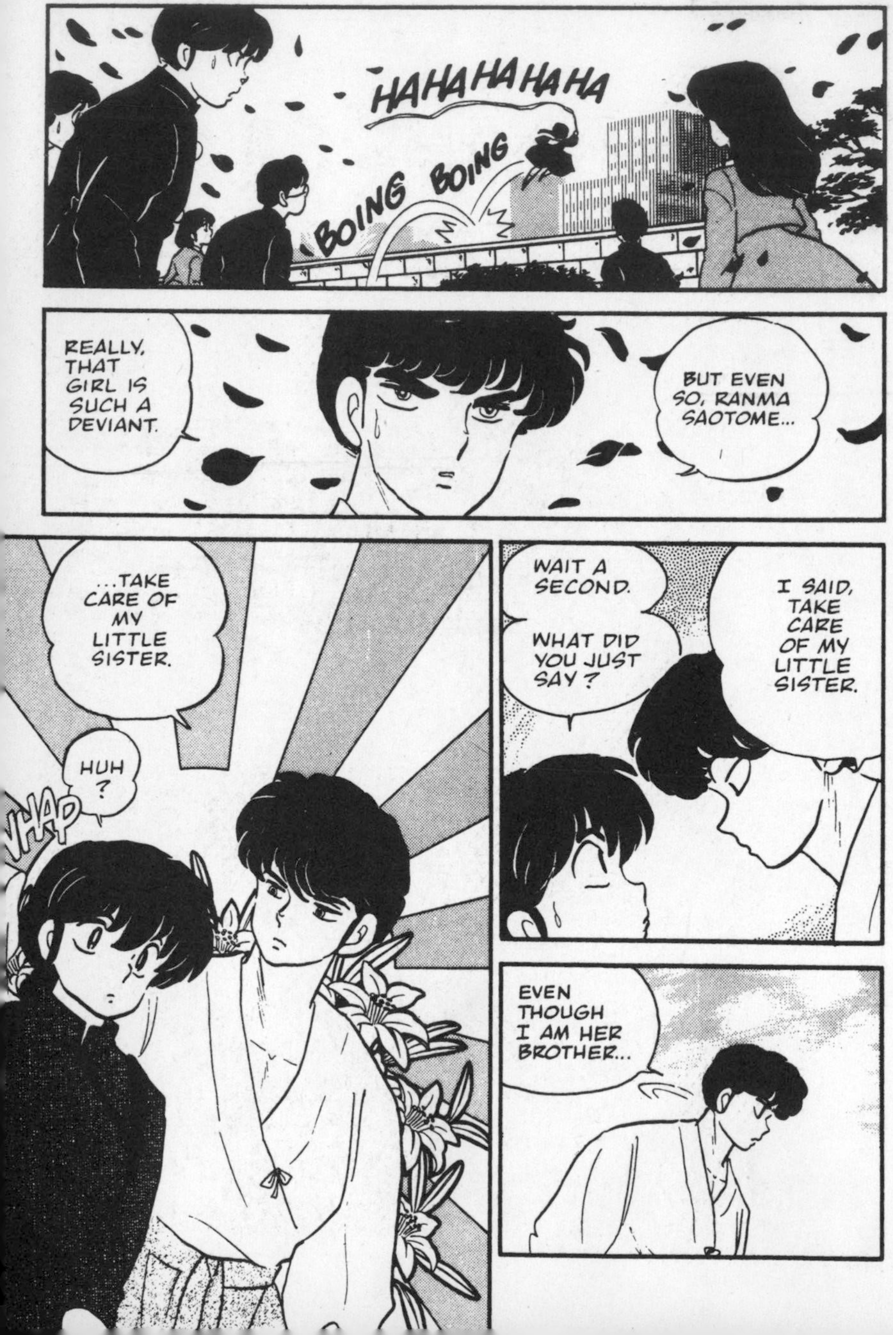
HAHAHAHAHA
BOING
BOING
REALLY, THAT GIRL IS SUCH A DEVIANT.
BUT EVEN SO, RANMA SAOTOME...
...TAKE CARE OF MY LITTLE SISTER.
HUH?
WHAP
WAIT A SECOND.
WHAT DID YOU JUST SAY?
I SAID, TAKE CARE OF MY LITTLE SISTER.
EVEN THOUGH I AM HER BROTHER...

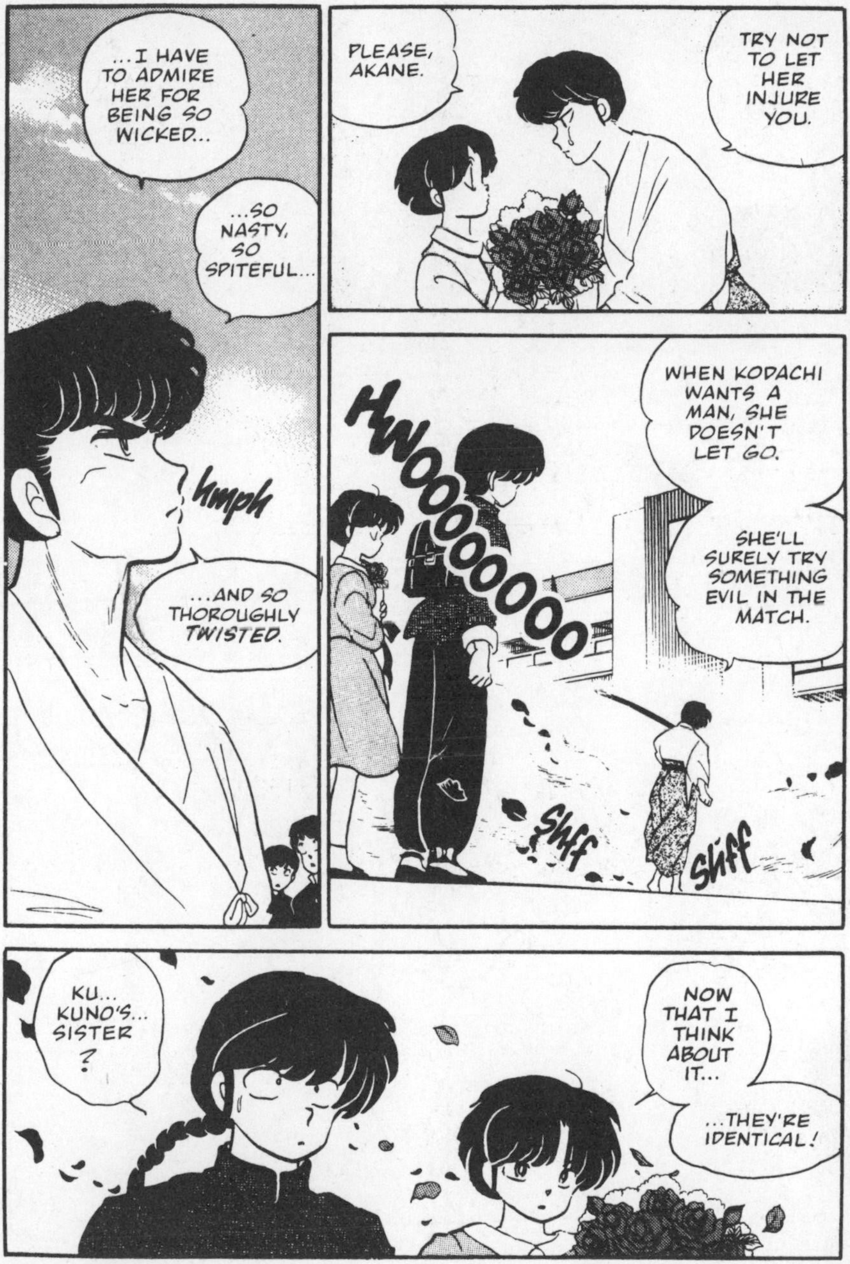
...I HAVE TO ADMIRE HER FOR BEING SO WICKED...
...SO NASTY, SO SPITEFUL...
hmph
...AND SO THOROUGHLY *TWISTED*.
PLEASE, AKANE.
TRY NOT TO LET HER INJURE YOU.
HWOOOOOOOO
WHEN KODACHI WANTS A MAN, SHE DOESN'T LET GO.
SHE'LL SURELY TRY SOMETHING EVIL IN THE MATCH.
shff
shff
KU... KUNO'S... SISTER ?
NOW THAT I THINK ABOUT IT...
...THEY'RE IDENTICAL!

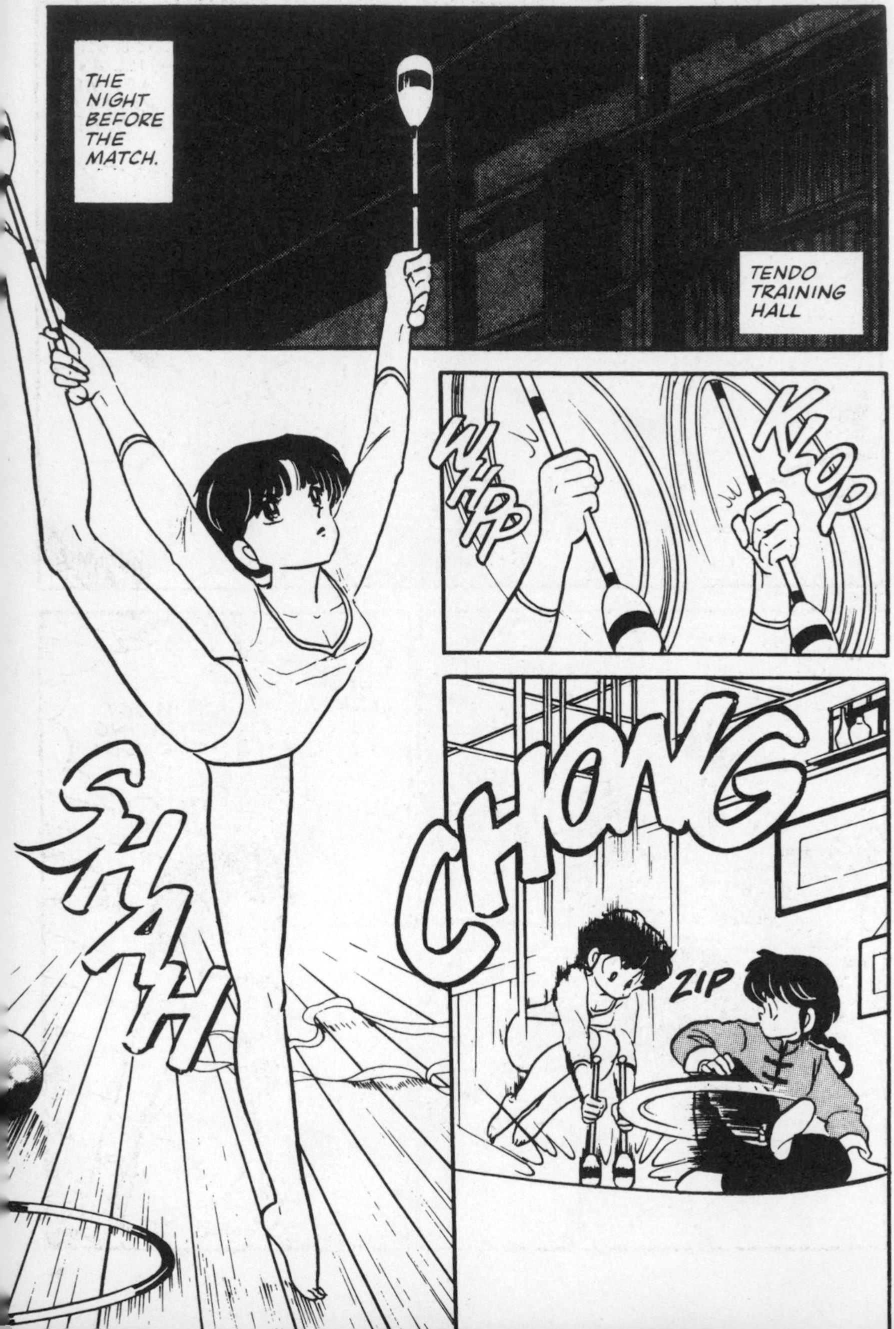
THE NIGHT BEFORE THE MATCH.
TENDO TRAINING HALL
SHAH
WHPP
KLOP
CHONG
ZIP

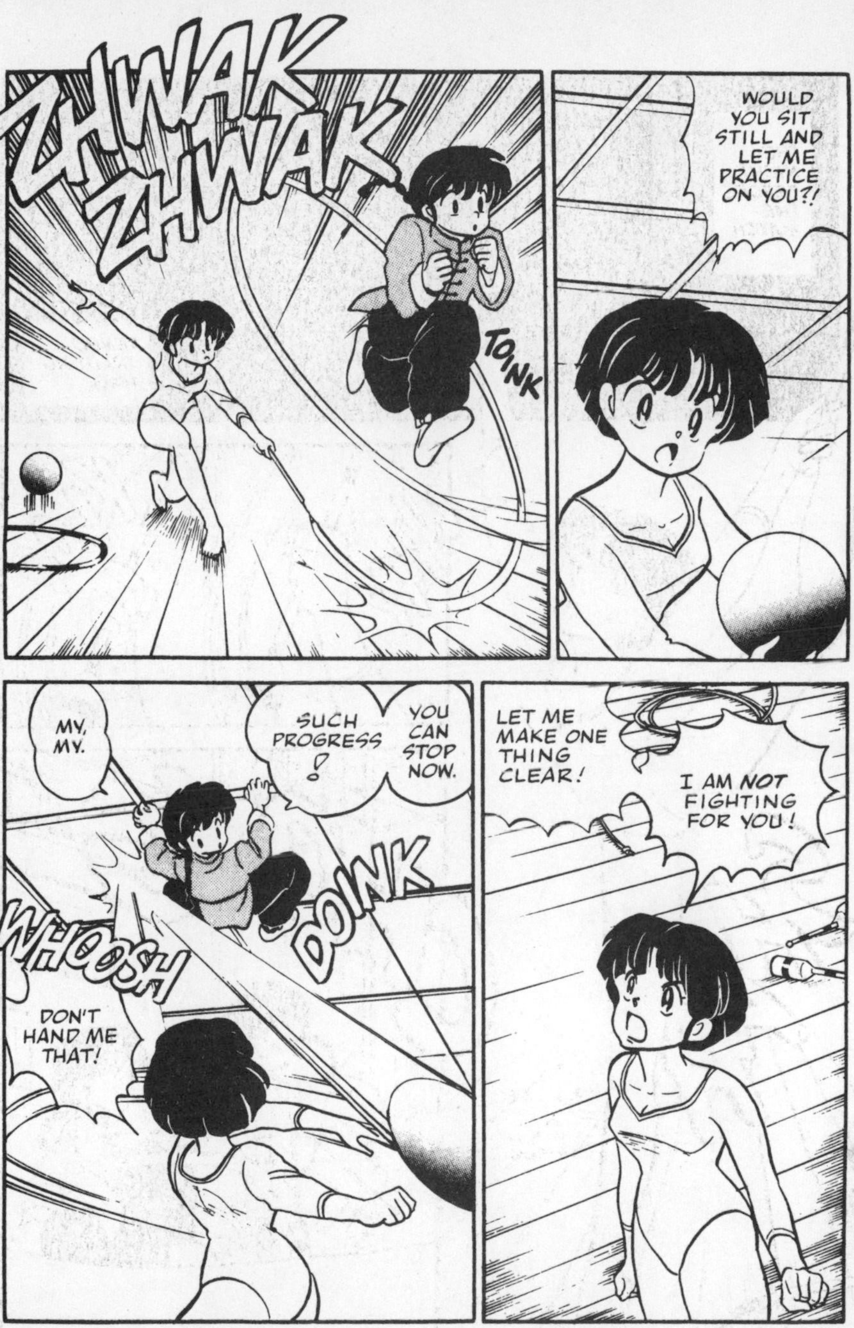
ZHWAK ZHWAK ZHWAK
TOINK
WOULD YOU SIT STILL AND LET ME PRACTICE ON YOU?!
MY, MY.
SUCH PROGRESS!
YOU CAN STOP NOW.
WHOOSH
DOINK
DON'T HAND ME THAT!
LET ME MAKE ONE THING CLEAR!
I AM *NOT* FIGHTING FOR YOU!

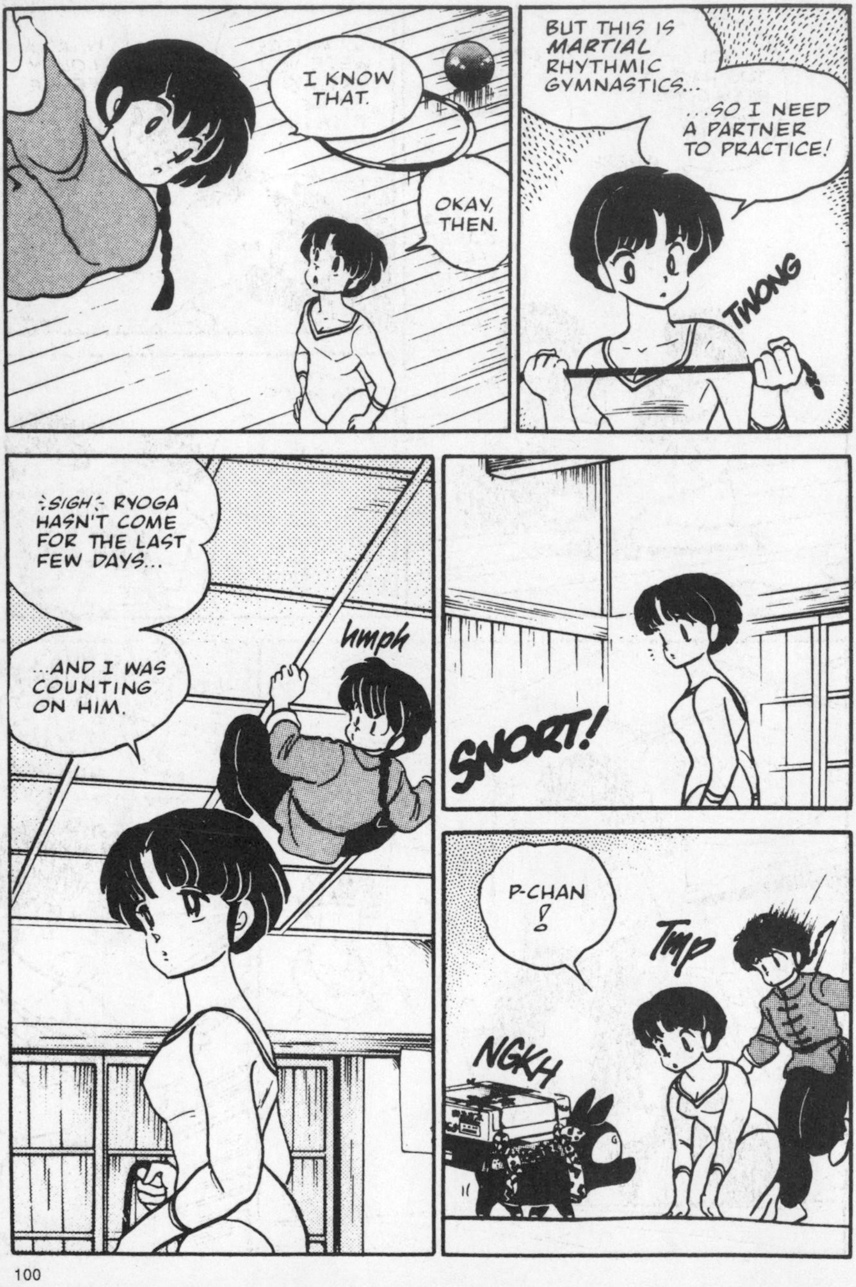
I KNOW THAT.
OKAY, THEN.
BUT THIS IS MARTIAL RHYTHMIC GYMNASTICS...
...SO I NEED A PARTNER TO PRACTICE!
TWONG
-:SIGH:- RYOGA HASN'T COME FOR THE LAST FEW DAYS...
...AND I WAS COUNTING ON HIM.
hmph
SNORT!
P-CHAN!
Tmp
NGKH

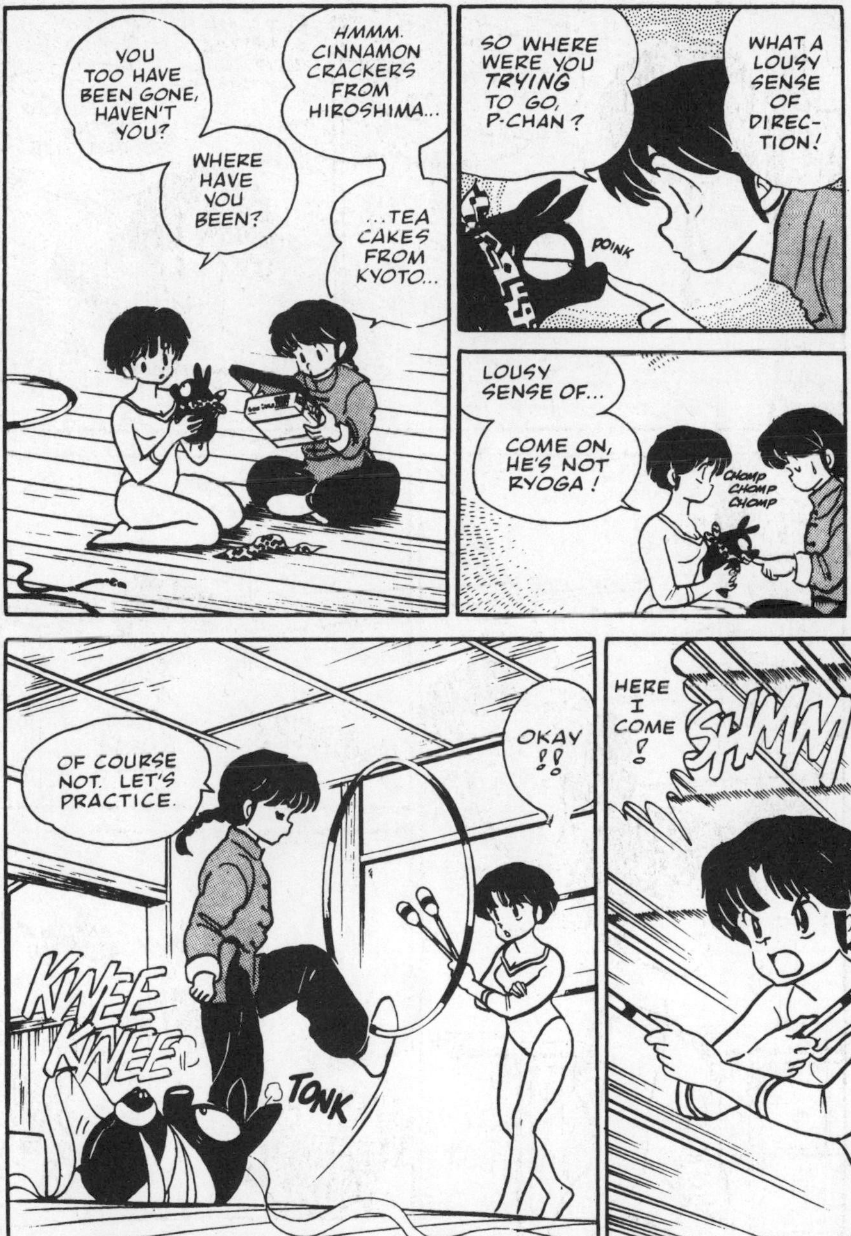
YOU TOO HAVE BEEN GONE, HAVEN'T YOU?
WHERE HAVE YOU BEEN?
HMMM. CINNAMON CRACKERS FROM HIROSHIMA...
...TEA CAKES FROM KYOTO...
SO WHERE WERE YOU TRYING TO GO, P-CHAN?
WHAT A LOUSY SENSE OF DIRECTION!
POINK
LOUSY SENSE OF...
COME ON, HE'S NOT RYOGA!
CHOMP CHOMP CHOMP
OF COURSE NOT. LET'S PRACTICE.
OKAY !!
KWEE KWEE
TONK
HERE I COME!
SHMM

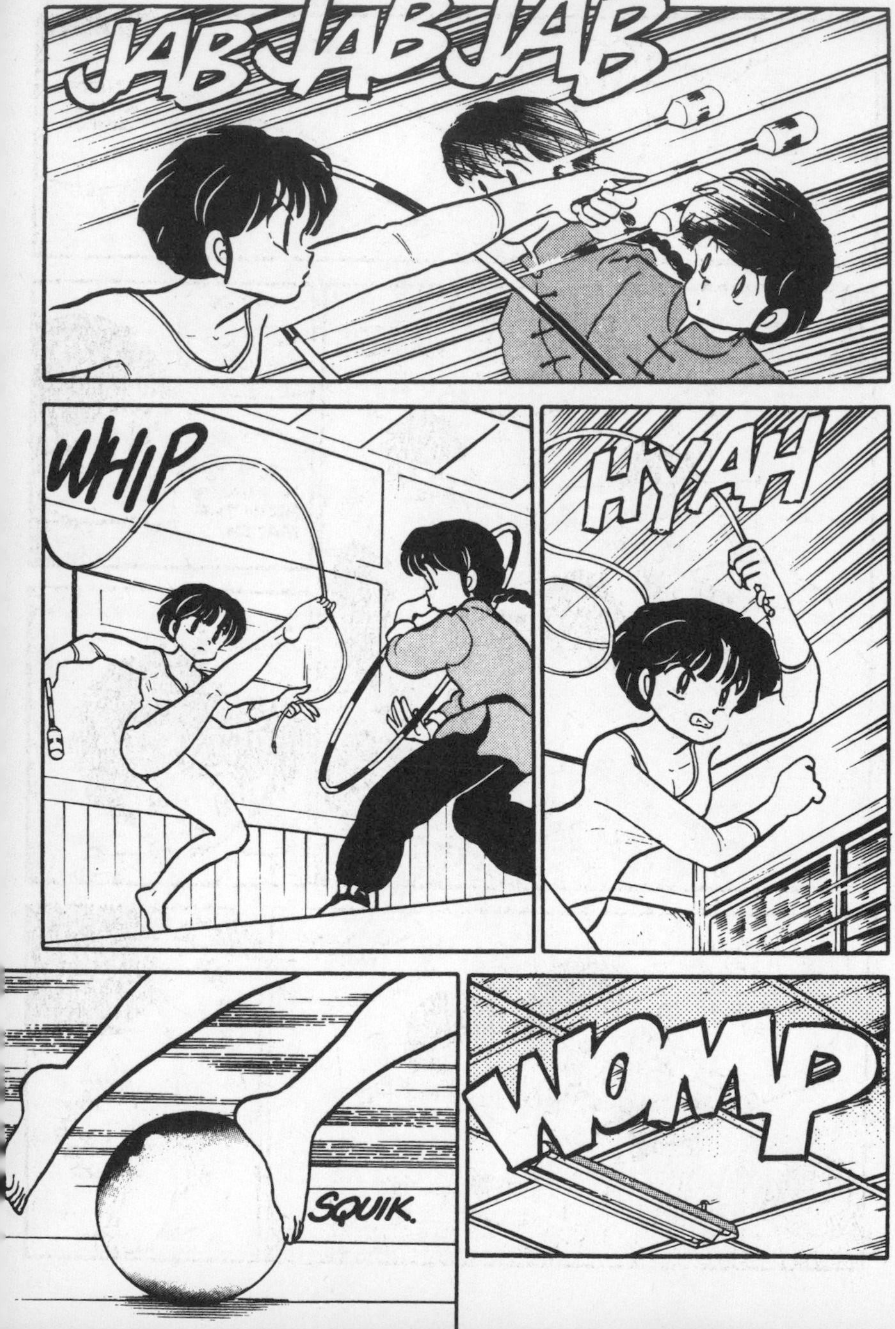
JAB JAB JAB
WHIP
HYAH
SQUIK.
WOMP

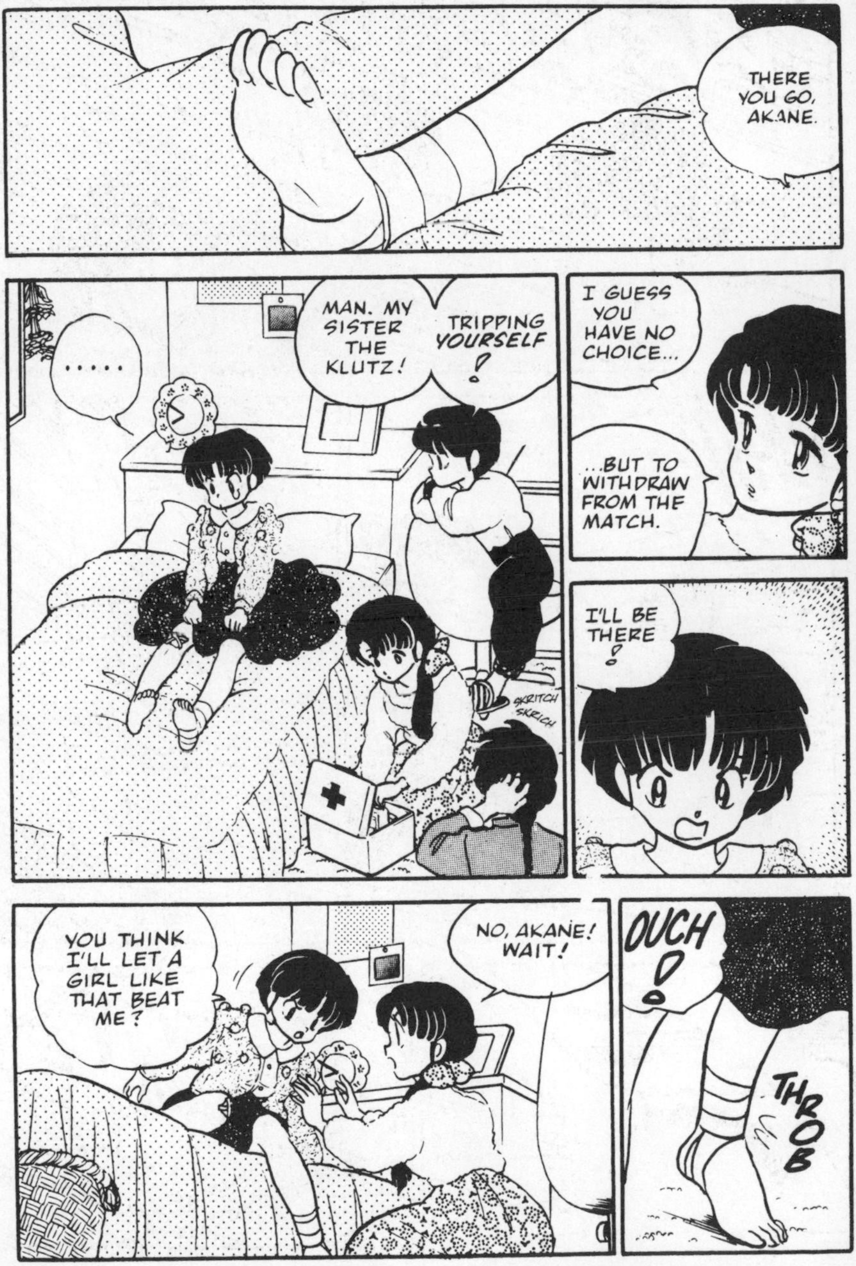

THERE YOU GO, AKANE.
.....
MAN. MY SISTER THE KLUTZ!
TRIPPING YOURSELF!
SKRITCH SKRICH
I GUESS YOU HAVE NO CHOICE...
...BUT TO WITHDRAW FROM THE MATCH.
I'LL BE THERE!
YOU THINK I'LL LET A GIRL LIKE THAT BEAT ME?
NO, AKANE! WAIT!
OUCH!
THROB

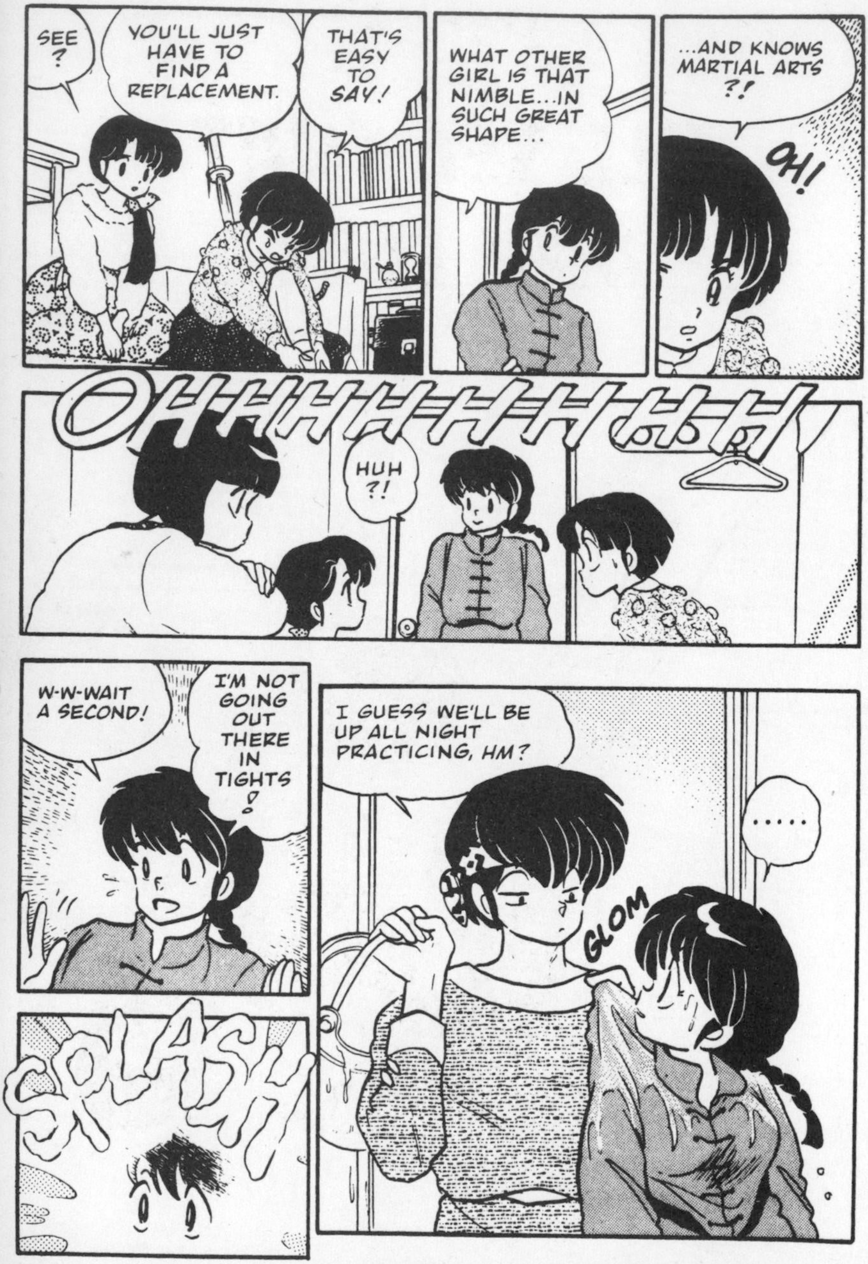
SEE?
YOU'LL JUST HAVE TO FIND A REPLACEMENT.
THAT'S EASY TO SAY!
WHAT OTHER GIRL IS THAT NIMBLE...IN SUCH GREAT SHAPE...
...AND KNOWS MARTIAL ARTS?!
OH!
OHHHHHHHHH!
HUH?!
W-W-WAIT A SECOND!
I'M NOT GOING OUT THERE IN TIGHTS!
SPLASH!
I GUESS WE'LL BE UP ALL NIGHT PRACTICING, HM?
.....
GLOM

Part 6

I'LL SEE THAT YOU LOSE

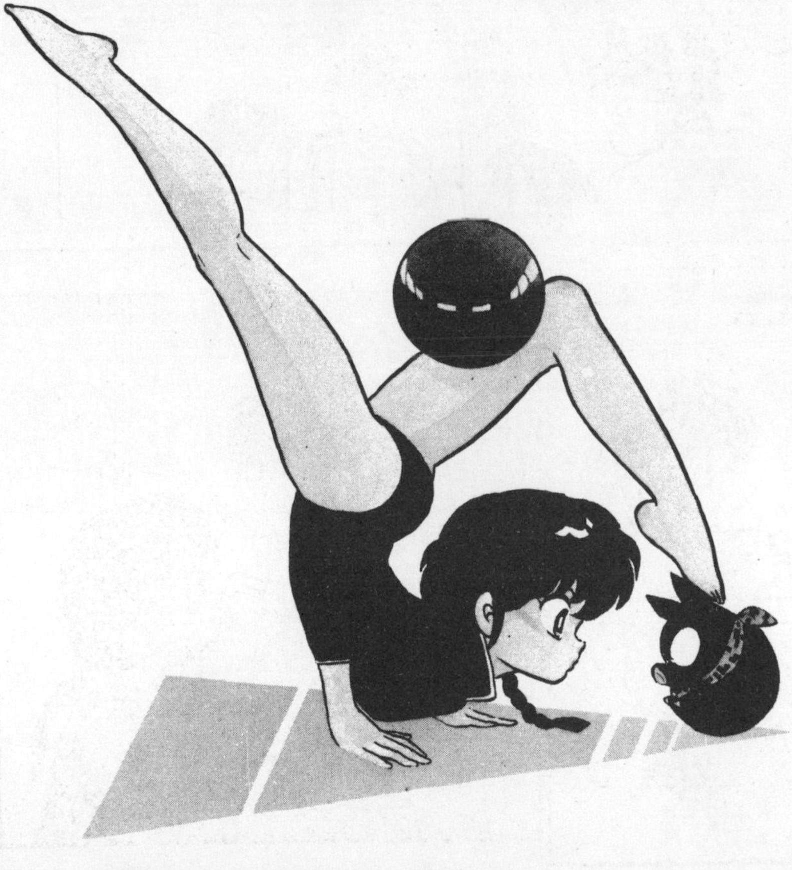

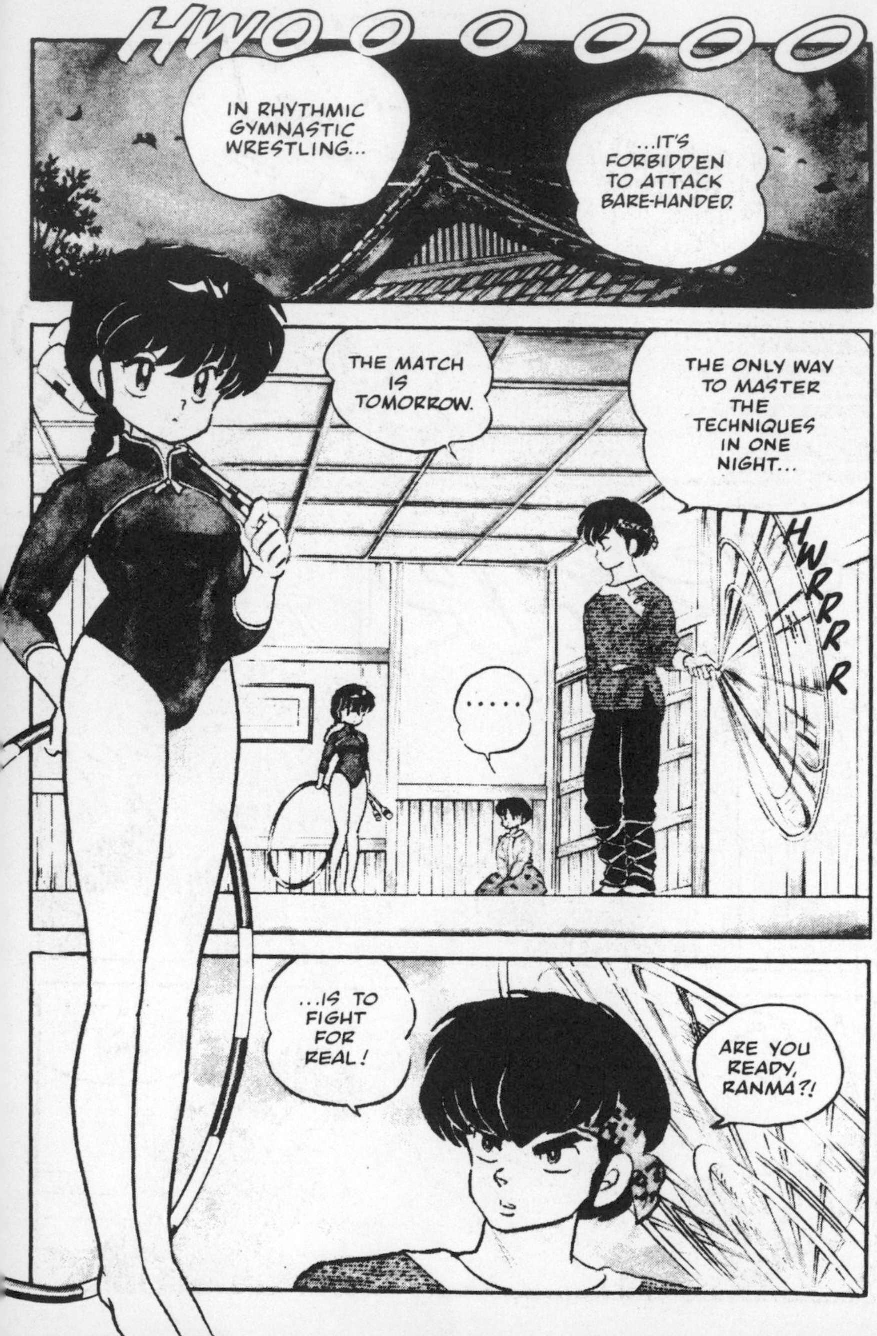
HWOOOOOO
IN RHYTHMIC GYMNASTIC WRESTLING...
...IT'S FORBIDDEN TO ATTACK BARE-HANDED.
THE MATCH IS TOMORROW.
......
THE ONLY WAY TO MASTER THE TECHNIQUES IN ONE NIGHT...
HWRRRR
...IS TO FIGHT FOR REAL!
ARE YOU READY, RANMA?!

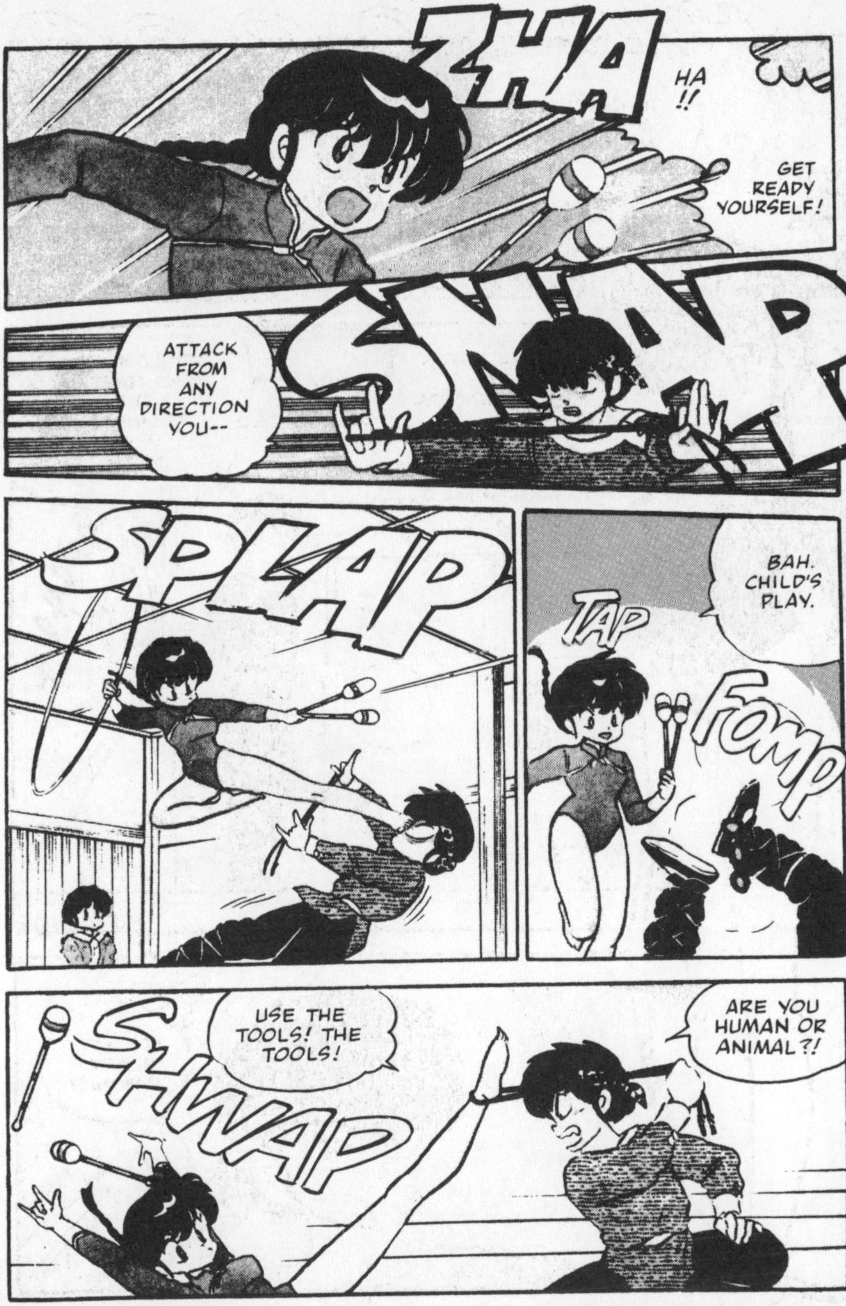
ZHA
HA !!
GET READY YOURSELF!
SNAP
ATTACK FROM ANY DIRECTION YOU--
SPLAP
TAP
BAH. CHILD'S PLAY.
FOMP
SHWAP
USE THE TOOLS! THE TOOLS!
ARE YOU HUMAN OR ANIMAL?!

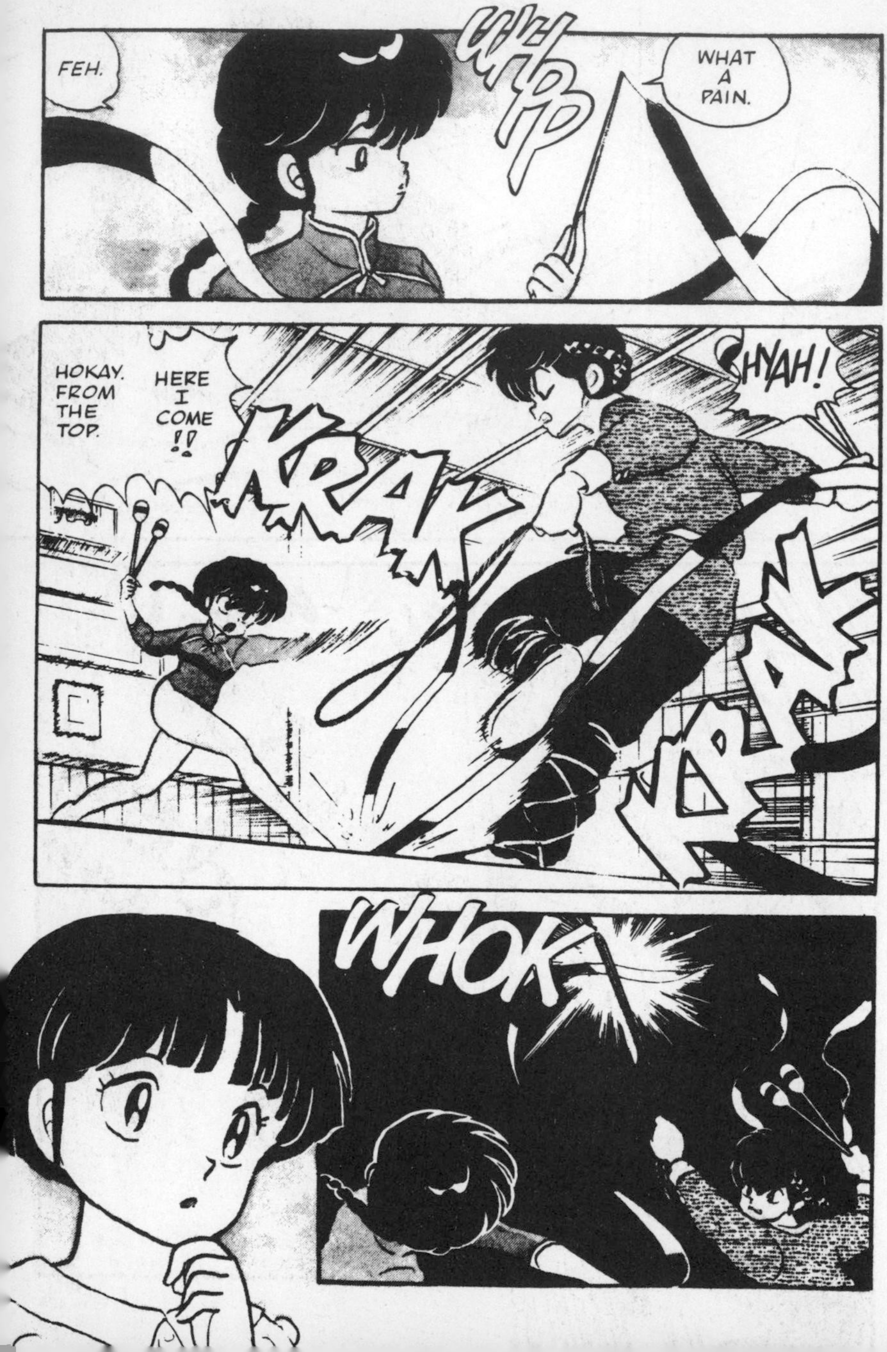
FEH.
whip
WHAT A PAIN.
HOKAY. FROM THE TOP.
HERE I COME!!
KRAK
SHYAH!
KRAK
WHOK

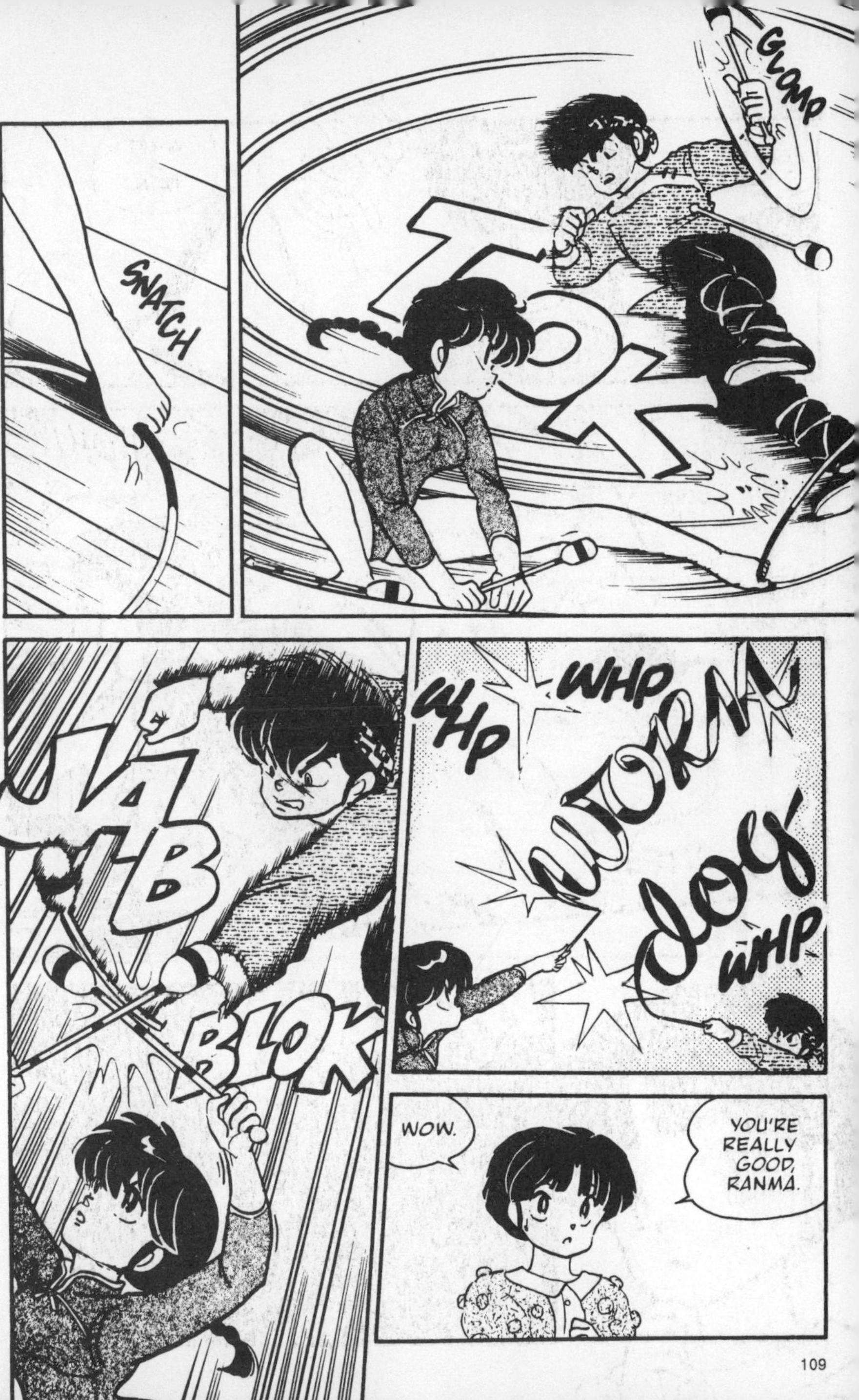

SNATCH
GLOMP
TOK
JAB
BLOK
WHP
WHP
WHP
WOW.
YOU'RE REALLY GOOD, RANMA.

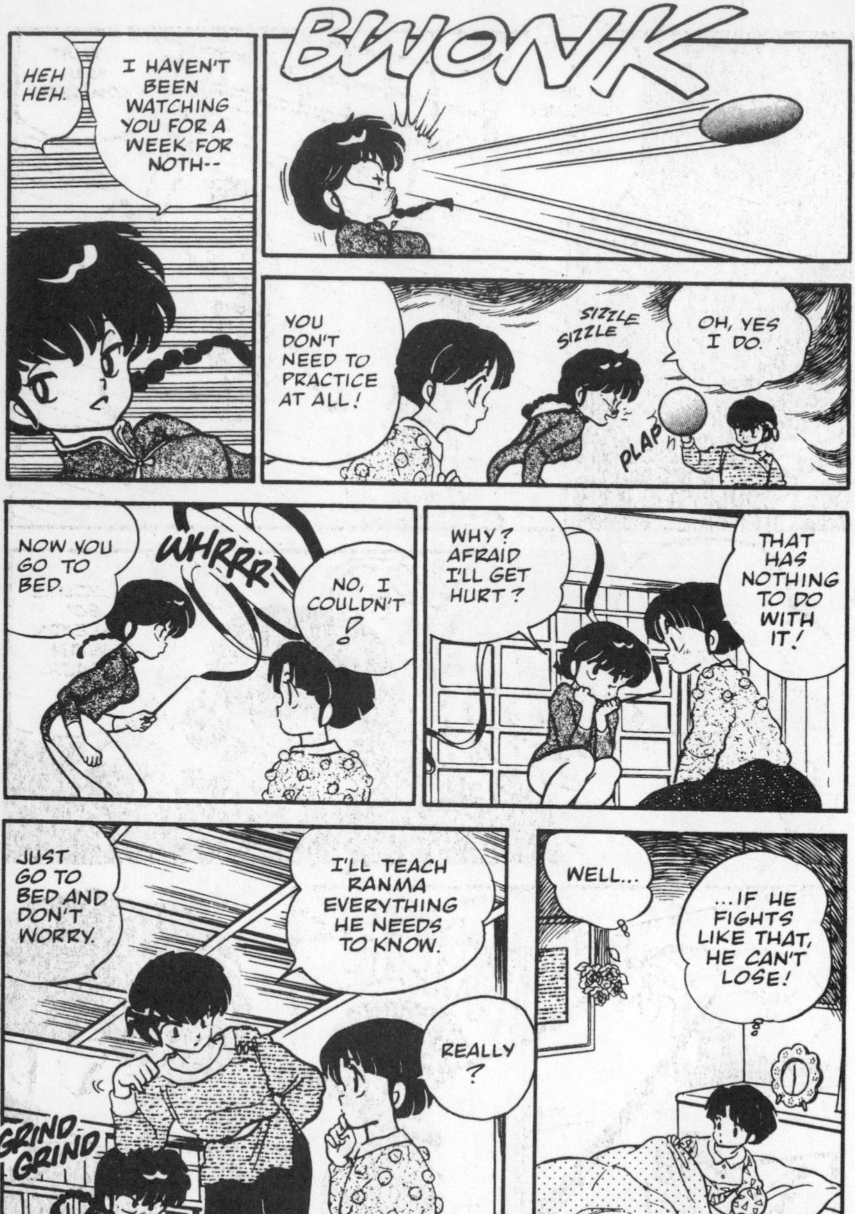
HEH HEH.
I HAVEN'T BEEN WATCHING YOU FOR A WEEK FOR NOTH--
BWONK
YOU DON'T NEED TO PRACTICE AT ALL!
SIZZLE SIZZLE
OH, YES I DO.
PLAP
NOW YOU GO TO BED.
WHRRR
NO, I COULDN'T!
WHY? AFRAID I'LL GET HURT?
THAT HAS NOTHING TO DO WITH IT!
JUST GO TO BED AND DON'T WORRY.
I'LL TEACH RANMA EVERYTHING HE NEEDS TO KNOW.
REALLY?
GRIND GRIND
WELL...
...IF HE FIGHTS LIKE THAT, HE CAN'T LOSE!

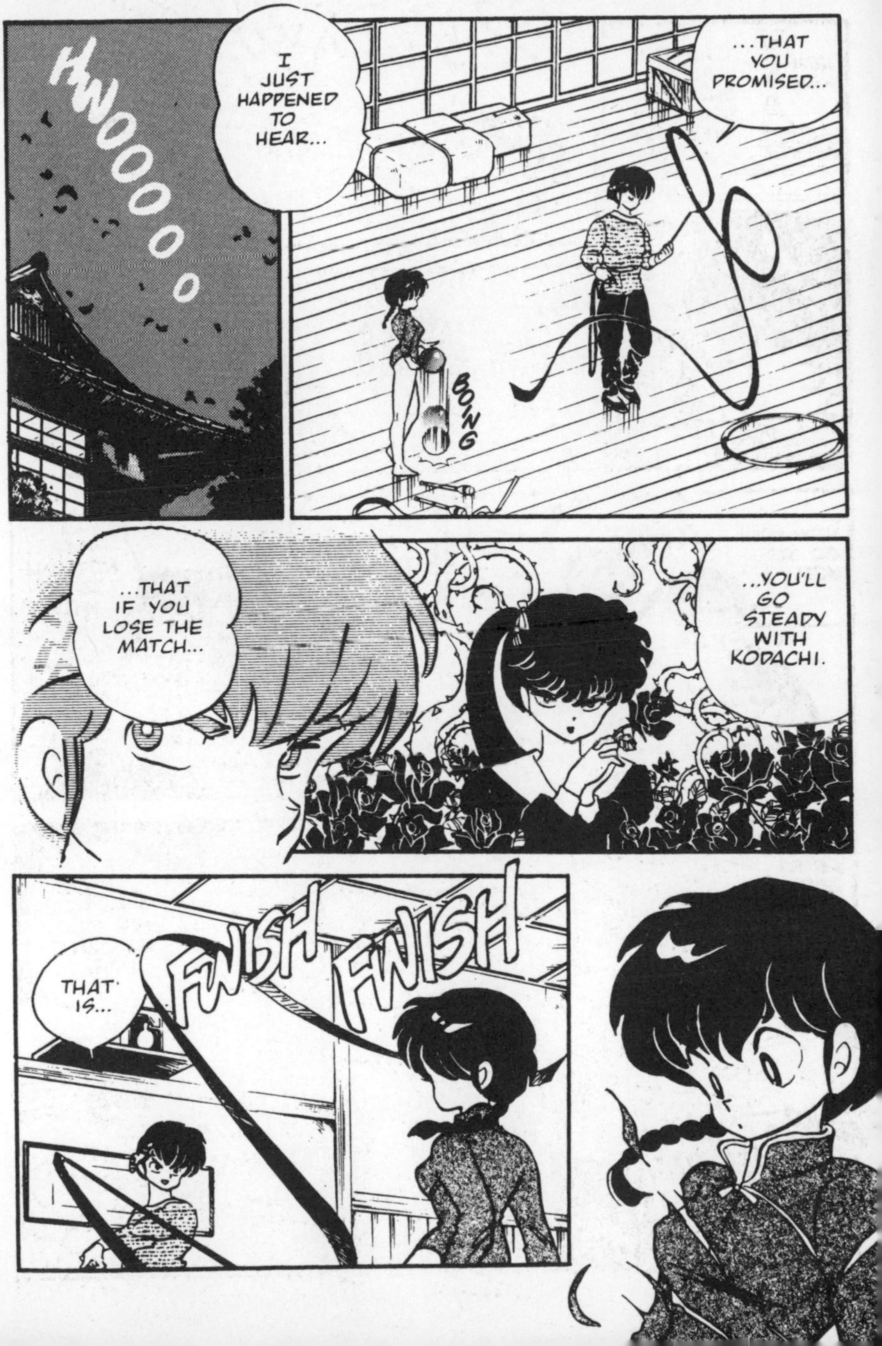
HWOOOOOO
I JUST HAPPENED TO HEAR...
...THAT YOU PROMISED...
BOING
...THAT IF YOU LOSE THE MATCH...
...YOU'LL GO STEADY WITH KODACHI.
THAT IS...
FWISH FWISH

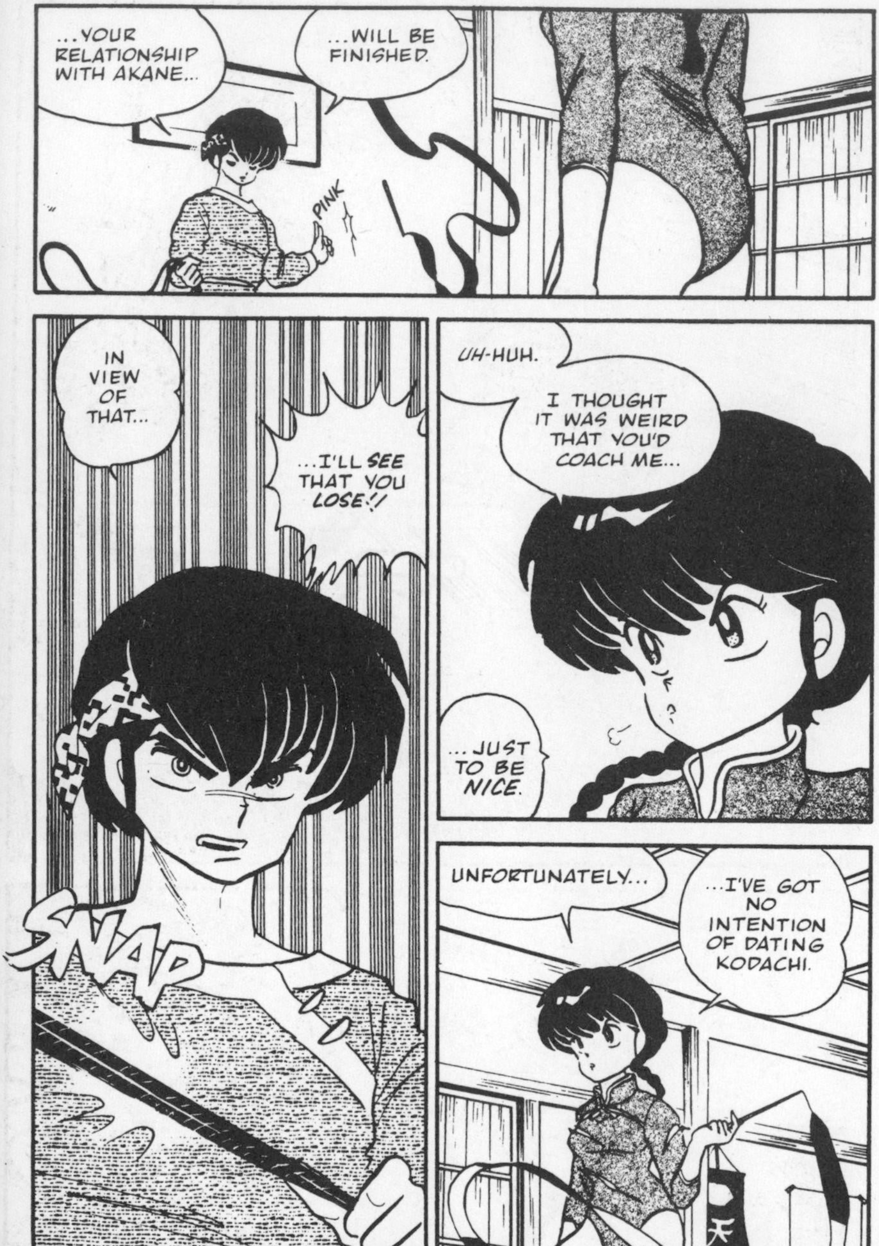
...YOUR RELATIONSHIP WITH AKANE...
...WILL BE FINISHED.
PINK
IN VIEW OF THAT...
...I'LL SEE THAT YOU LOSE!!
SNAP
UH-HUH.
I THOUGHT IT WAS WEIRD THAT YOU'D COACH ME...
...JUST TO BE NICE.
UNFORTUNATELY...
...I'VE GOT NO INTENTION OF DATING KODACHI.

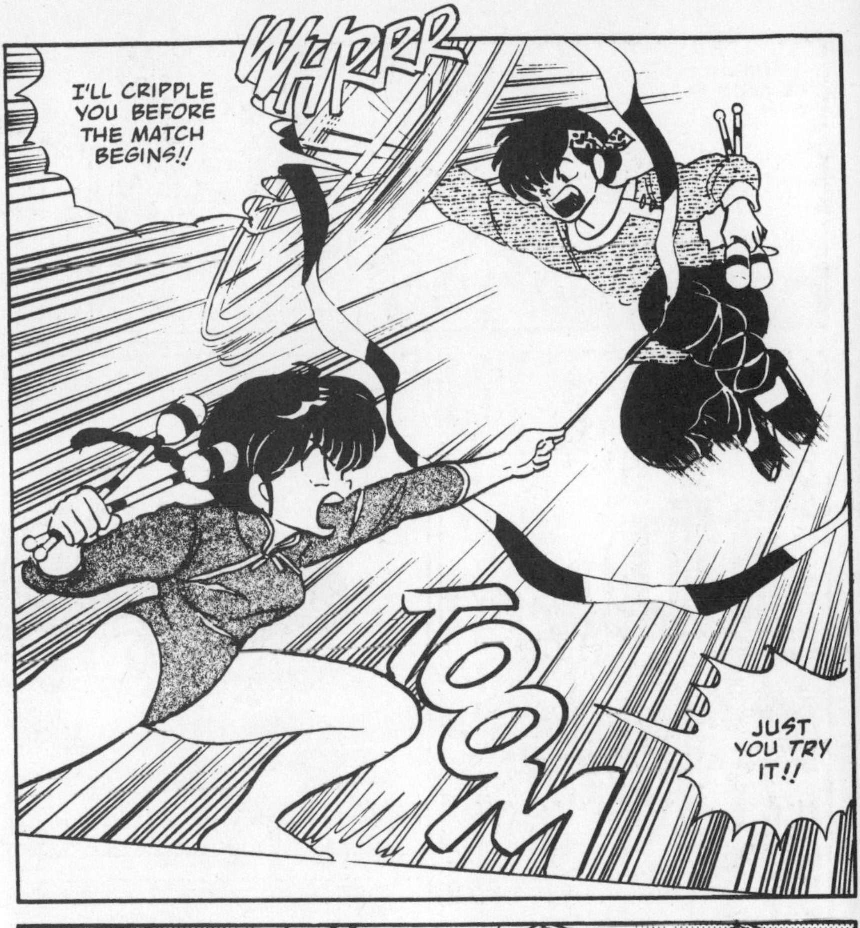
WHRRR
I'LL CRIPPLE YOU BEFORE THE MATCH BEGINS!!
TOOM
JUST YOU TRY IT!!
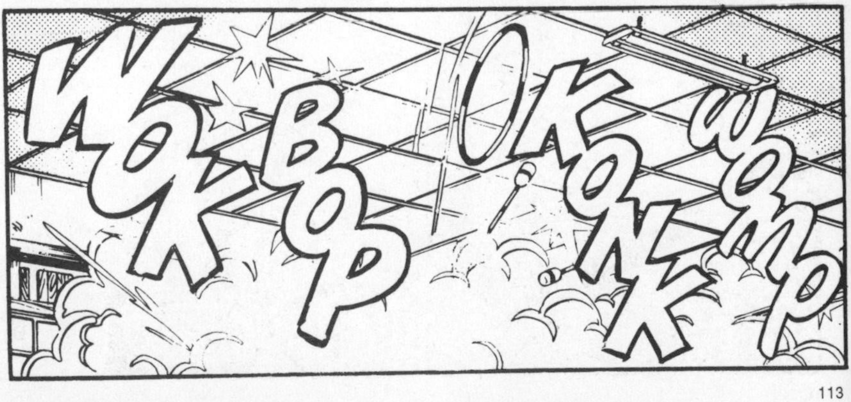
WOK
BOP
BOKONK
WOMP

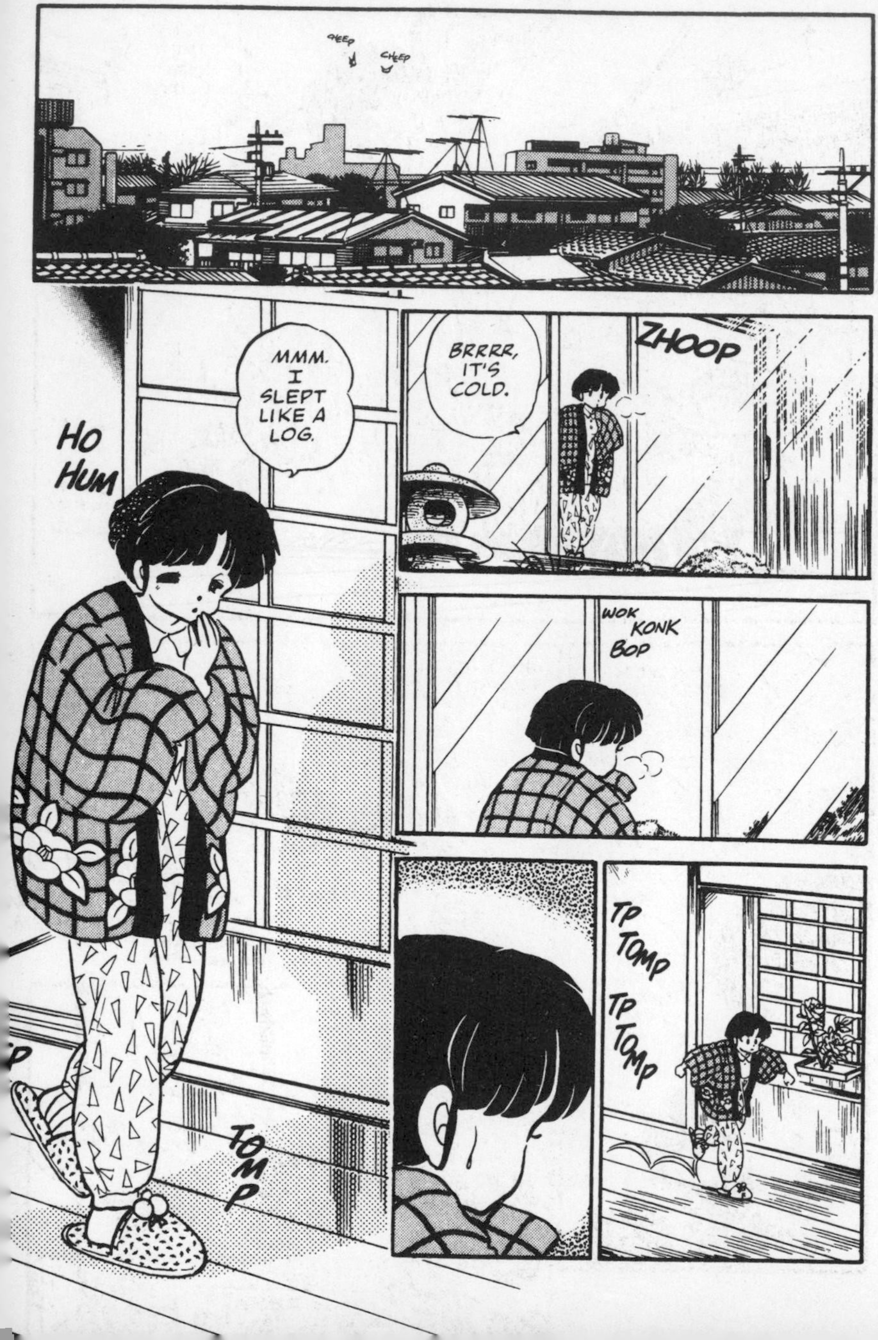
CHEEP
CHEEP
HO HUM
MMM. I SLEPT LIKE A LOG.
TOMP
BRRRR, IT'S COLD.
ZHOOP
WOK KONK BOP
TP TOMP TP TOMP

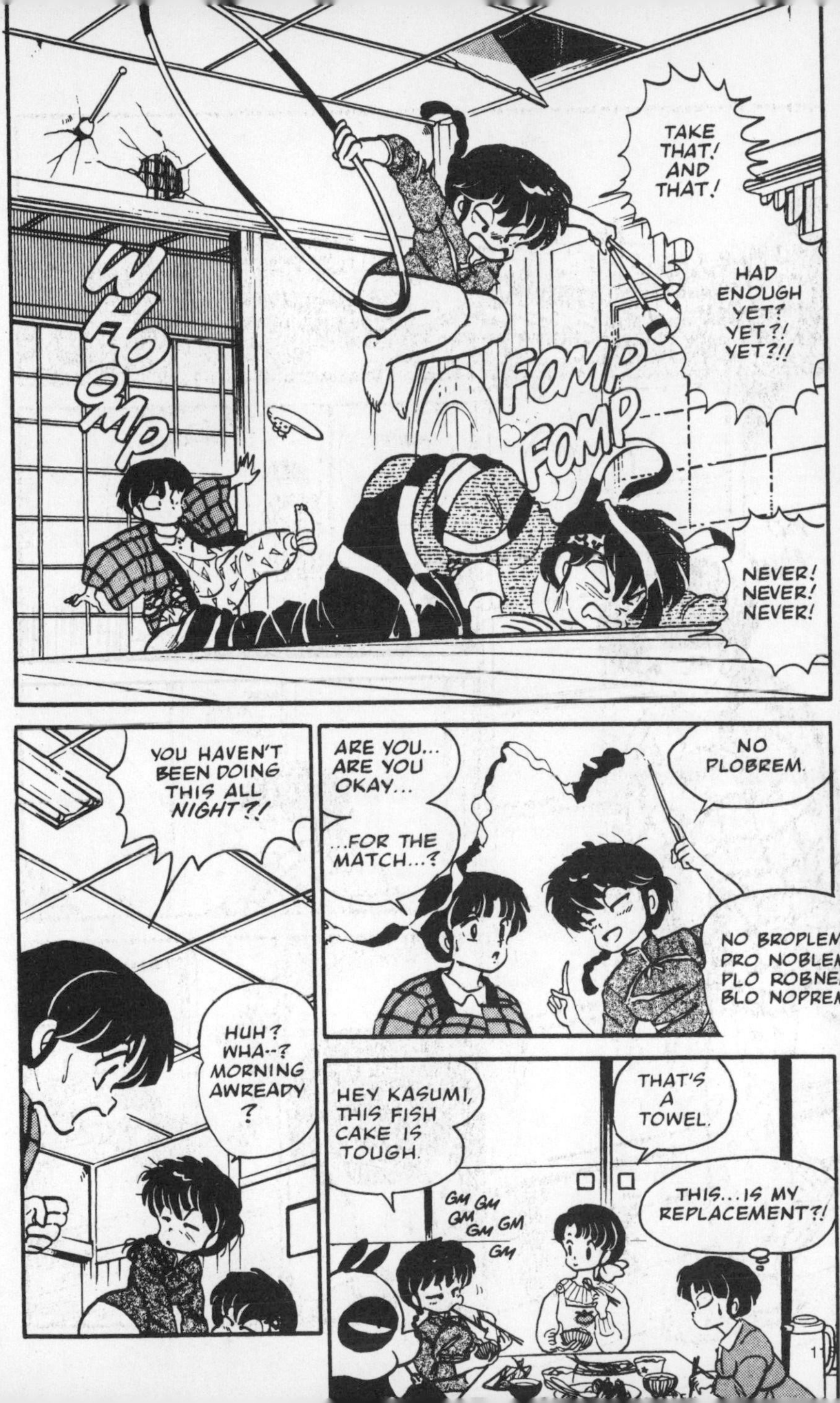
TAKE THAT! AND THAT!
HAD ENOUGH YET? YET?! YET?!!
WHOMP
FOMP FOMP
NEVER! NEVER! NEVER!
YOU HAVEN'T BEEN DOING THIS ALL NIGHT?!
HUH? WHA--? MORNING AWREADY ?
ARE YOU... ARE YOU OKAY...
...FOR THE MATCH...?
NO PLOBREM.
NO BROPLEM. PRO NOBLEM. PLO ROBNEM BLO NOPREM.
HEY KASUMI, THIS FISH CAKE IS TOUGH.
THAT'S A TOWEL.
GM GM GM GM GM GM
THIS...IS MY REPLACEMENT?!

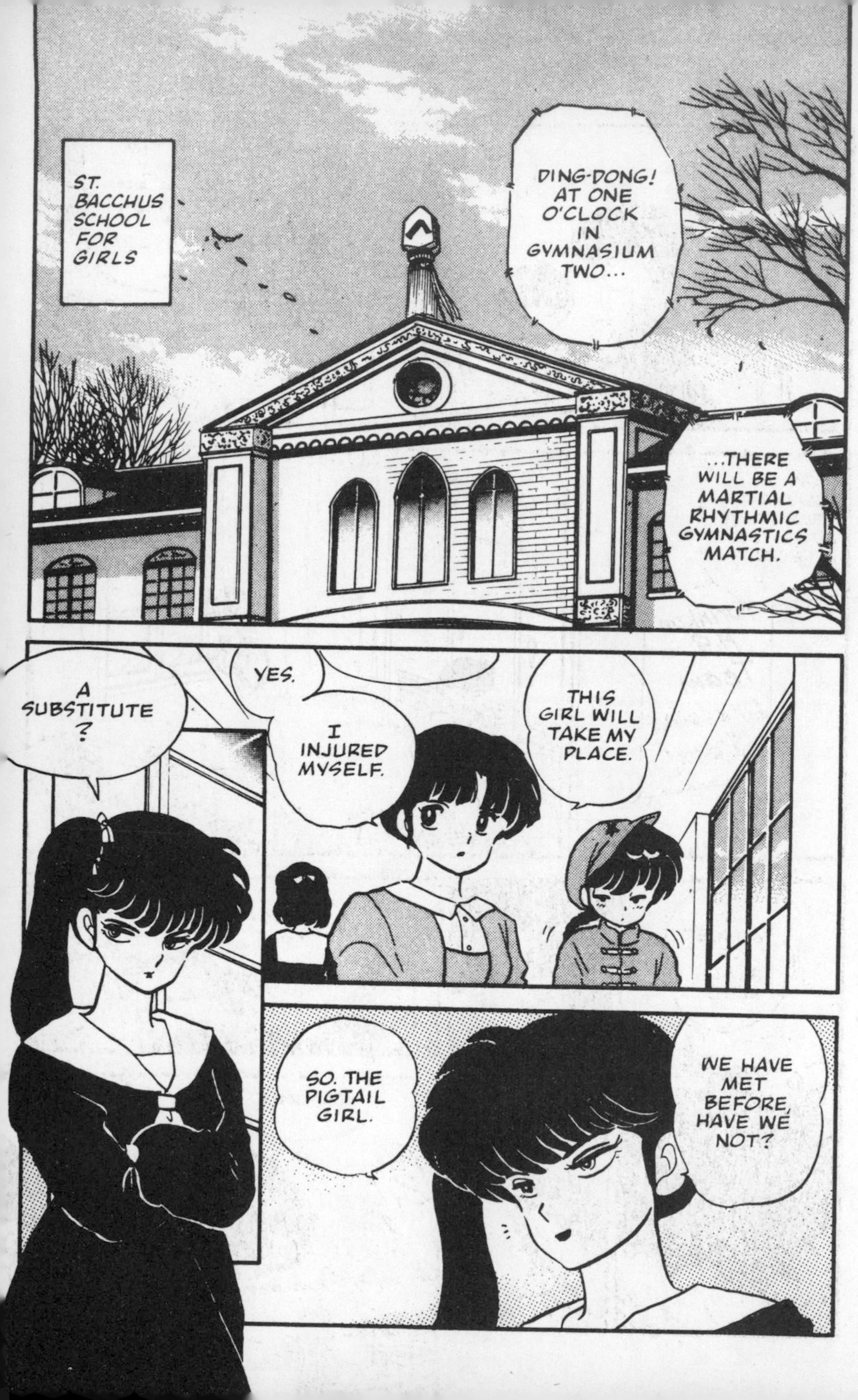
ST. BACCHUS SCHOOL FOR GIRLS
DING-DONG! AT ONE O'CLOCK IN GYMNASIUM TWO...
...THERE WILL BE A MARTIAL RHYTHMIC GYMNASTICS MATCH.
A SUBSTITUTE?
YES.
I INJURED MYSELF.
THIS GIRL WILL TAKE MY PLACE.
SO. THE PIGTAIL GIRL.
WE HAVE MET BEFORE, HAVE WE NOT?

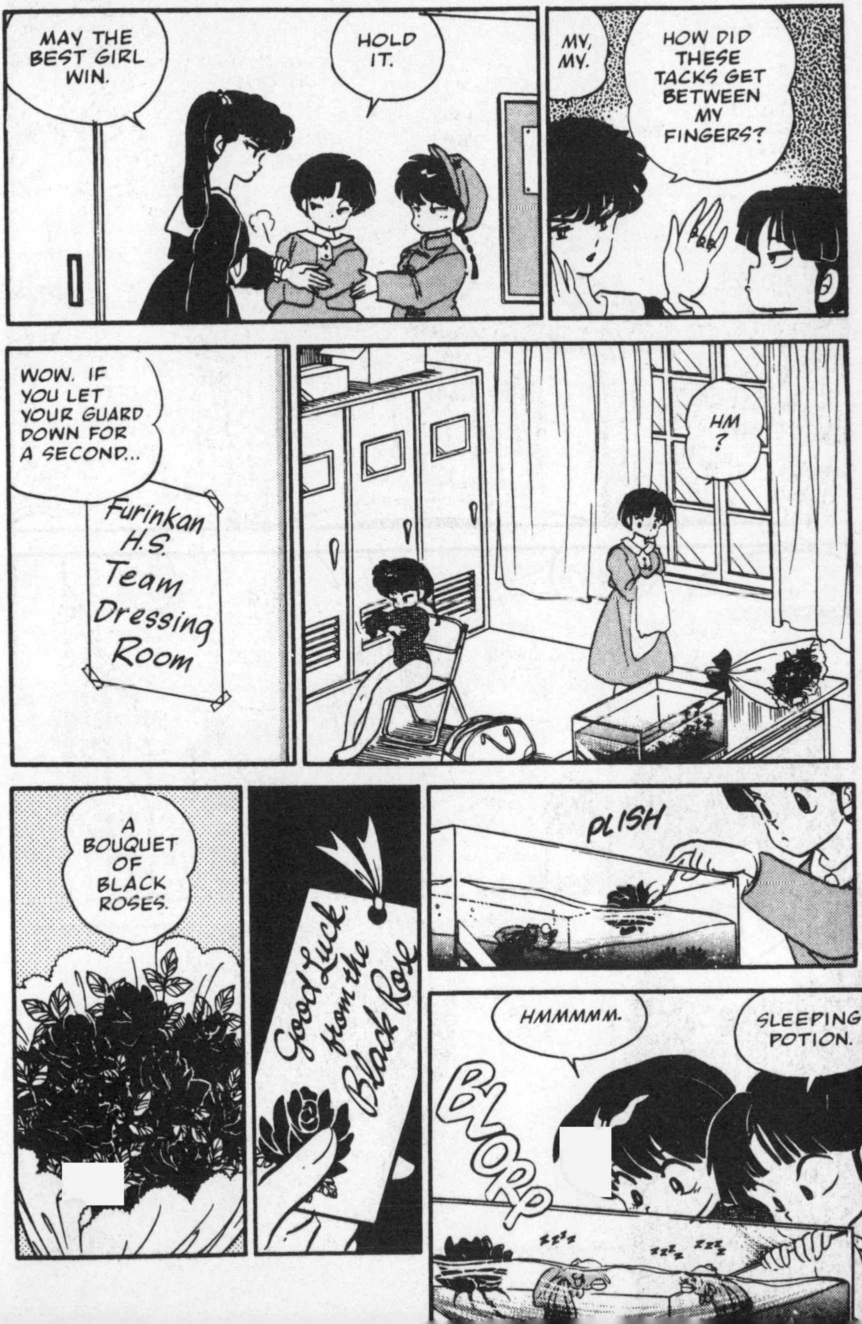

MAY THE BEST GIRL WIN.
HOLD IT.
MY, MY.
HOW DID THESE TACKS GET BETWEEN MY FINGERS?
WOW. IF YOU LET YOUR GUARD DOWN FOR A SECOND...
Furinkan H.S. Team Dressing Room
HM ?
A BOUQUET OF BLACK ROSES.
Good Luck from the Black Rose
PLISH
HMMMMM.
SLEEPING POTION.
BLORP

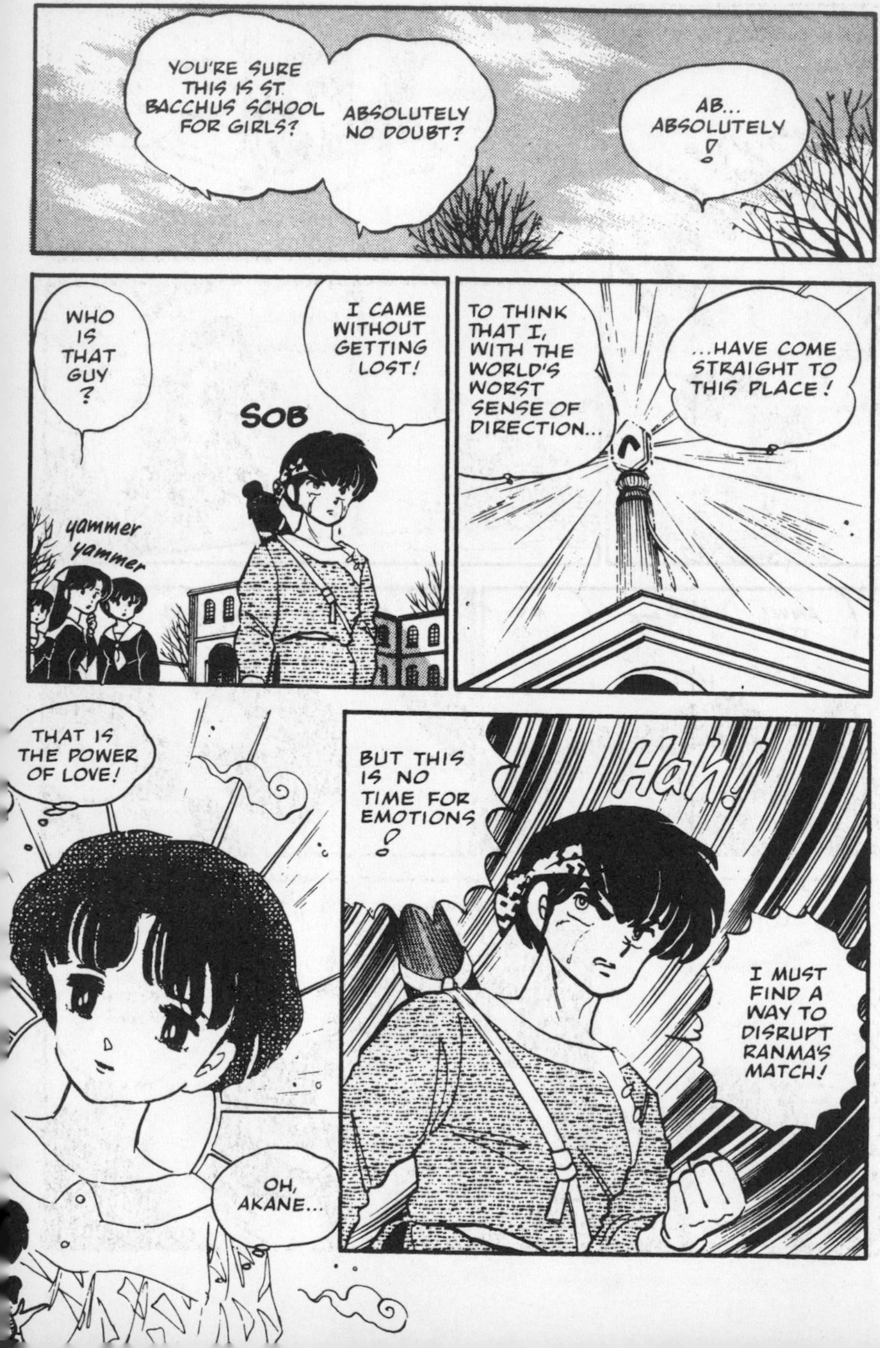

YOU'RE SURE THIS IS ST. BACCHUS SCHOOL FOR GIRLS?
ABSOLUTELY NO DOUBT?
AB... ABSOLUTELY!
WHO IS THAT GUY?
I CAME WITHOUT GETTING LOST!
SOB
yammer yammer
TO THINK THAT I, WITH THE WORLD'S WORST SENSE OF DIRECTION...
...HAVE COME STRAIGHT TO THIS PLACE!
THAT IS THE POWER OF LOVE!
OH, AKANE...
BUT THIS IS NO TIME FOR EMOTIONS!
HAH!
I MUST FIND A WAY TO DISRUPT RANMA'S MATCH!

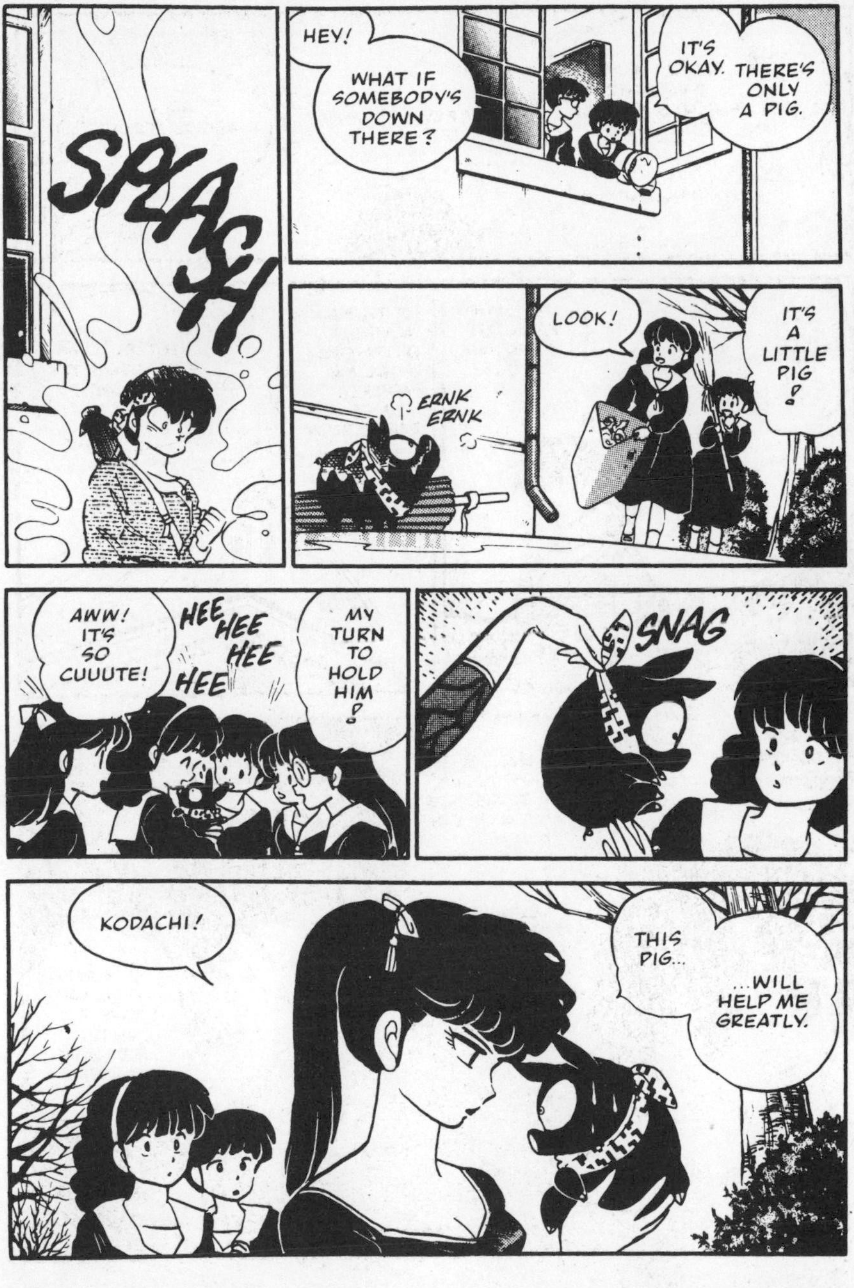
SPLASH
HEY!
WHAT IF SOMEBODY'S DOWN THERE?
IT'S OKAY.
THERE'S ONLY A PIG.
ERNK ERNK
LOOK!
IT'S A LITTLE PIG!
AWW! IT'S SO CUUUTE!
HEE HEE HEE HEE
MY TURN TO HOLD HIM!
SNAG
KODACHI!
THIS PIG...
...WILL HELP ME GREATLY.

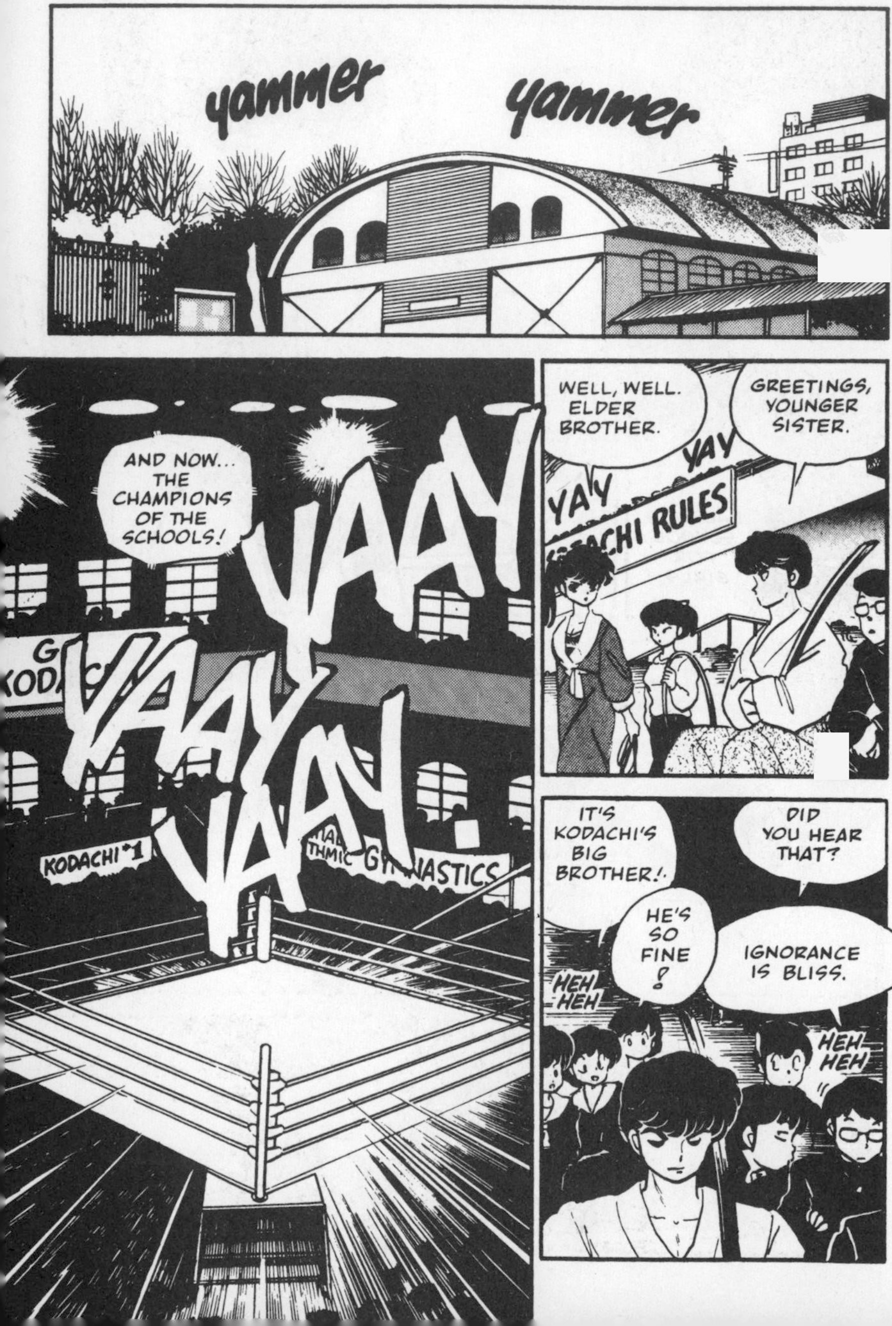
yammer yammer
AND NOW... THE CHAMPIONS OF THE SCHOOLS!
YAAY
YAAY
YAAY
KODACHI #1
WELL, WELL. ELDER BROTHER.
GREETINGS, YOUNGER SISTER.
YAY YAY
IT'S KODACHI'S BIG BROTHER!
DID YOU HEAR THAT?
HEH HEH
HE'S SO FINE!
IGNORANCE IS BLISS.
HEH HEH

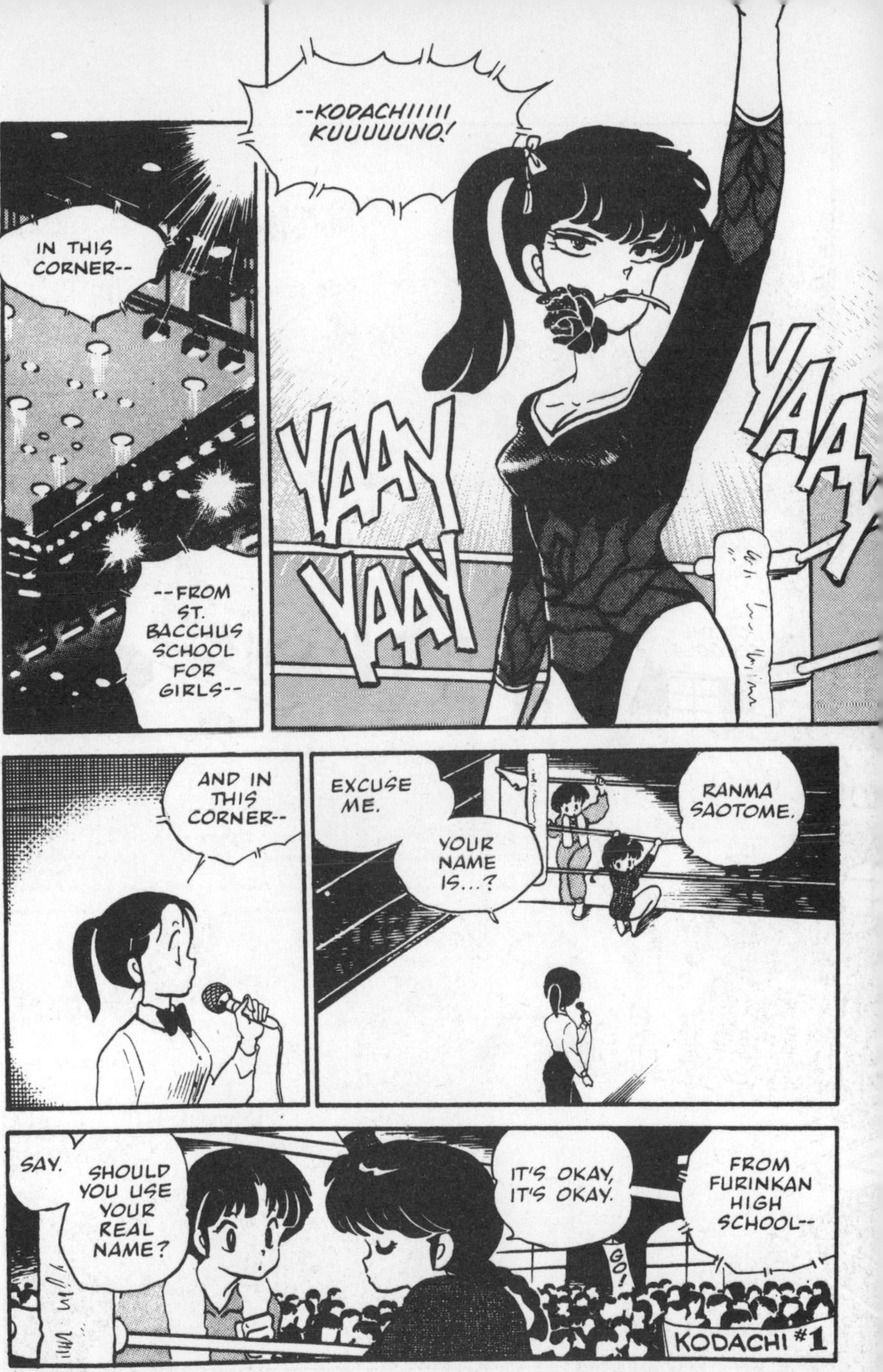
IN THIS CORNER--
--FROM ST. BACCHUS SCHOOL FOR GIRLS--
--KODACHI!!!!! KUUUUUNO!
YAAY YAAY
YAA
AND IN THIS CORNER--
EXCUSE ME.
YOUR NAME IS...?
RANMA SAOTOME.
SAY.
SHOULD YOU USE YOUR REAL NAME?
IT'S OKAY, IT'S OKAY.
FROM FURINKAN HIGH SCHOOL--
GO!
KODACHI #1

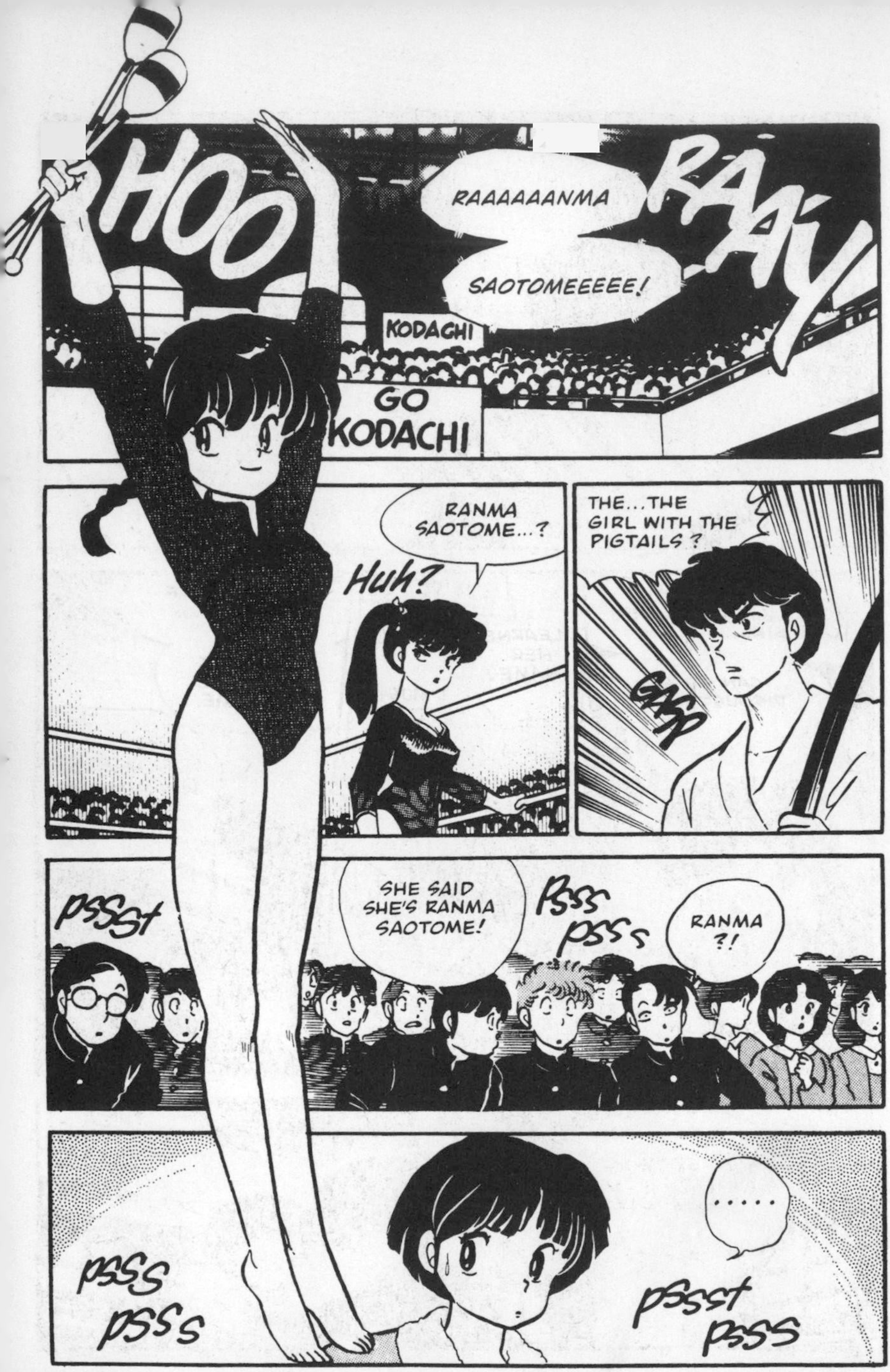
HOO
RAAAAAANMA
SAOTOMEEEEE!
RAAY
KODACHI
GO KODACHI
RANMA SAOTOME...?
Huh?
THE...THE GIRL WITH THE PIGTAILS?
pssst
SHE SAID SHE'S RANMA SAOTOME!
Psss psss
RANMA ?!
.....
psss psss
pssst psss

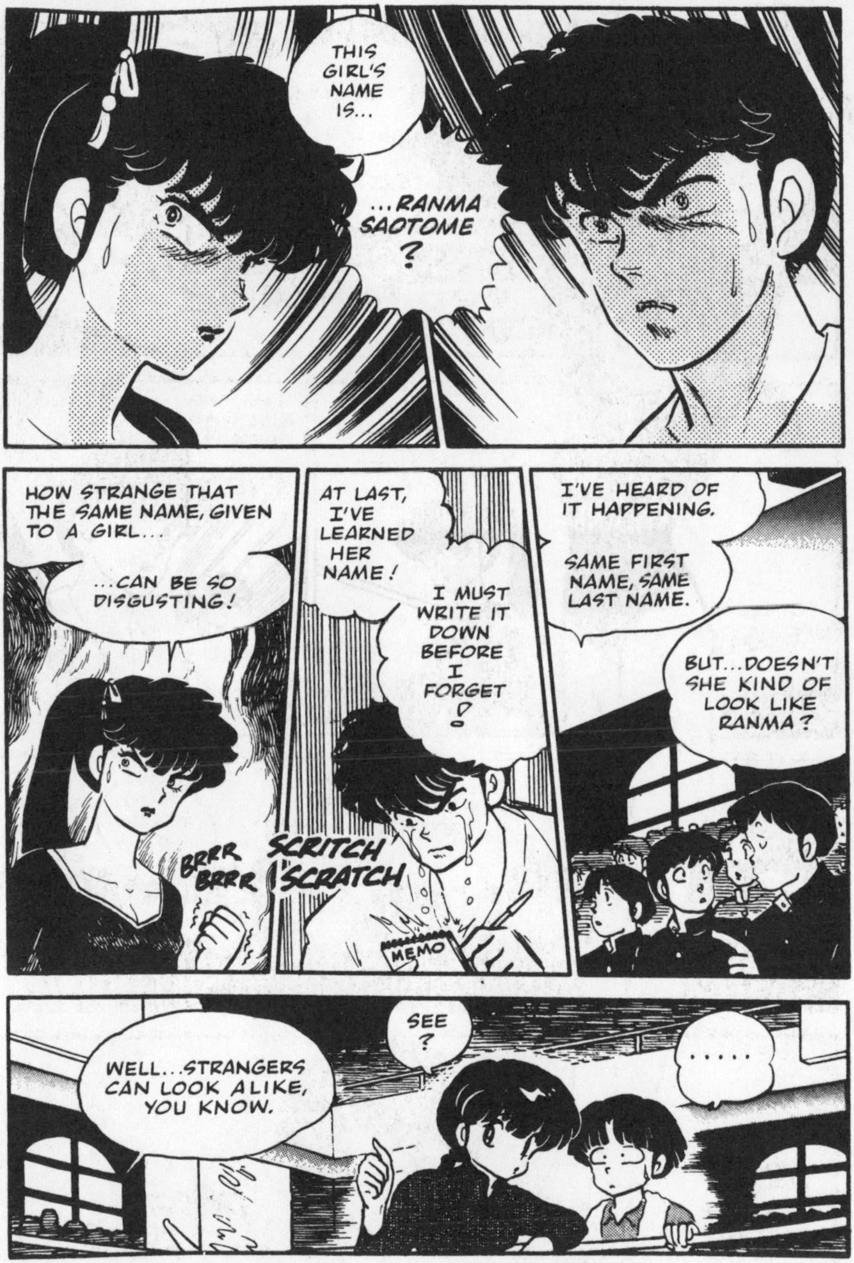
THIS GIRL'S NAME IS...
...RANMA SAOTOME ?
HOW STRANGE THAT THE SAME NAME, GIVEN TO A GIRL...
...CAN BE SO DISGUSTING!
BRRR BRRR
AT LAST, I'VE LEARNED HER NAME!
I MUST WRITE IT DOWN BEFORE I FORGET !
SCRITCH SCRATCH
MEMO
I'VE HEARD OF IT HAPPENING.
SAME FIRST NAME, SAME LAST NAME.
BUT...DOESN'T SHE KIND OF LOOK LIKE RANMA?
WELL...STRANGERS CAN LOOK ALIKE, YOU KNOW.
SEE ?
.....

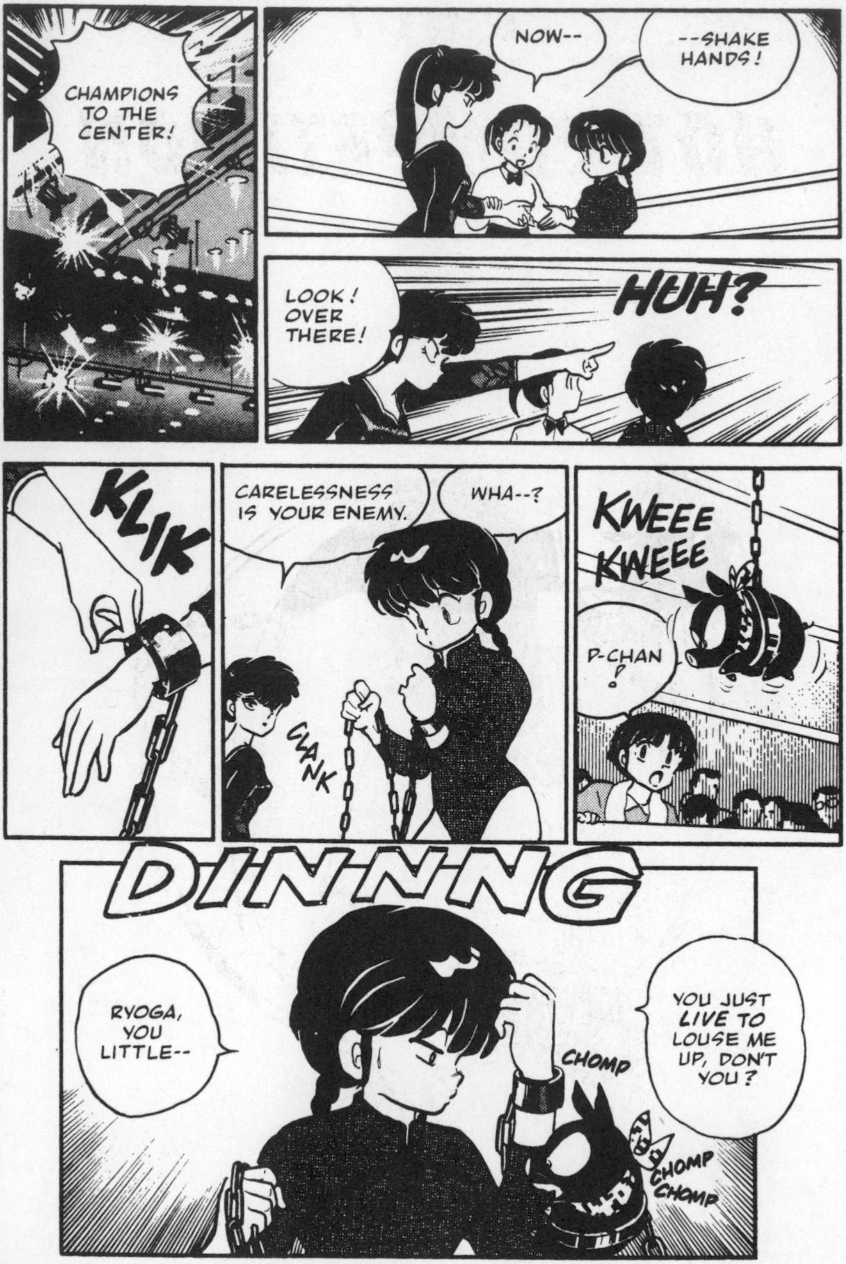
CHAMPIONS TO THE CENTER!
NOW--
--SHAKE HANDS!
LOOK! OVER THERE!
HUH?
KLIK
CARELESSNESS IS YOUR ENEMY.
WHA--?
CLANK
KWEEE KWEEE
P-CHAN!
DINNNG
RYOGA, YOU LITTLE--
YOU JUST LIVE TO LOUSE ME UP, DON'T YOU?
CHOMP
CHOMP CHOMP

Part 7
HOT COMPETITION

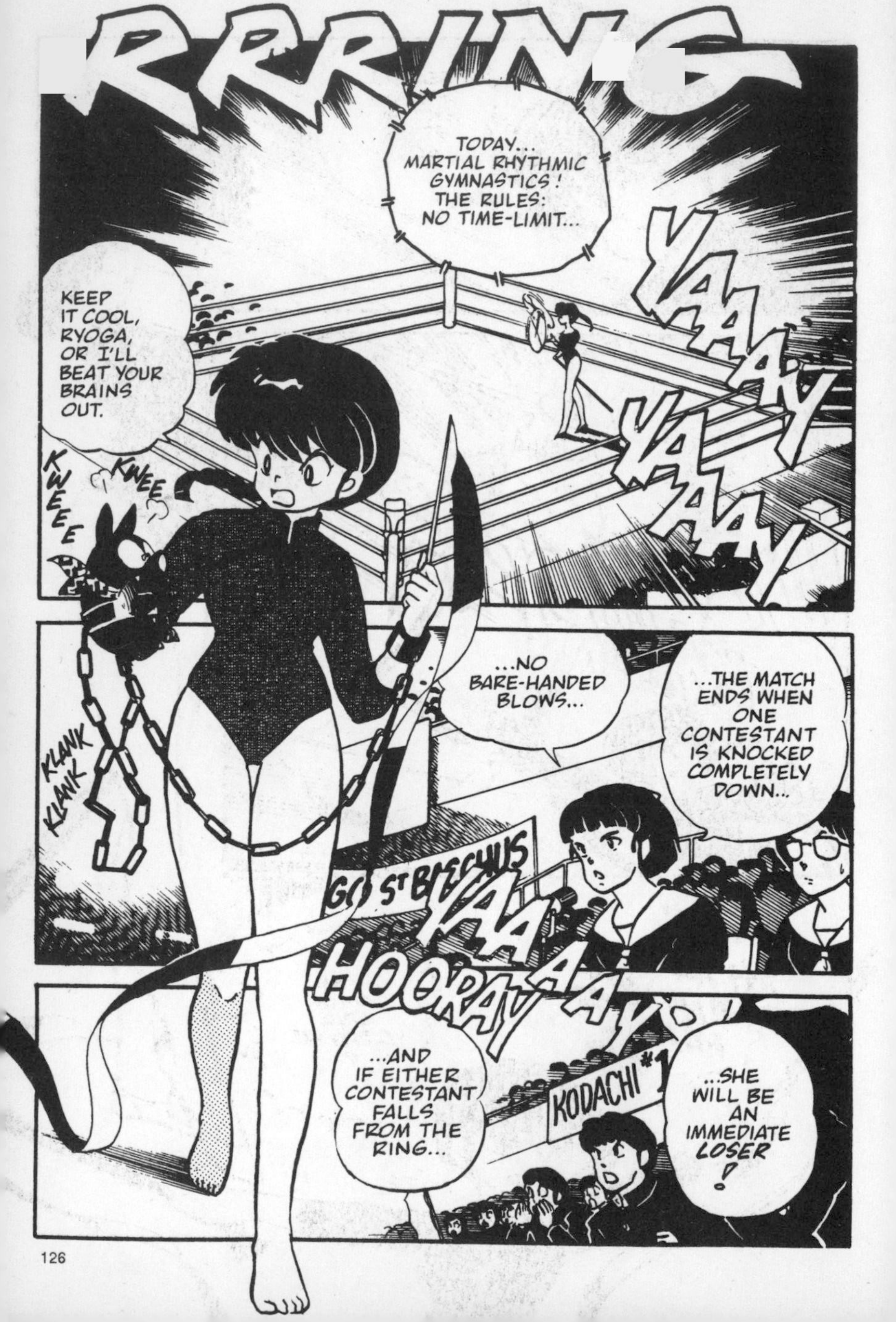

RRRING
TODAY... MARTIAL RHYTHMIC GYMNASTICS! THE RULES: NO TIME-LIMIT...
KEEP IT COOL, RYOGA, OR I'LL BEAT YOUR BRAINS OUT.
YAAAY
KWEEEE
KWEEE
YAAAAY
KLANK KLANK
...NO BARE-HANDED BLOWS...
...THE MATCH ENDS WHEN ONE CONTESTANT IS KNOCKED COMPLETELY DOWN...
YAAAAAY
HOORAY
...AND IF EITHER CONTESTANT FALLS FROM THE RING...
KODACHI #1
...SHE WILL BE AN IMMEDIATE LOSER!

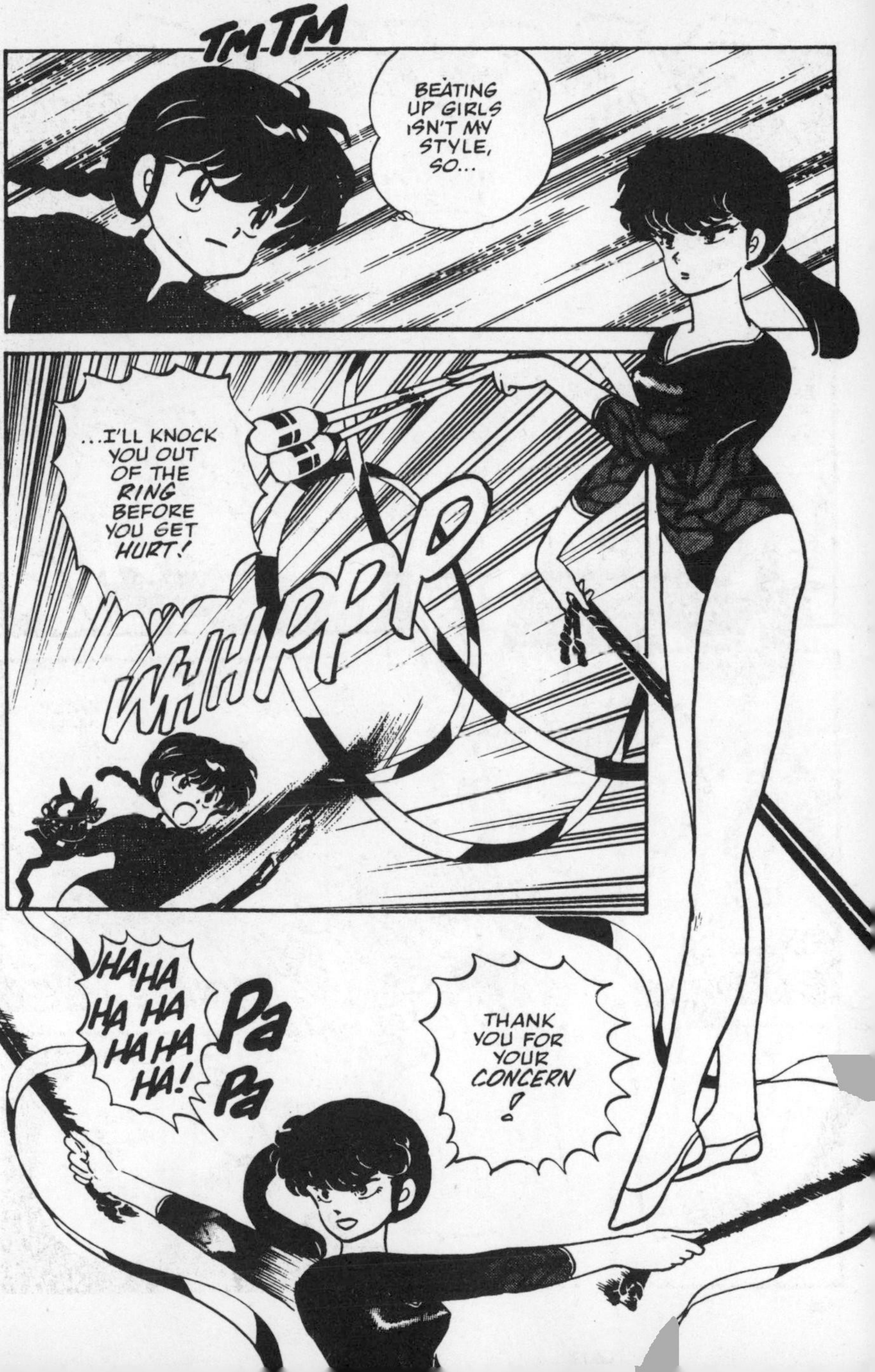
TM-TM
BEATING UP GIRLS ISN'T MY STYLE, SO...
...I'LL KNOCK YOU OUT OF THE RING BEFORE YOU GET HURT!
WHHPPP
HA HA HA HA HA HA HA!
Pa Pa
THANK YOU FOR YOUR CONCERN!

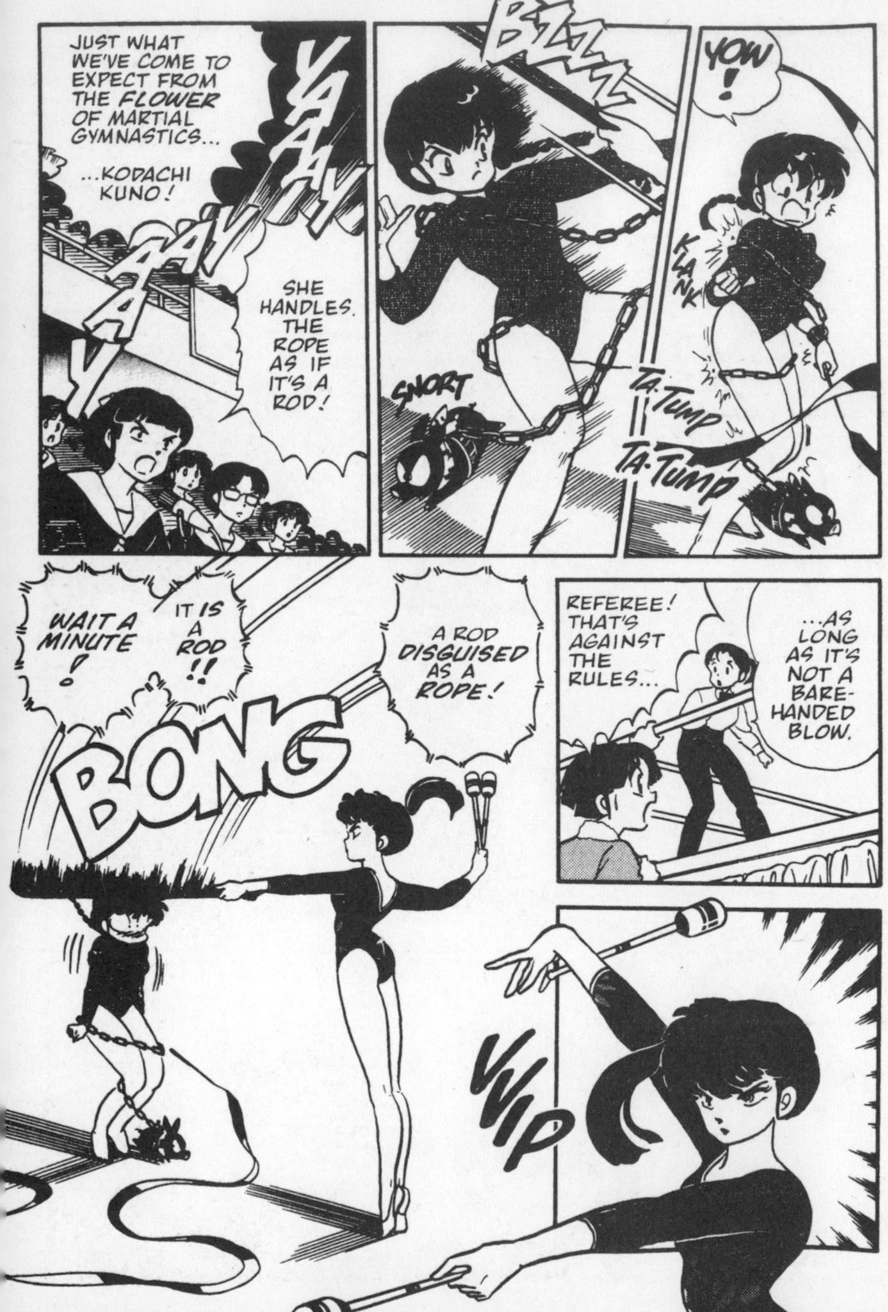
JUST WHAT WE'VE COME TO EXPECT FROM THE *FLOWER* OF MARTIAL GYMNASTICS...
...KODACHI KUNO!
YAAAAAAAY
SHE HANDLES THE ROPE AS IF IT'S A ROD!
BZZZZ
SNORT
YOW!
KLANK
TA-TUMP
TA-TUMP
WAIT A MINUTE!
IT *IS* A ROD!!
A ROD *DISGUISED* AS A *ROPE*!
BONG
REFEREE! THAT'S AGAINST THE RULES...
...AS LONG AS IT'S NOT A BARE-HANDED BLOW.
VVIP

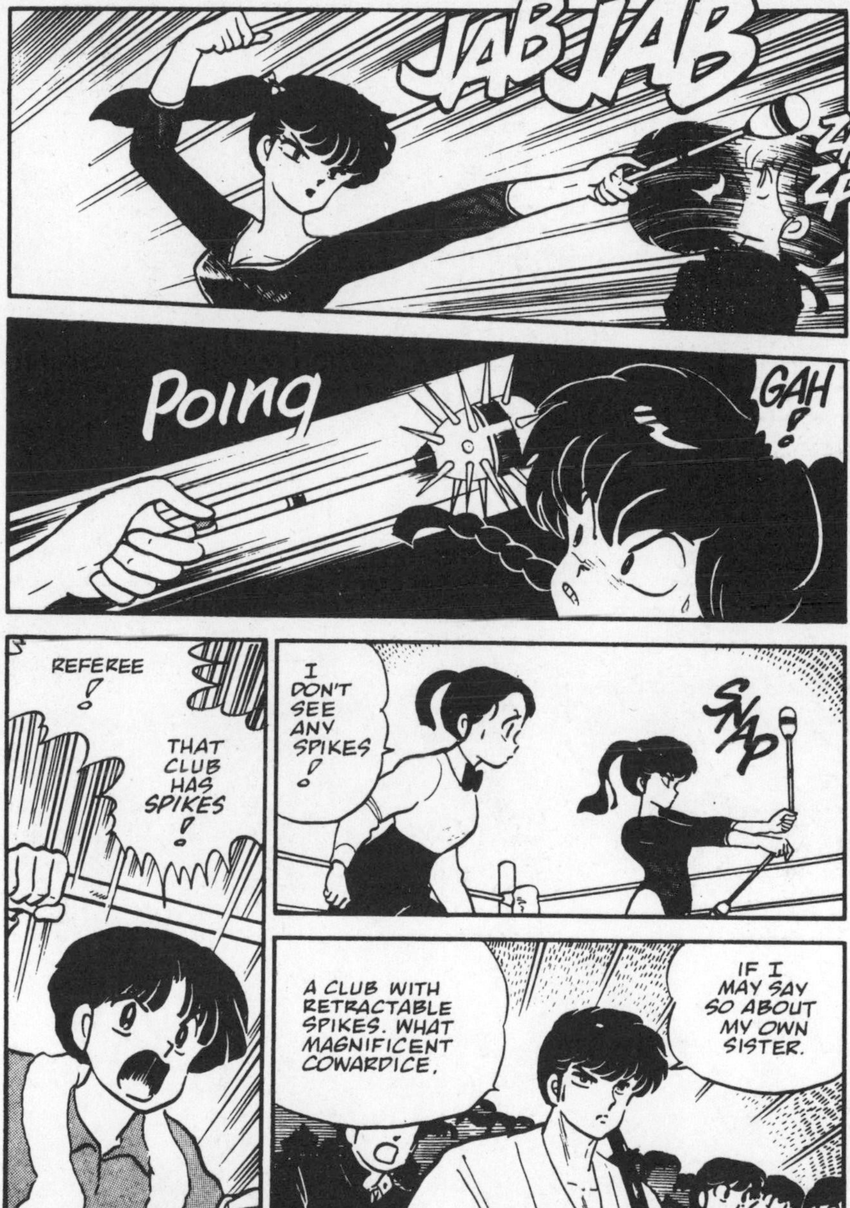
JAB JAB
ZP
ZP
Poing
GAH!
REFEREE!
THAT CLUB HAS SPIKES!
I DON'T SEE ANY SPIKES!
SNAP
A CLUB WITH RETRACTABLE SPIKES. WHAT MAGNIFICENT COWARDICE,
IF I MAY SAY SO ABOUT MY OWN SISTER.

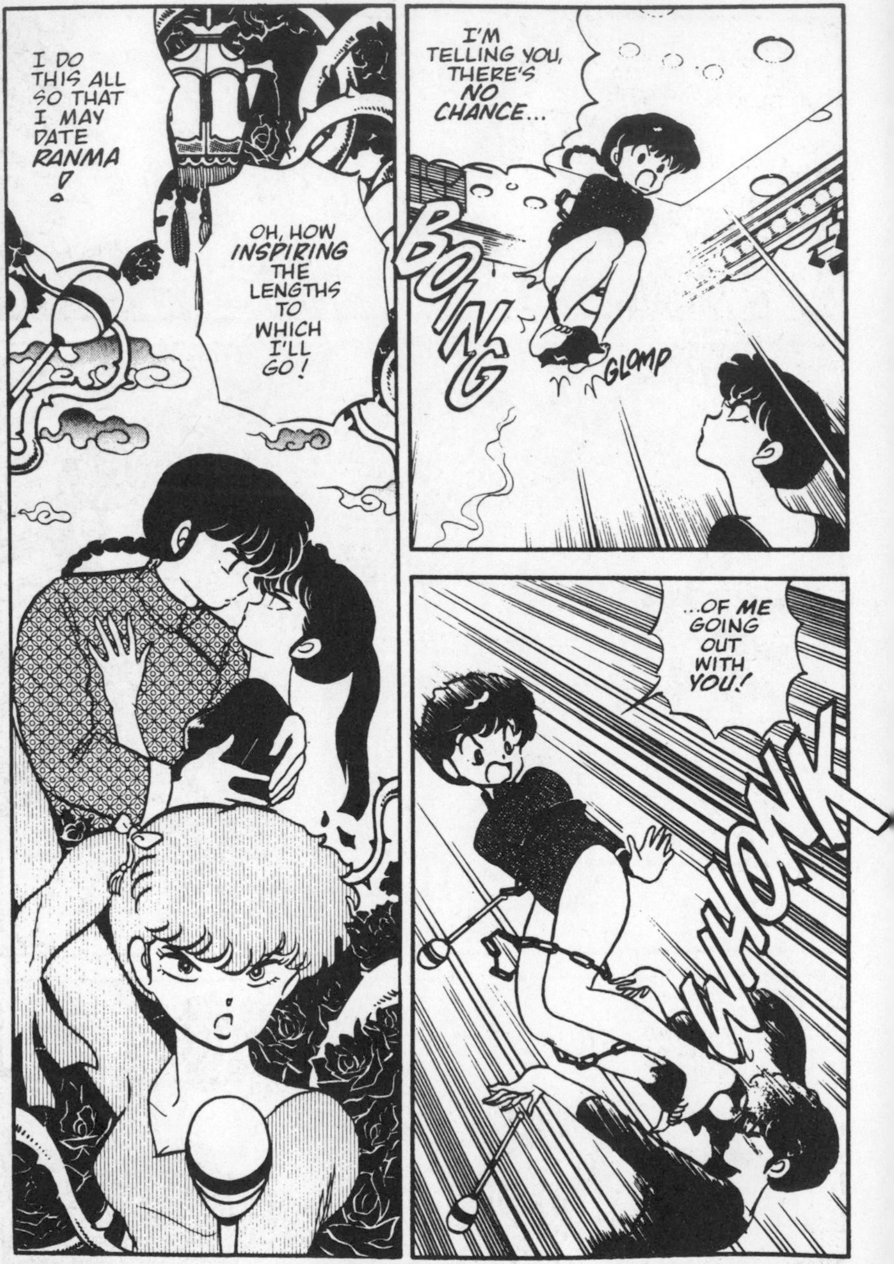

I DO THIS ALL SO THAT I MAY DATE RANMA!
OH, HOW INSPIRING THE LENGTHS TO WHICH I'LL GO!
I'M TELLING YOU, THERE'S NO CHANCE...
BOING
GLOMP
...OF ME GOING OUT WITH YOU!
WHOK

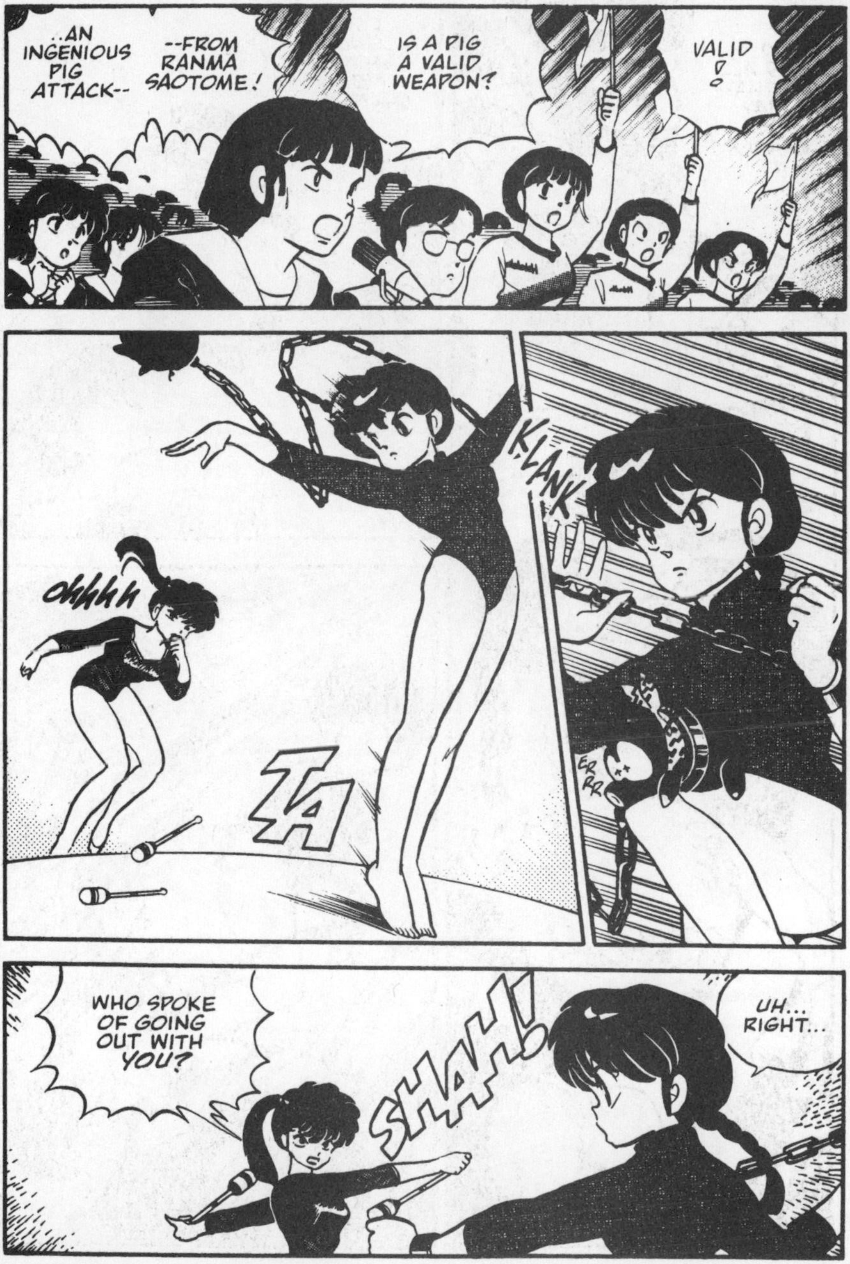
..AN INGENIOUS PIG ATTACK--
--FROM RANMA SAOTOME!
IS A PIG A VALID WEAPON?
VALID!
OHHHH
TA
KLANK
ERRR
WHO SPOKE OF GOING OUT WITH YOU?
SHAH!
UH... RIGHT...

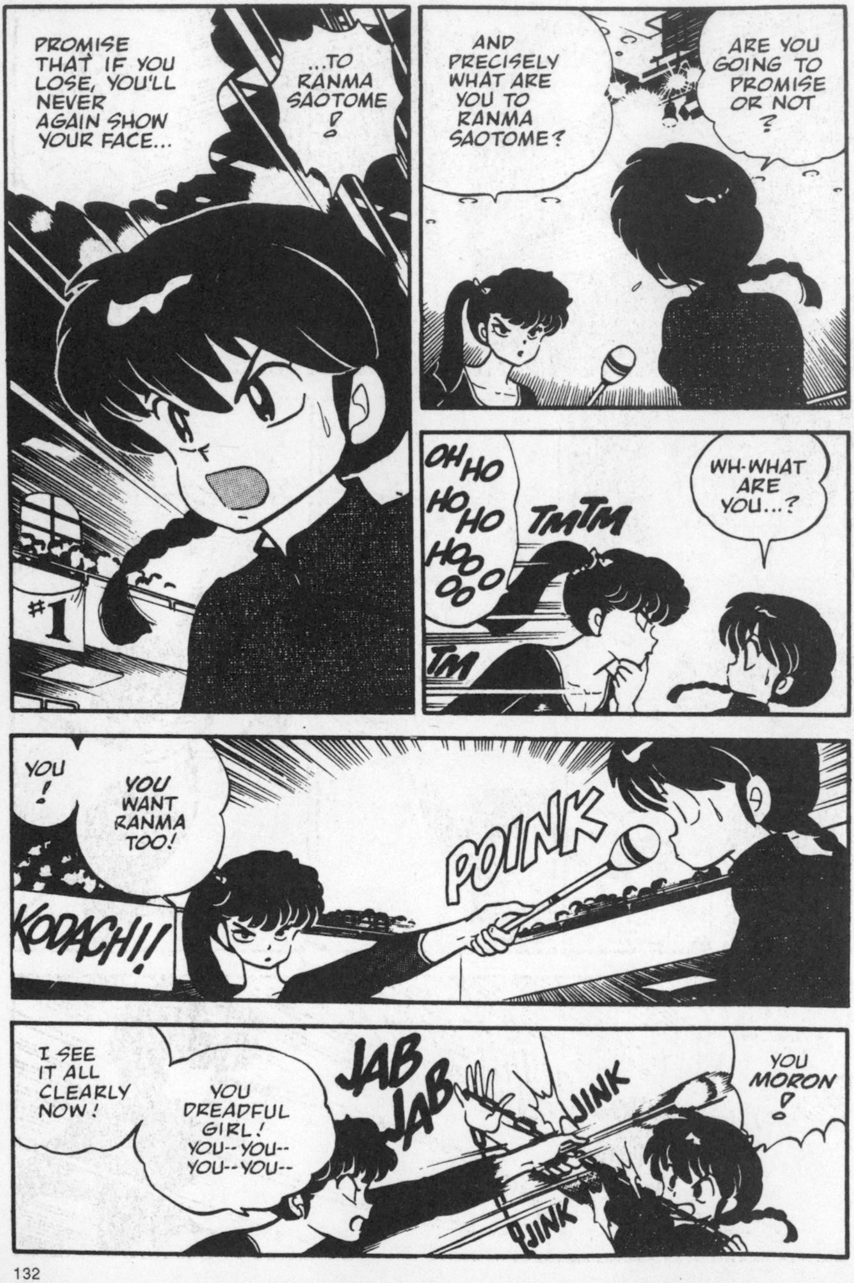
PROMISE THAT IF YOU LOSE, YOU'LL NEVER AGAIN SHOW YOUR FACE...
...TO RANMA SAOTOME!
AND PRECISELY WHAT ARE YOU TO RANMA SAOTOME?
ARE YOU GOING TO PROMISE OR NOT?
OH HO HO HO HOOOOO
TMTM
TM
WH-WHAT ARE YOU...?
YOU!
YOU WANT RANMA TOO!
KODACHI!!
POINK
I SEE IT ALL CLEARLY NOW!
YOU DREADFUL GIRL! YOU--YOU-- YOU--YOU--
JAB JAB
JINK
JINK
YOU MORON!

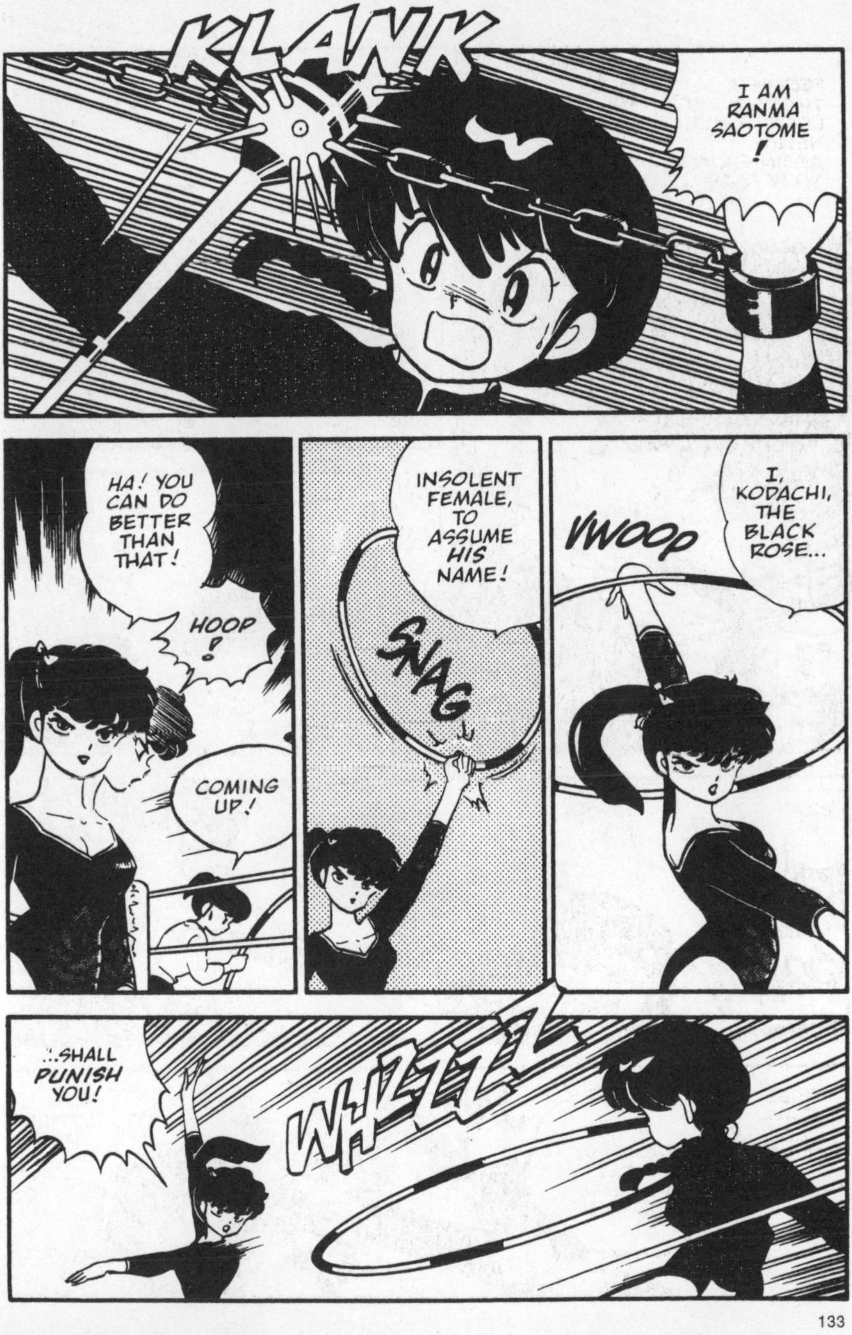
KLANK
I AM RANMA SAOTOME!
HA! YOU CAN DO BETTER THAN THAT!
HOOP!
COMING UP!
INSOLENT FEMALE, TO ASSUME HIS NAME!
SNAG
VWOOP
I, KODACHI, THE BLACK ROSE...
...SHALL PUNISH YOU!
WHZZZZ

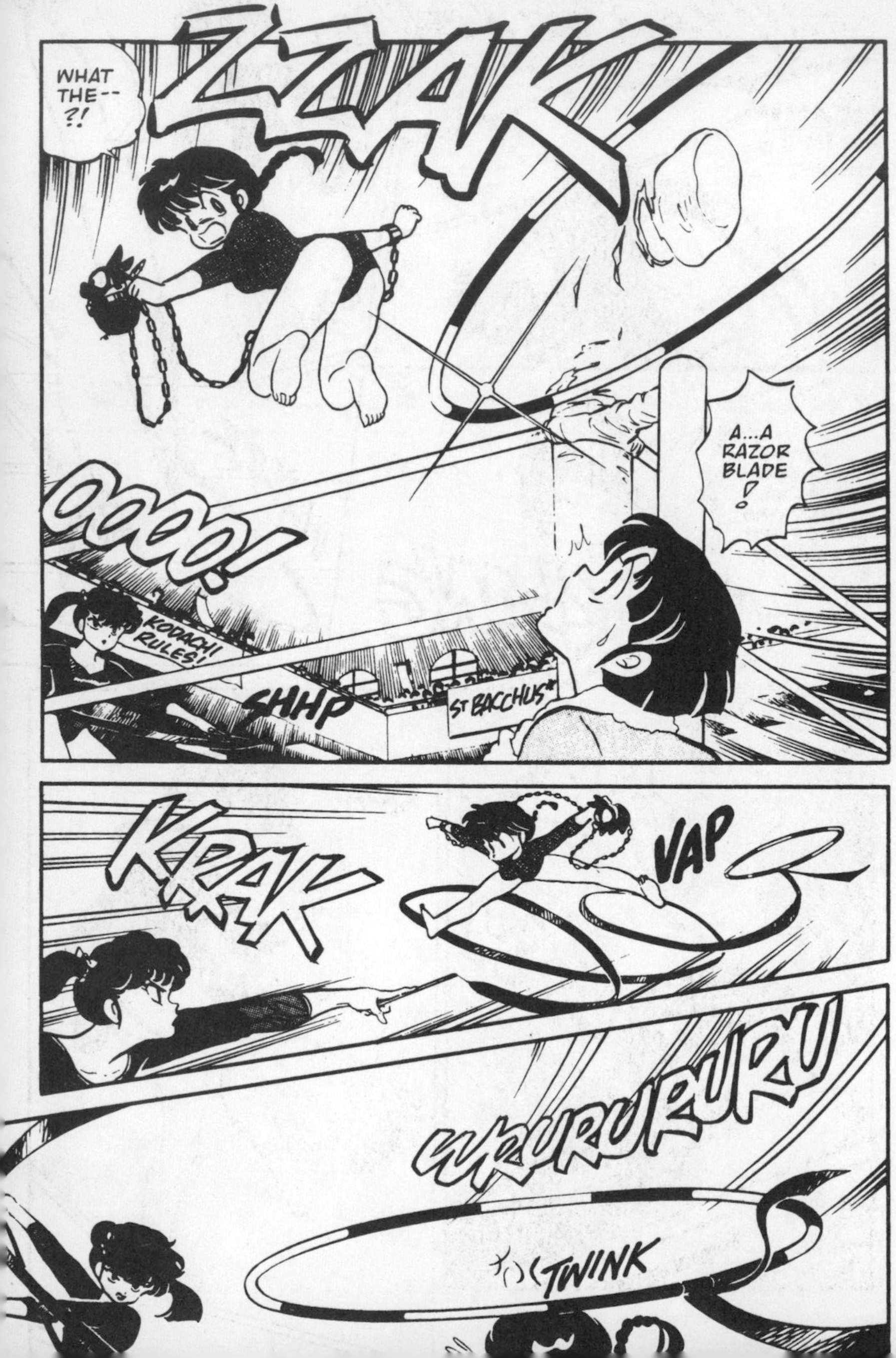
ZZAK
WHAT THE-- ?!
A...A RAZOR BLADE !
OOOO!
KODACHI RULES!
SHHP
ST BACCHUS
KRAK
VAP
URURURURURU
TWINK

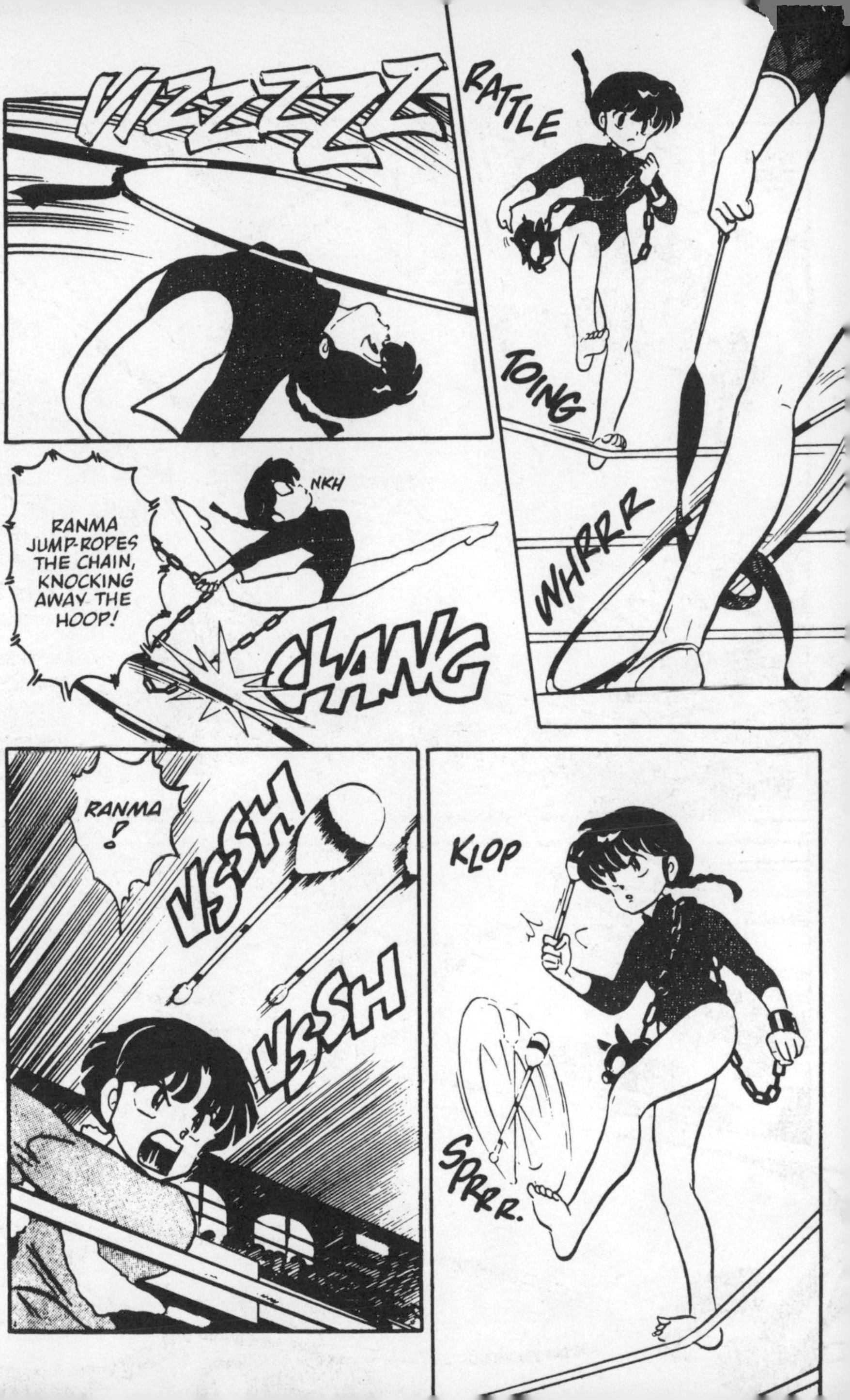
VIZZZZZ
RATTLE
TOING
WHRRR
NKH
RANMA JUMP-ROPES THE CHAIN, KNOCKING AWAY THE HOOP!
CLANG
RANMA!
VSSH
VSSH
KLOP
SPRRR.

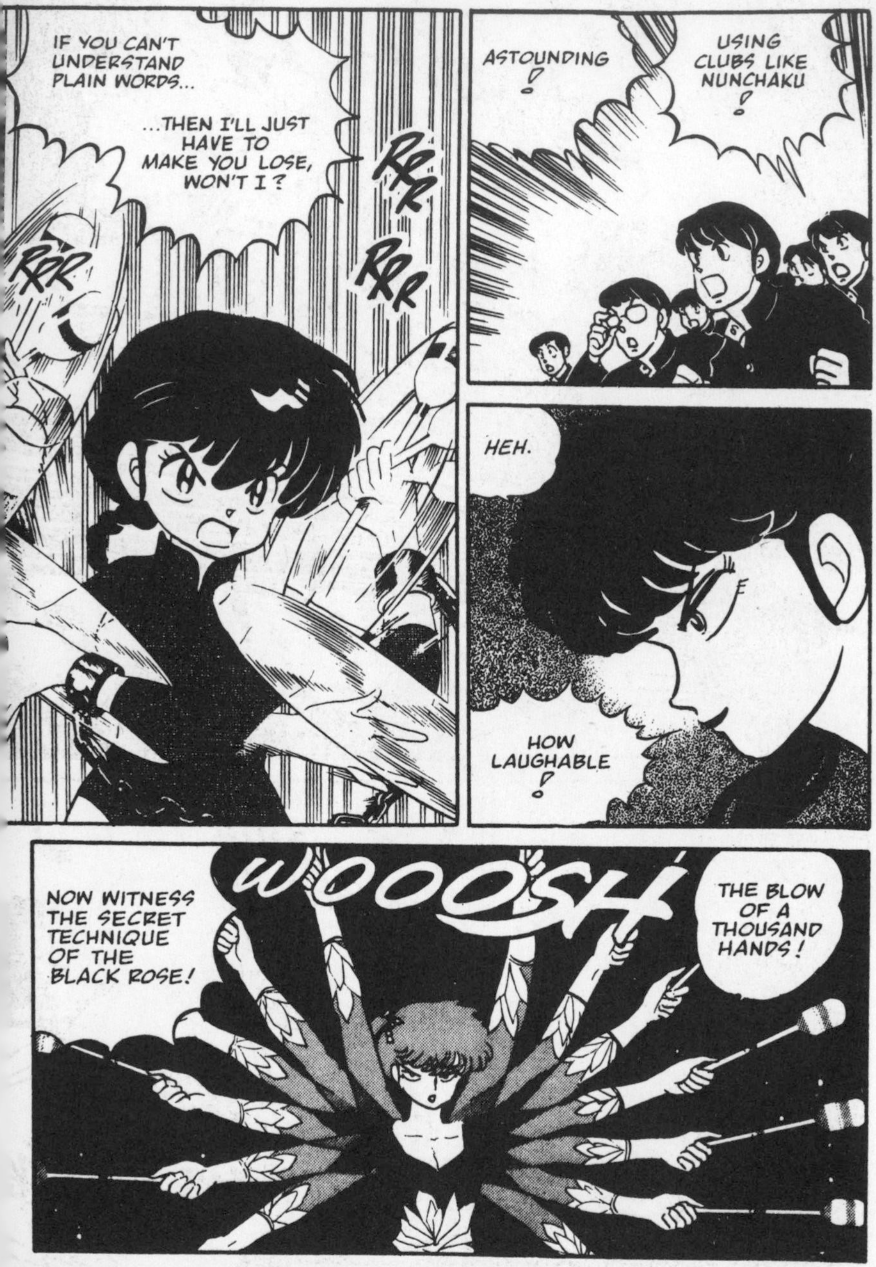
IF YOU CAN'T UNDERSTAND PLAIN WORDS...
...THEN I'LL JUST HAVE TO MAKE YOU LOSE, WON'T I?
RRR
RRR
RRR
ASTOUNDING!
USING CLUBS LIKE NUNCHAKU!
HEH.
HOW LAUGHABLE!
NOW WITNESS THE SECRET TECHNIQUE OF THE BLACK ROSE!
WOOOSH
THE BLOW OF A THOUSAND HANDS!

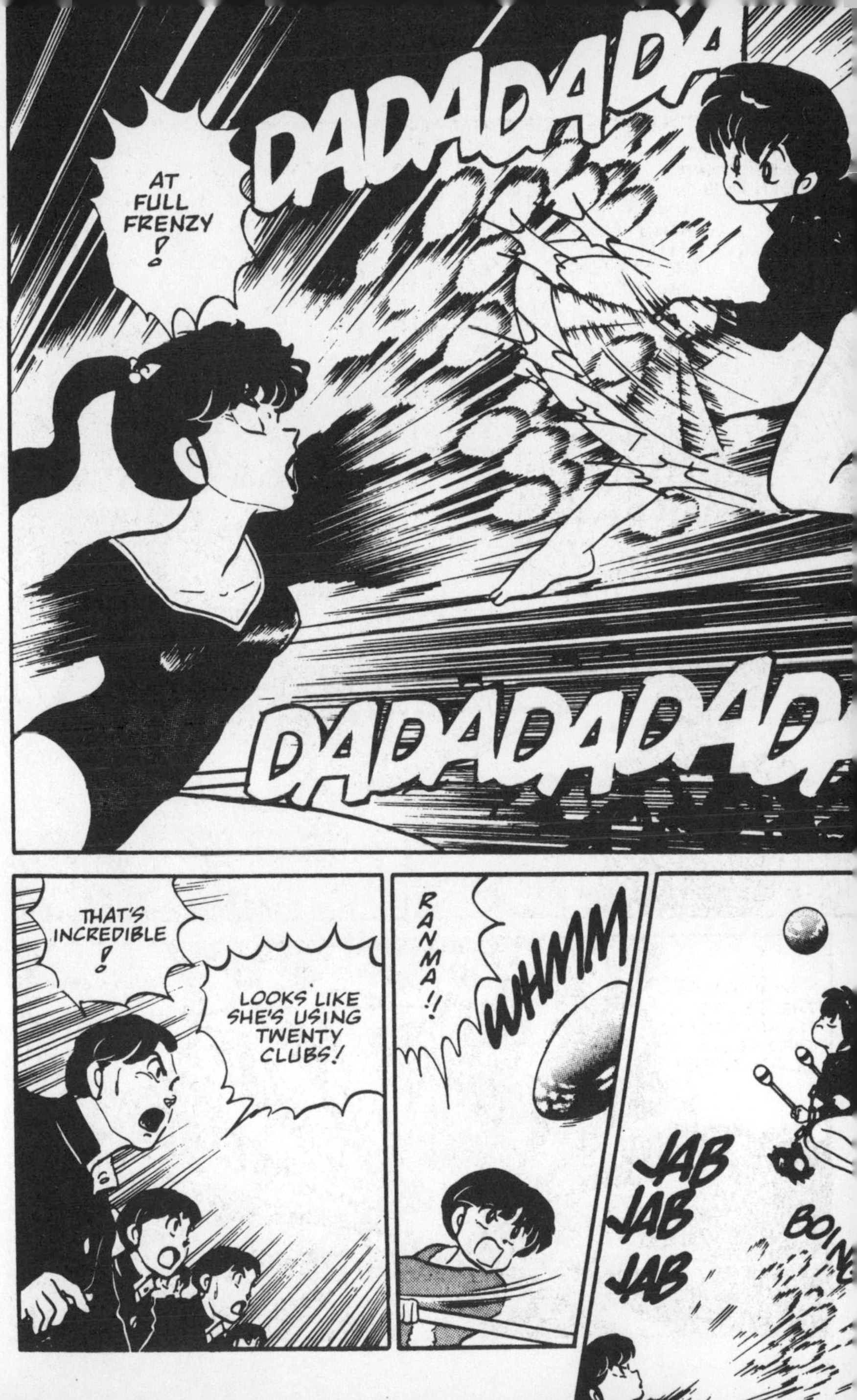
DADADADA
AT FULL FRENZY!
DADADADADA
JAB JAB JAB
BOIN
RANMA!!
WHMM
THAT'S INCREDIBLE!
LOOKS LIKE SHE'S USING TWENTY CLUBS!

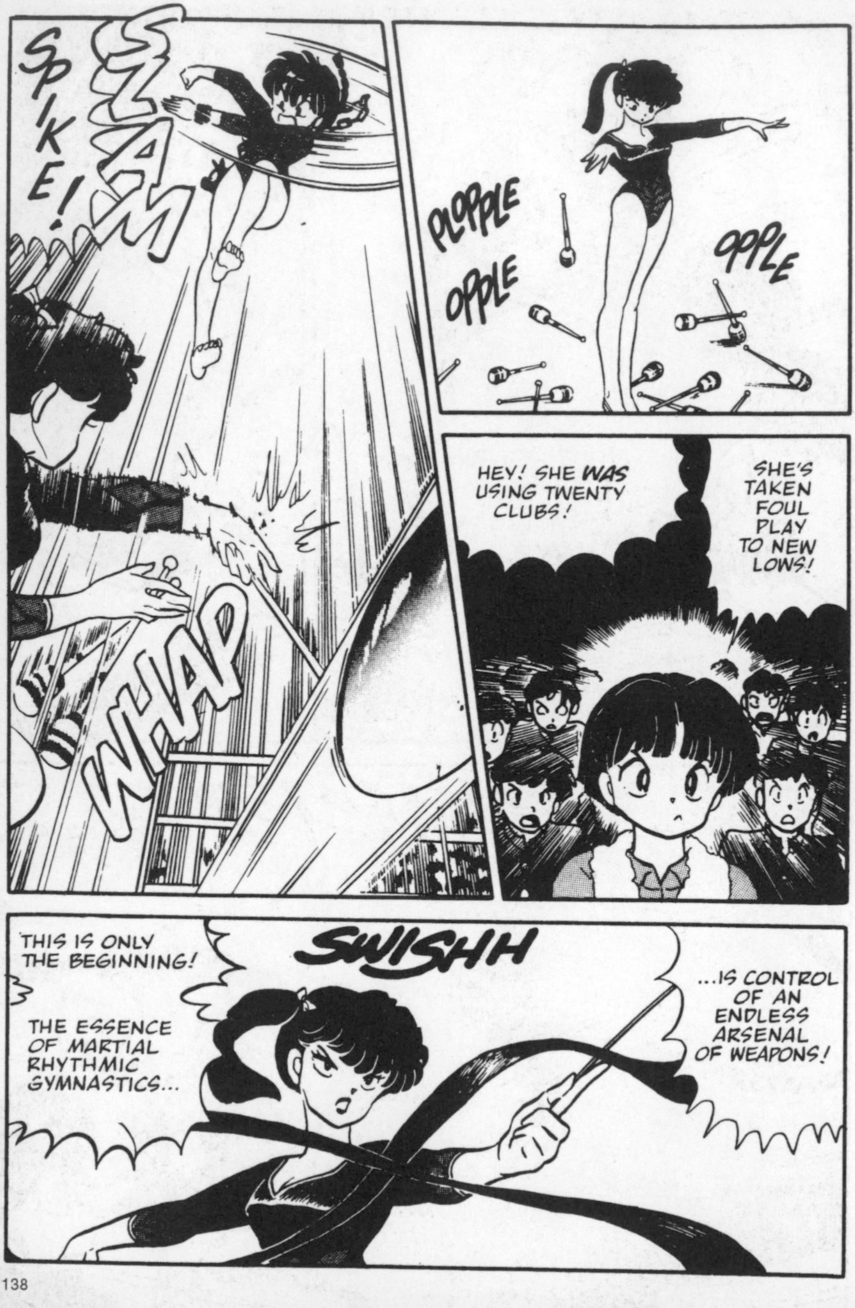
SPIKE!
SLAM
WHAP
PLOPPLE
OPPLE
OPPLE
HEY! SHE WAS USING TWENTY CLUBS!
SHE'S TAKEN FOUL PLAY TO NEW LOWS!
THIS IS ONLY THE BEGINNING!
SWISHH
THE ESSENCE OF MARTIAL RHYTHMIC GYMNASTICS...
...IS CONTROL OF AN ENDLESS ARSENAL OF WEAPONS!

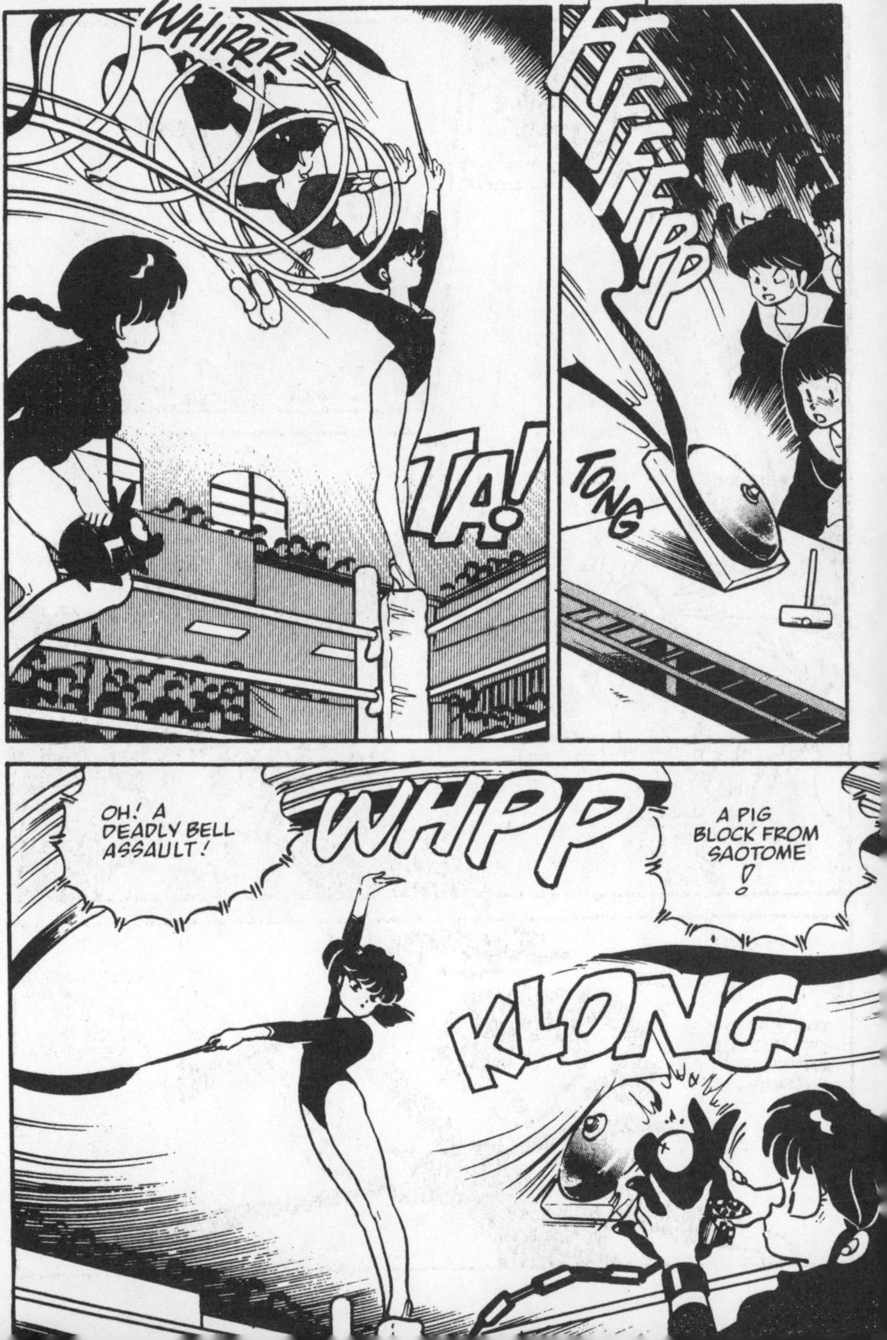
WHIRRR
TA!
FFFFFPP
TONG
OH! A DEADLY BELL ASSAULT!
WHPP
A PIG BLOCK FROM SAOTOME!
KLONG

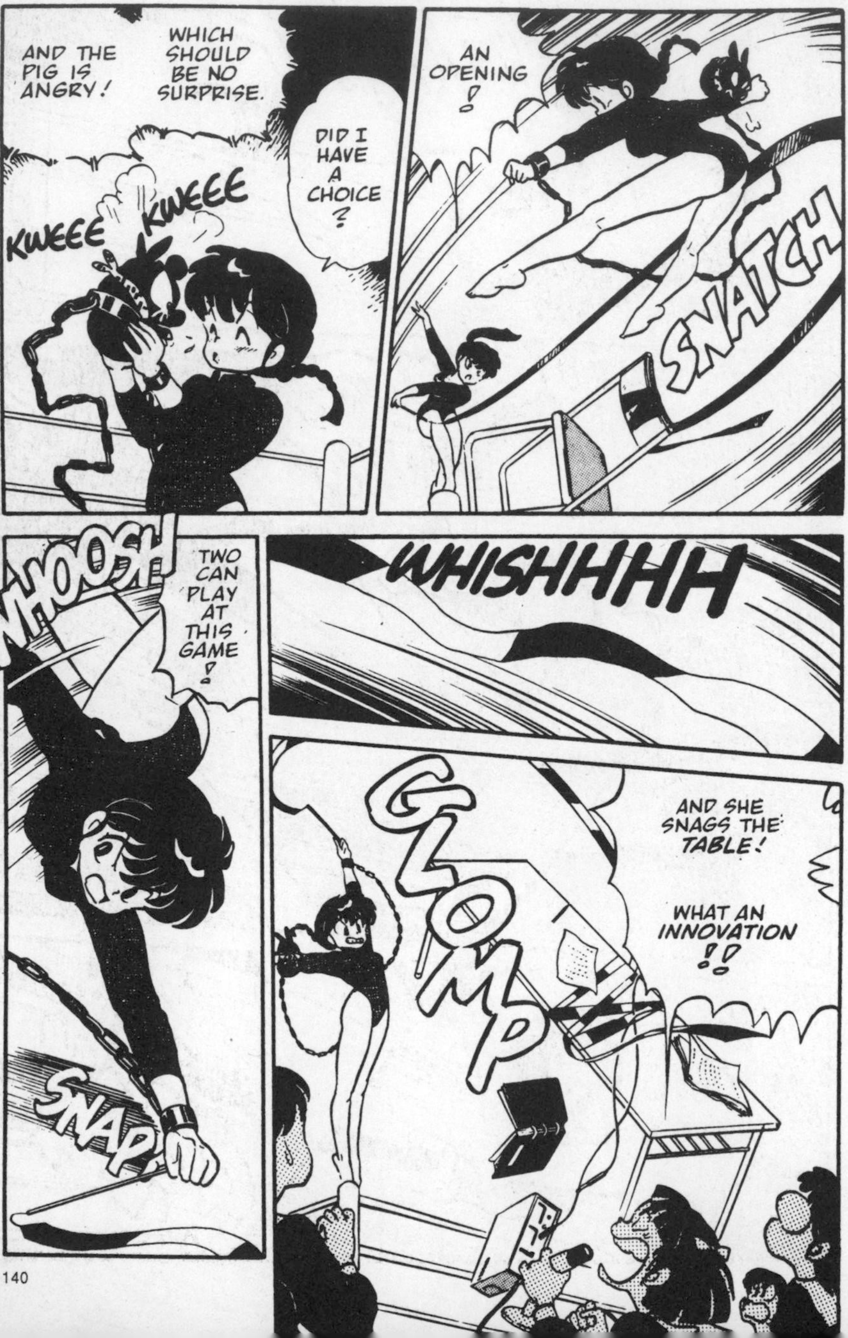
AND THE PIG IS ANGRY!
WHICH SHOULD BE NO SURPRISE.
DID I HAVE A CHOICE?
KWEEE KWEEE
AN OPENING!
SNATCH
WHOOSH
TWO CAN PLAY AT THIS GAME!
SNAP
WHISHHHH
GLOMP
AND SHE SNAGS THE TABLE!
WHAT AN INNOVATION!!

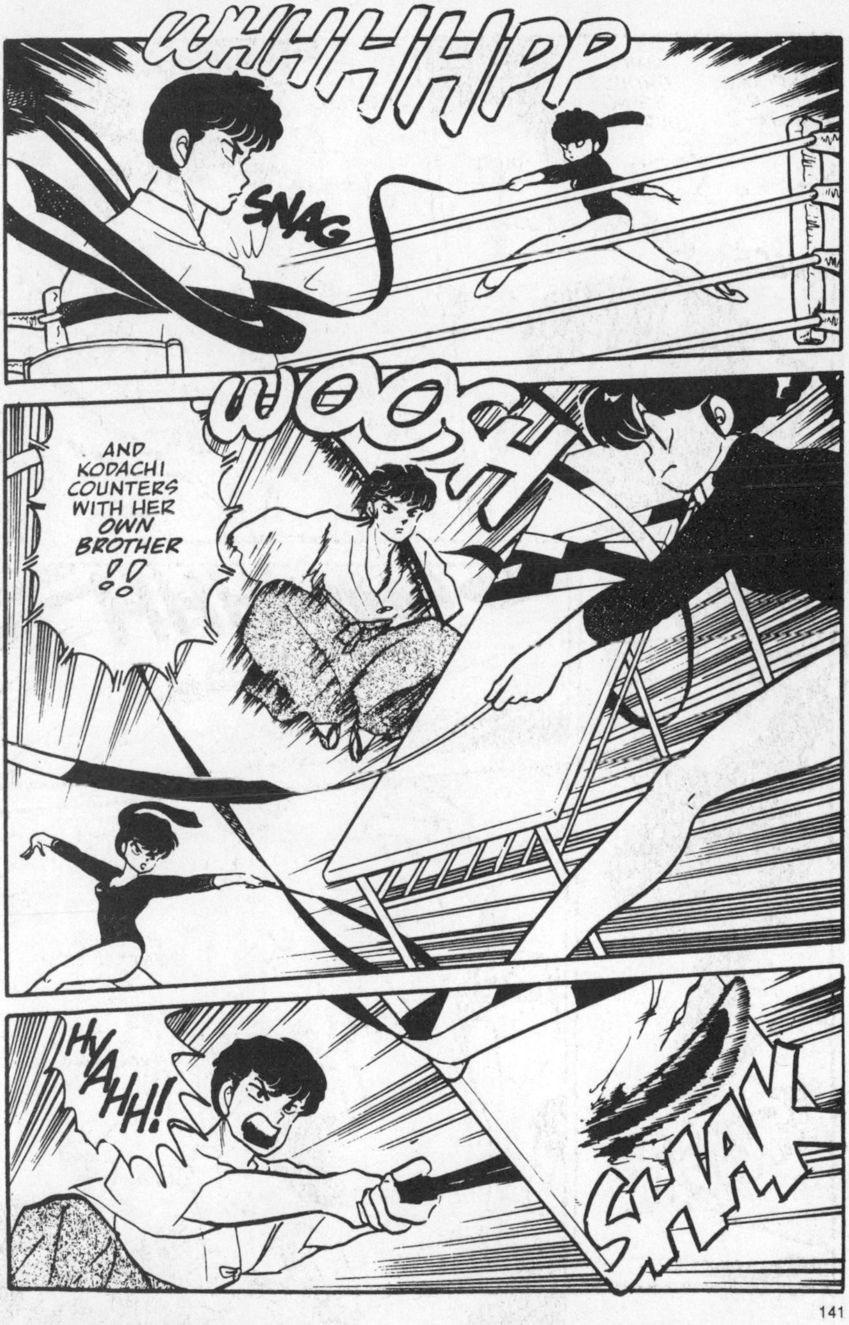
WHHHHPP
SNAG
WOOOSH
AND KODACHI COUNTERS WITH HER OWN BROTHER !!
HYAHH!
SHAK

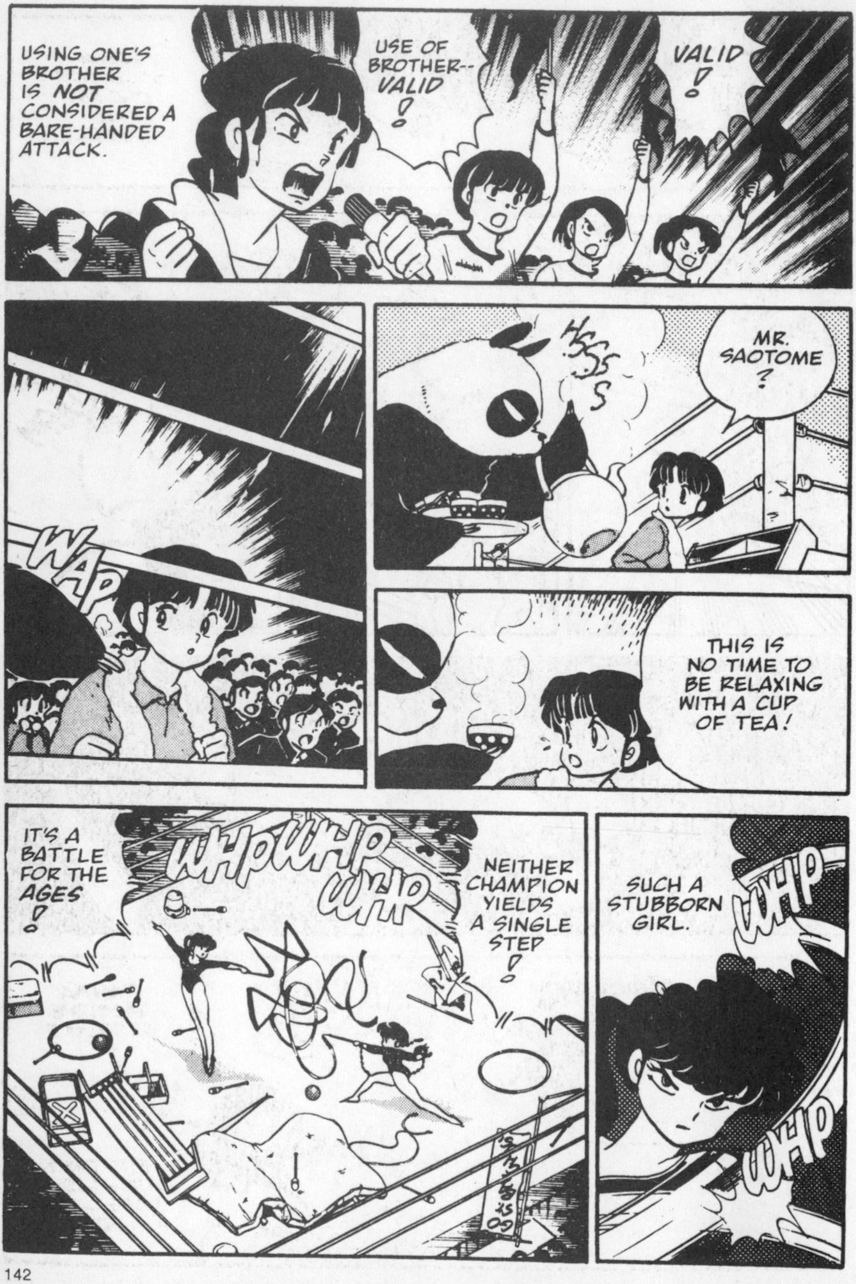
USING ONE'S BROTHER IS NOT CONSIDERED A BARE-HANDED ATTACK.
USE OF BROTHER-- VALID!
VALID!
WAP
HSSSS
MR. SAOTOME?
THIS IS NO TIME TO BE RELAXING WITH A CUP OF TEA!
IT'S A BATTLE FOR THE AGES!
WHPWHP
WHP
NEITHER CHAMPION YIELDS A SINGLE STEP!
SUCH A STUBBORN GIRL.
WHP
WHP

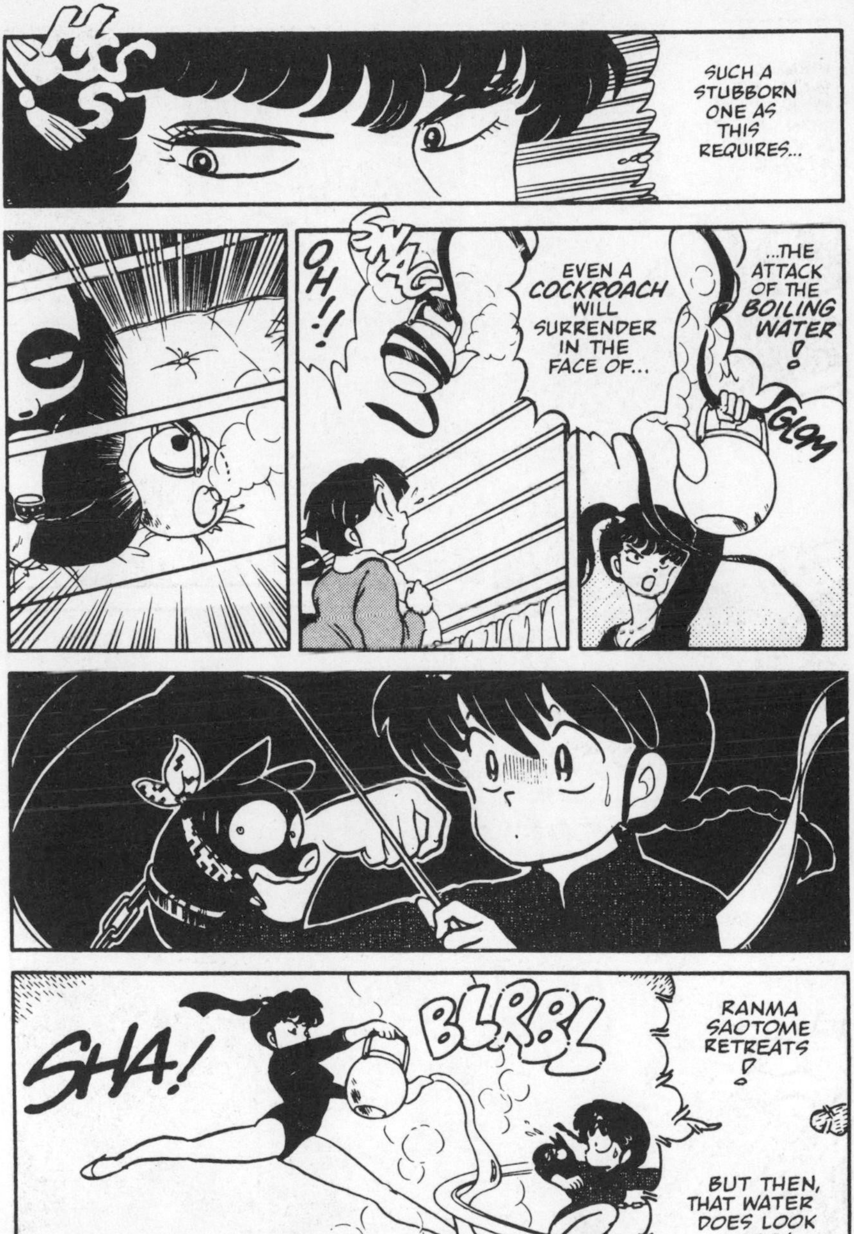
HISS
SUCH A STUBBORN ONE AS THIS REQUIRES...
OH!!
SNAG
EVEN A COCKROACH WILL SURRENDER IN THE FACE OF...
...THE ATTACK OF THE BOILING WATER!
GLOM
SHA!
BLRBL
RANMA SAOTOME RETREATS!
BUT THEN, THAT WATER DOES LOOK HOT!

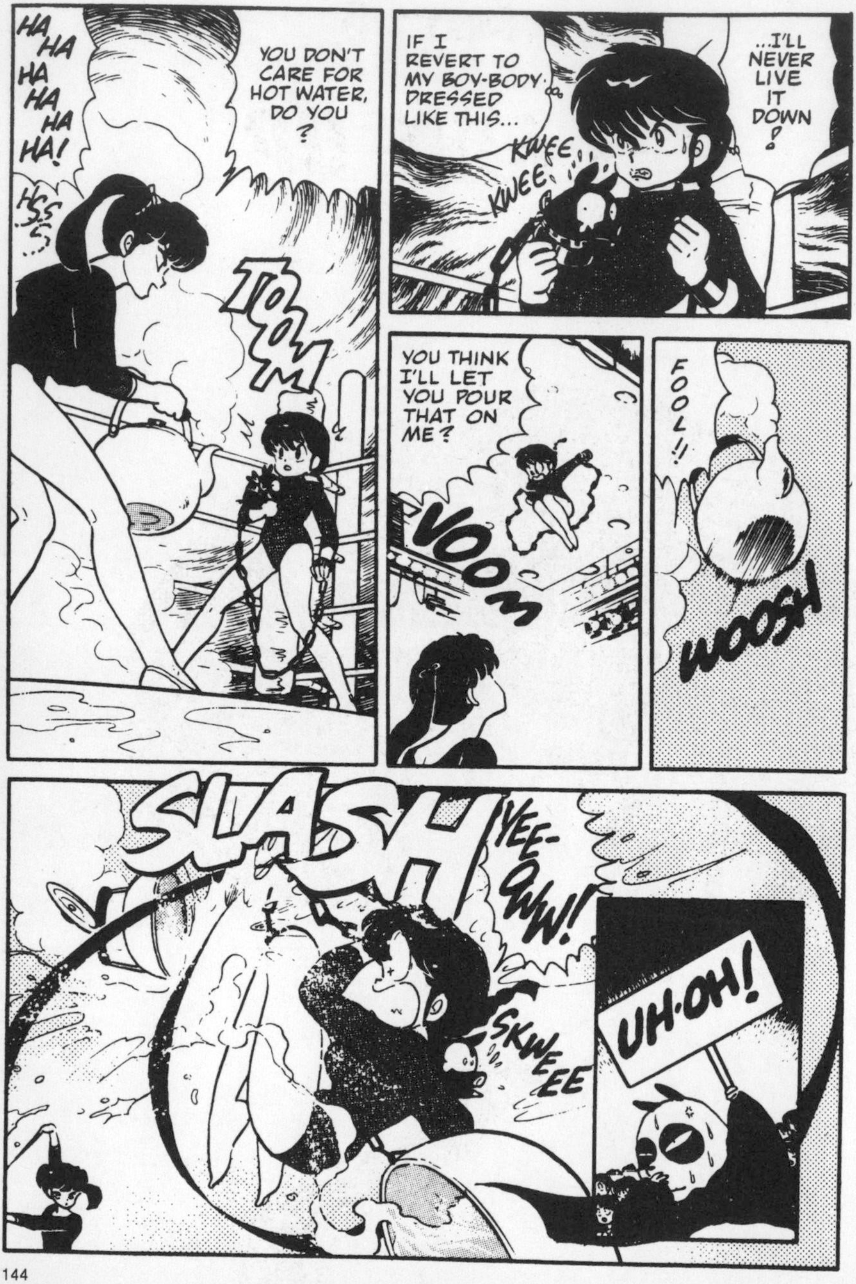
HA HA HA HA HA HA!
YOU DON'T CARE FOR HOT WATER, DO YOU?
HSSS
TOOOM
IF I REVERT TO MY BOY-BODY DRESSED LIKE THIS...
...I'LL NEVER LIVE IT DOWN!
KWEE KWEE
YOU THINK I'LL LET YOU POUR THAT ON ME?
VOOOM
FOOL!!
WOOSH
SLASH
YEE-OWW!
SKWEEEE
UH-OH!

Part 8

I GIVE UP

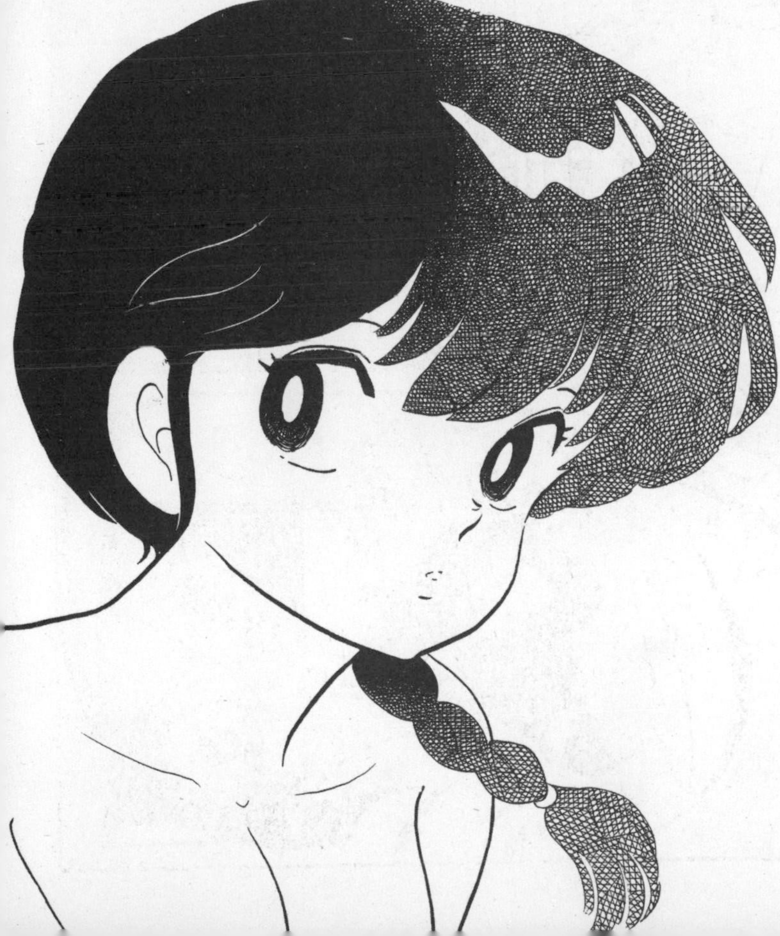

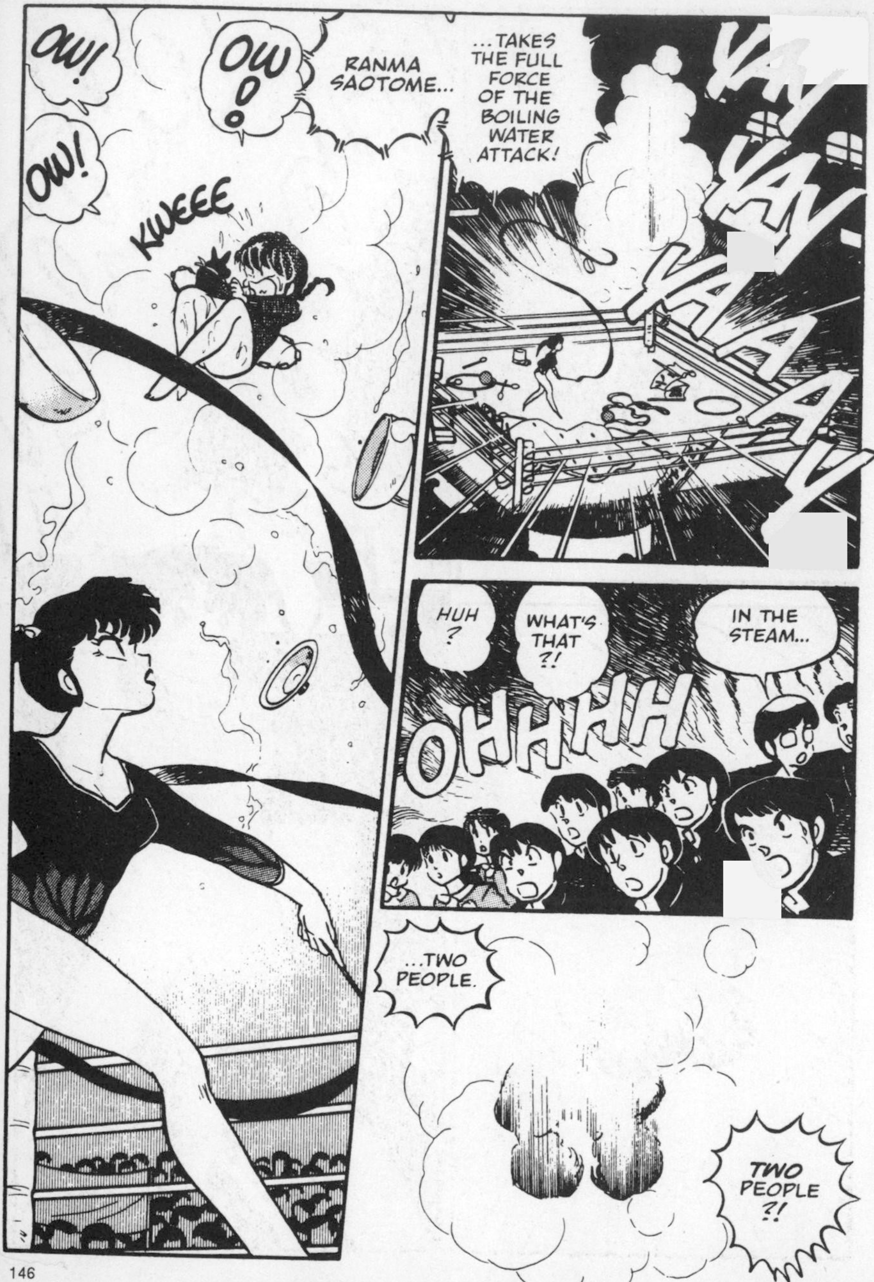
OW!
OW!
OW!
OW!
KWEEE
RANMA SAOTOME...
...TAKES THE FULL FORCE OF THE BOILING WATER ATTACK!
YAN YAN YAAAAN
HUH?
WHAT'S THAT?!
IN THE STEAM...
OHHHH
...TWO PEOPLE.
TWO PEOPLE?!

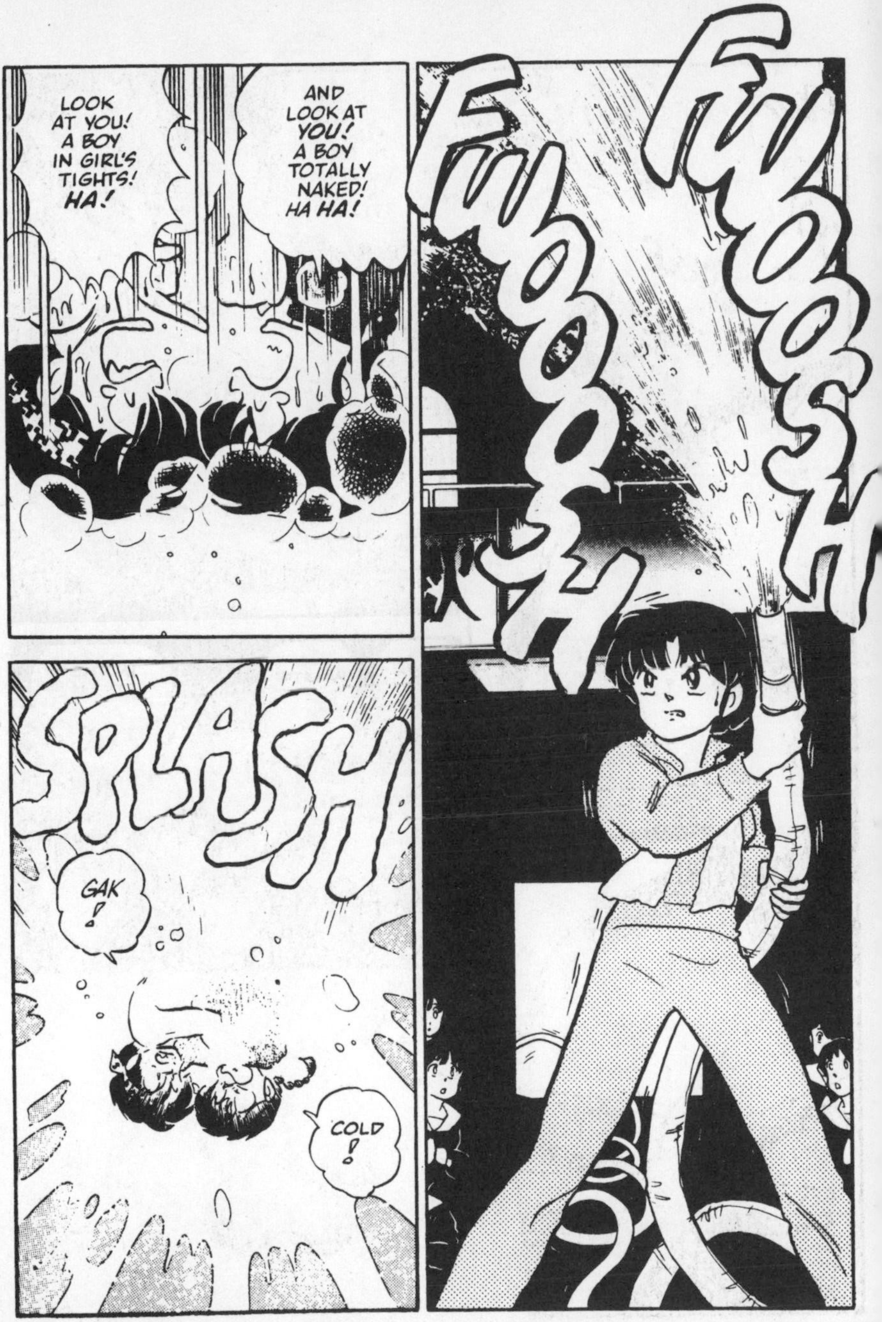
LOOK AT YOU! A BOY IN GIRL'S TIGHTS! HA!
AND LOOK AT YOU! A BOY TOTALLY NAKED! HA HA!
SPLASH
GAK!
COLD!
FWOOOSH
FWOOOSH

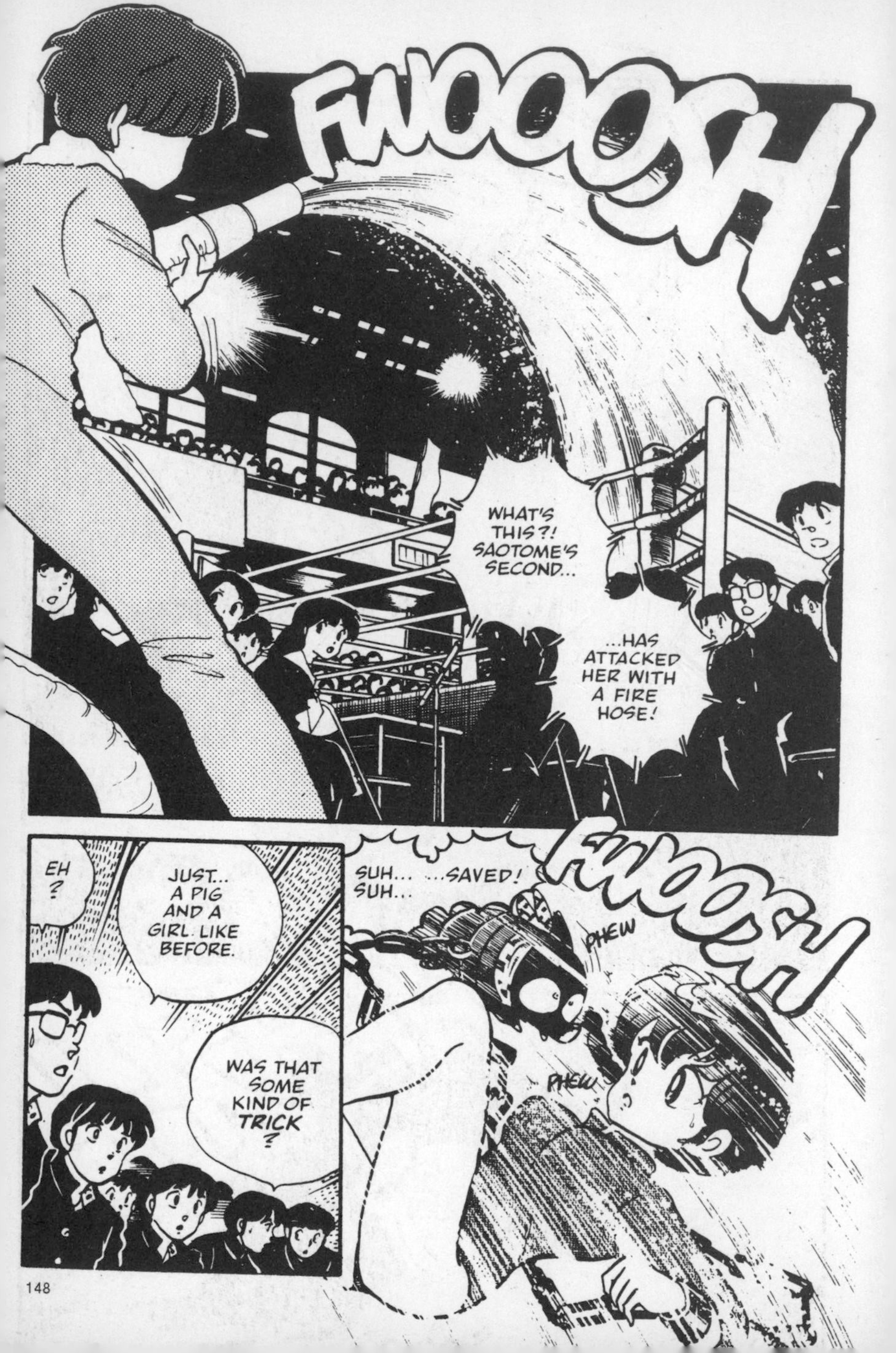
FWOOOSH
WHAT'S THIS?! SAOTOME'S SECOND...
...HAS ATTACKED HER WITH A FIRE HOSE!
EH ?
JUST... A PIG AND A GIRL. LIKE BEFORE.
WAS THAT SOME KIND OF TRICK ?
SUH... SUH...
...SAVED!
FWOOSH
PHEW
PHEW

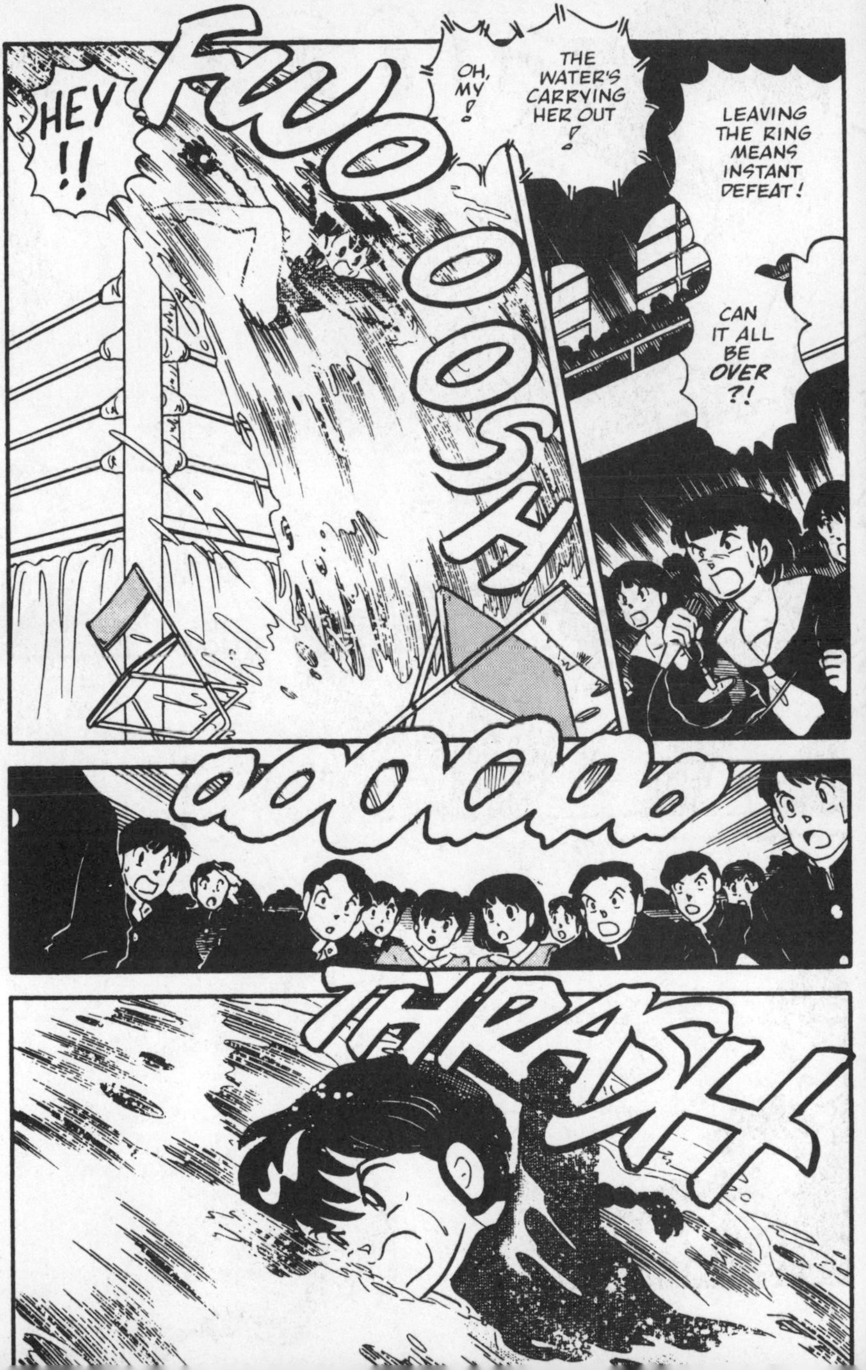
HEY!!
FWOOOOSH
OH, MY!
THE WATER'S CARRYING HER OUT!
LEAVING THE RING MEANS INSTANT DEFEAT!
CAN IT ALL BE OVER?!
AAAAAA
THRASH

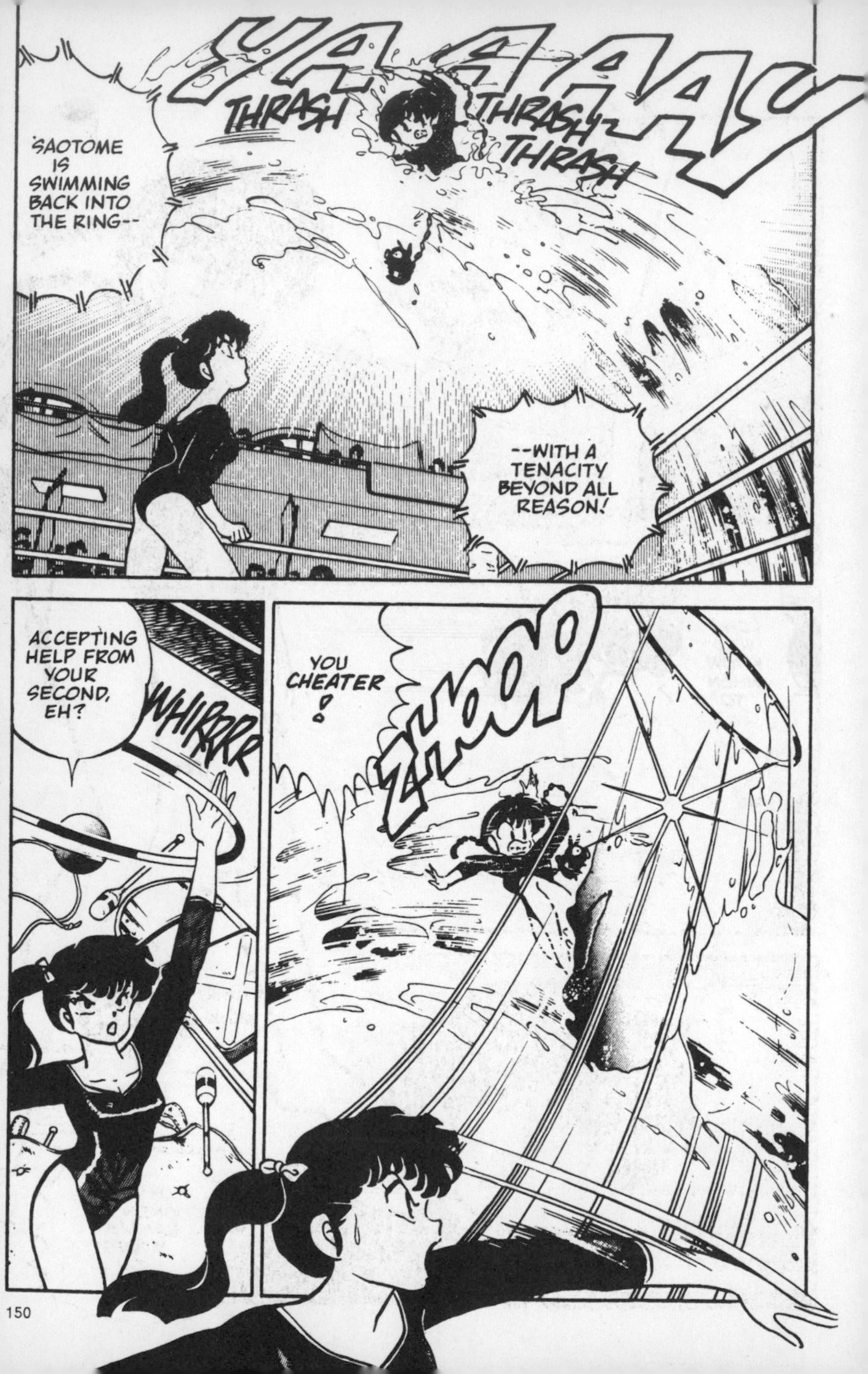
YAAAAY
THRASH THRASH THRASH THRASH
SAOTOME IS SWIMMING BACK INTO THE RING--
--WITH A TENACITY BEYOND ALL REASON!
ACCEPTING HELP FROM YOUR SECOND, EH?
WHIRRRR
YOU CHEATER!
ZHOOP

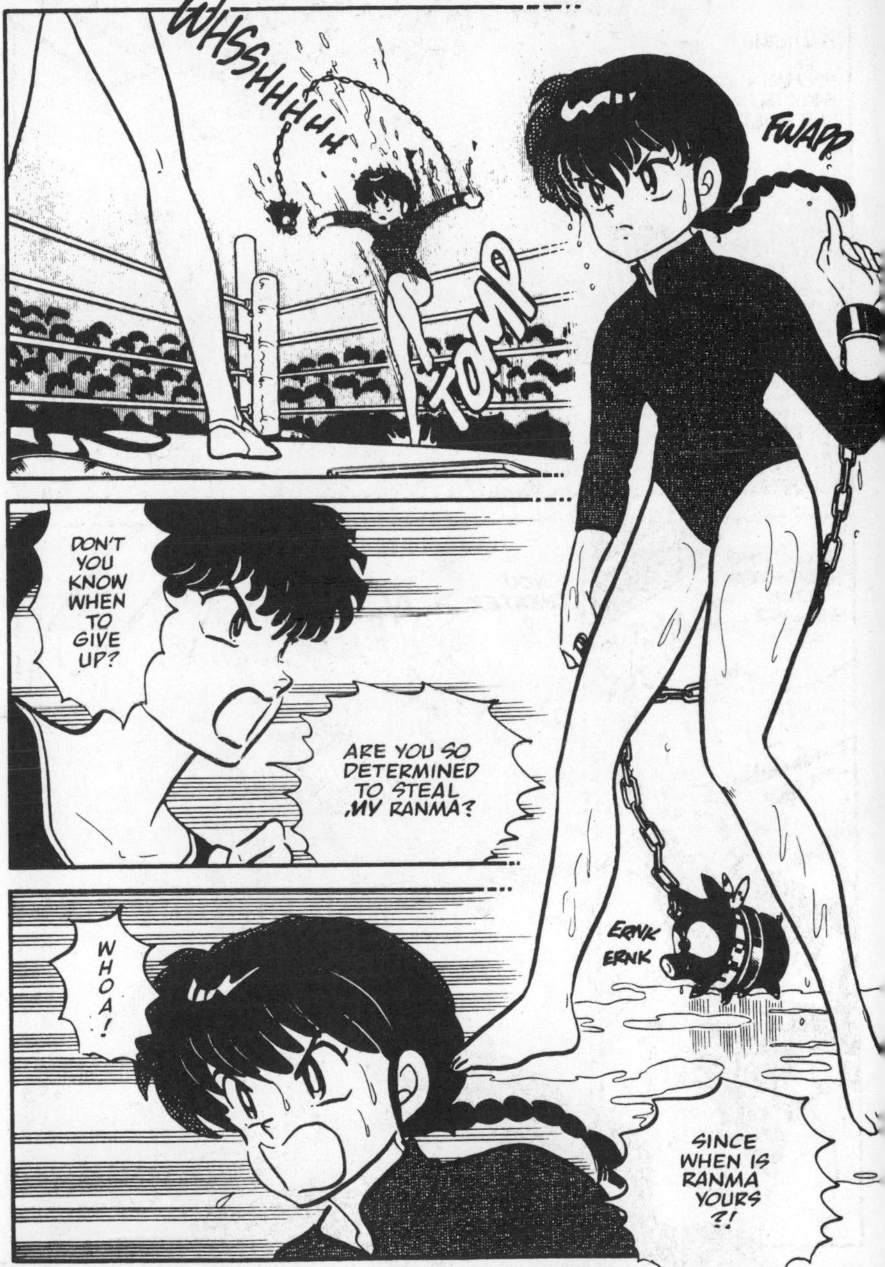
WHSSHHHHH
TOMP
FWAPP
DON'T YOU KNOW WHEN TO GIVE UP?
ARE YOU SO DETERMINED TO STEAL MY RANMA?
ERNK ERNK
WHOA!
SINCE WHEN IS RANMA YOURS ?!

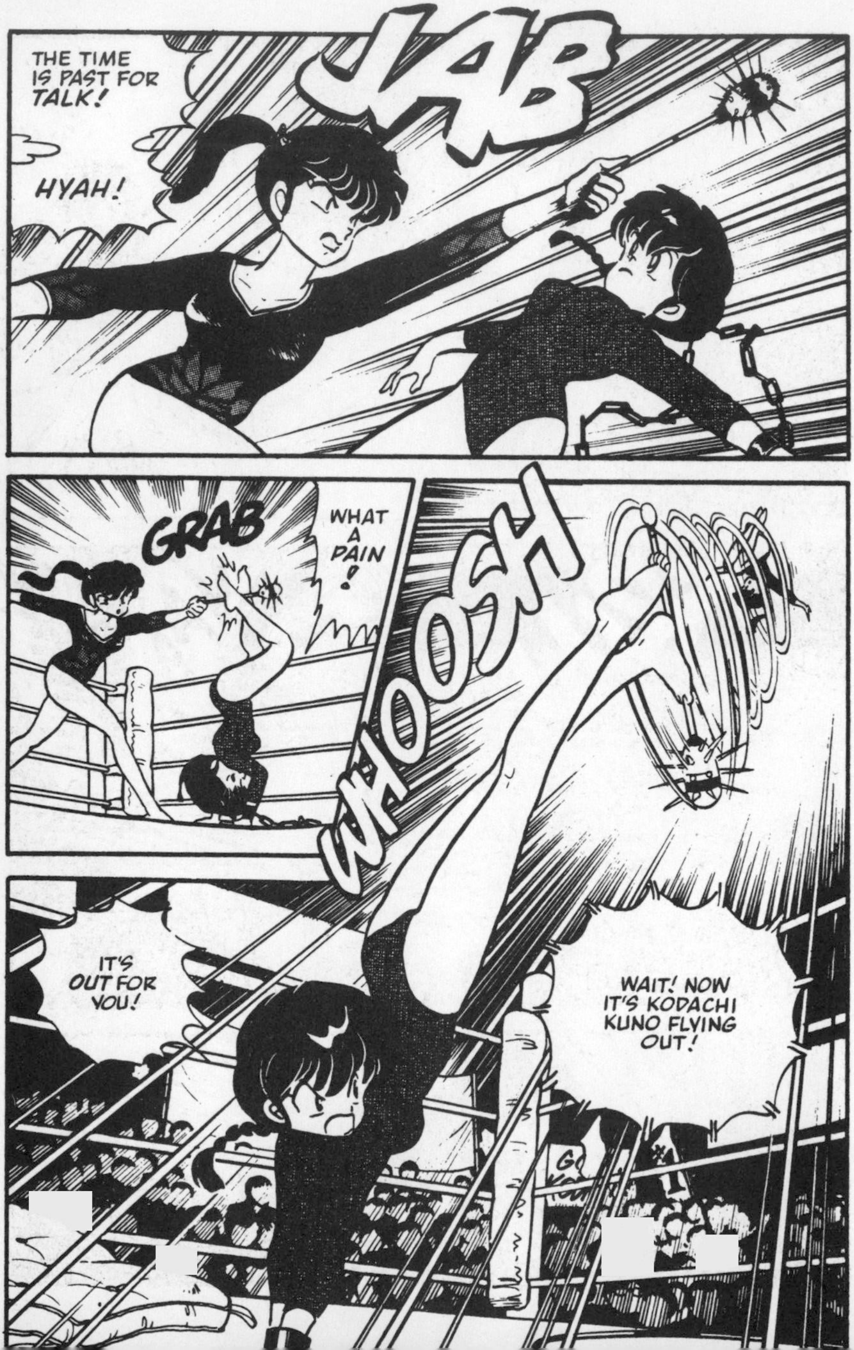
THE TIME IS PAST FOR TALK!
JAB
HYAH!
GRAB
WHAT A PAIN!
WHOOSH
IT'S OUT FOR YOU!
WAIT! NOW IT'S KODACHI KUNO FLYING OUT!

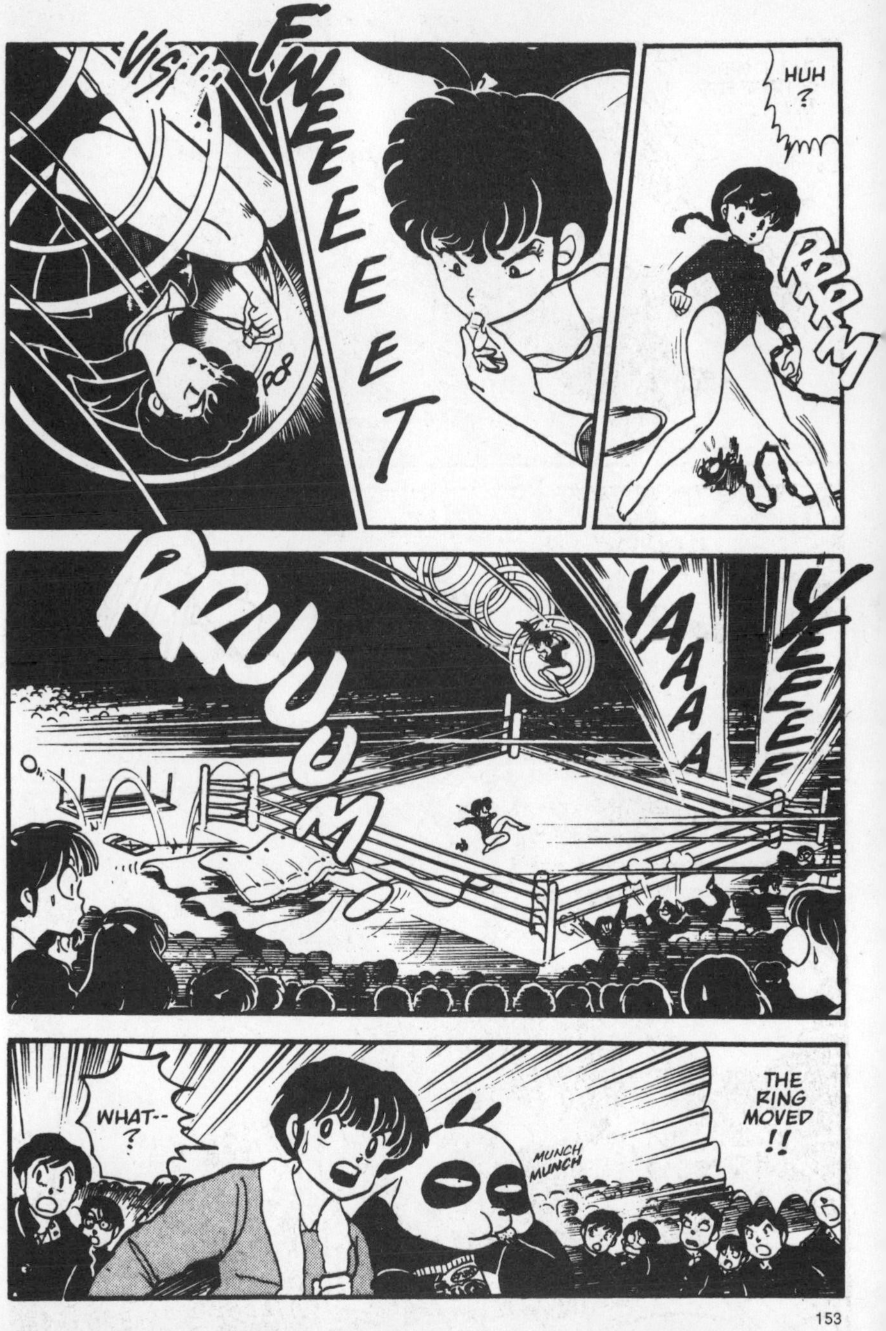
VISH...
POP
FWEEEEEET
HUH ?
RAAAM
RAUUUM
YAAAAA
YEEEEEE
WHAT-- ?
MUNCH MUNCH
THE RING MOVED !!

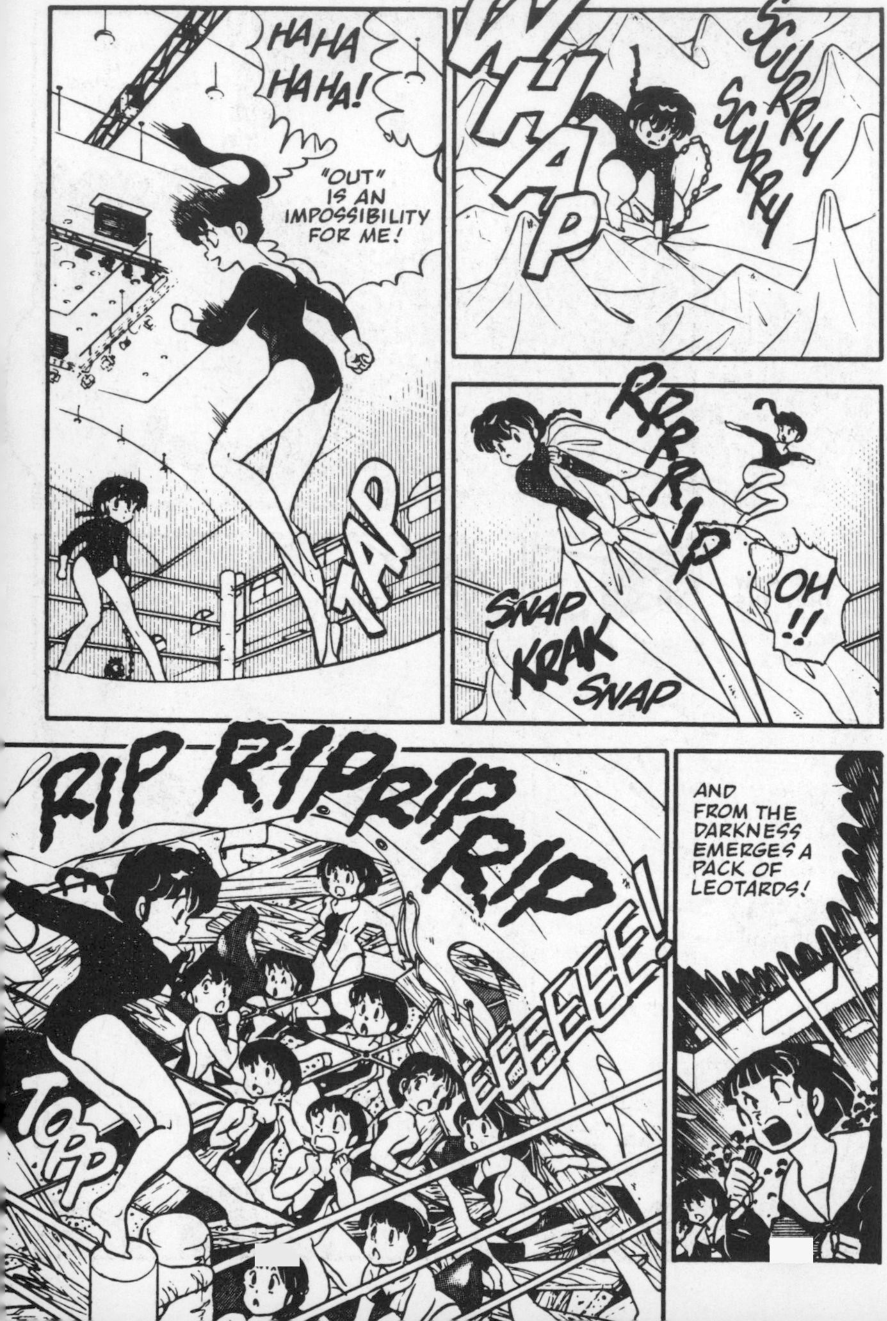
HAHA HAHA!
"OUT" IS AN IMPOSSIBILITY FOR ME!
TAP
WHAP
SCURRY SCURRY
RRRRIP
OH!!
SNAP KRAK SNAP
RIP RIPRIPRIP
EEEEEE!
TOPP
AND FROM THE DARKNESS EMERGES A PACK OF LEOTARDS!

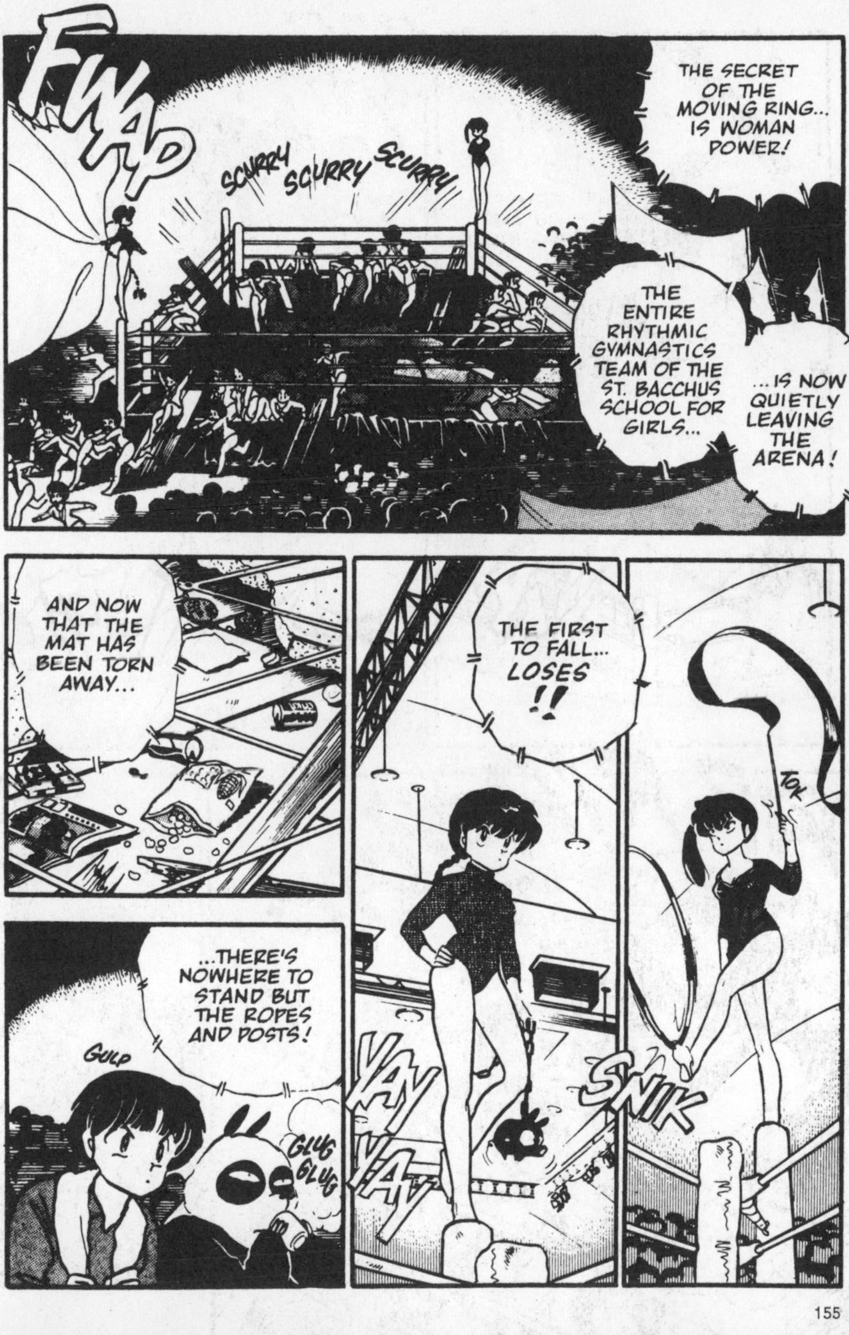
FWAP
SCURRY
SCURRY
SCURRY
THE SECRET OF THE MOVING RING... IS WOMAN POWER!
THE ENTIRE RHYTHMIC GYMNASTICS TEAM OF THE ST. BACCHUS SCHOOL FOR GIRLS...
...IS NOW QUIETLY LEAVING THE ARENA!
AND NOW THAT THE MAT HAS BEEN TORN AWAY...
...THERE'S NOWHERE TO STAND BUT THE ROPES AND POSTS!
GULP
GLUG GLUG
THE FIRST TO FALL... LOSES!!
YAY YAY
TOK
SNIK

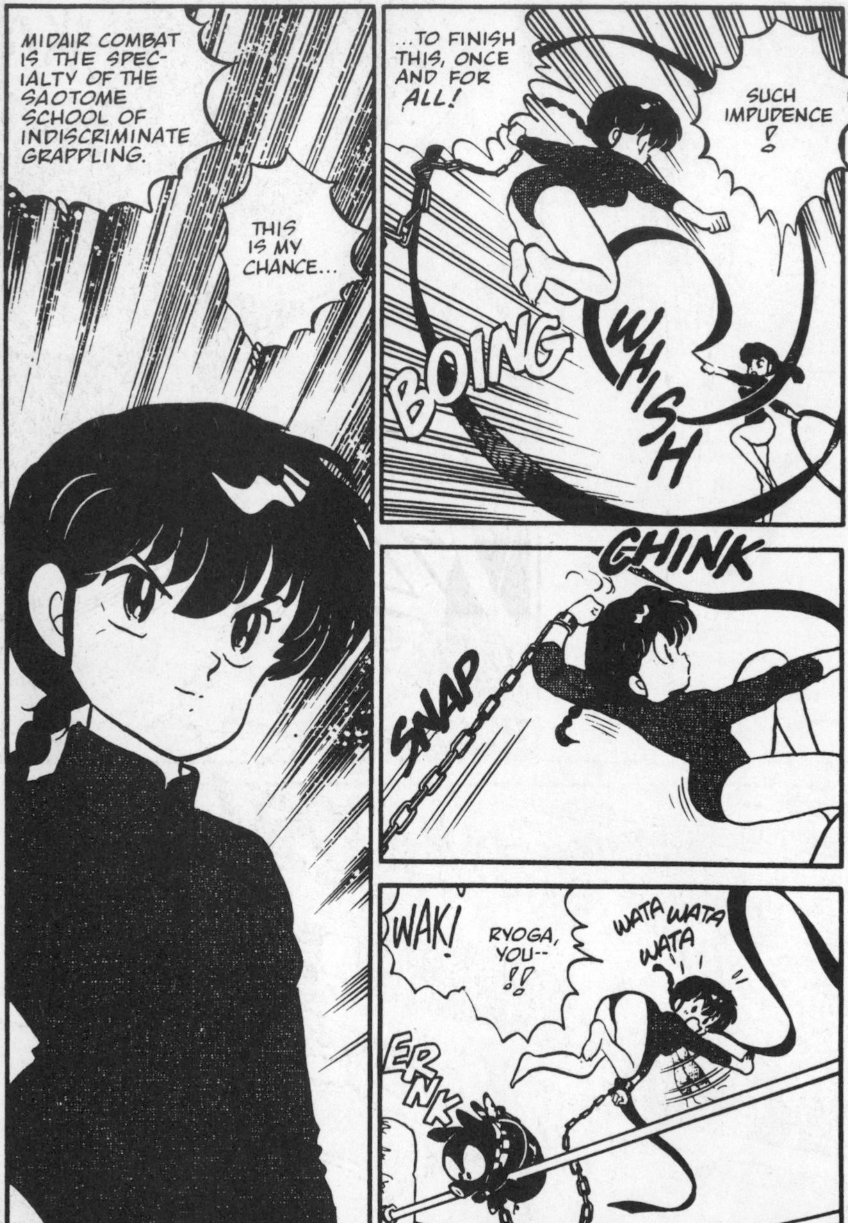
MIDAIR COMBAT IS THE SPECIALTY OF THE SAOTOME SCHOOL OF INDISCRIMINATE GRAPPLING.
THIS IS MY CHANCE...
...TO FINISH THIS, ONCE AND FOR ALL!
SUCH IMPUDENCE!
BOING
WHISH
CHINK
SNAP
WAK!
RYOGA, YOU--!!
WATA WATA WATA
ERNK

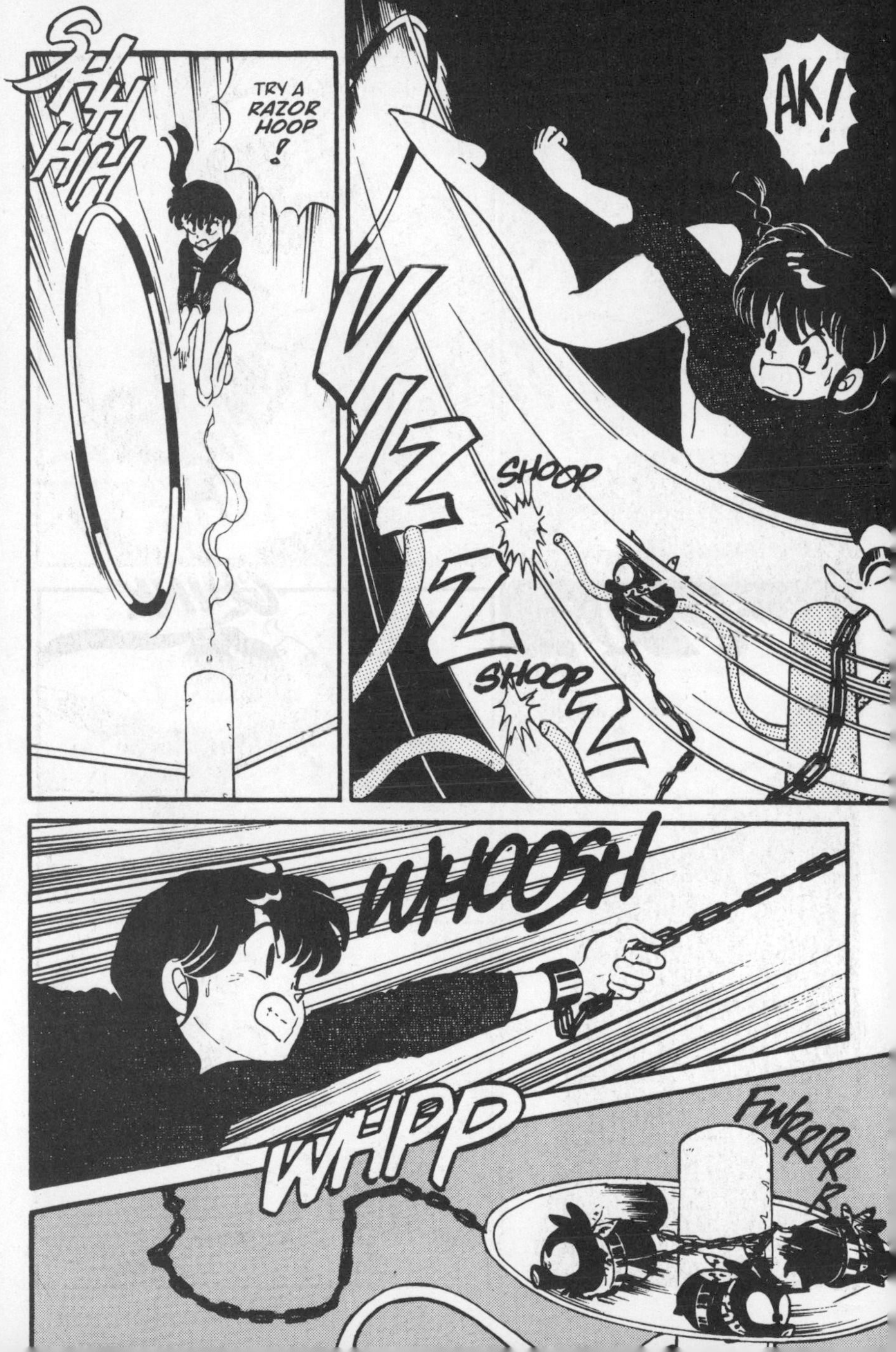
SHHHH
TRY A RAZOR HOOP!
AK!
VZZZZ
SHOOP
SHOOP
WHOOSH
WHPP
FWRRRRR

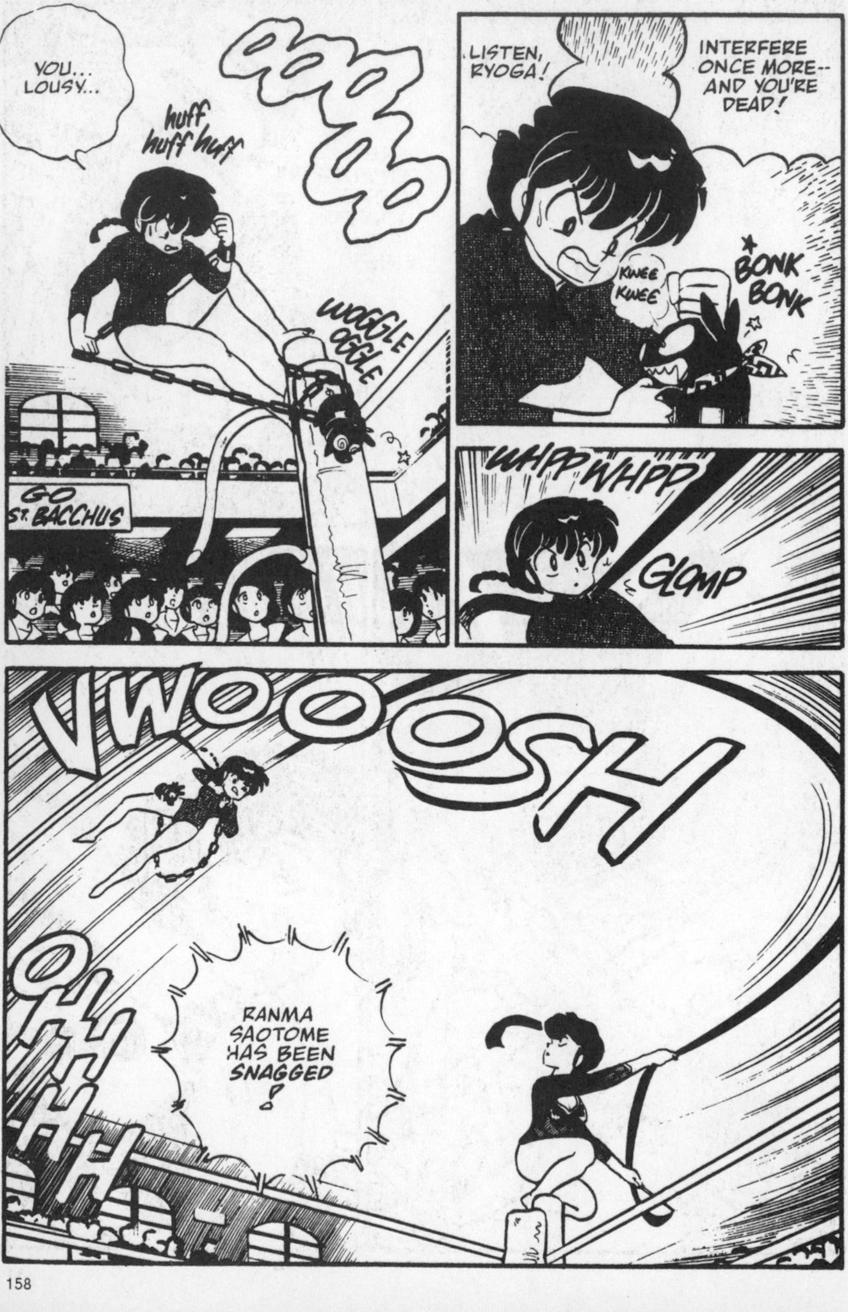
YOU... LOUSY...
huff huff huff
WOGGLE OGGLE
GO ST. BACCHUS
LISTEN, RYOGA!
INTERFERE ONCE MORE-- AND YOU'RE DEAD!
KWEE KWEE
BONK BONK
WHPP WHPP
GLOMP
VWOOOSH
OHHHH
RANMA SAOTOME HAS BEEN SNAGGED!

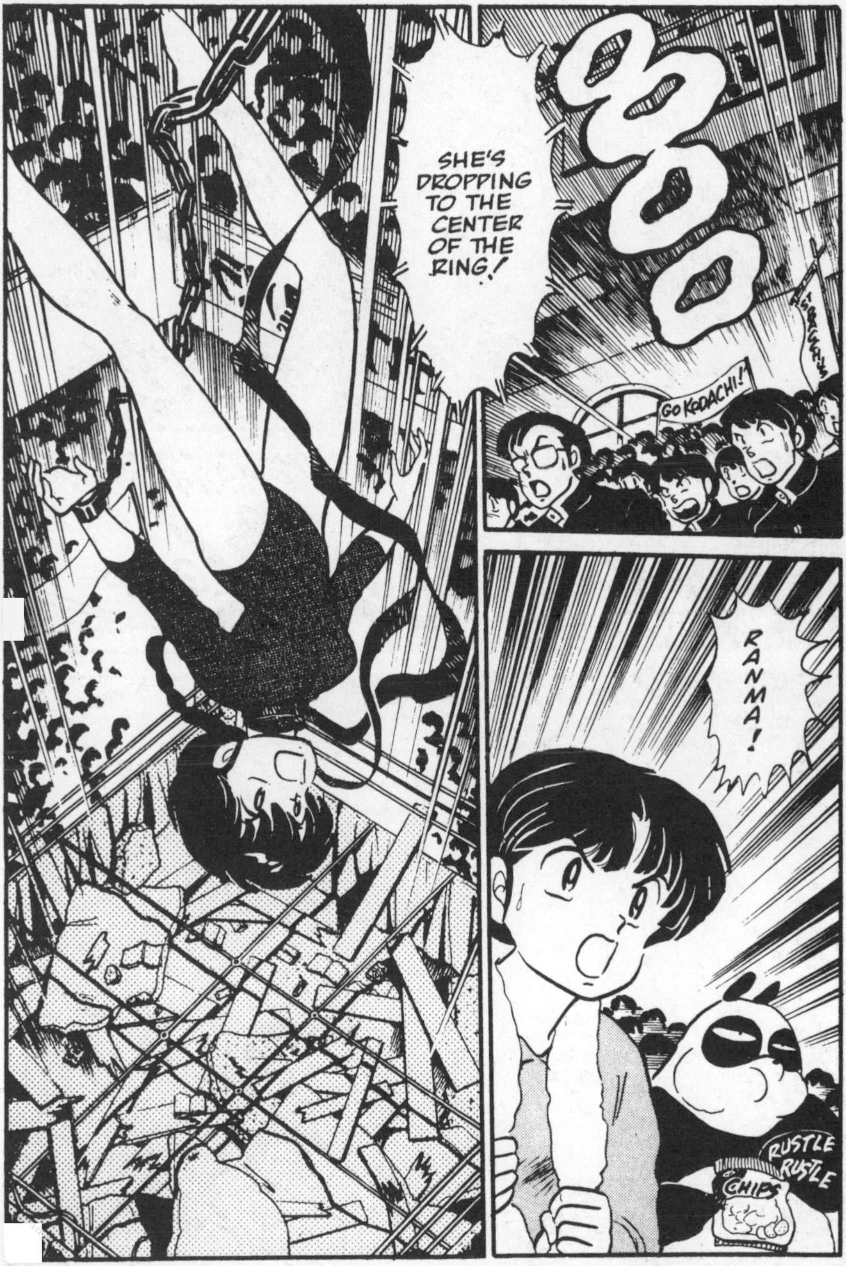
SHE'S DROPPING TO THE CENTER OF THE RING!
OOOO
GO KODACHI!
RANMA!
RUSTLE RUSTLE
CHIPS

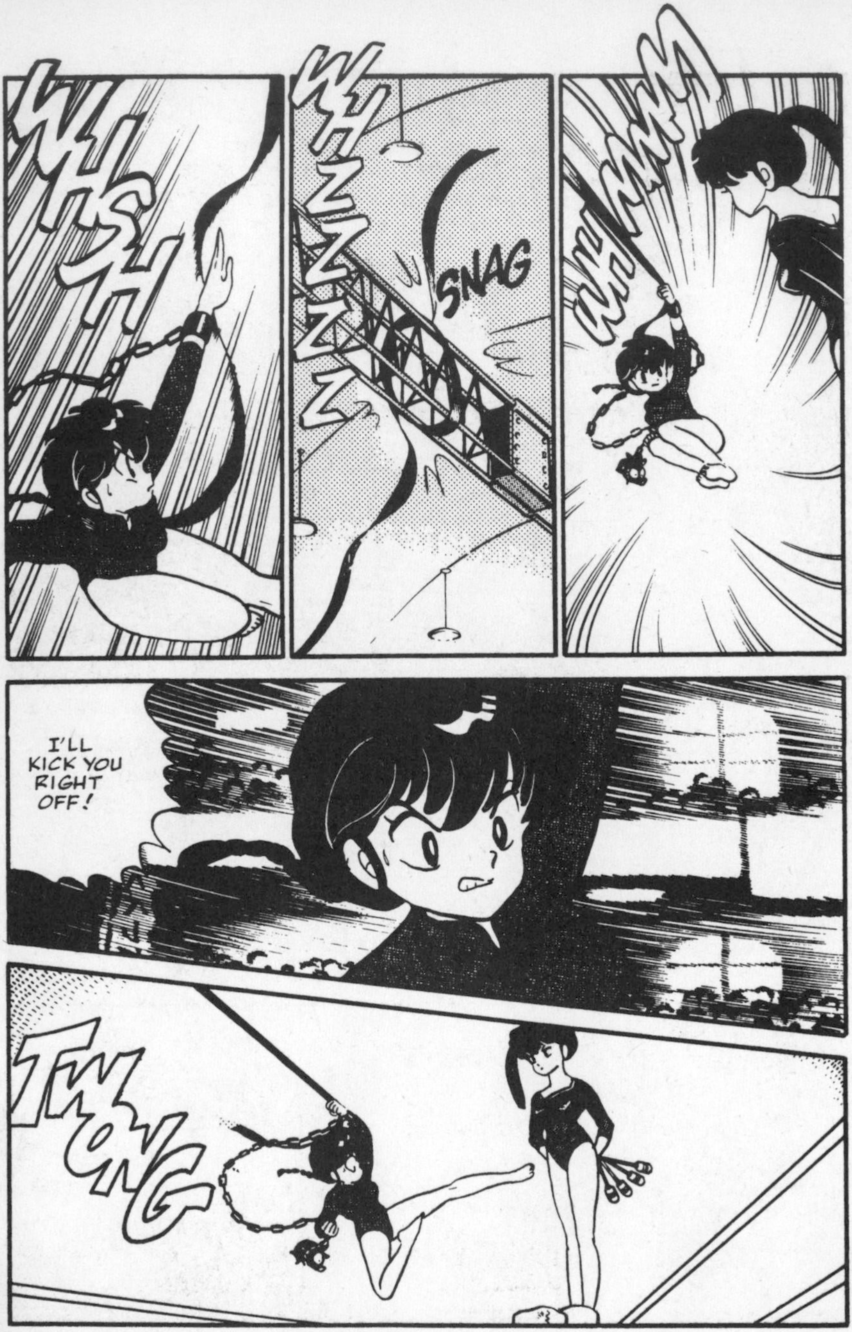
WHISH
WHZZZZZ
SNAG
I'LL KICK YOU RIGHT OFF!
TWONG

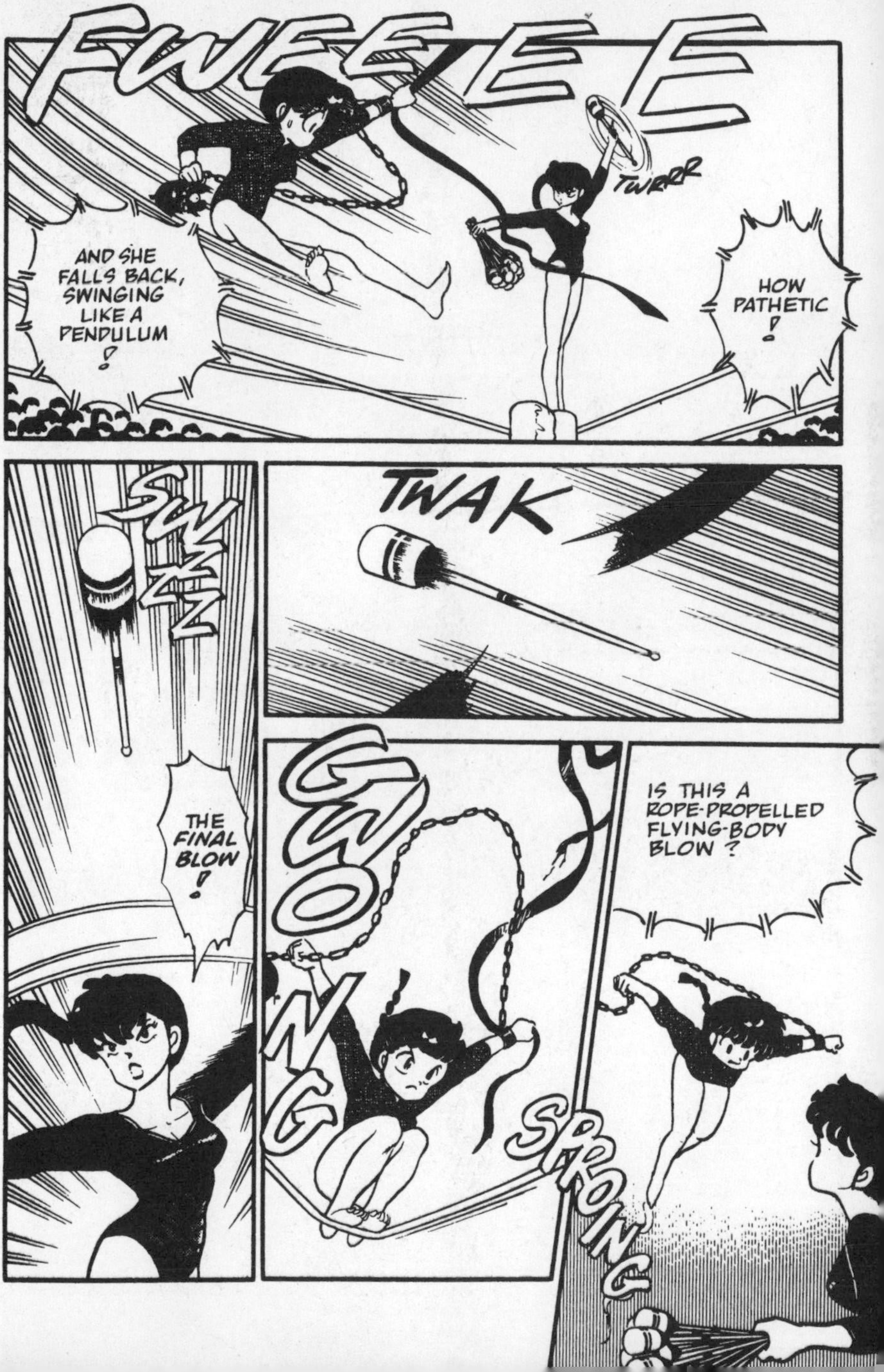
FWEEEE
TWIRRR
AND SHE FALLS BACK, SWINGING LIKE A PENDULUM!
HOW PATHETIC!
SWZZ
TWAK
THE FINAL BLOW!
GWONG
SPROING
IS THIS A ROPE-PROPELLED FLYING-BODY BLOW?

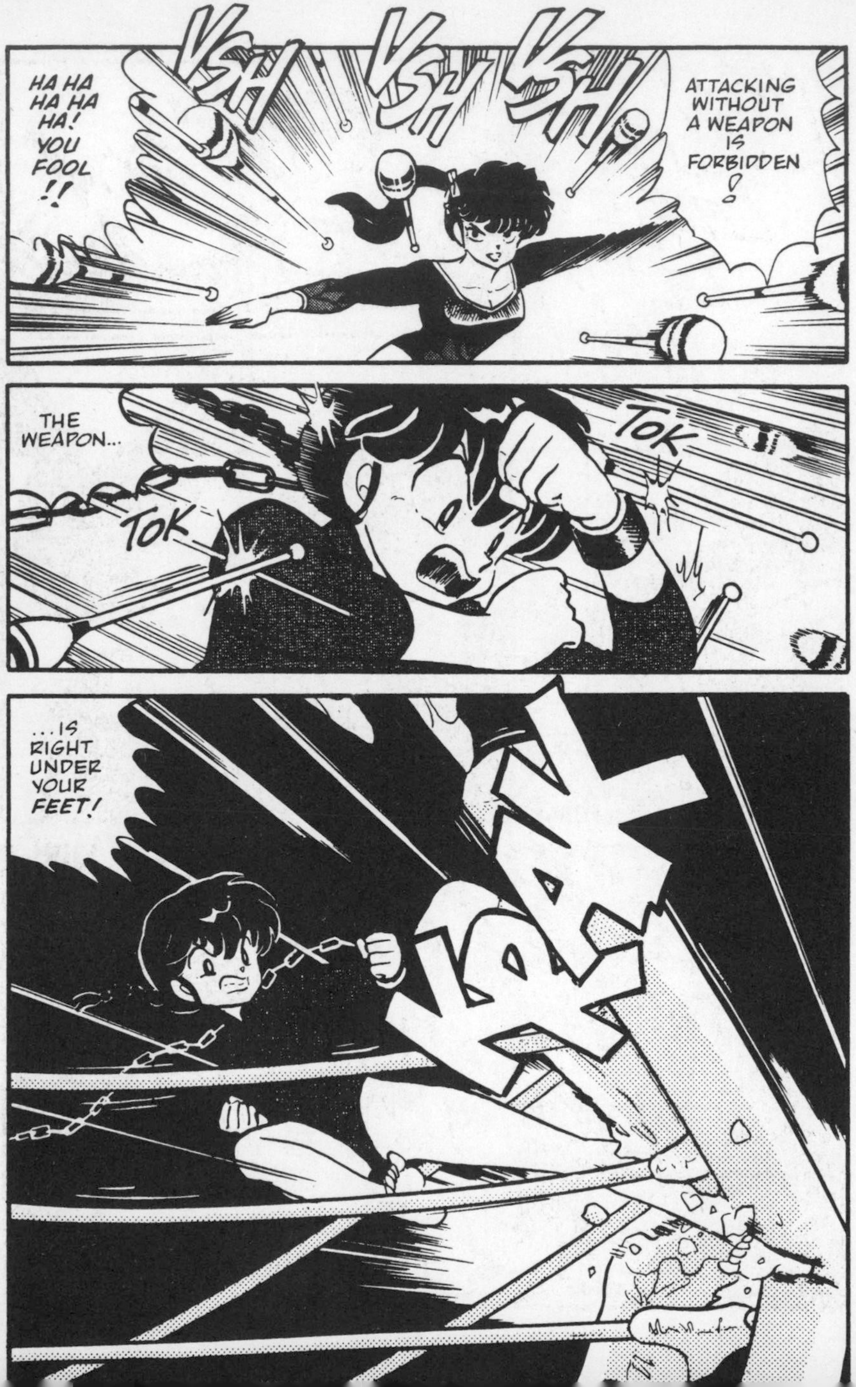
HA HA HA HA HA! YOU FOOL !!
VSH VSH VSH
ATTACKING WITHOUT A WEAPON IS FORBIDDEN!
THE WEAPON...
TOK
TOK
...IS RIGHT UNDER YOUR FEET!

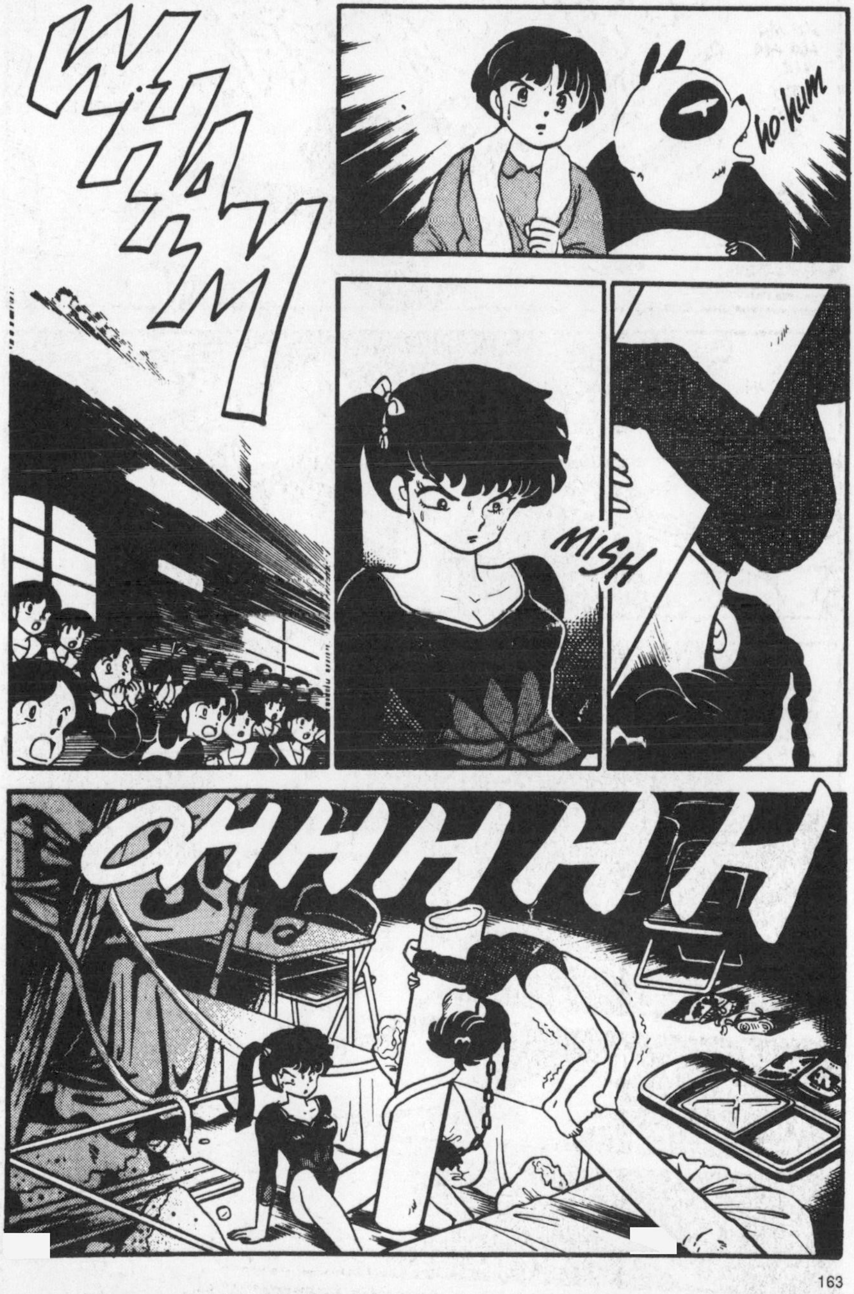
WHAM
ho-hum
MISH
OHHHHH

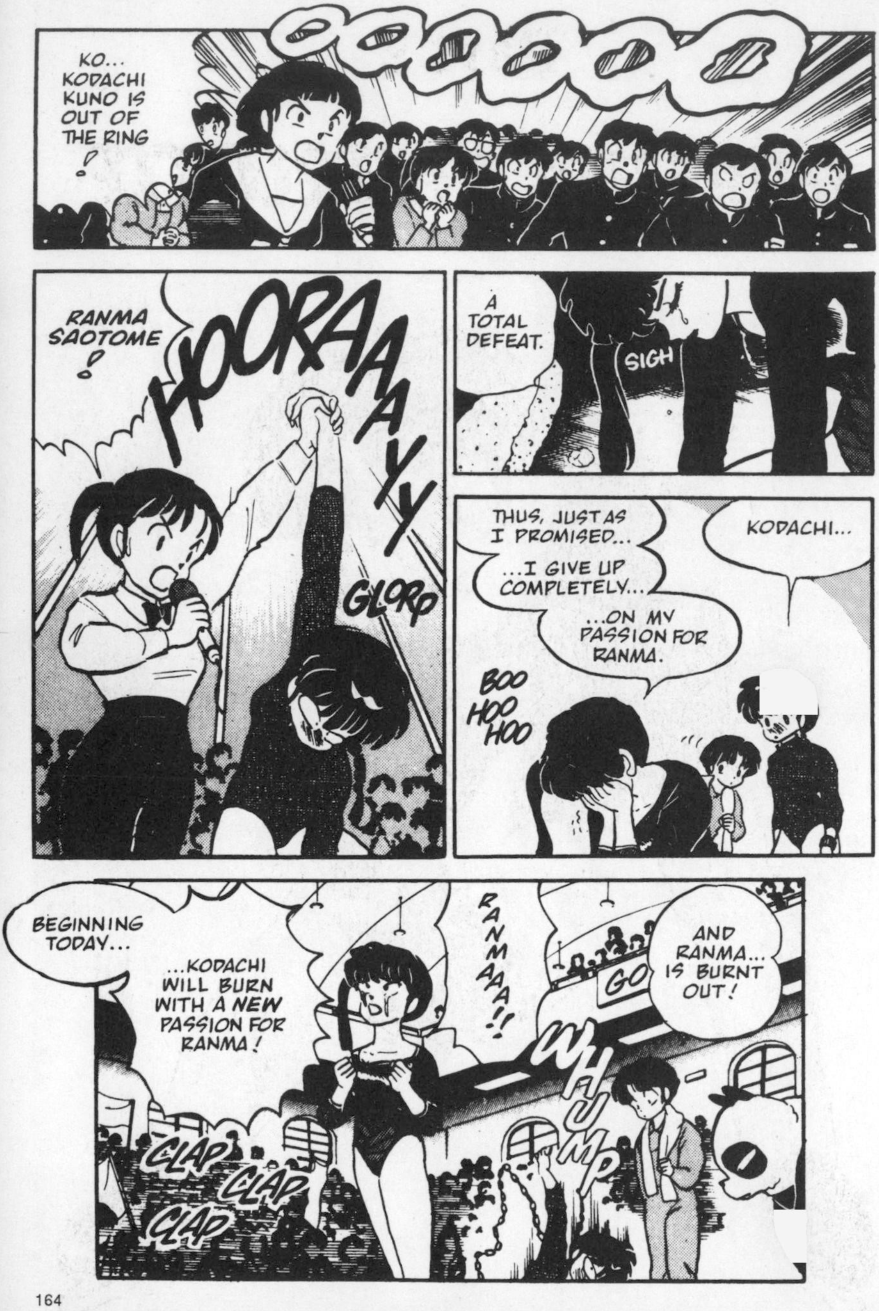

KO... KODACHI KUNO IS OUT OF THE RING!
OOOOOO
RANMA SAOTOME!
HOORAAAYY
GLORP
A TOTAL DEFEAT.
SIGH
THUS, JUST AS I PROMISED...
...I GIVE UP COMPLETELY...
...ON MY PASSION FOR RANMA.
KODACHI...
BOO HOO HOO
BEGINNING TODAY...
...KODACHI WILL BURN WITH A NEW PASSION FOR RANMA!
RANMAAAA!!
GO
AND RANMA... IS BURNT OUT!
WHUMP
CLAP CLAP CLAP

Part 9

DARLING CHARLOTTE

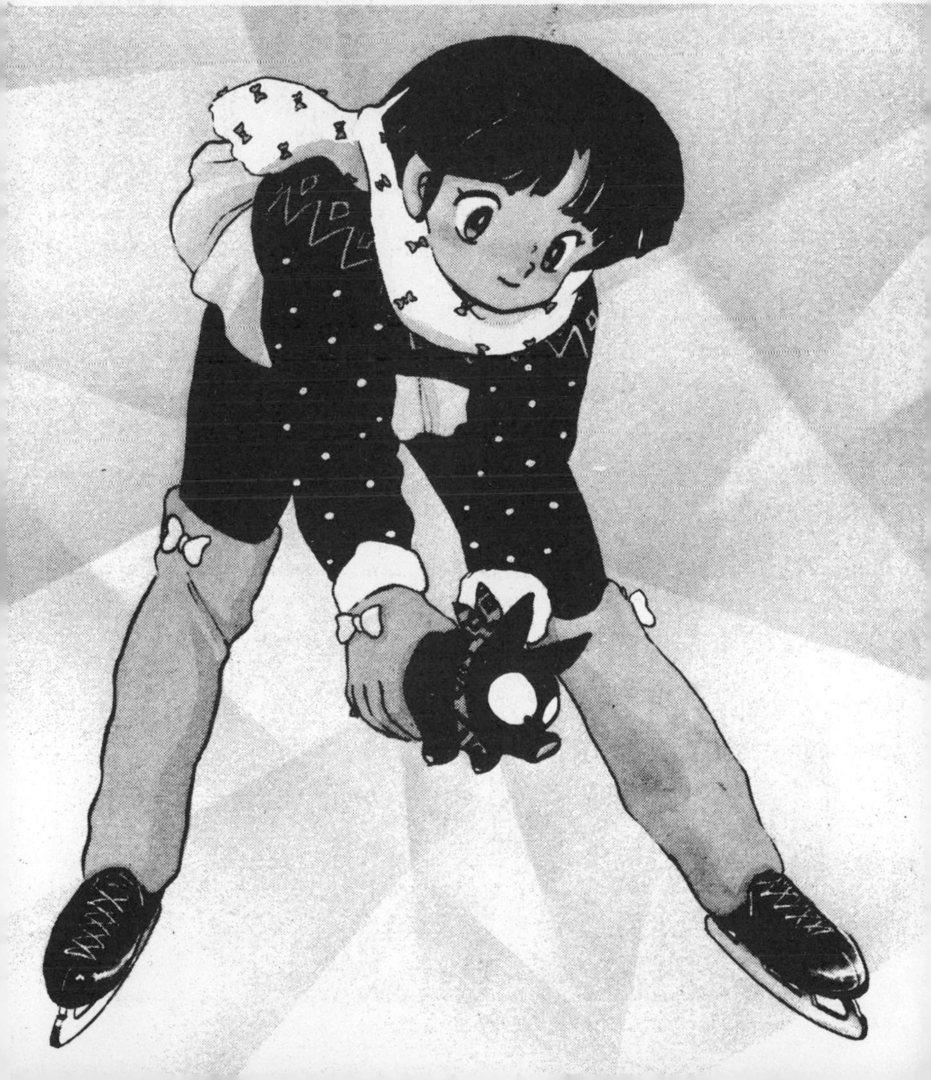

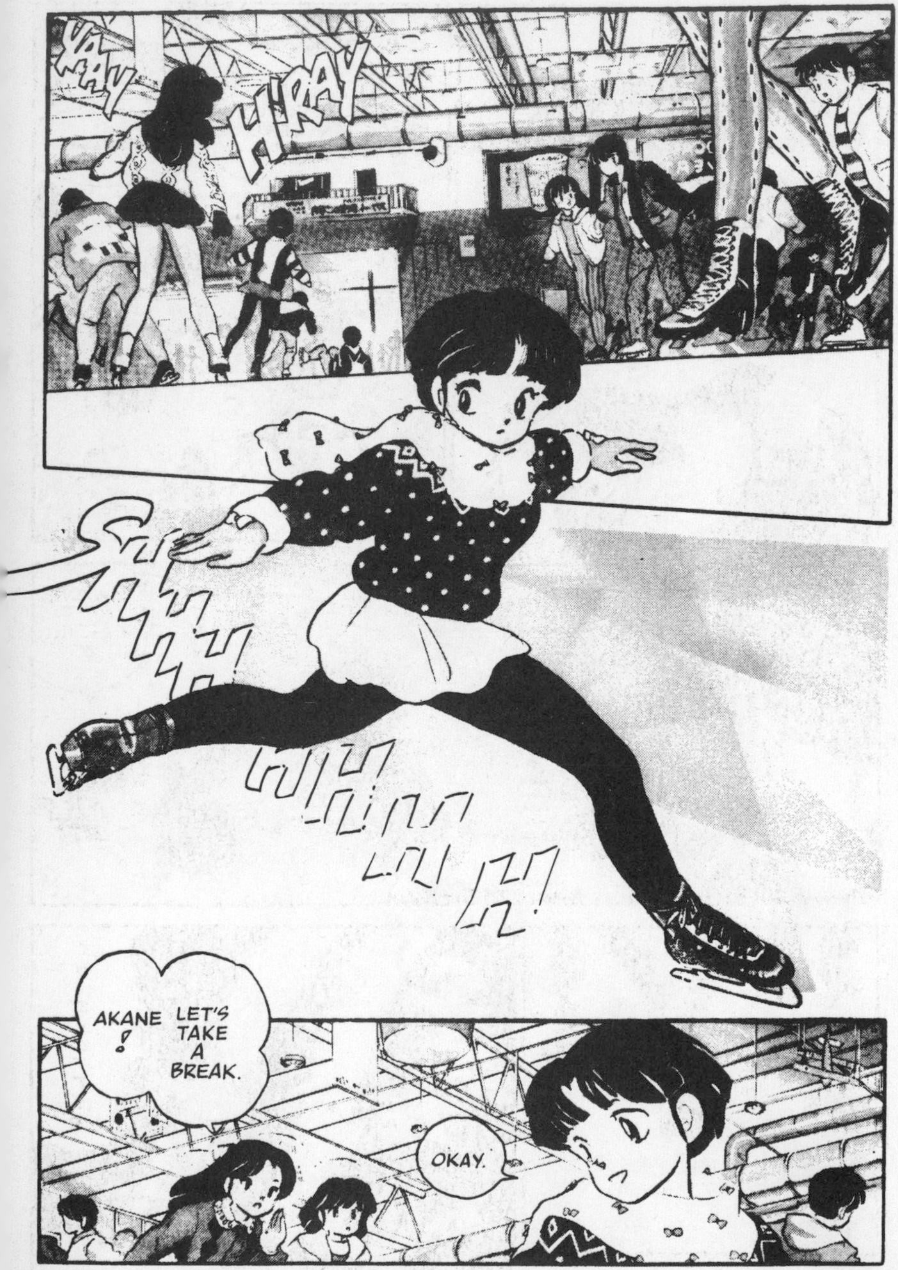
YAY
H-RAY
SWISHHH!
WHHHRRR!
AKANE! LET'S TAKE A BREAK.
OKAY.

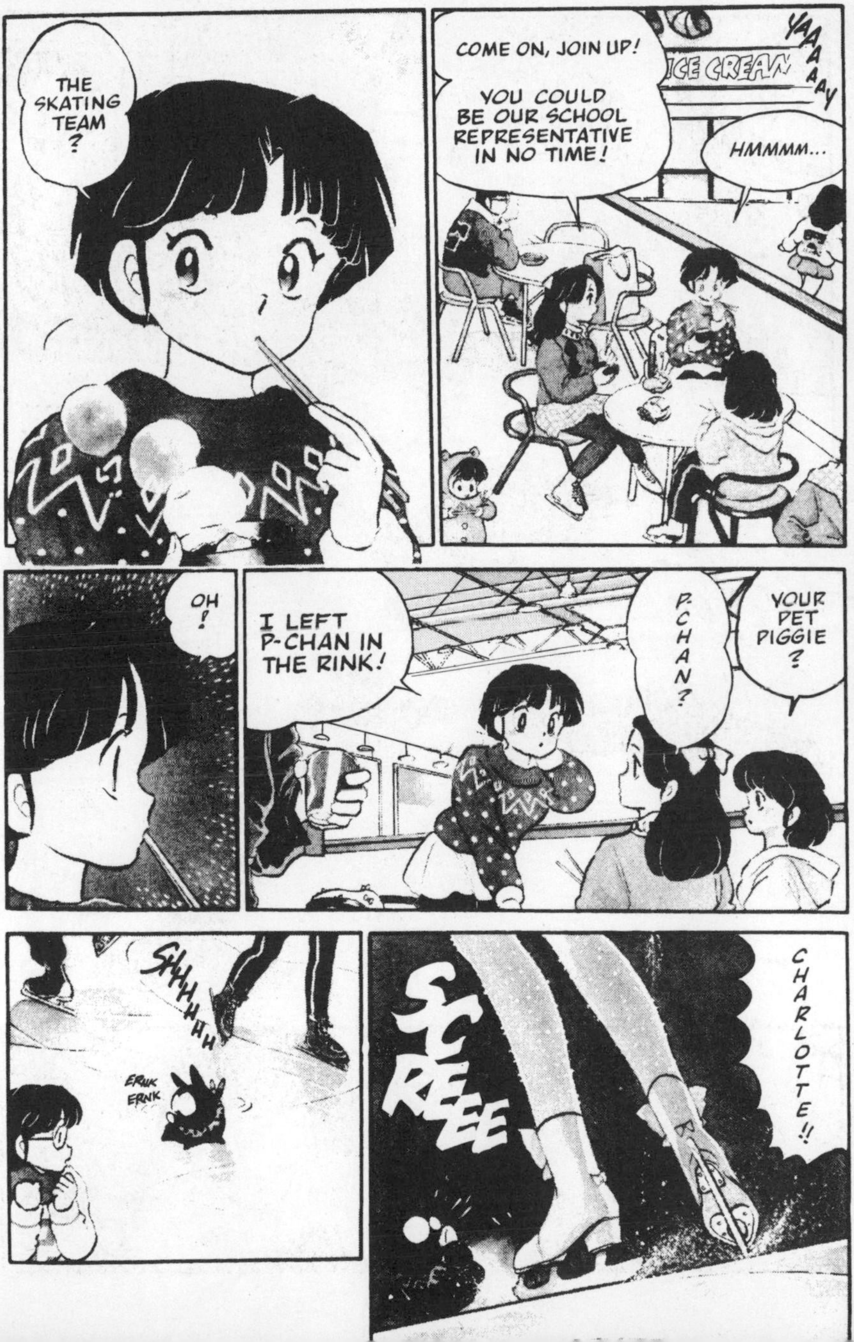
THE SKATING TEAM?
COME ON, JOIN UP!
YOU COULD BE OUR SCHOOL REPRESENTATIVE IN NO TIME!
ICE CREAM
YAAAAAAY
HMMMM...
OH!
I LEFT P-CHAN IN THE RINK!
P-CHAN?
YOUR PET PIGGIE?
SHHHHHH
ERNK ERNK
SCREEEE
CHARLOTTE!!

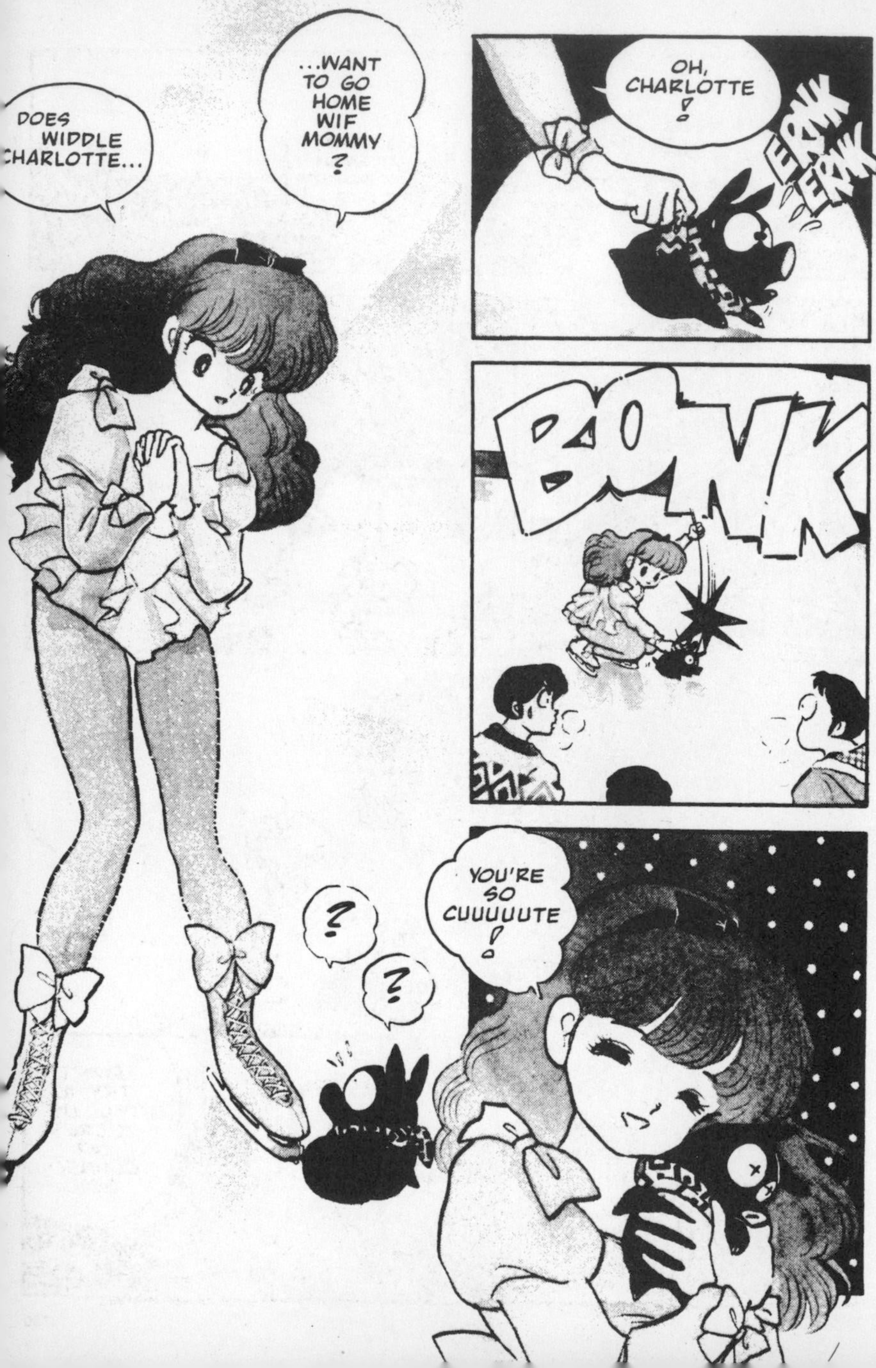
DOES WIDDLE CHARLOTTE...
...WANT TO GO HOME WIF MOMMY?
?
?
OH, CHARLOTTE!
ERK ERK
BONK
YOU'RE SO CUUUUUTE!

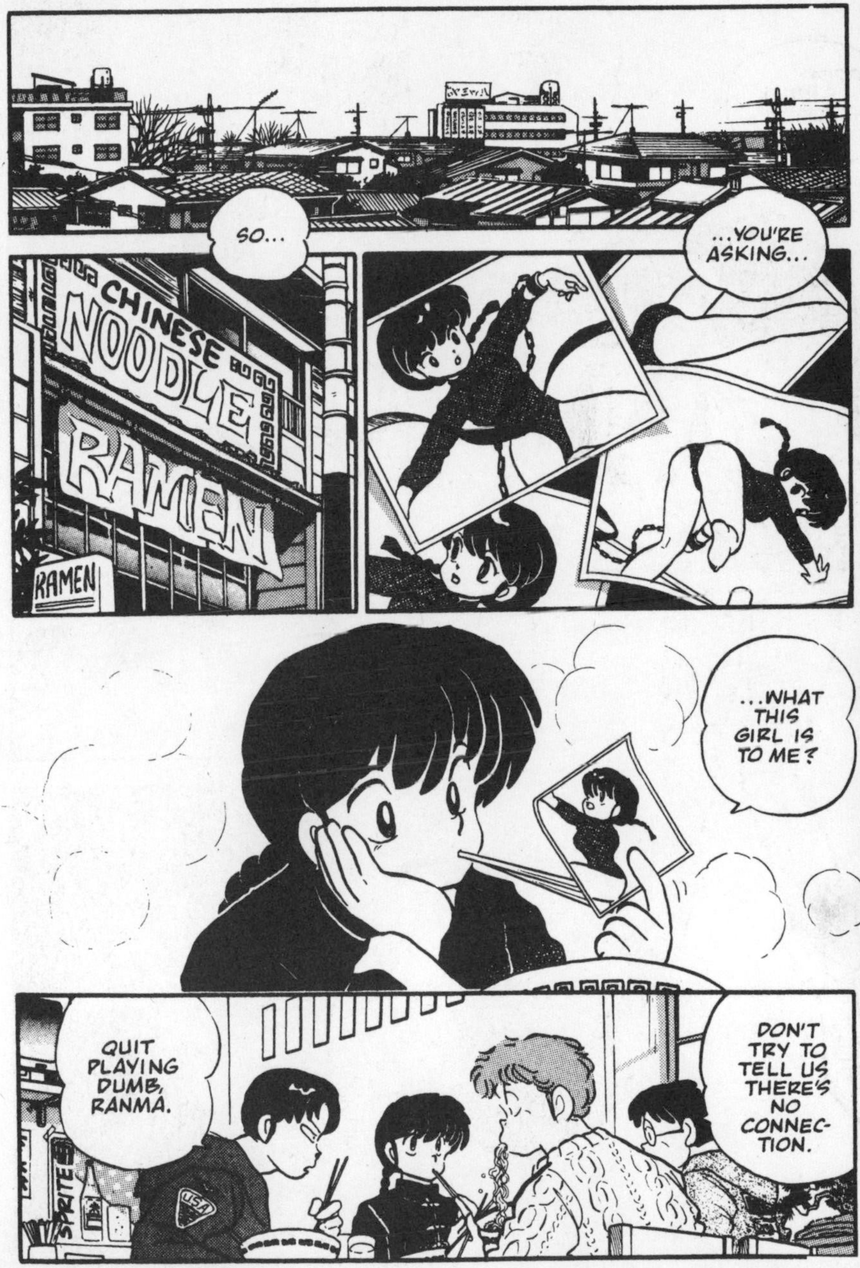
SO...
CHINESE NOODLE
RAMEN
RAMEN
...YOU'RE ASKING...
...WHAT THIS GIRL IS TO ME?
QUIT PLAYING DUMB, RANMA.
SPRITE
USA
DON'T TRY TO TELL US THERE'S NO CONNECTION.

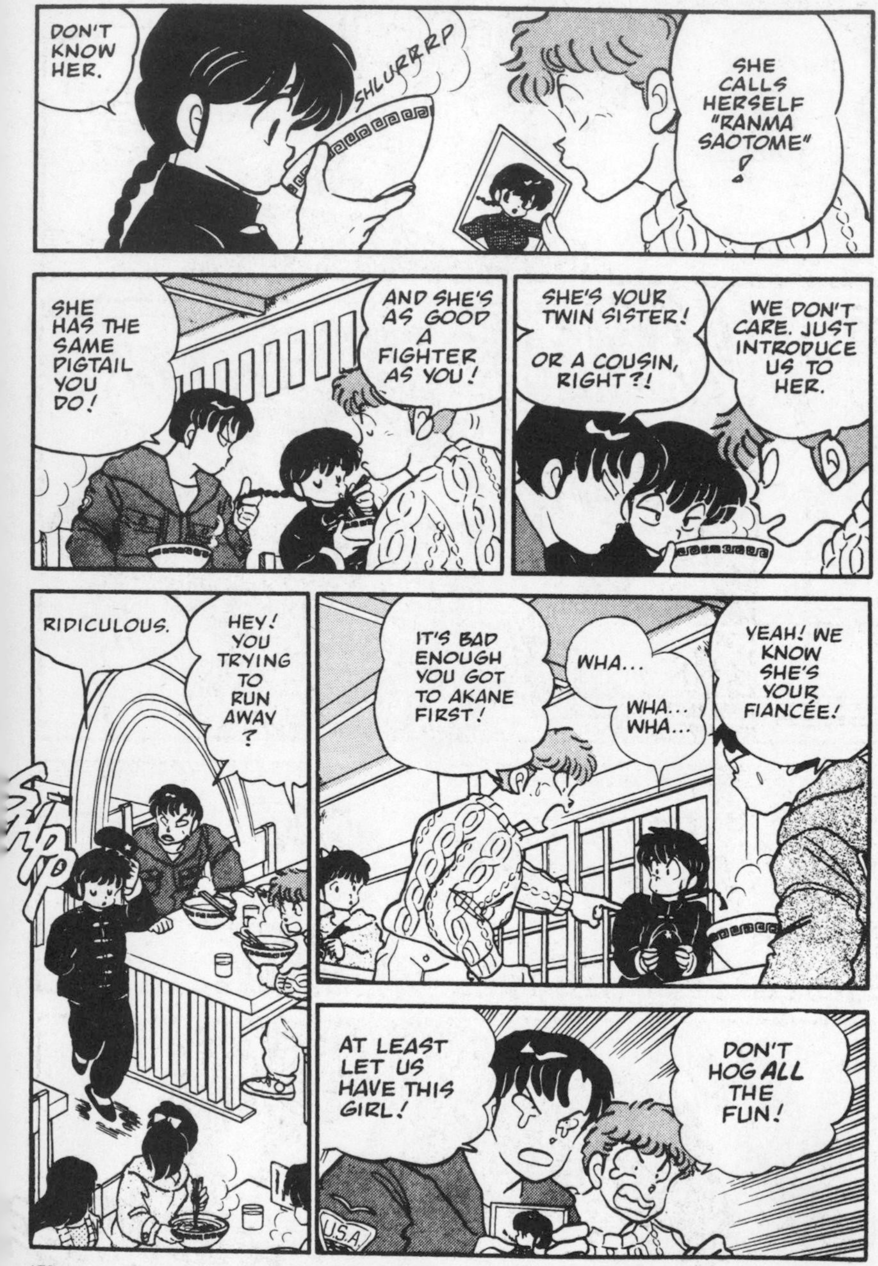

DON'T KNOW HER.
SHLURRRP
SHE CALLS HERSELF "RANMA SAOTOME"!
SHE HAS THE SAME PIGTAIL YOU DO!
AND SHE'S AS GOOD A FIGHTER AS YOU!
SHE'S YOUR TWIN SISTER!
OR A COUSIN, RIGHT?!
WE DON'T CARE. JUST INTRODUCE US TO HER.
RIDICULOUS.
HEY! YOU TRYING TO RUN AWAY?
IT'S BAD ENOUGH YOU GOT TO AKANE FIRST!
WHA...
WHA... WHA...
YEAH! WE KNOW SHE'S YOUR FIANCÉE!
AT LEAST LET US HAVE THIS GIRL!
U.S.A.
DON'T HOG ALL THE FUN!

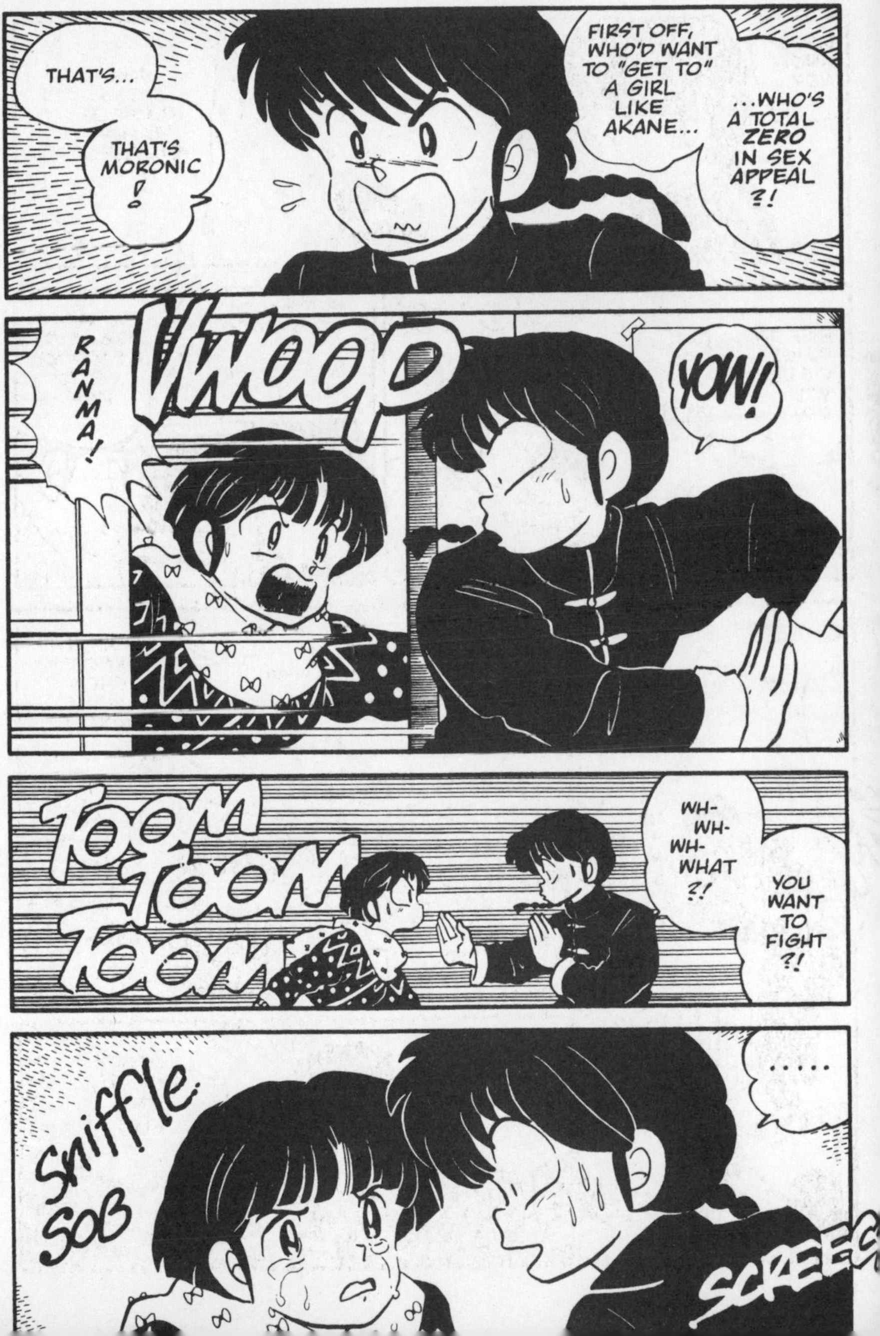
THAT'S...
THAT'S MORONIC!
FIRST OFF, WHO'D WANT TO "GET TO" A GIRL LIKE AKANE...
...WHO'S A TOTAL ZERO IN SEX APPEAL?!
RANMA!
VWOOP
YOW!
TOOM TOOM TOOM
WH-WH-WH-WHAT?!
YOU WANT TO FIGHT?!
.....
Sniffle
SOB
SCREEC

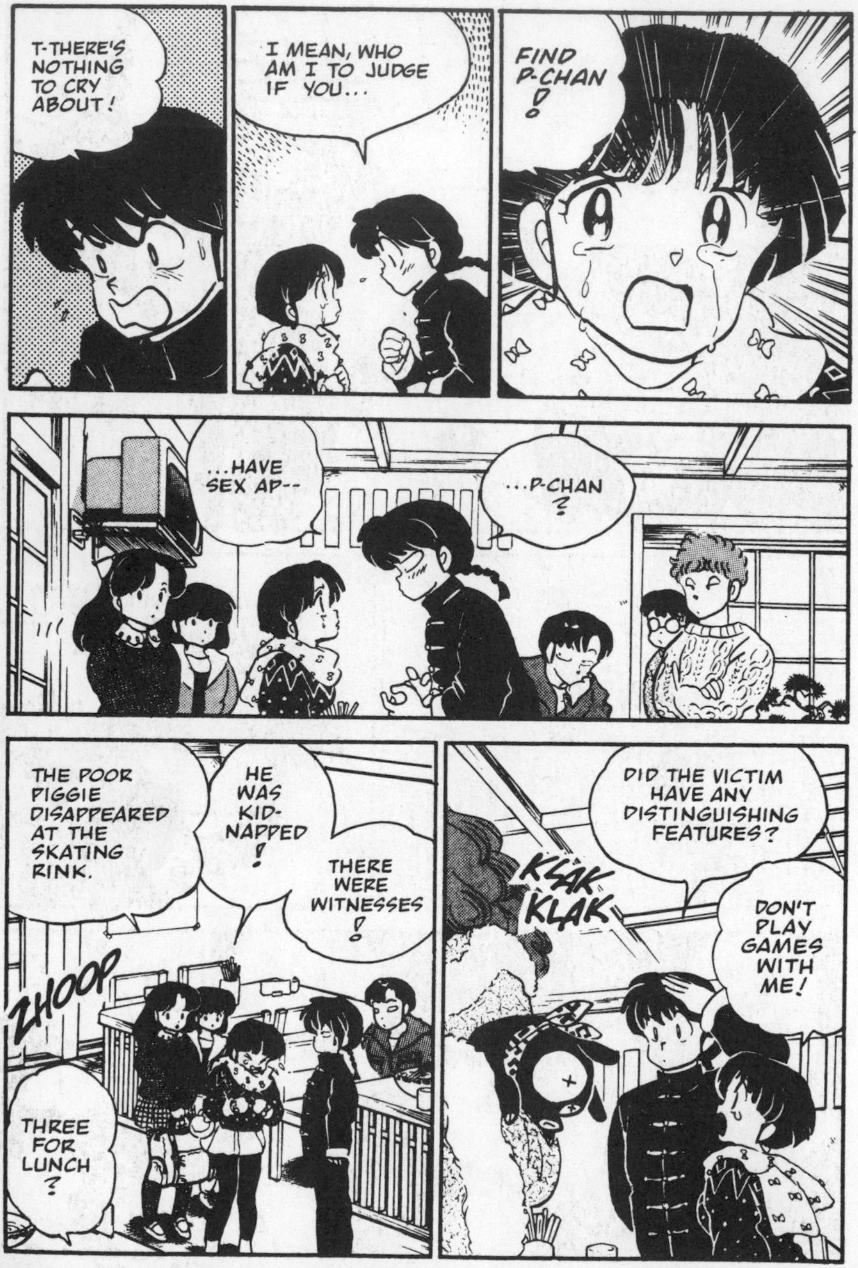
T-THERE'S NOTHING TO CRY ABOUT!
I MEAN, WHO AM I TO JUDGE IF YOU...
FIND P-CHAN!
...HAVE SEX AP--
...P-CHAN?
THE POOR PIGGIE DISAPPEARED AT THE SKATING RINK.
HE WAS KID-NAPPED!
THERE WERE WITNESSES!
ZHOOP
THREE FOR LUNCH?
DID THE VICTIM HAVE ANY DISTINGUISHING FEATURES?
KLAK KLAK
DON'T PLAY GAMES WITH ME!

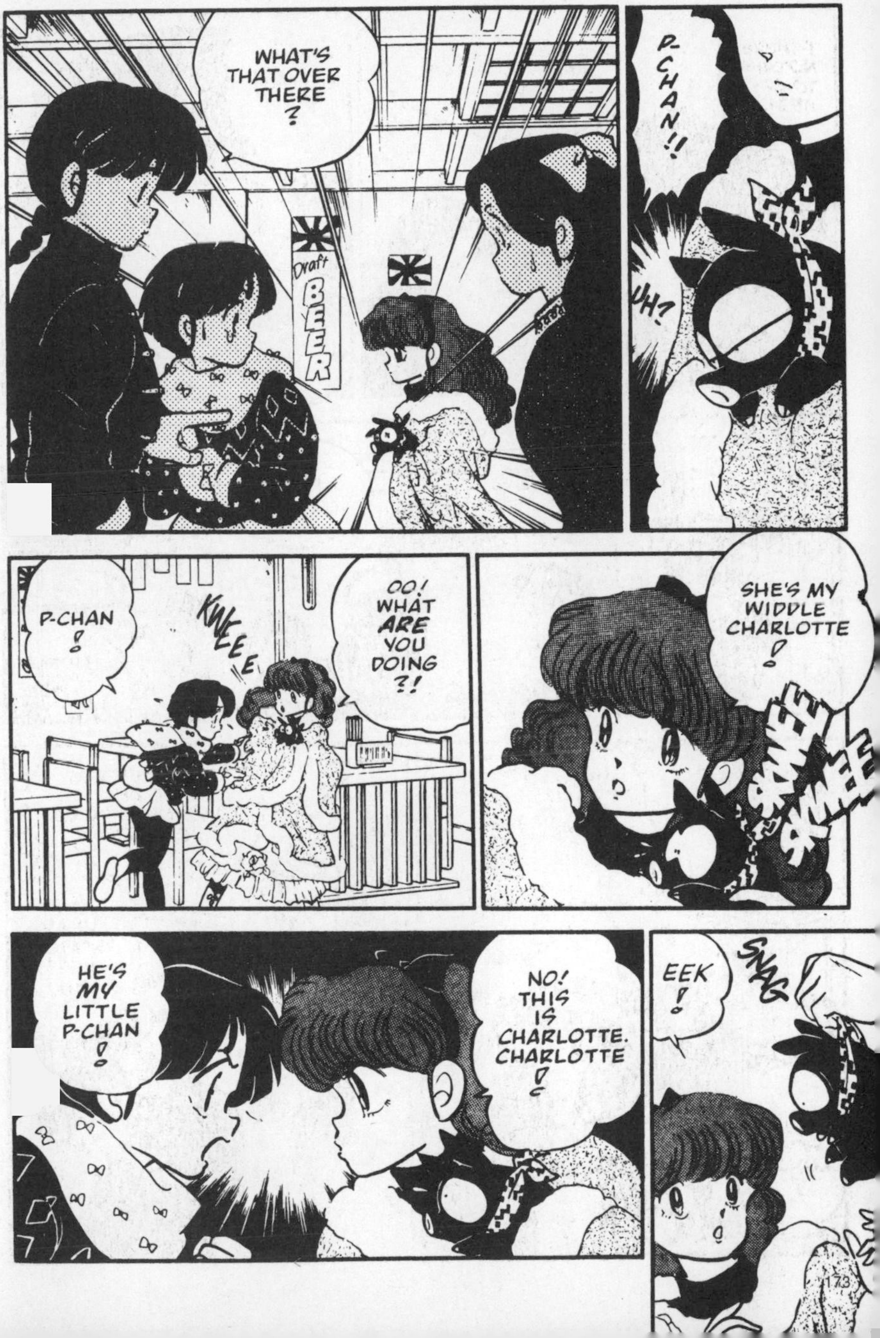

WHAT'S THAT OVER THERE ?
Draft BEER
P-CHAN!!
UH?
P-CHAN !
KWEEEE
OO! WHAT ARE YOU DOING ?!
SHE'S MY WIDDLE CHARLOTTE !
SKWEE SKWEE
HE'S MY LITTLE P-CHAN !
NO! THIS IS CHARLOTTE. CHARLOTTE !
EEK !
SNAG

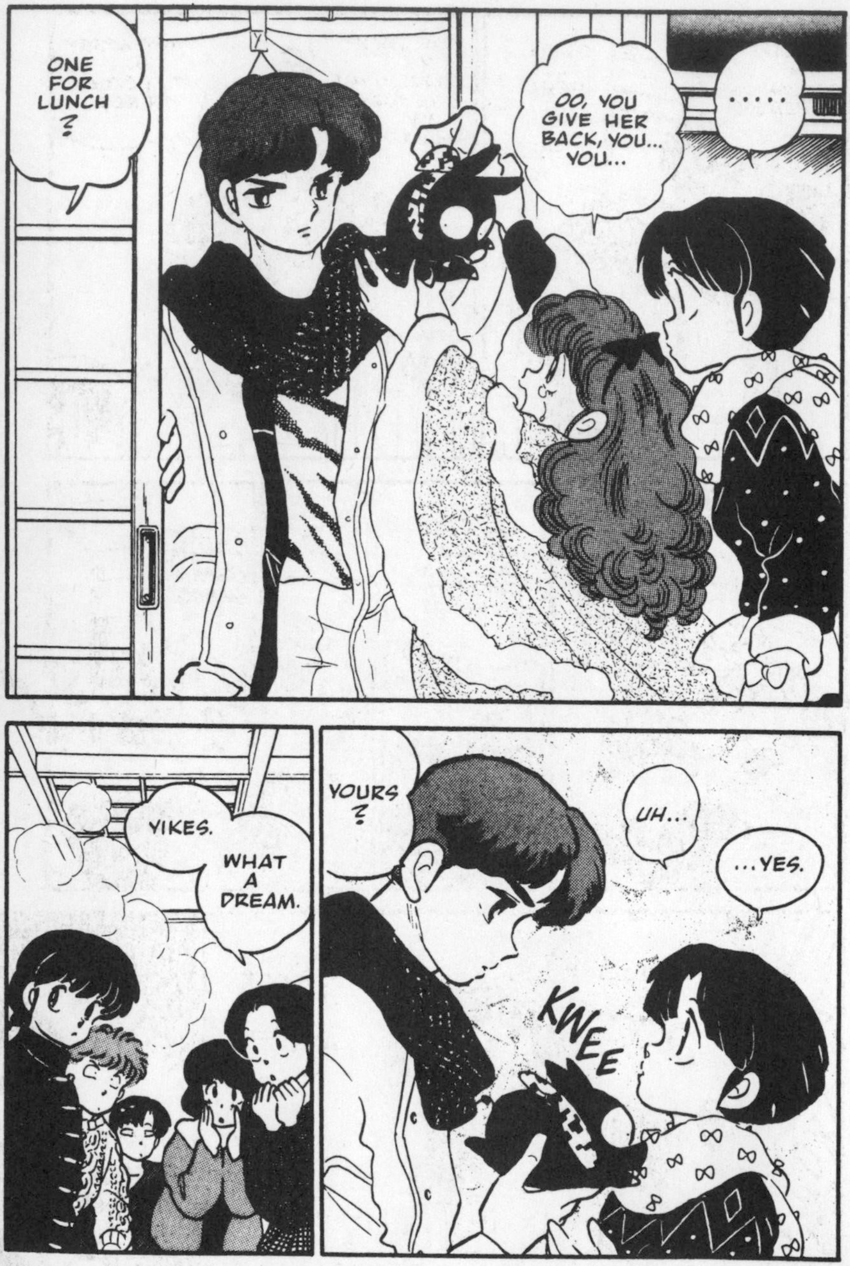
.....
OO, YOU GIVE HER BACK, YOU... YOU...
ONE FOR LUNCH?
YOURS?
UH...
...YES.
KWEE
YIKES.
WHAT A DREAM.

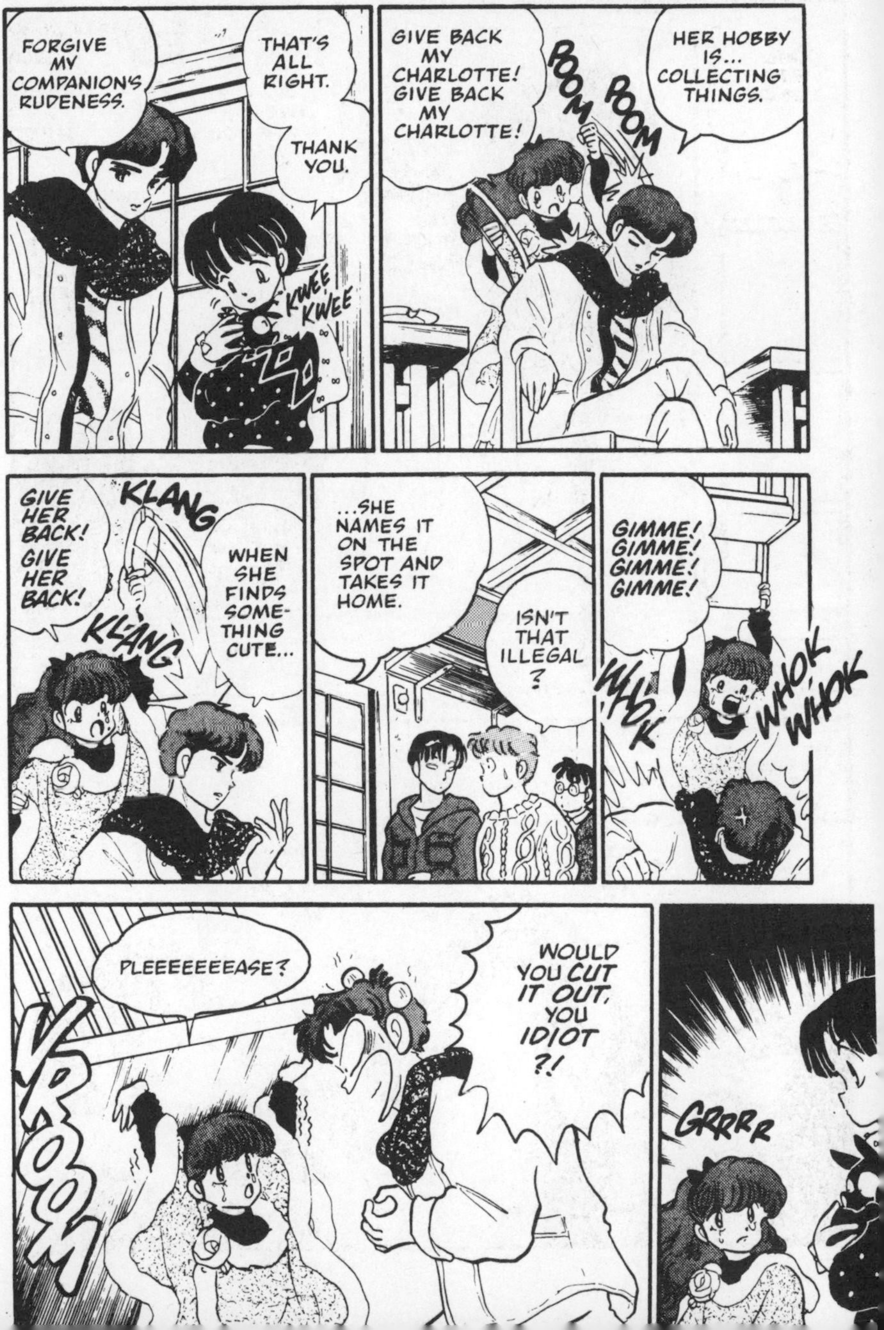

FORGIVE MY COMPANION'S RUDENESS.
THAT'S ALL RIGHT.
THANK YOU.
KWEE KWEE
GIVE BACK MY CHARLOTTE! GIVE BACK MY CHARLOTTE!
POOM POOM
HER HOBBY IS... COLLECTING THINGS.
GIVE HER BACK! GIVE HER BACK!
KLANG
KLANG
WHEN SHE FINDS SOME-THING CUTE...
...SHE NAMES IT ON THE SPOT AND TAKES IT HOME.
ISN'T THAT ILLEGAL?
GIMME! GIMME! GIMME! GIMME!
WHOK
WHOK WHOK
PLEEEEEEEASE?
VROOM
WOULD YOU CUT IT OUT, YOU IDIOT?!
GRRRR

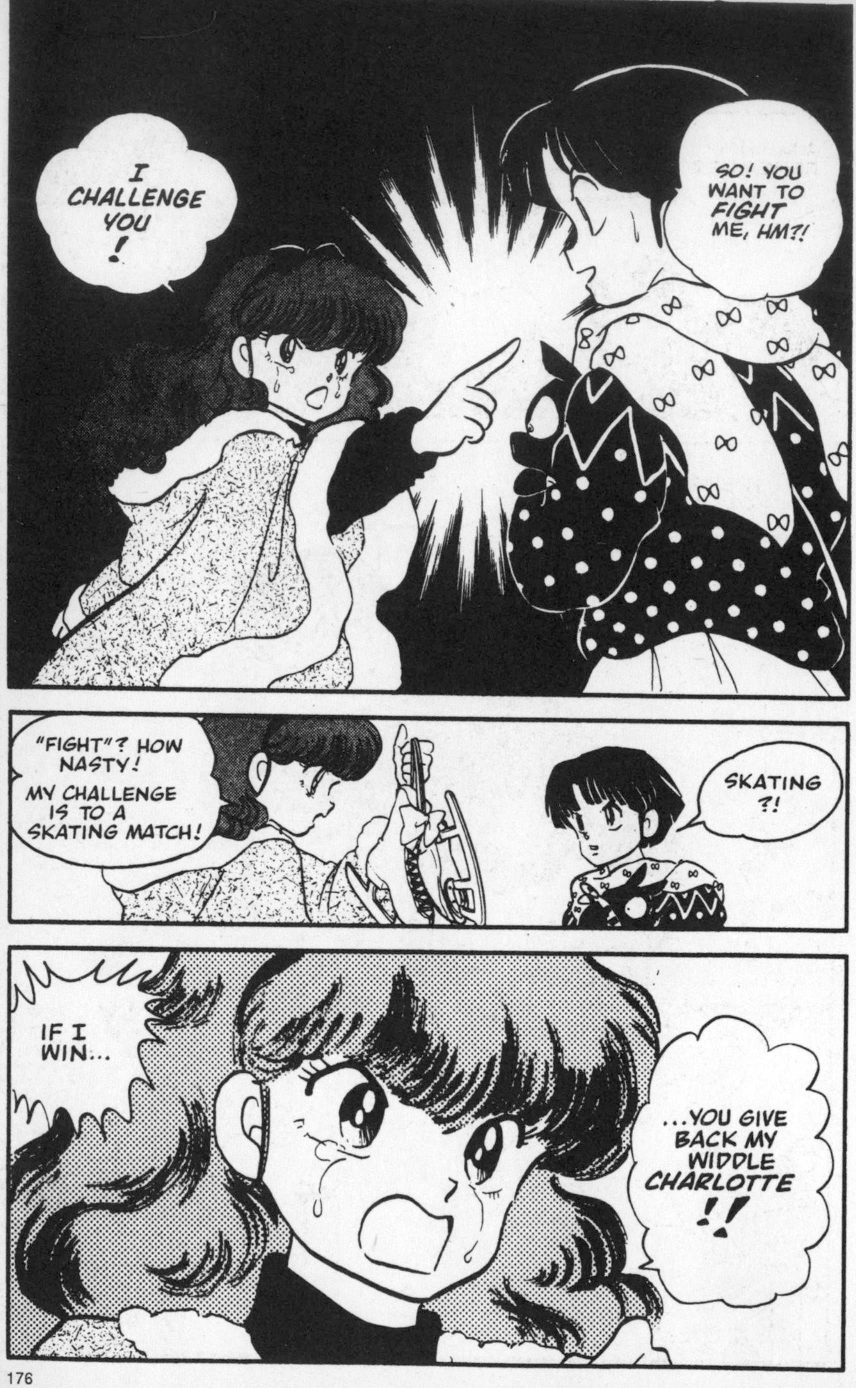
I CHALLENGE YOU!
SO! YOU WANT TO FIGHT ME, HM?!
"FIGHT"? HOW NASTY!
MY CHALLENGE IS TO A SKATING MATCH!
SKATING?!
IF I WIN...
...YOU GIVE BACK MY WIDDLE CHARLOTTE!!

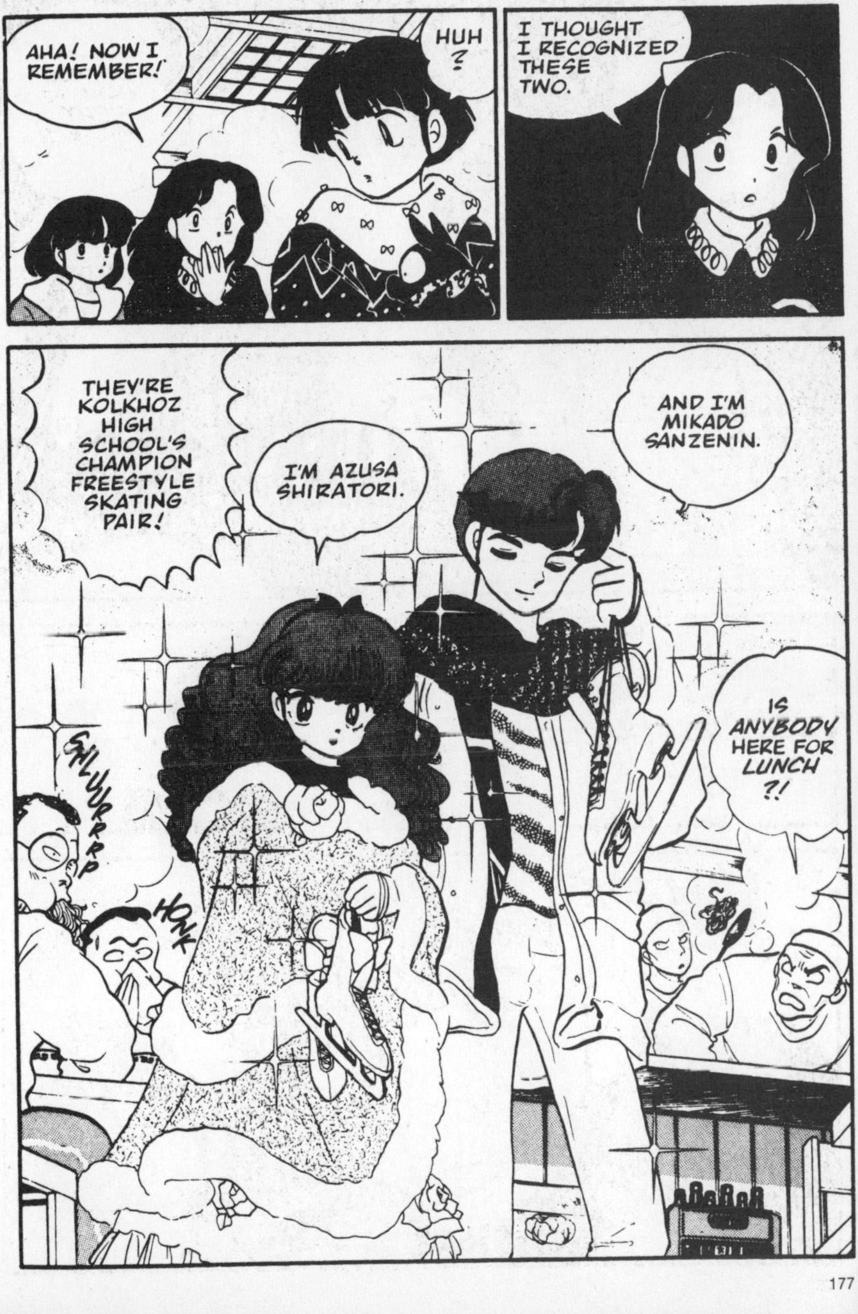
AHA! NOW I REMEMBER!
HUH ?
I THOUGHT I RECOGNIZED THESE TWO.
THEY'RE KOLKHOZ HIGH SCHOOL'S CHAMPION FREESTYLE SKATING PAIR!
I'M AZUSA SHIRATORI.
AND I'M MIKADO SANZENIN.
SHLUURRRP
HONK
IS ANYBODY HERE FOR LUNCH ?!

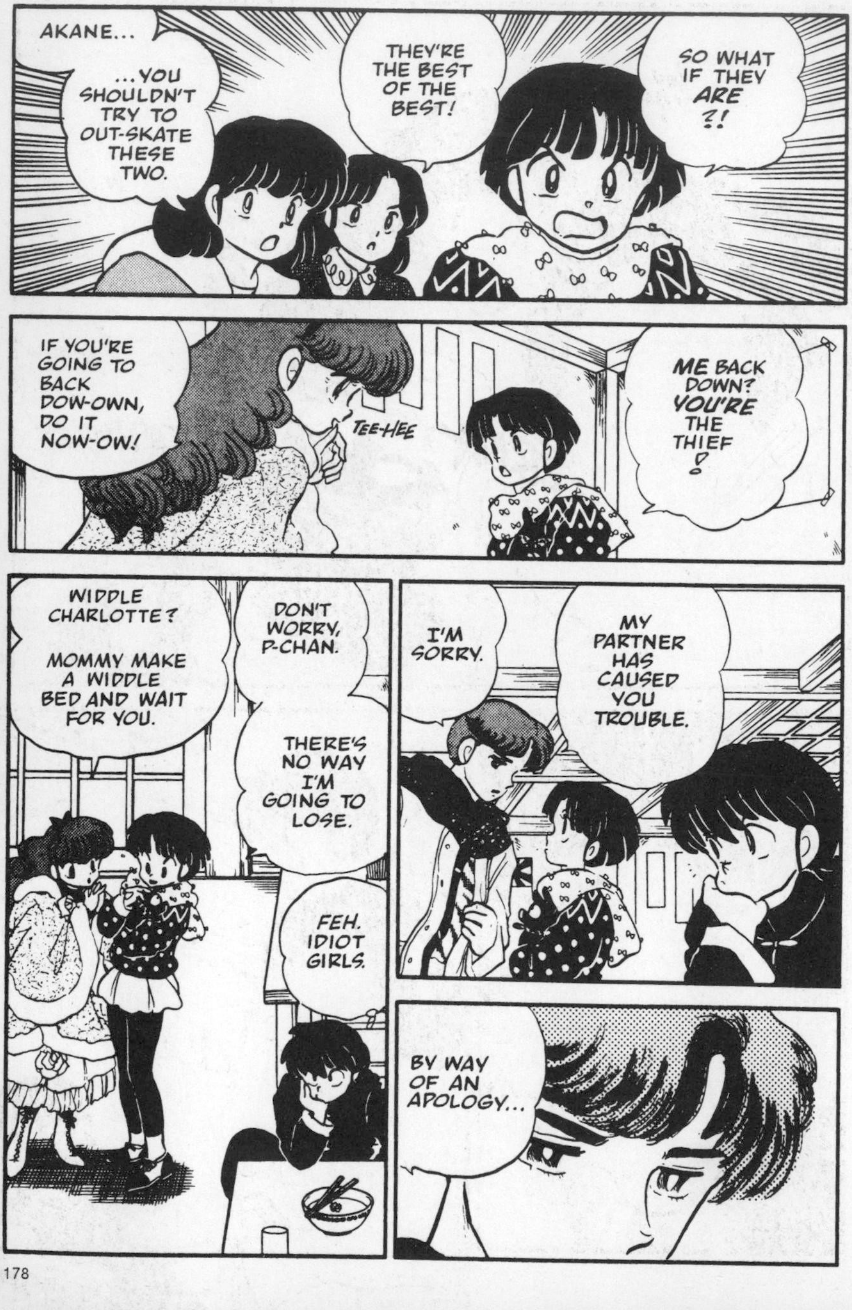
AKANE...
...YOU SHOULDN'T TRY TO OUT-SKATE THESE TWO.
THEY'RE THE BEST OF THE BEST!
SO WHAT IF THEY ARE?!
IF YOU'RE GOING TO BACK DOW-OWN, DO IT NOW-OW!
TEE-HEE
ME BACK DOWN? YOU'RE THE THIEF!
WIDDLE CHARLOTTE?
MOMMY MAKE A WIDDLE BED AND WAIT FOR YOU.
DON'T WORRY, P-CHAN.
THERE'S NO WAY I'M GOING TO LOSE.
FEH. IDIOT GIRLS.
I'M SORRY.
MY PARTNER HAS CAUSED YOU TROUBLE.
BY WAY OF AN APOLOGY...

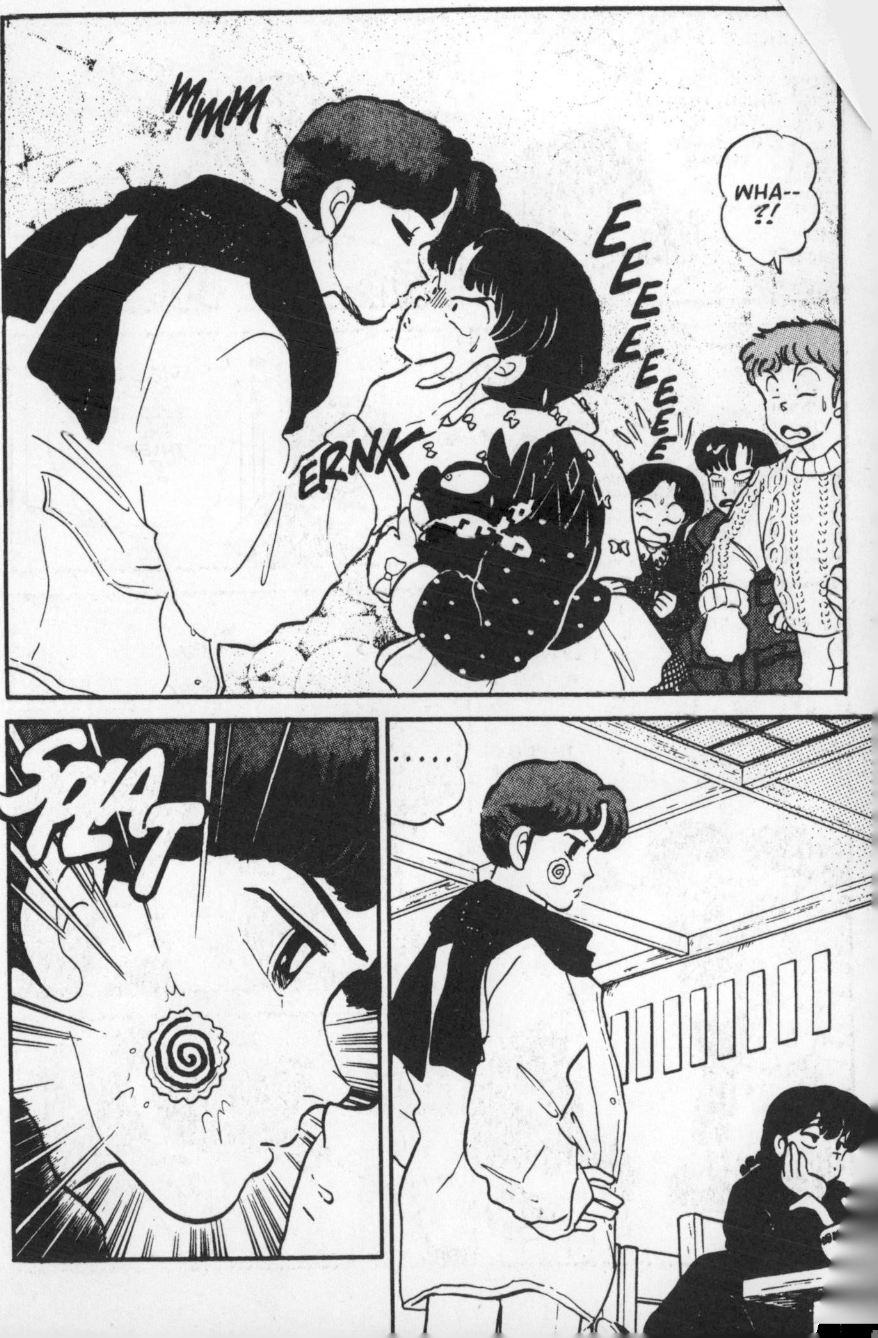
MMM
ERNK
EEEEEEEEE
WHA-- ?!
SPLAT
......

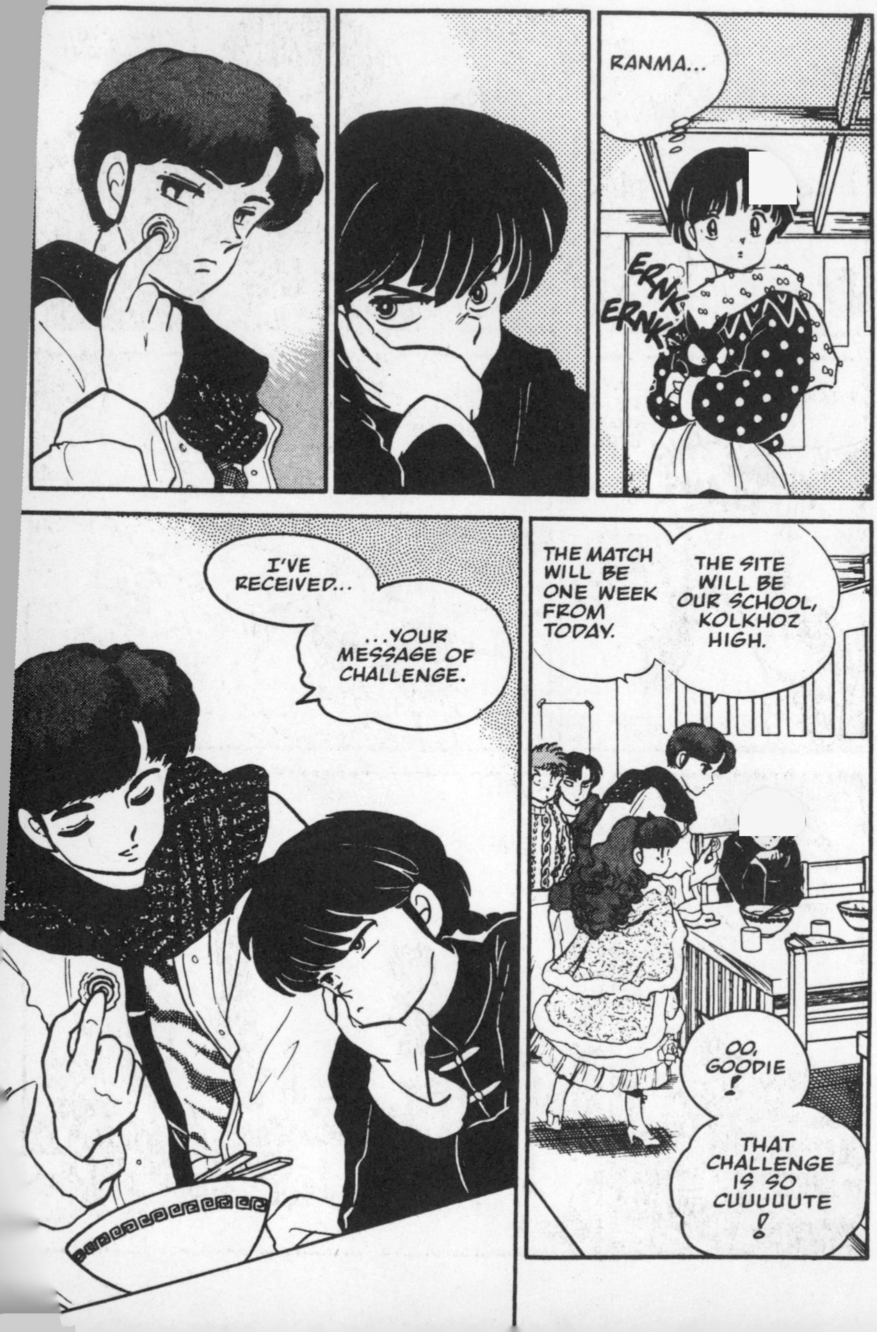
RANMA...
ERNK
ERNK
I'VE RECEIVED...
...YOUR MESSAGE OF CHALLENGE.
THE MATCH WILL BE ONE WEEK FROM TODAY.
THE SITE WILL BE OUR SCHOOL, KOLKHOZ HIGH.
OO, GOODIE!
THAT CHALLENGE IS SO CUUUUUTE!

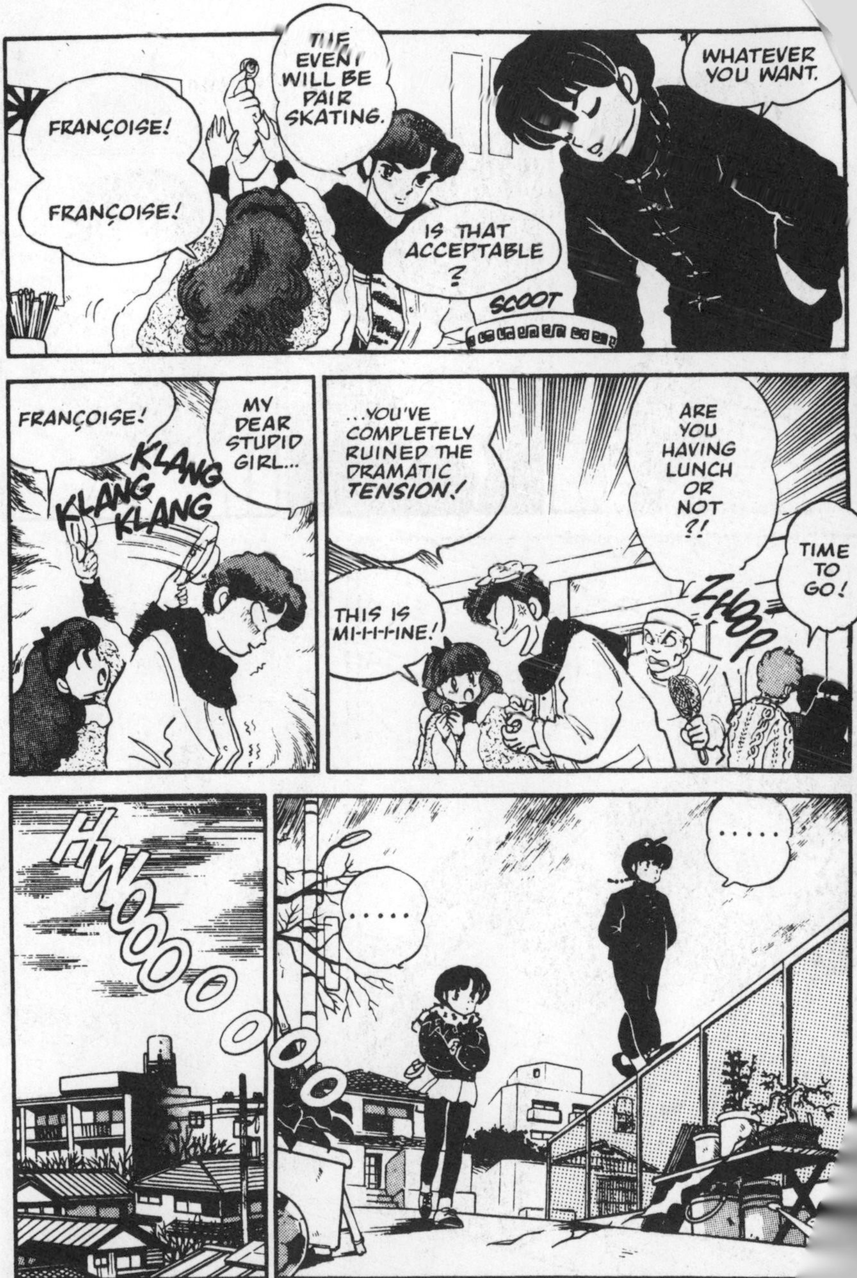
FRANÇOISE!
FRANÇOISE!
THE EVENT WILL BE PAIR SKATING.
IS THAT ACCEPTABLE ?
SCOOT
WHATEVER YOU WANT.
FRANÇOISE!
KLANG KLANG KLANG
MY DEAR STUPID GIRL...
...YOU'VE COMPLETELY RUINED THE DRAMATIC TENSION!
THIS IS MI-I-I-I-INE!
ARE YOU HAVING LUNCH OR NOT ?!
ZHOOP
TIME TO GO!
HWOOOOOOOOO
.....
.....

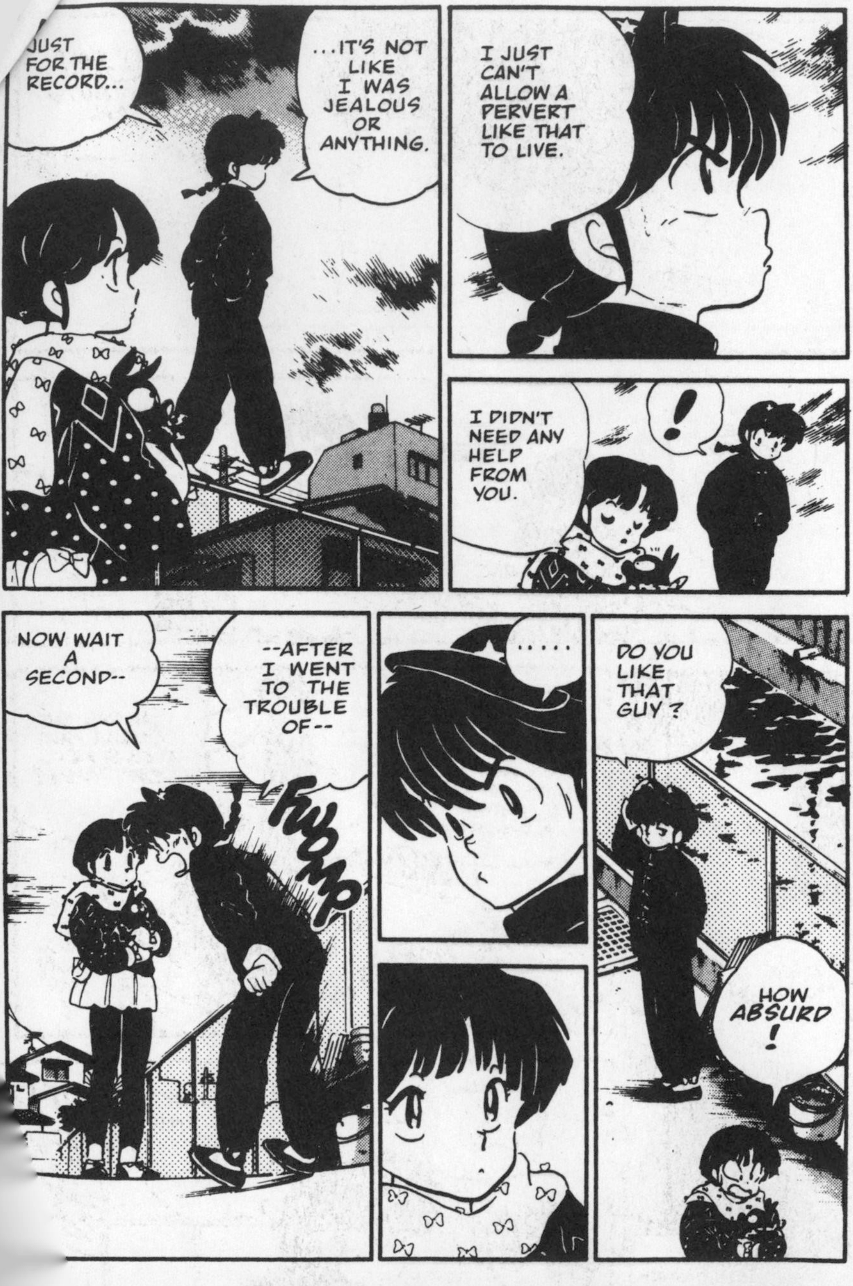
JUST FOR THE RECORD...
...IT'S NOT LIKE I WAS JEALOUS OR ANYTHING.
I JUST CAN'T ALLOW A PERVERT LIKE THAT TO LIVE.
I DIDN'T NEED ANY HELP FROM YOU.
!
NOW WAIT A SECOND--
--AFTER I WENT TO THE TROUBLE OF--
FWOMP
.....
DO YOU LIKE THAT GUY ?
HOW ABSURD !

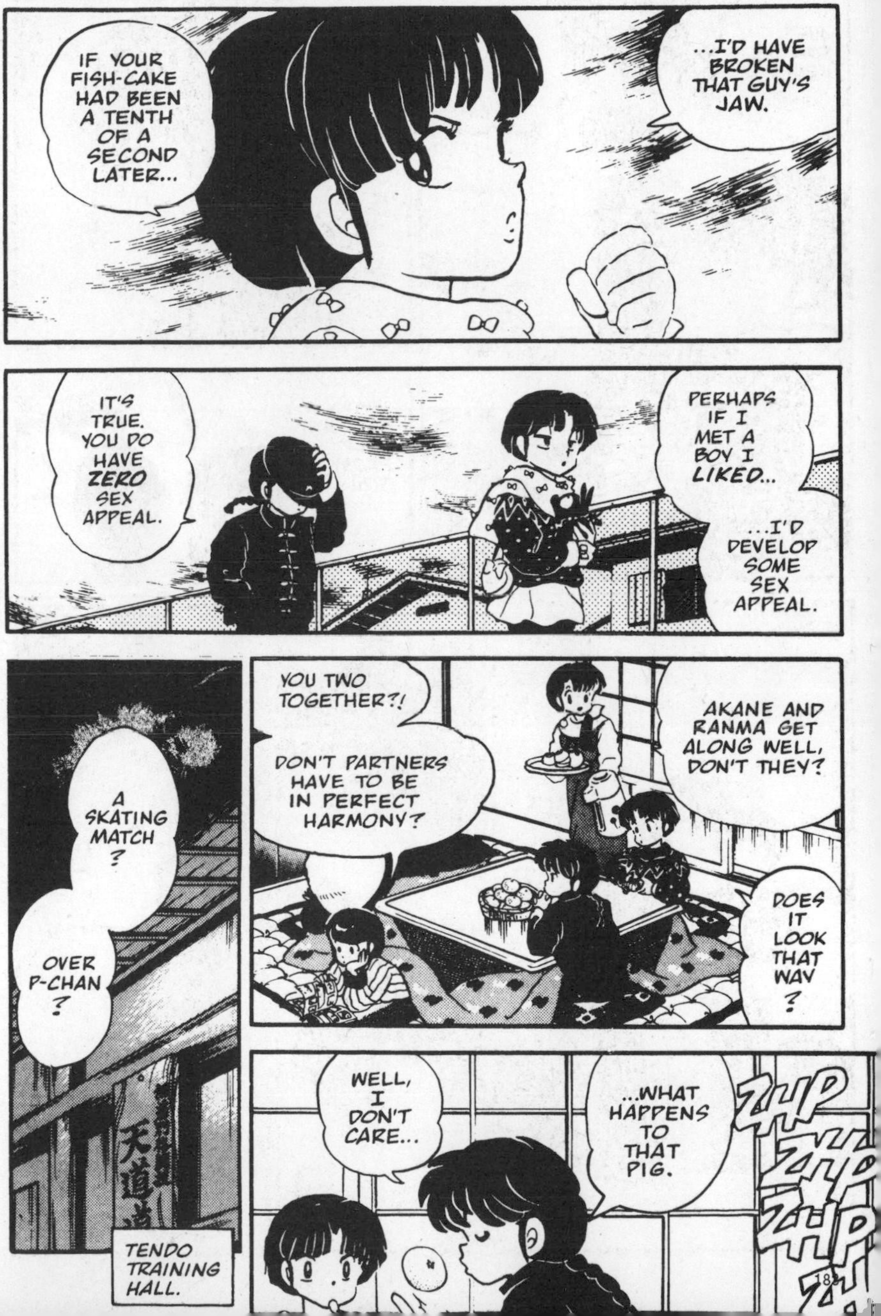
IF YOUR FISH-CAKE HAD BEEN A TENTH OF A SECOND LATER...
...I'D HAVE BROKEN THAT GUY'S JAW.
IT'S TRUE. YOU DO HAVE ZERO SEX APPEAL.
PERHAPS IF I MET A BOY I LIKED...
...I'D DEVELOP SOME SEX APPEAL.
A SKATING MATCH?
OVER P-CHAN?
TENDO TRAINING HALL.
YOU TWO TOGETHER?!
AKANE AND RANMA GET ALONG WELL, DON'T THEY?
DON'T PARTNERS HAVE TO BE IN PERFECT HARMONY?
DOES IT LOOK THAT WAY?
WELL, I DON'T CARE...
...WHAT HAPPENS TO THAT PIG.
ZHP ZHP ZHP ZHP

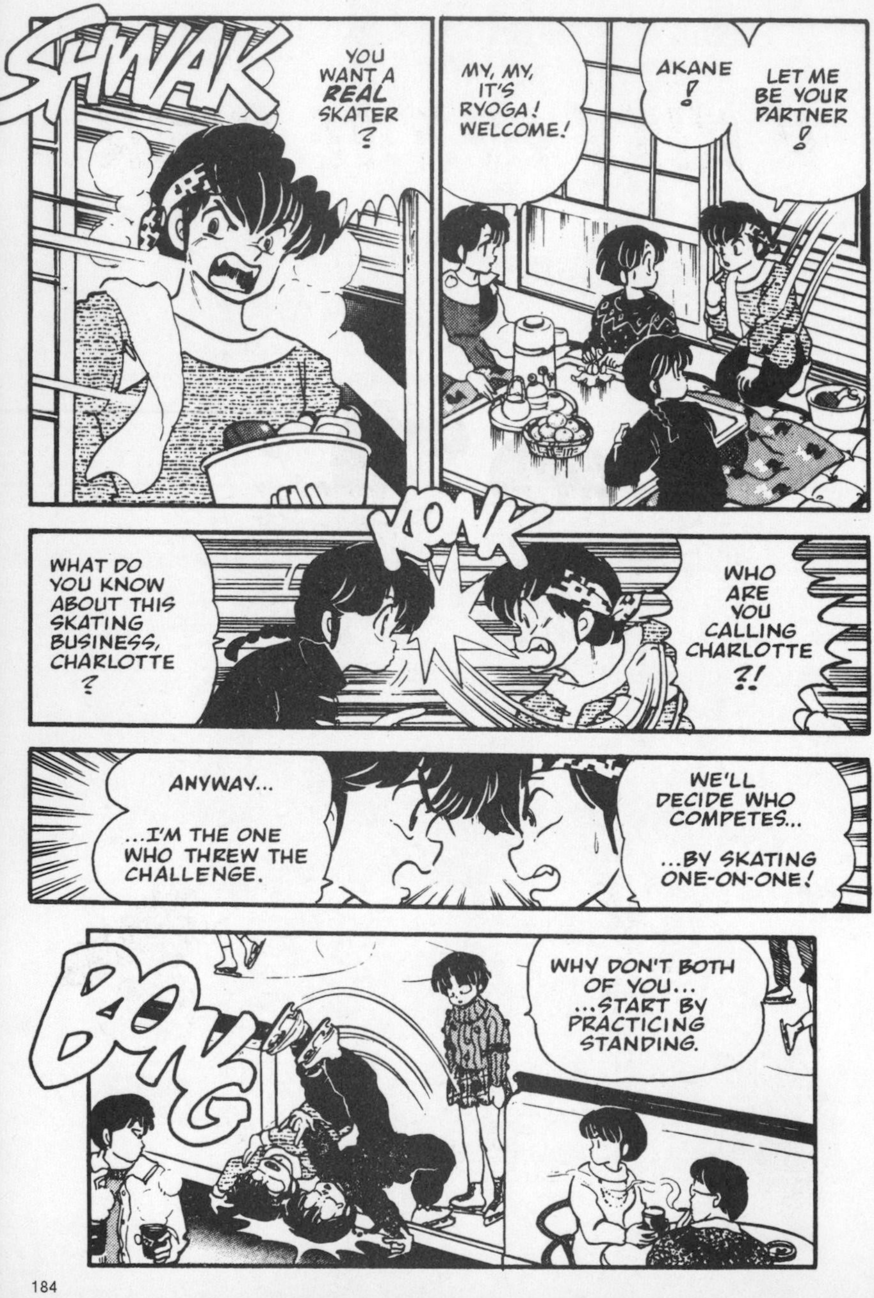
SHWAK
YOU WANT A REAL SKATER?
MY, MY, IT'S RYOGA! WELCOME!
AKANE!
LET ME BE YOUR PARTNER!
KONK
WHAT DO YOU KNOW ABOUT THIS SKATING BUSINESS, CHARLOTTE?
WHO ARE YOU CALLING CHARLOTTE?!
ANYWAY...
...I'M THE ONE WHO THREW THE CHALLENGE.
WE'LL DECIDE WHO COMPETES...
...BY SKATING ONE-ON-ONE!
BONG
WHY DON'T BOTH OF YOU... ...START BY PRACTICING STANDING.

Part 10

A KISS IN THE RINK

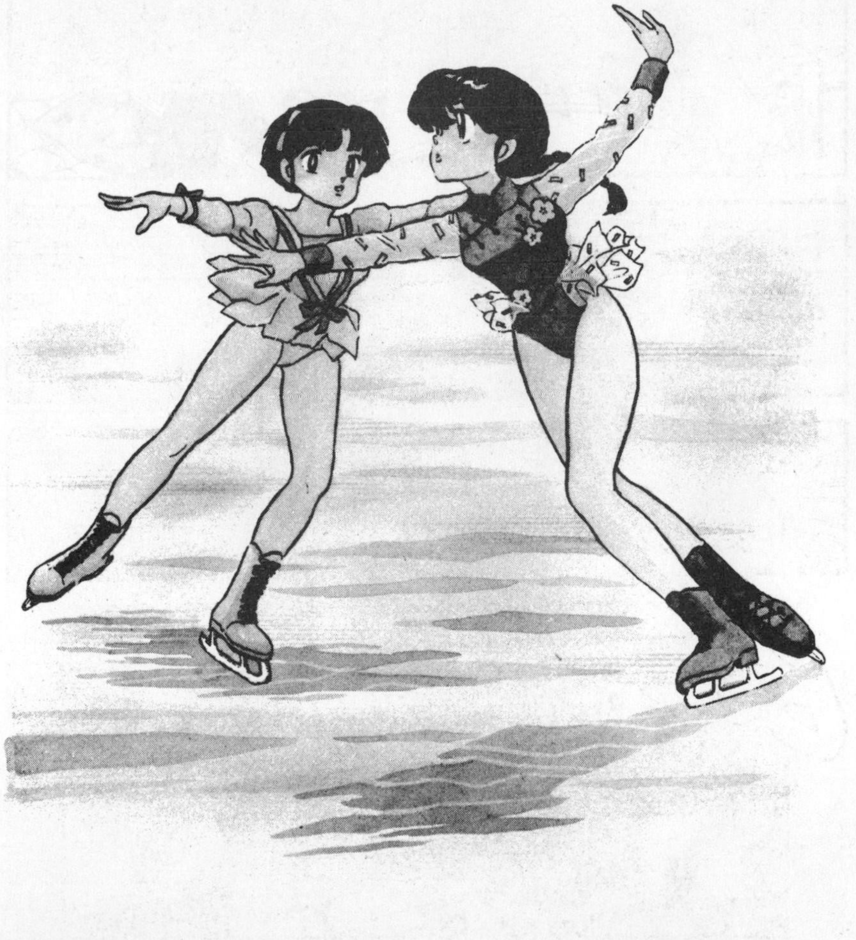

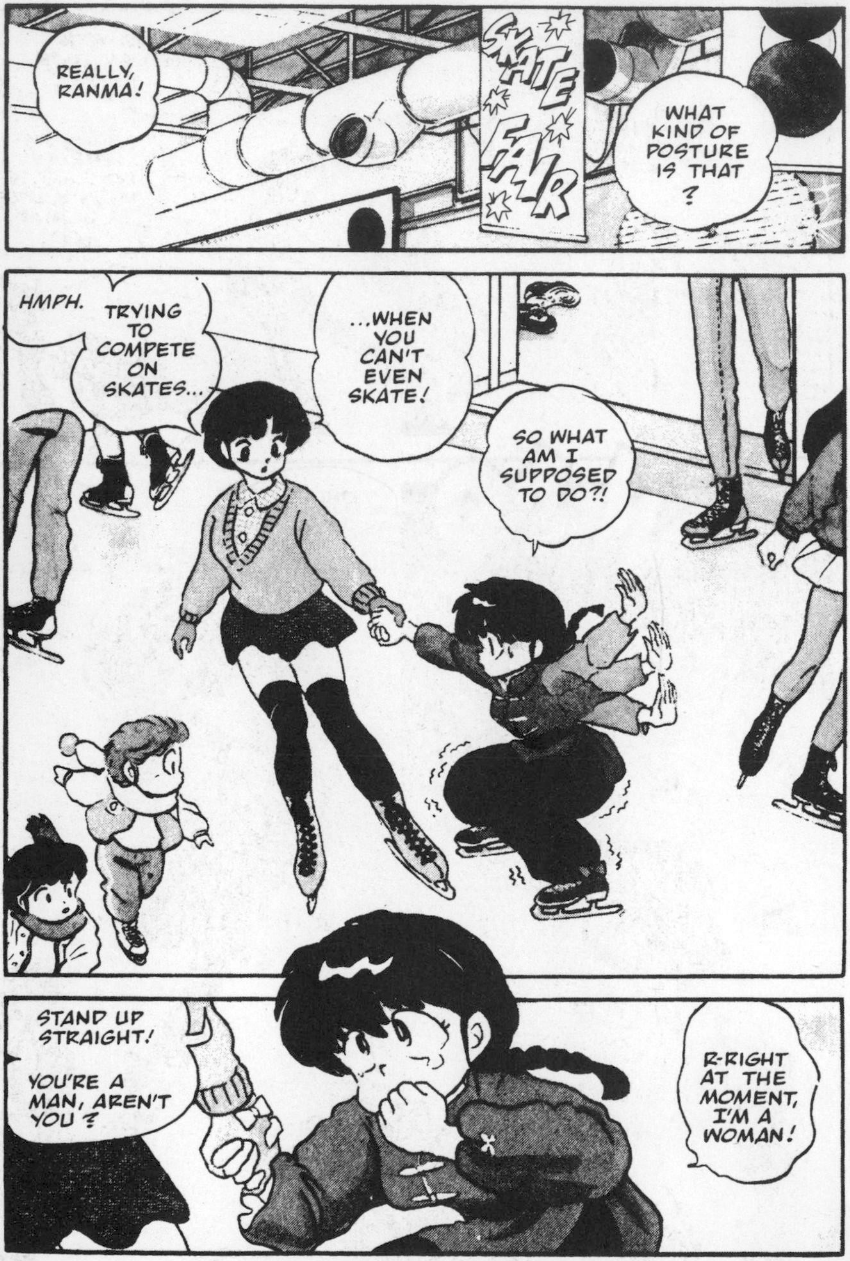
REALLY, RANMA!
SKATE FAIR
WHAT KIND OF POSTURE IS THAT ?
HMPH.
TRYING TO COMPETE ON SKATES...
...WHEN YOU CAN'T EVEN SKATE!
SO WHAT AM I SUPPOSED TO DO?!
STAND UP STRAIGHT!
YOU'RE A MAN, AREN'T YOU ?
R-RIGHT AT THE MOMENT, I'M A WOMAN!

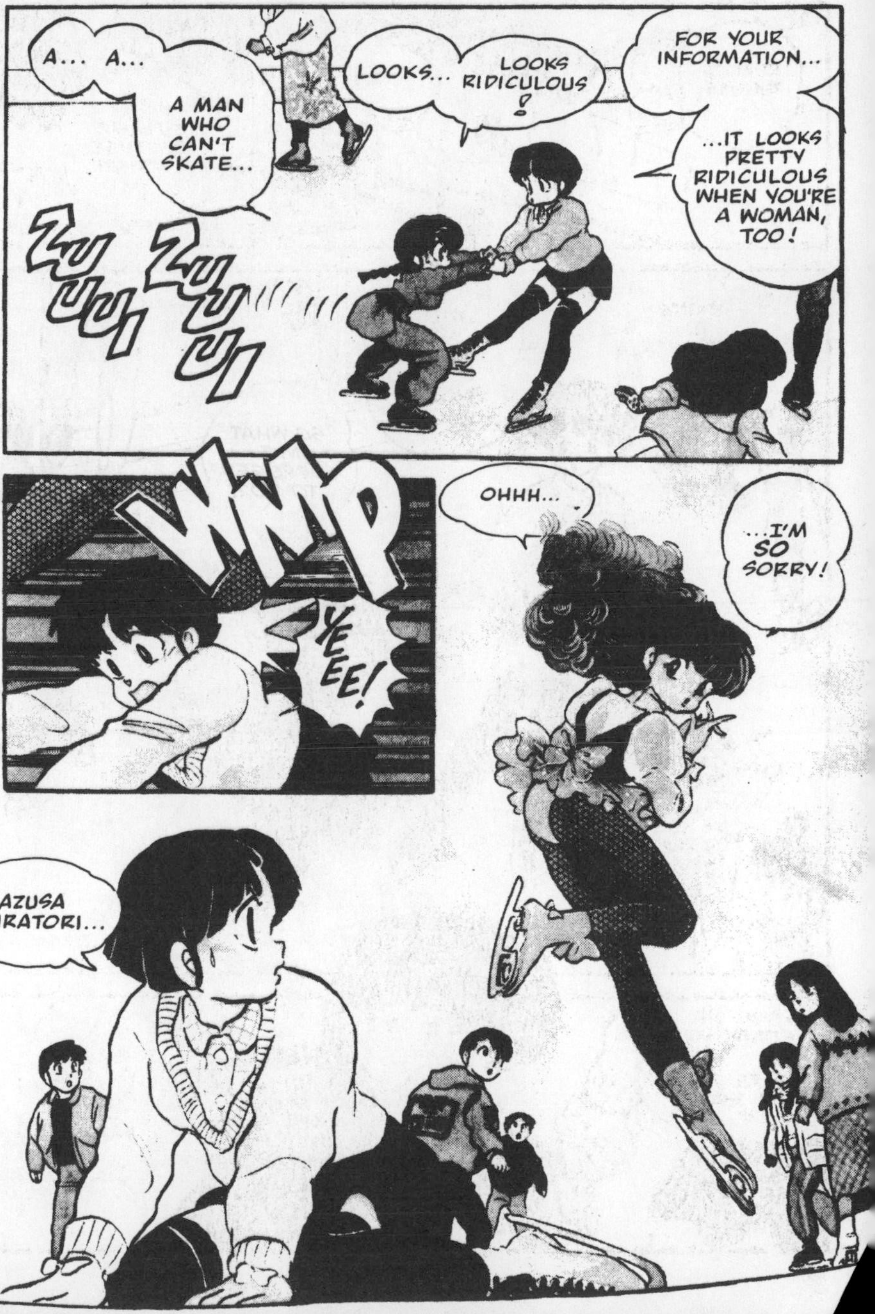
A... A...
A MAN WHO CAN'T SKATE...
LOOKS... LOOKS RIDICULOUS!
FOR YOUR INFORMATION...
...IT LOOKS PRETTY RIDICULOUS WHEN YOU'RE A WOMAN, TOO!
ZUUUI
ZUUUI
WMP
YEEEE!
OHHH...
...I'M SO SORRY!
AZUSA SHIRATORI...

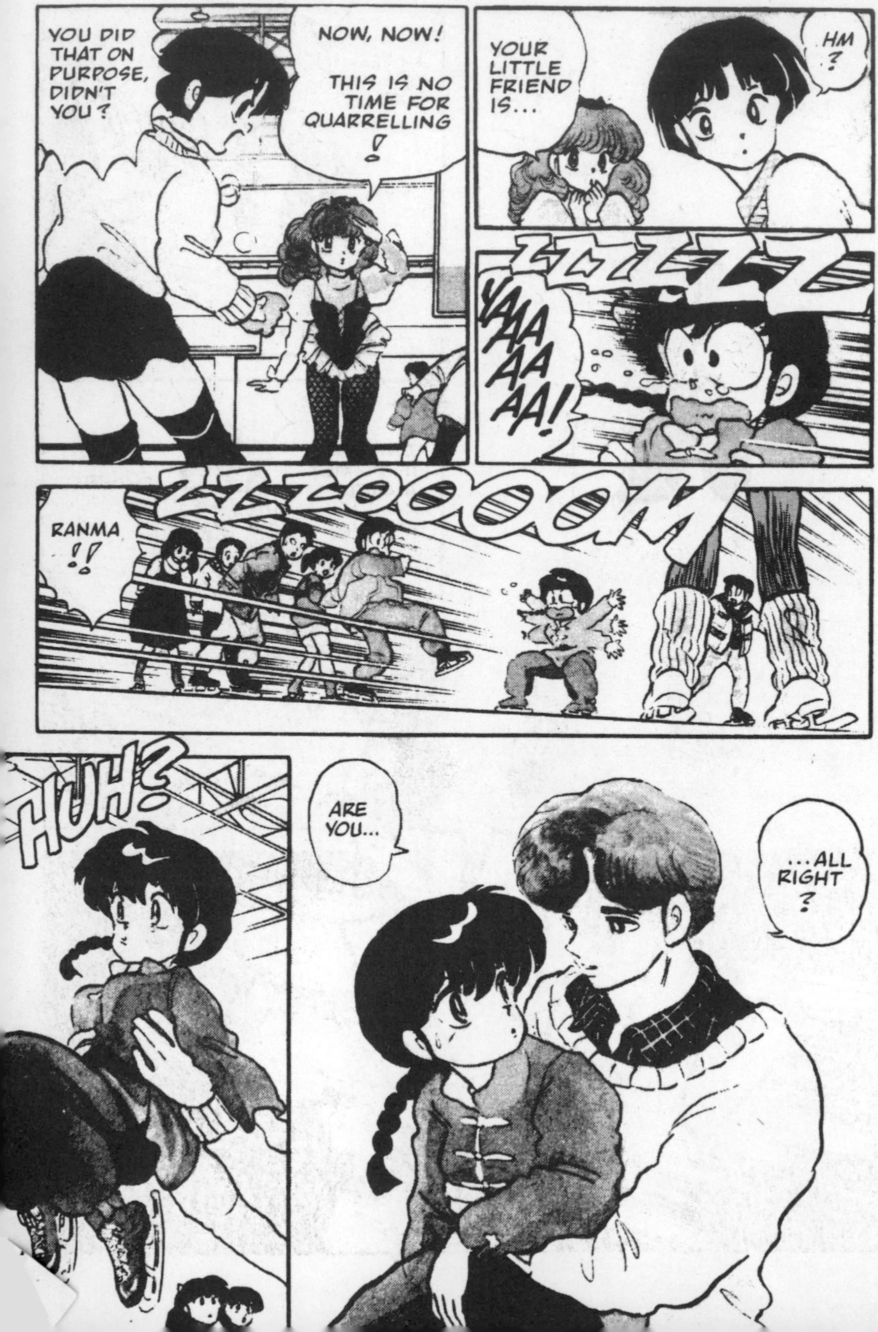
YOU DID THAT ON PURPOSE, DIDN'T YOU?
NOW, NOW!
THIS IS NO TIME FOR QUARRELLING!
YOUR LITTLE FRIEND IS...
HM?
ZZZZZZ
YAAAAAAAAA!
ZZZOOOOOM
RANMA!!
HUH?
ARE YOU...
...ALL RIGHT?

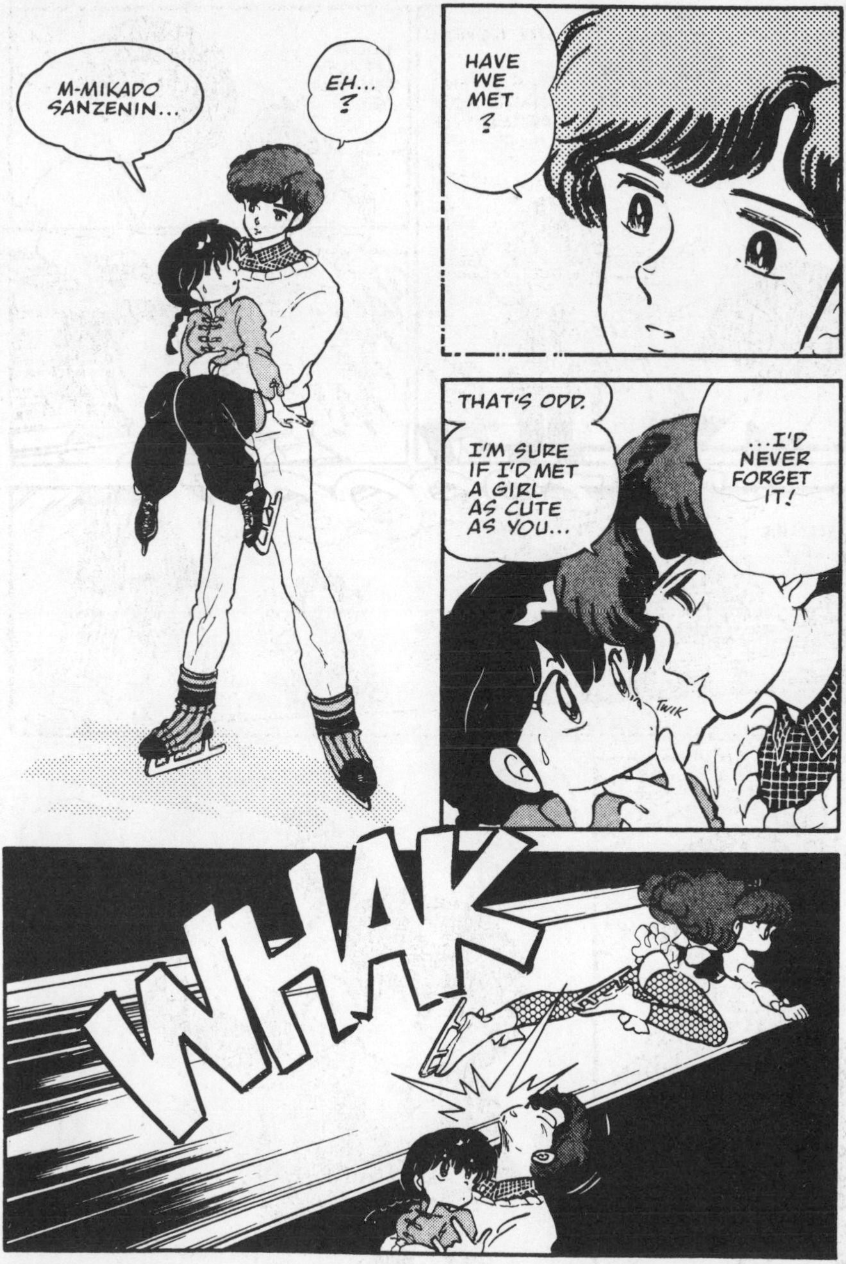
M-MIKADO SANZENIN...
EH...?
HAVE WE MET?
THAT'S ODD.
I'M SURE IF I'D MET A GIRL AS CUTE AS YOU...
...I'D NEVER FORGET IT!
TWIK
WHAK

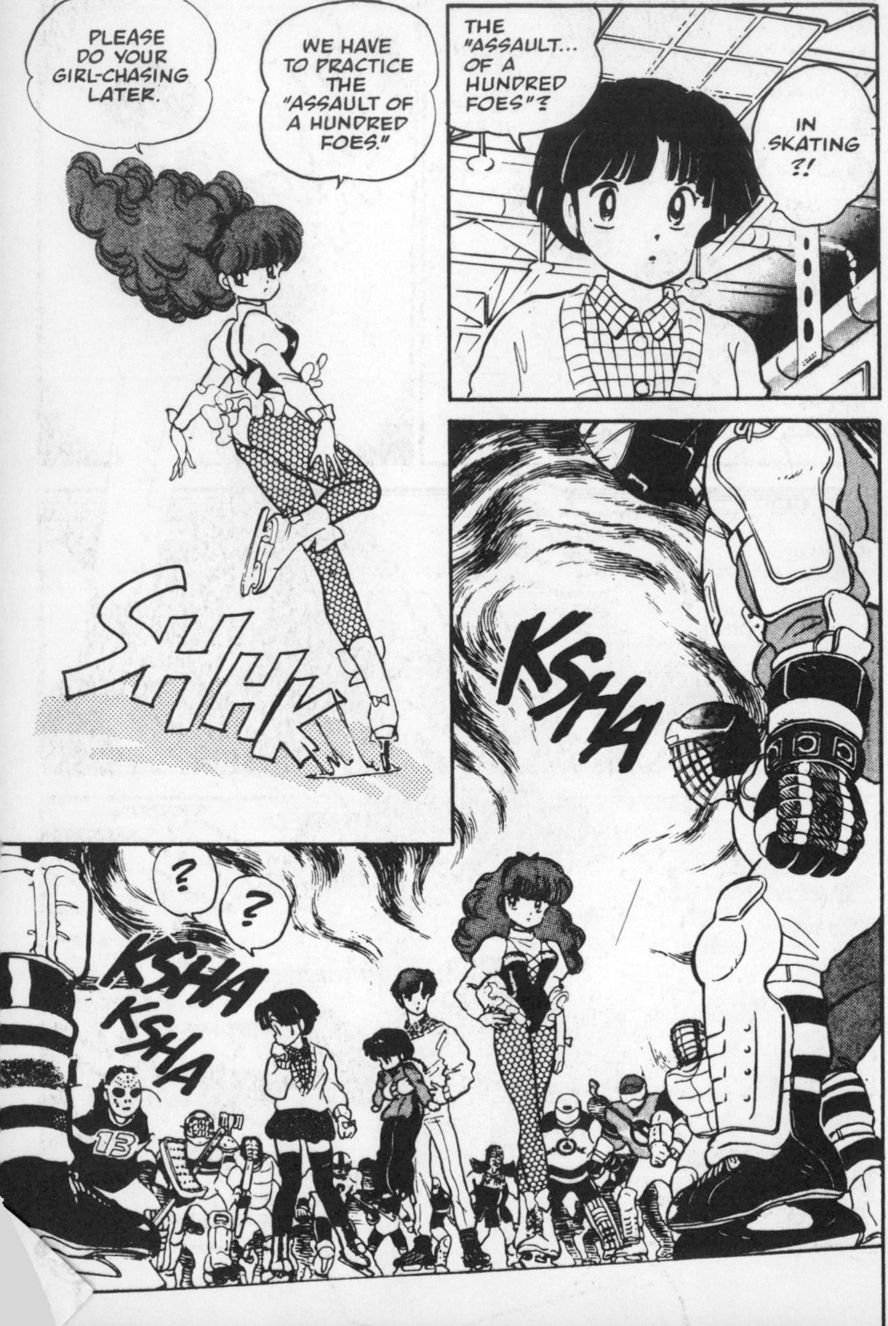
PLEASE DO YOUR GIRL-CHASING LATER.
WE HAVE TO PRACTICE THE "ASSAULT OF A HUNDRED FOES."
SHHK
THE "ASSAULT... OF A HUNDRED FOES"?
IN SKATING ?!
KSHA
?
?
KSHA KSHA KSHA

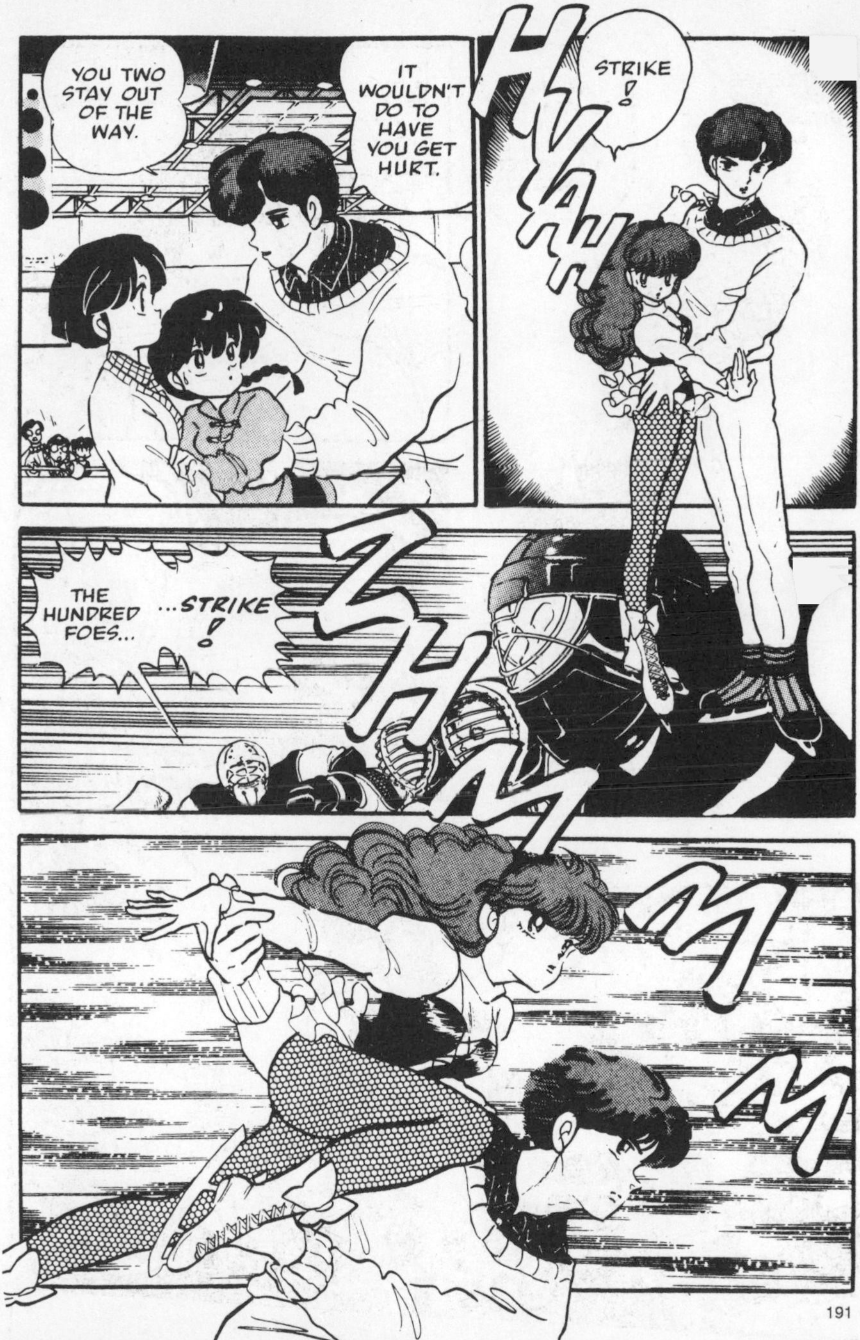
YOU TWO STAY OUT OF THE WAY.
IT WOULDN'T DO TO HAVE YOU GET HURT.
HYAAH
STRIKE!
THE HUNDRED FOES...
...STRIKE!
ZHMMMM

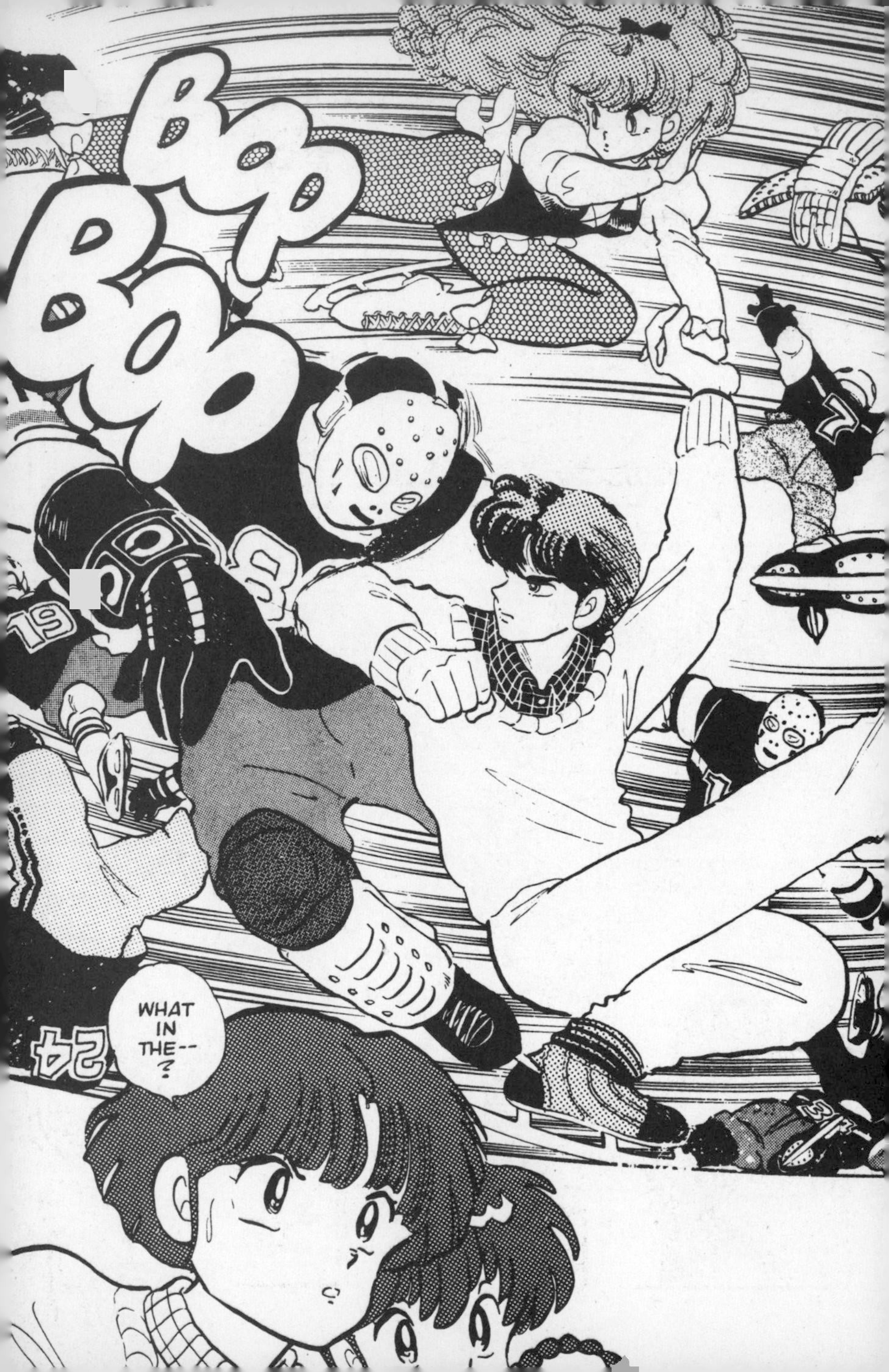
BOP BOP BOP
WHAT IN THE--?

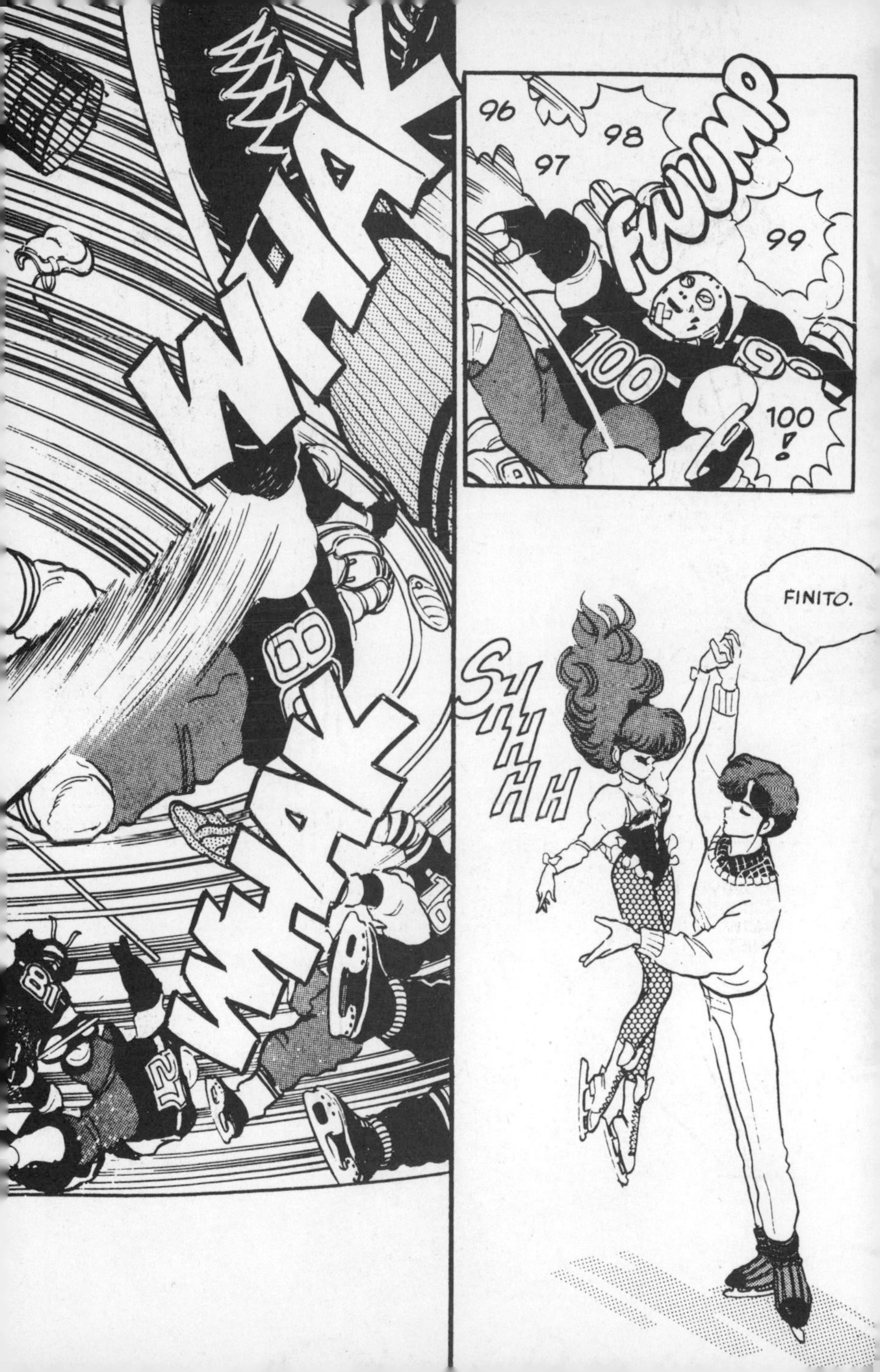
WHAK
WHAK
96
97
98
FWUMP
99
100!
SHHHH
FINITO.

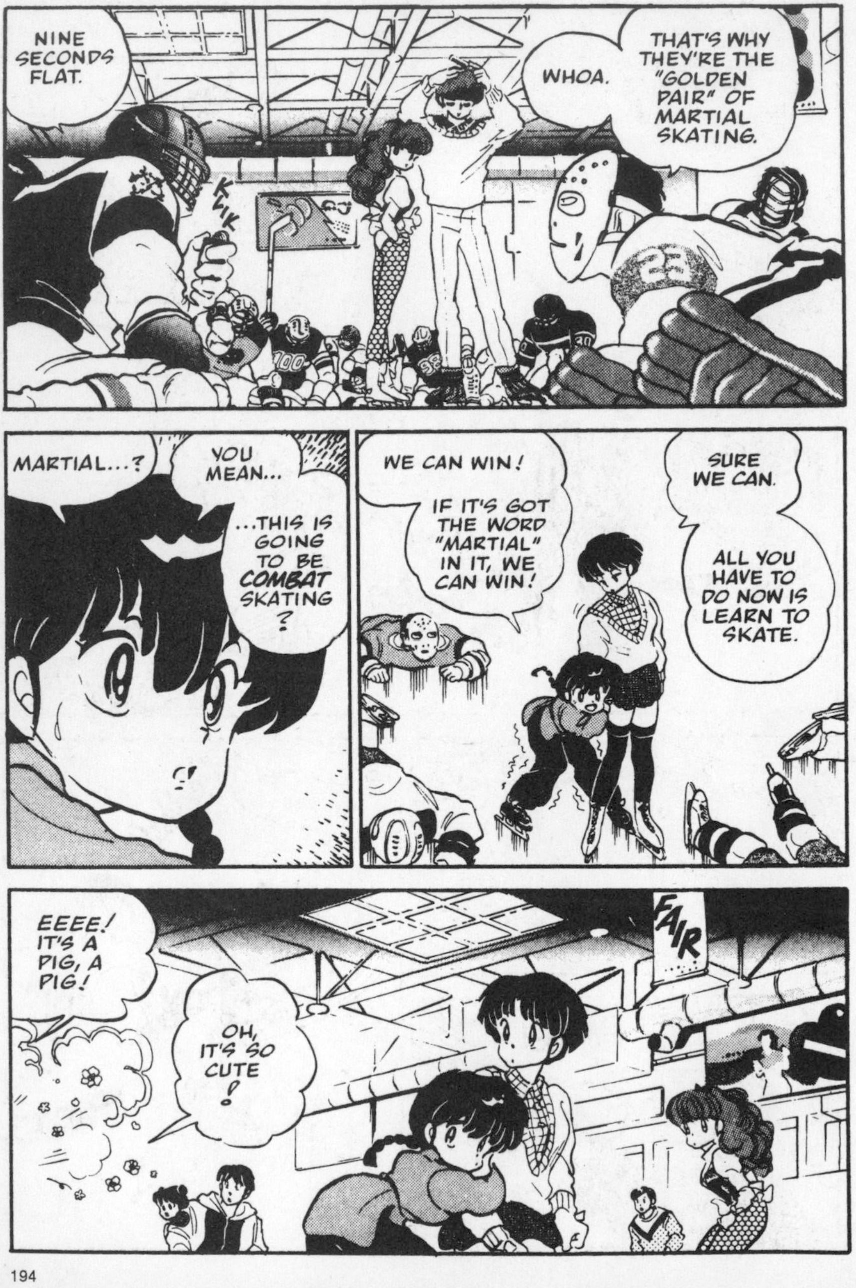
NINE SECONDS FLAT.
KVIK
WHOA.
THAT'S WHY THEY'RE THE "GOLDEN PAIR" OF MARTIAL SKATING.
MARTIAL...?
YOU MEAN...
...THIS IS GOING TO BE COMBAT SKATING?
WE CAN WIN!
IF IT'S GOT THE WORD "MARTIAL" IN IT, WE CAN WIN!
SURE WE CAN.
ALL YOU HAVE TO DO NOW IS LEARN TO SKATE.
EEEE! IT'S A PIG, A PIG!
OH, IT'S SO CUTE!
FAIR

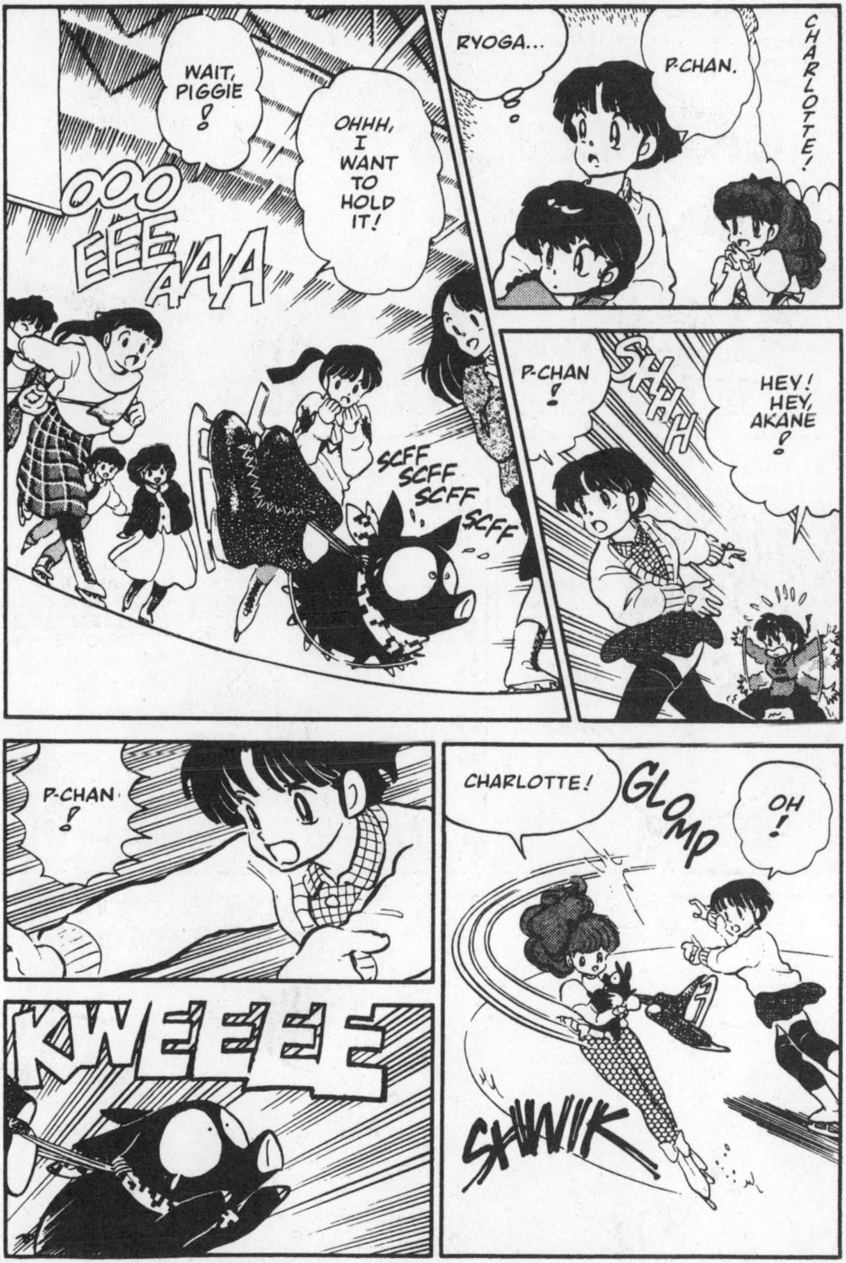
WAIT, PIGGIE!
OHHH, I WANT TO HOLD IT!
OOO EEE AAA
SCFF SCFF SCFF SCFF
RYOGA...
P-CHAN.
CHARLOTTE!
P-CHAN!
SHHH
HEY! HEY, AKANE!
P-CHAN!
KWEEEE
CHARLOTTE!
GLOMP
OH!
SHWIK

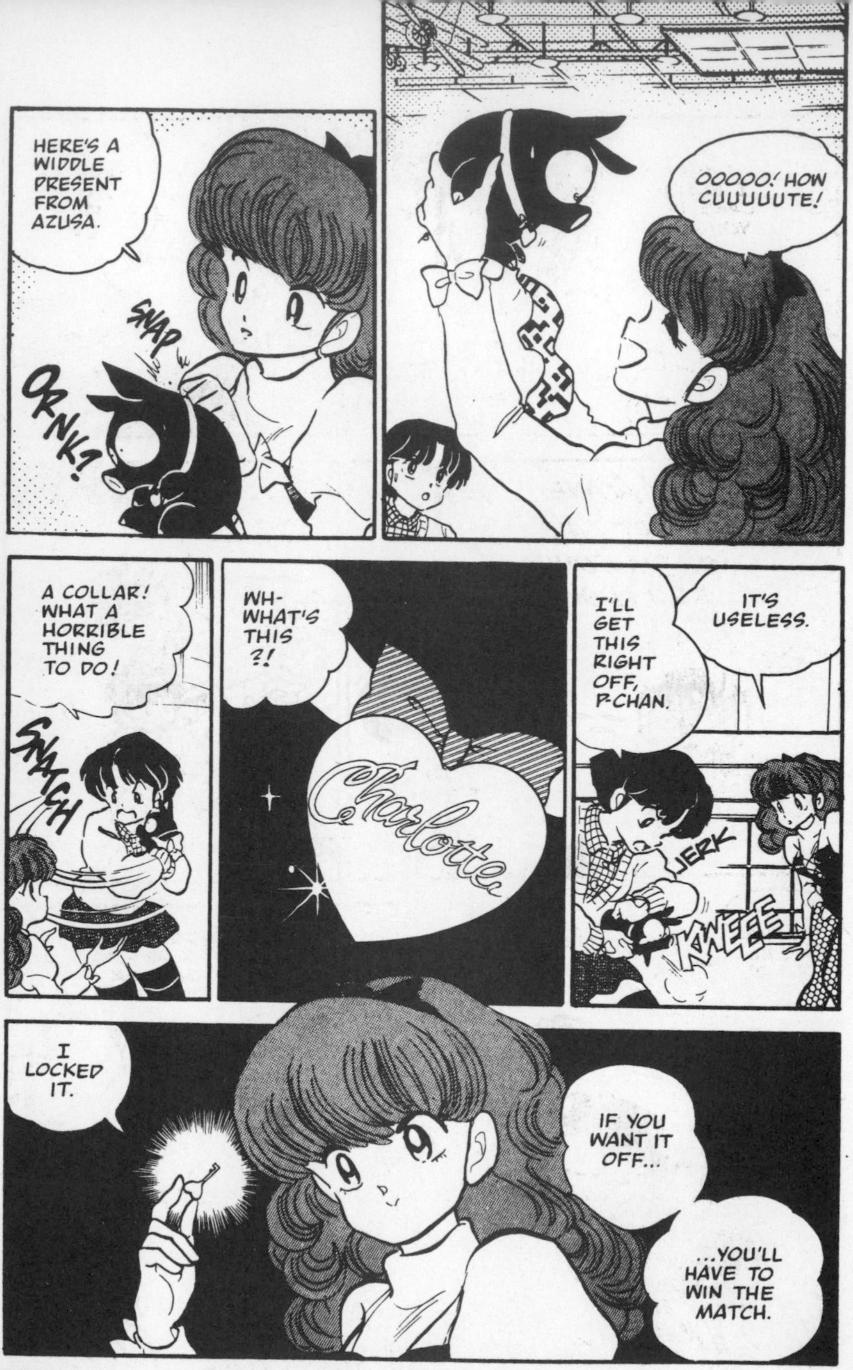
HERE'S A WIDDLE PRESENT FROM AZUSA.
SNAP
ORNK!?
OOOOO! HOW CUUUUUTE!
A COLLAR! WHAT A HORRIBLE THING TO DO!
SNATCH
WH-WHAT'S THIS ?!
Charlotte
I'LL GET THIS RIGHT OFF, P-CHAN.
IT'S USELESS.
JERK
KWEEEE
I LOCKED IT.
IF YOU WANT IT OFF...
...YOU'LL HAVE TO WIN THE MATCH.

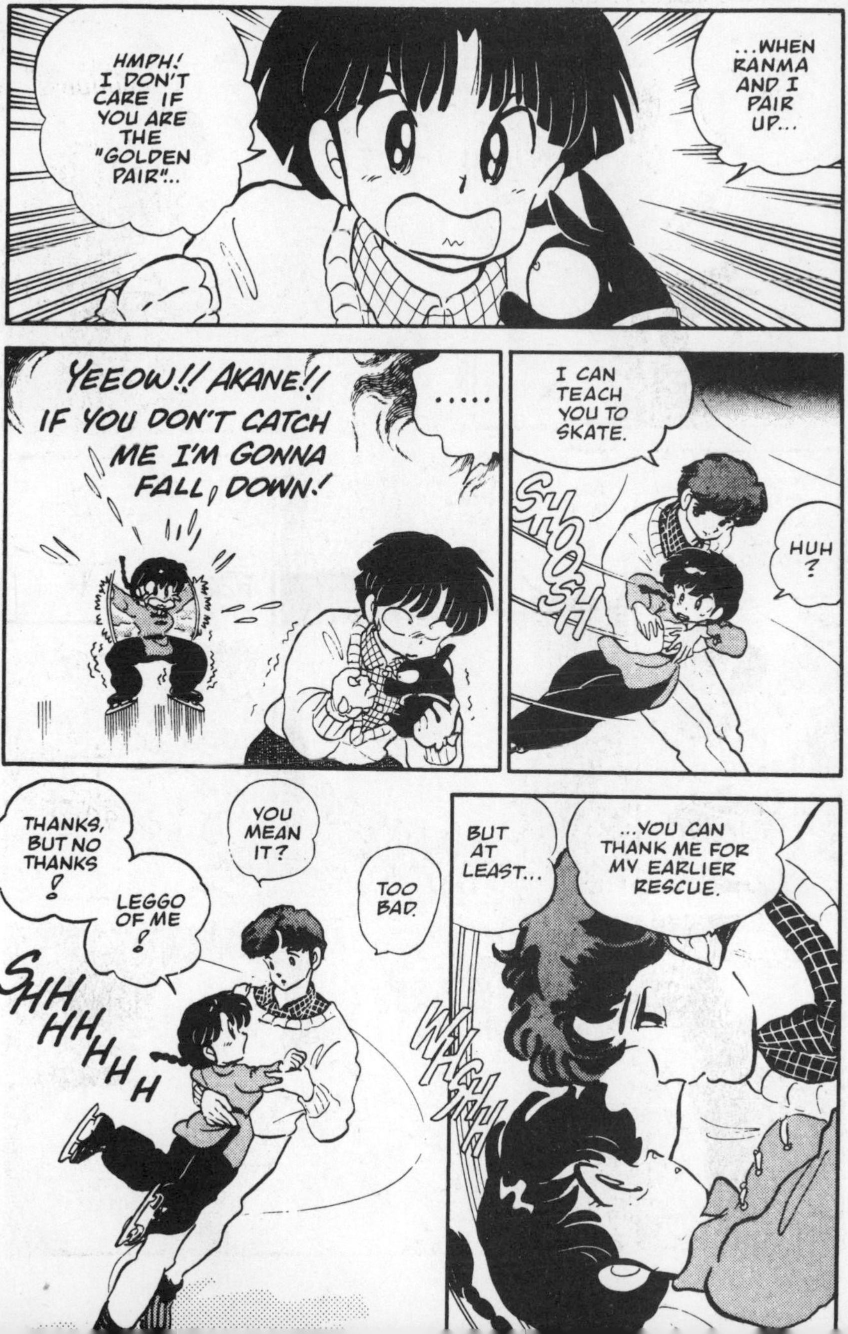
HMPH! I DON'T CARE IF YOU ARE THE "GOLDEN PAIR"...
...WHEN RANMA AND I PAIR UP...
YEEOW!! AKANE!! IF YOU DON'T CATCH ME I'M GONNA FALL DOWN!
.....
I CAN TEACH YOU TO SKATE.
SHOOSH
HUH?
THANKS, BUT NO THANKS!
LEGGO OF ME!
YOU MEAN IT?
TOO BAD.
SHHHHHHH
BUT AT LEAST...
...YOU CAN THANK ME FOR MY EARLIER RESCUE.

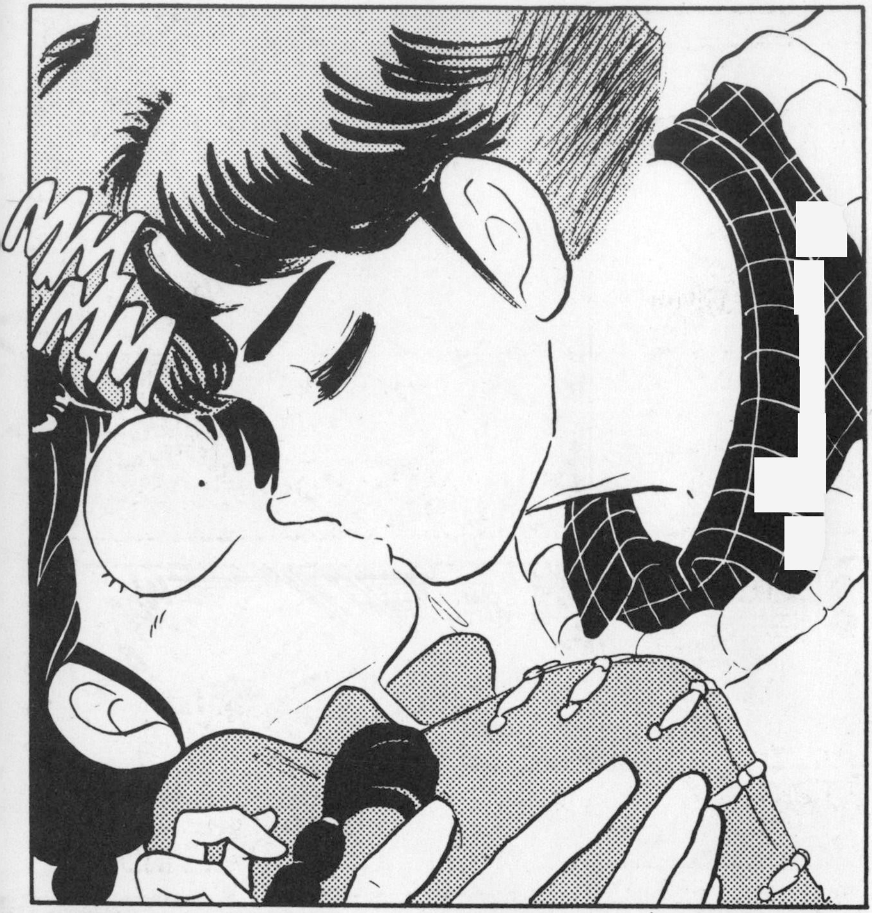
MMMM

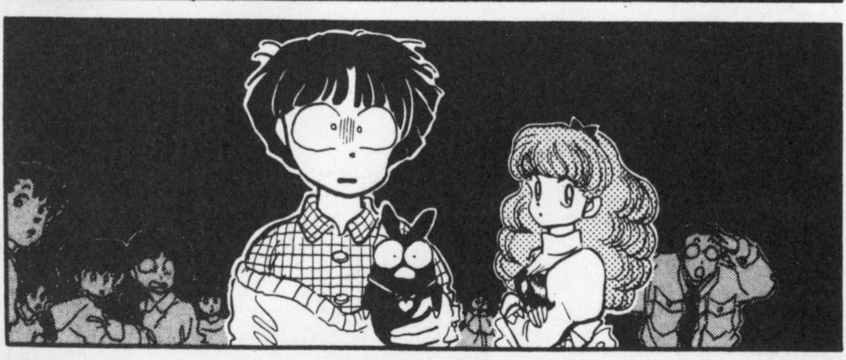

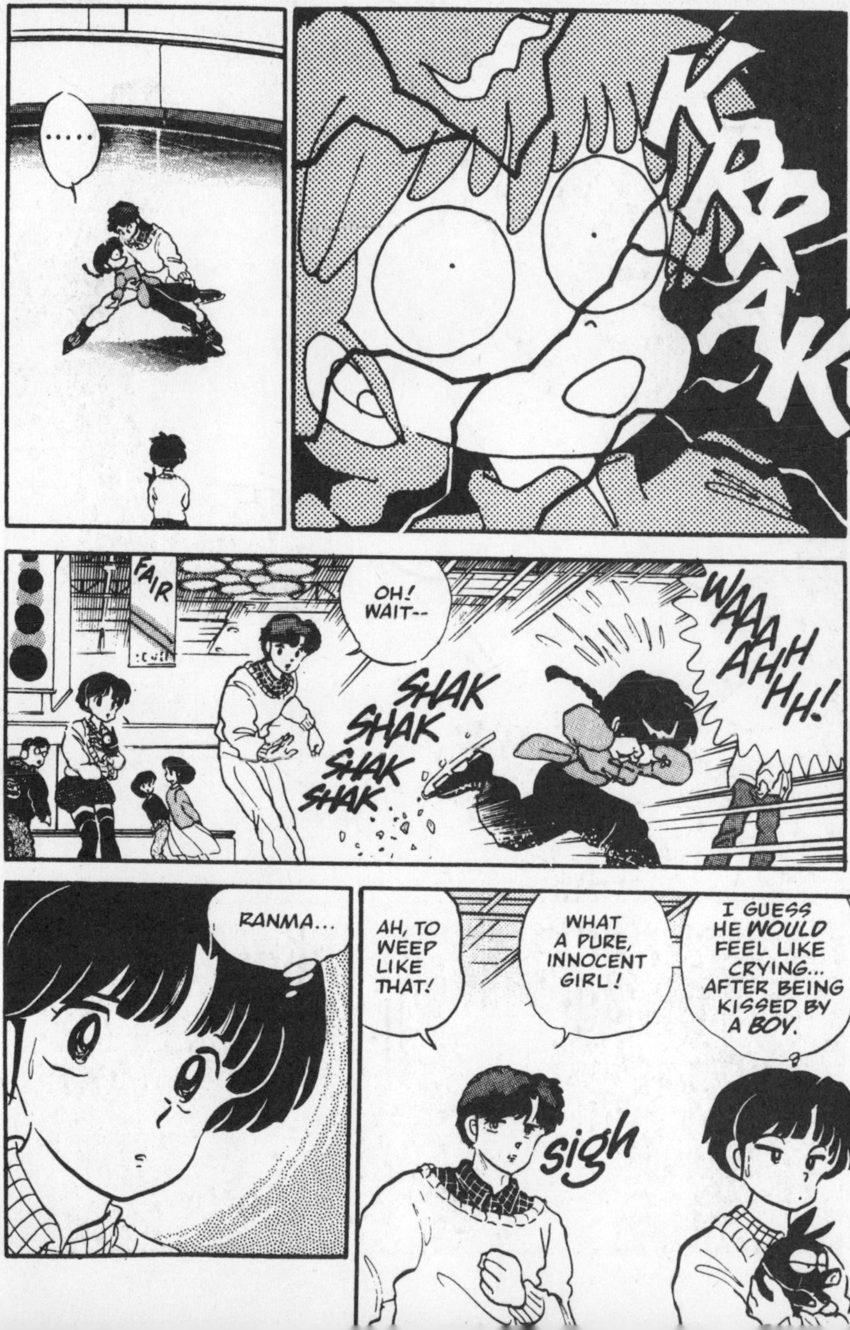
......
KRRAK
FAIR
OH! WAIT--
SHAK SHAK SHAK SHAK
WAAAAHH AHHHH!
RANMA...
AH, TO WEEP LIKE THAT!
WHAT A PURE, INNOCENT GIRL!
I GUESS HE WOULD FEEL LIKE CRYING... AFTER BEING KISSED BY A BOY.
sigh

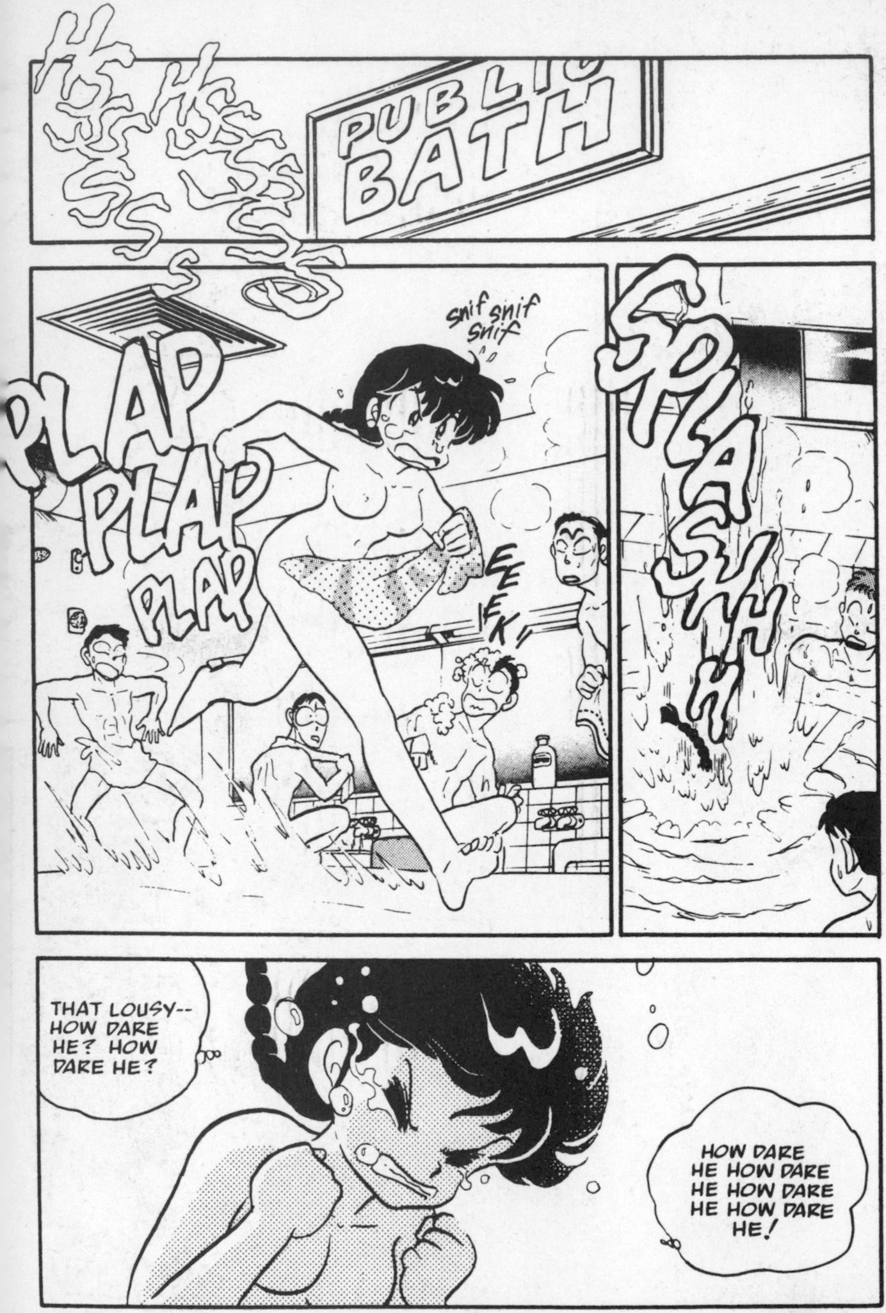

PUBLIC BATH
HSSSSS HSSSSS
snif snif snif
PLAP PLAP PLAP PLAP
EEEEK
SPLASHHH
THAT LOUSY-- HOW DARE HE? HOW DARE HE?
HOW DARE HE HOW DARE HE HOW DARE HE HOW DARE HE!

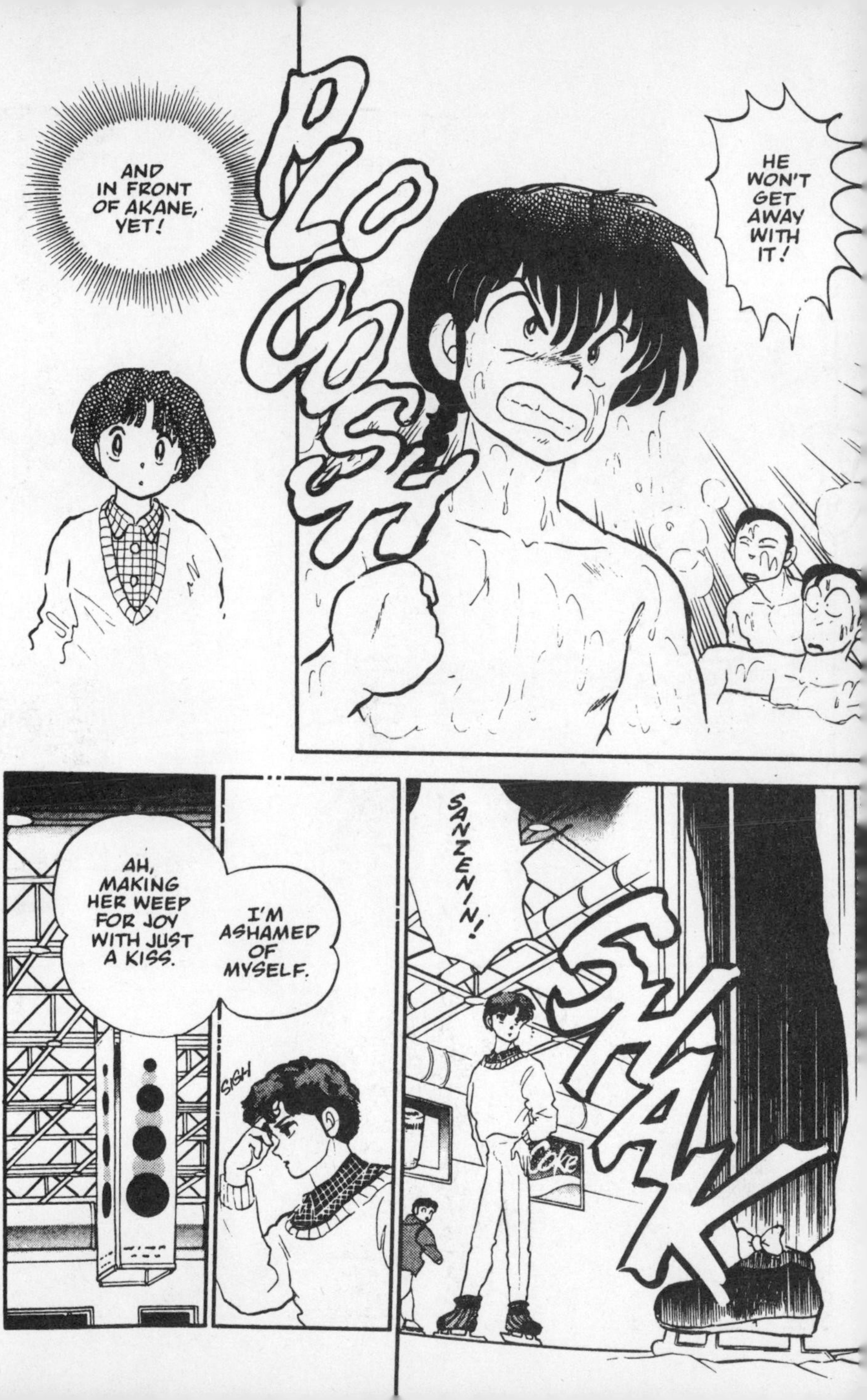
AND IN FRONT OF AKANE, YET!
PLOOSH
HE WON'T GET AWAY WITH IT!
AH, MAKING HER WEEP FOR JOY WITH JUST A KISS.
I'M ASHAMED OF MYSELF.
SIGH
SANZENIN!
SMAK
Coke

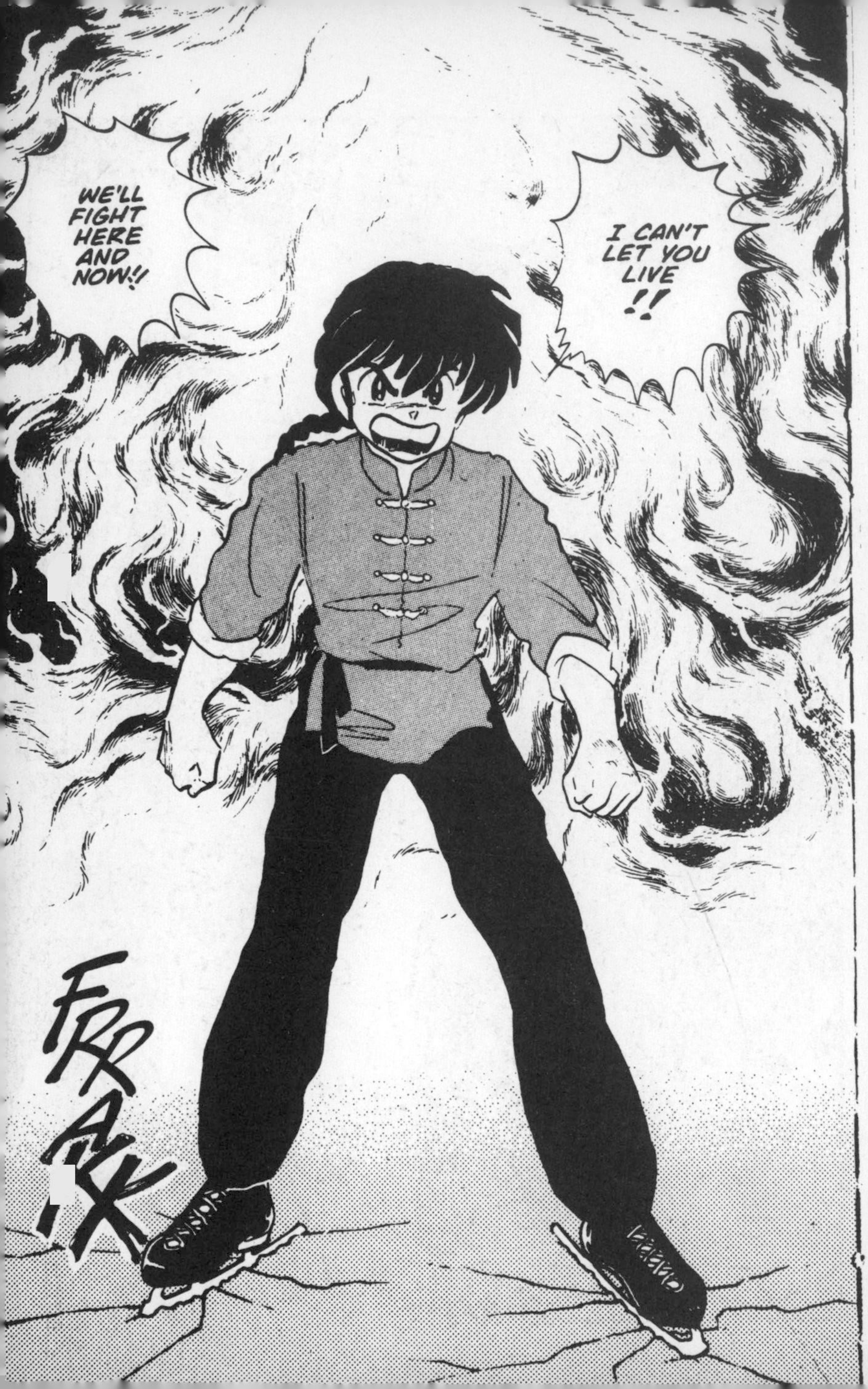
WE'LL FIGHT HERE AND NOW!!
I CAN'T LET YOU LIVE !!
FRRANK

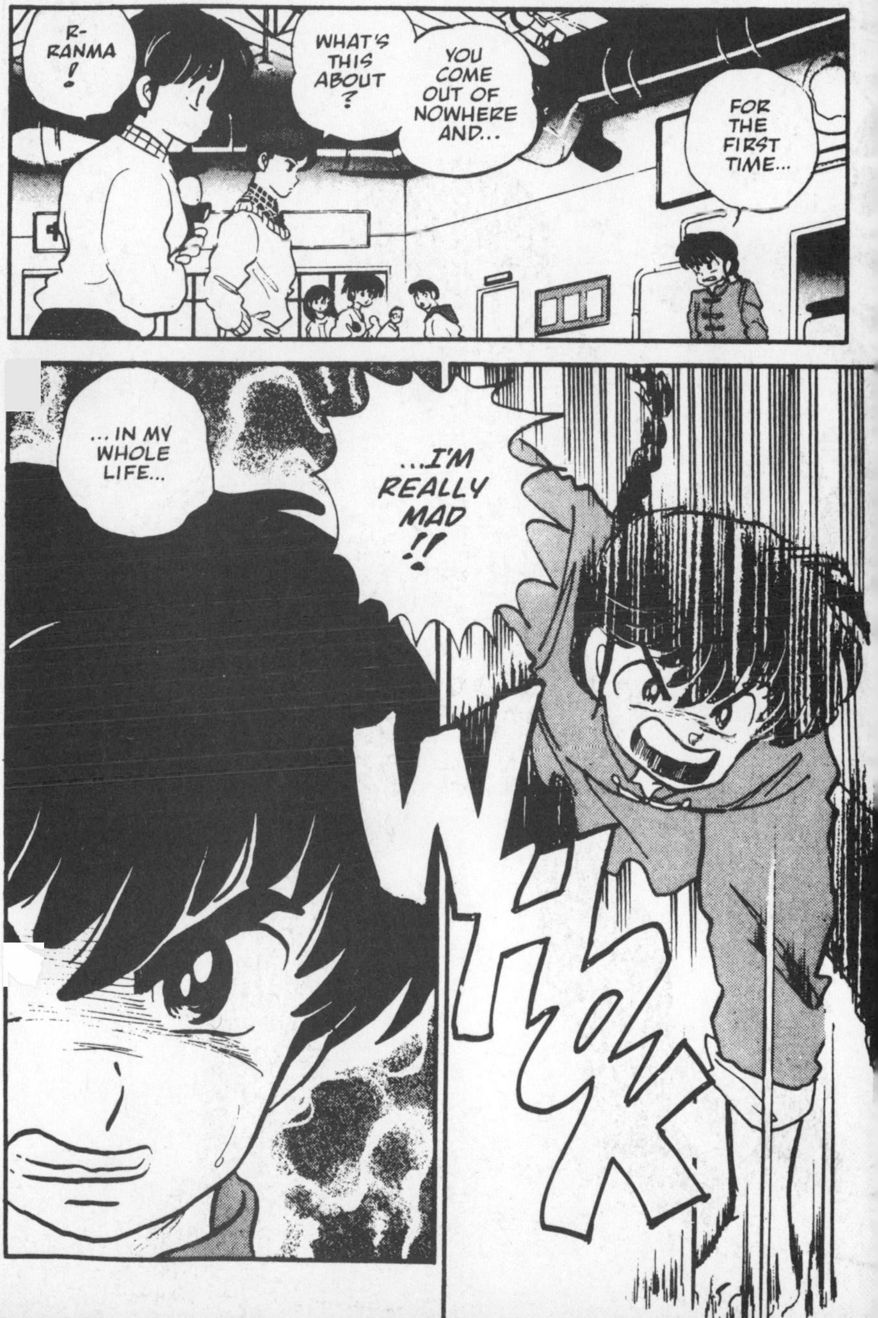
R-RANMA!
WHAT'S THIS ABOUT?
YOU COME OUT OF NOWHERE AND...
FOR THE FIRST TIME...
...IN MY WHOLE LIFE...
...I'M REALLY MAD!!

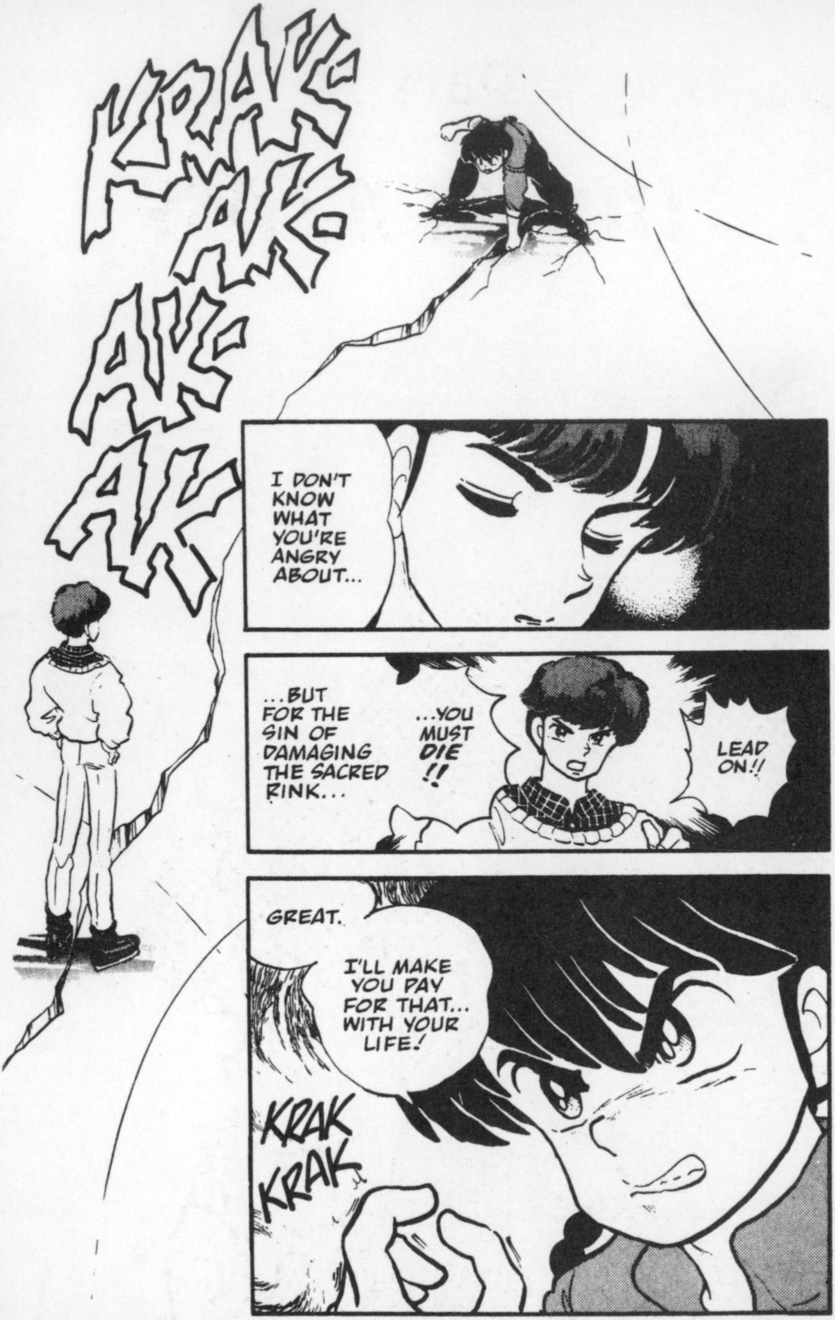
KRAKAK-AK-AK
I DON'T KNOW WHAT YOU'RE ANGRY ABOUT...
...BUT FOR THE SIN OF DAMAGING THE SACRED RINK...
...YOU MUST DIE!!
LEAD ON!!
GREAT.
I'LL MAKE YOU PAY FOR THAT... WITH YOUR LIFE!
KRAK KRAK

Part 11

LIPS AT A LOSS

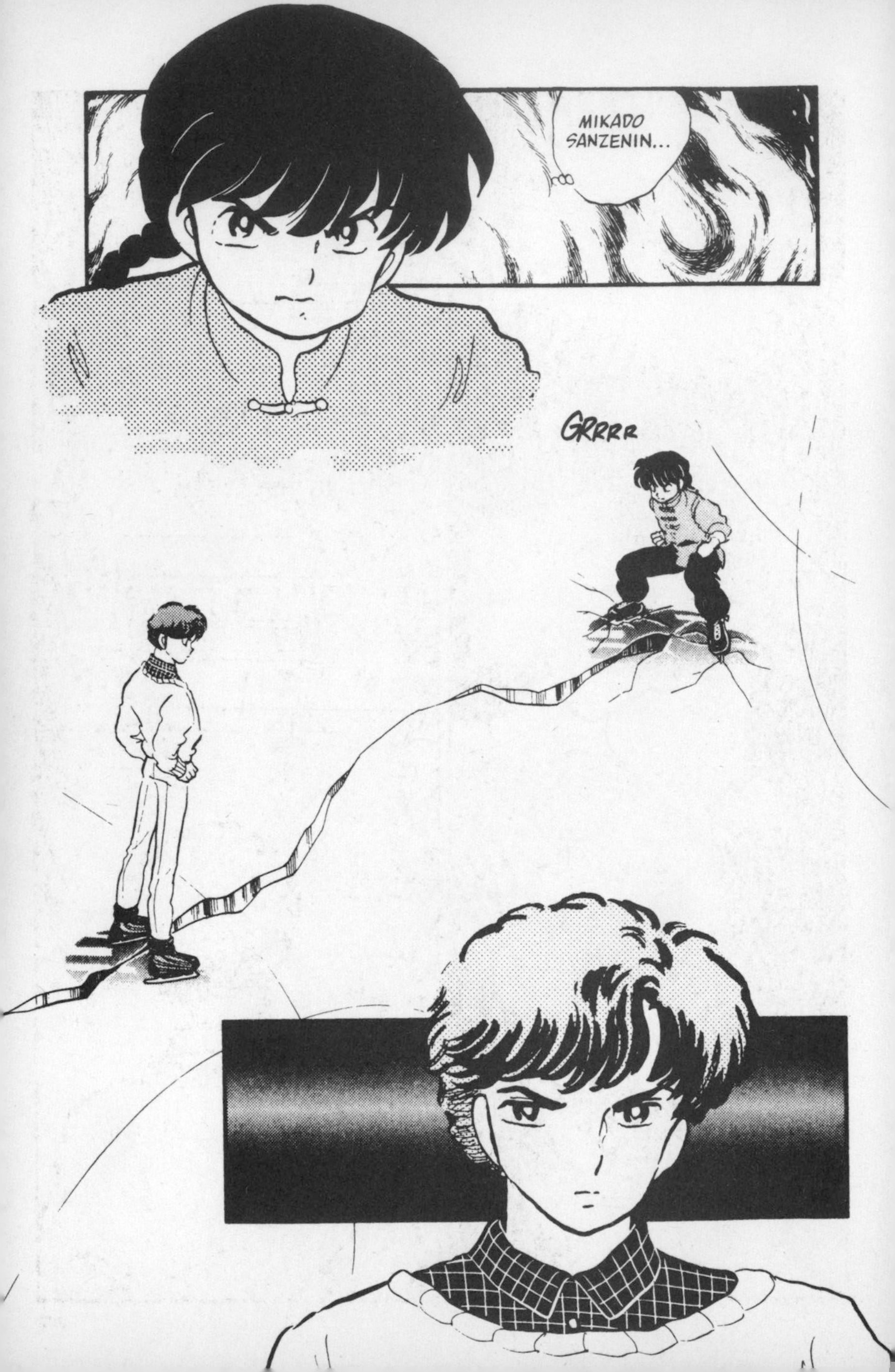
MIKADO SANZENIN...
GRRRR

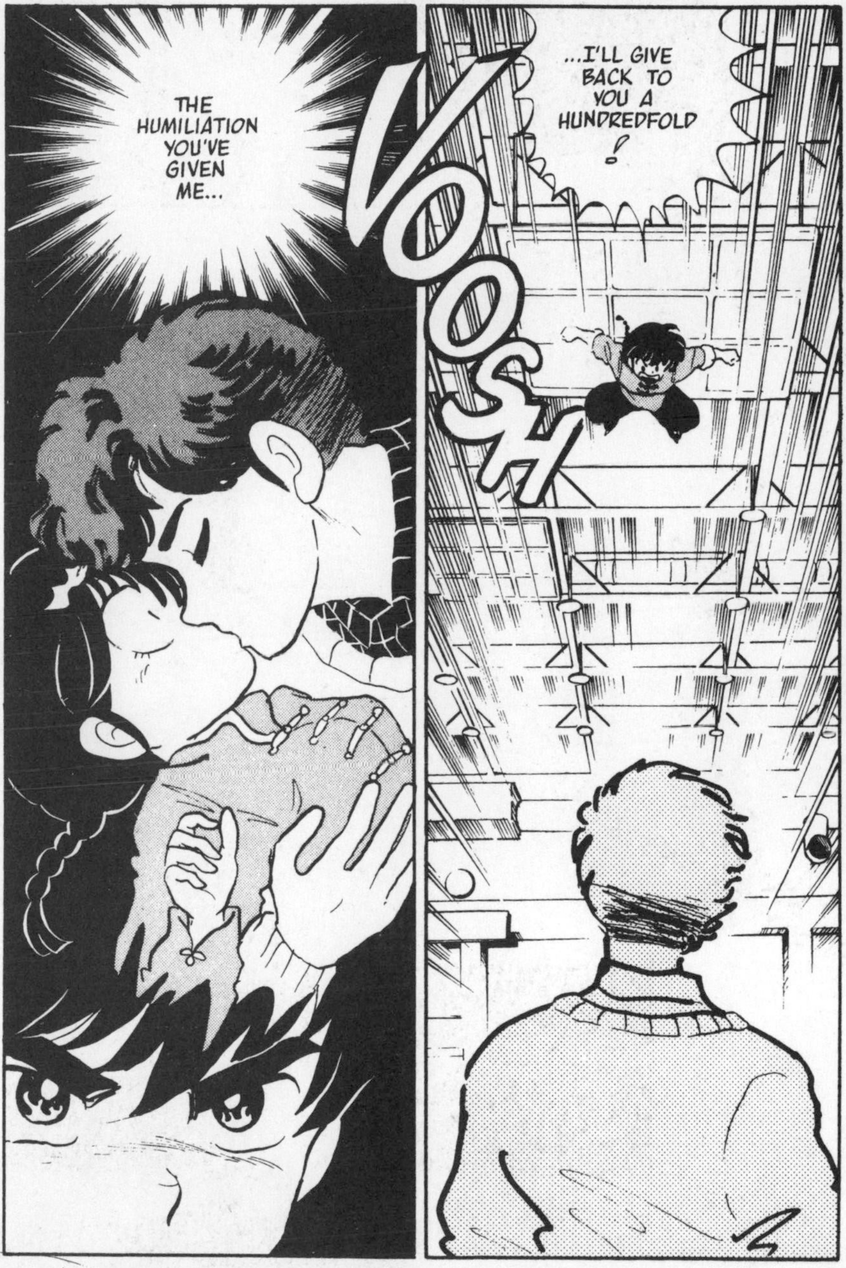
THE HUMILIATION YOU'VE GIVEN ME...
VOOSH
...I'LL GIVE BACK TO YOU A HUNDREDFOLD!

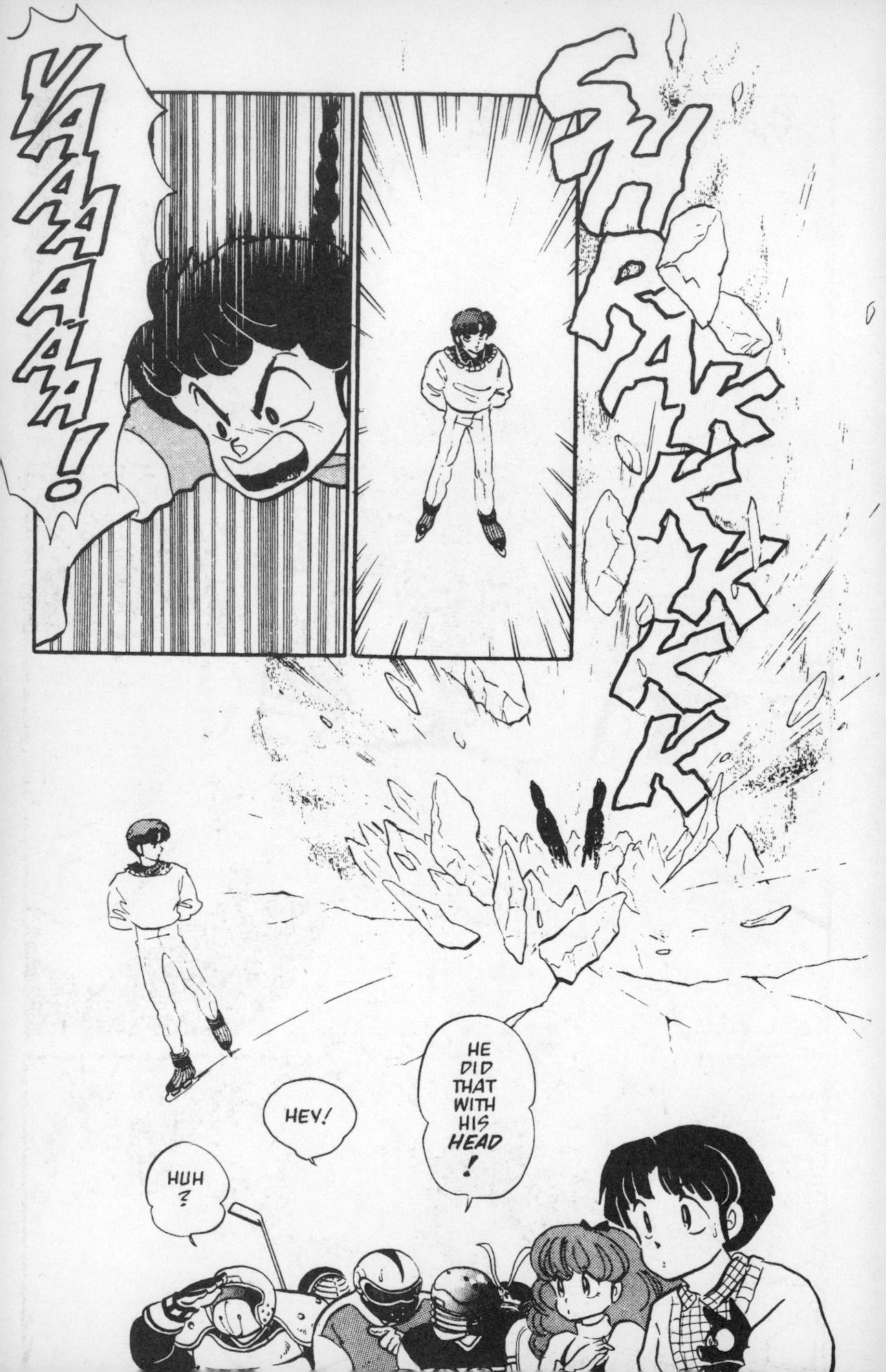
YAAAAAAA!
SHAKKKKK
HEY!
HUH?
HE DID THAT WITH HIS HEAD!

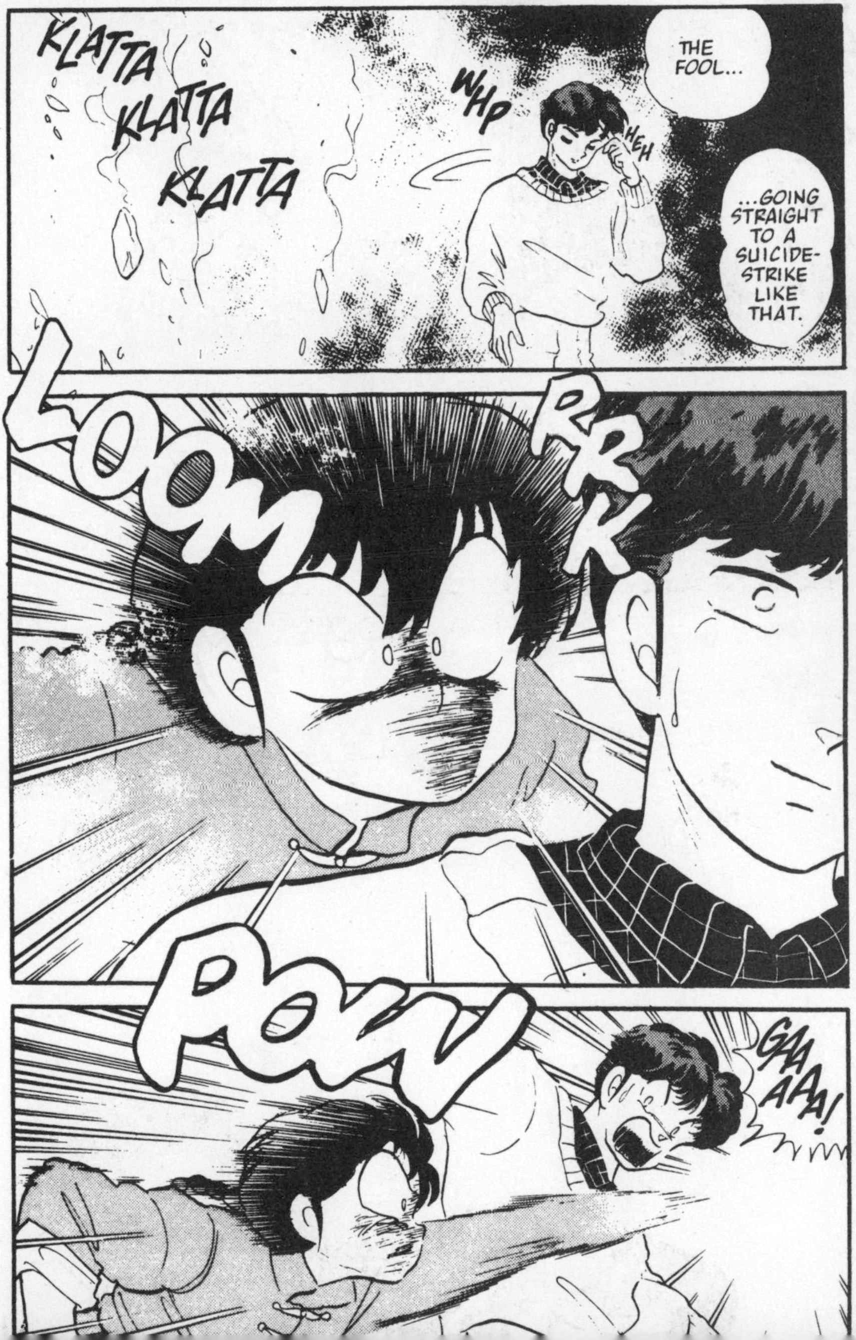
KLATTA
KLATTA
KLATTA
WHP
THE FOOL...
HEH
...GOING STRAIGHT TO A SUICIDE-STRIKE LIKE THAT.
LOOM
RRK
POW
GAAAAAA!

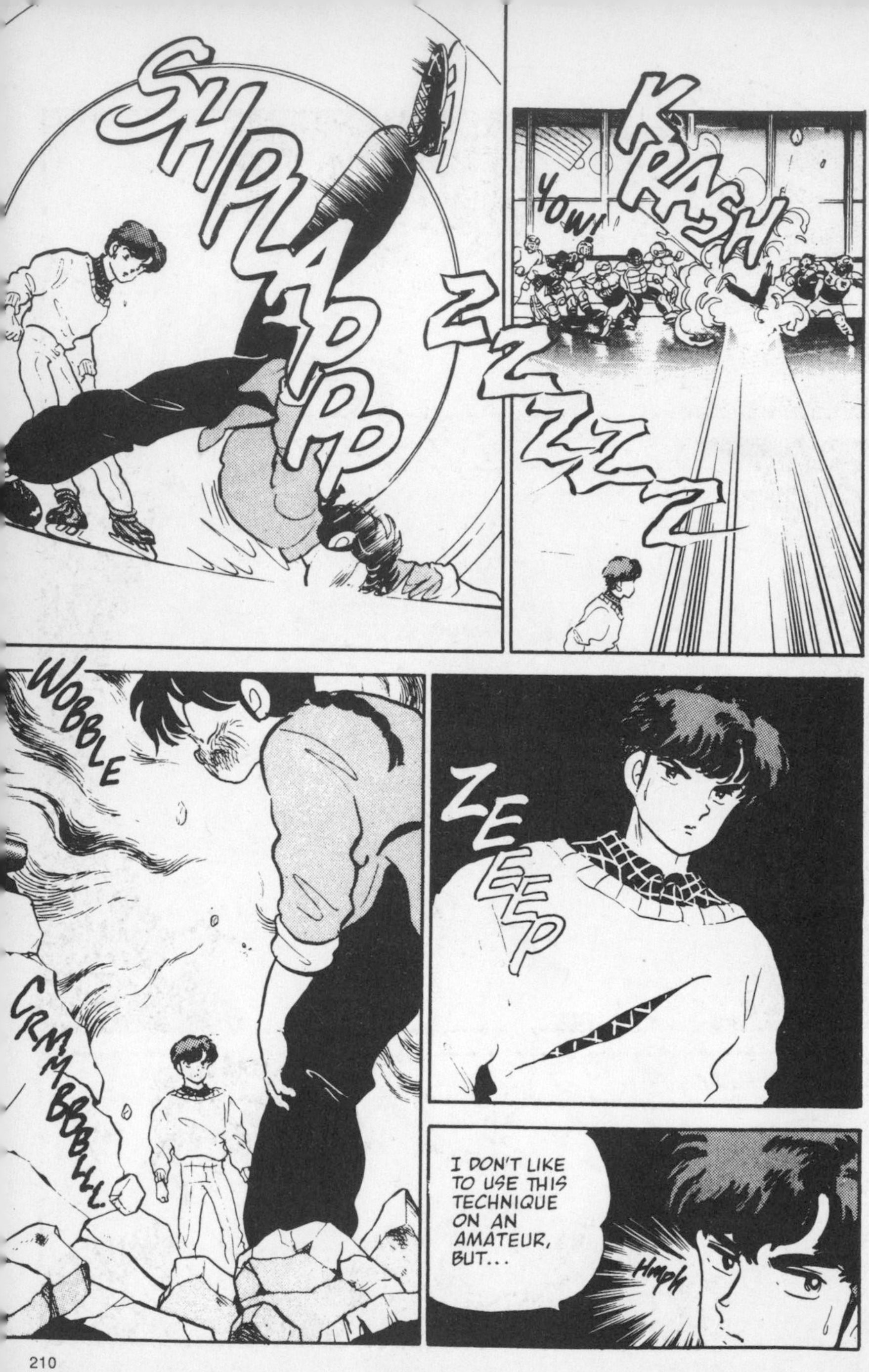
SHPLAPP
ZZZZZ
KRASH
YOW!
WOBBLE
CRMMBBBLLL
ZEEEP
I DON'T LIKE TO USE THIS TECHNIQUE ON AN AMATEUR, BUT...
Hmph

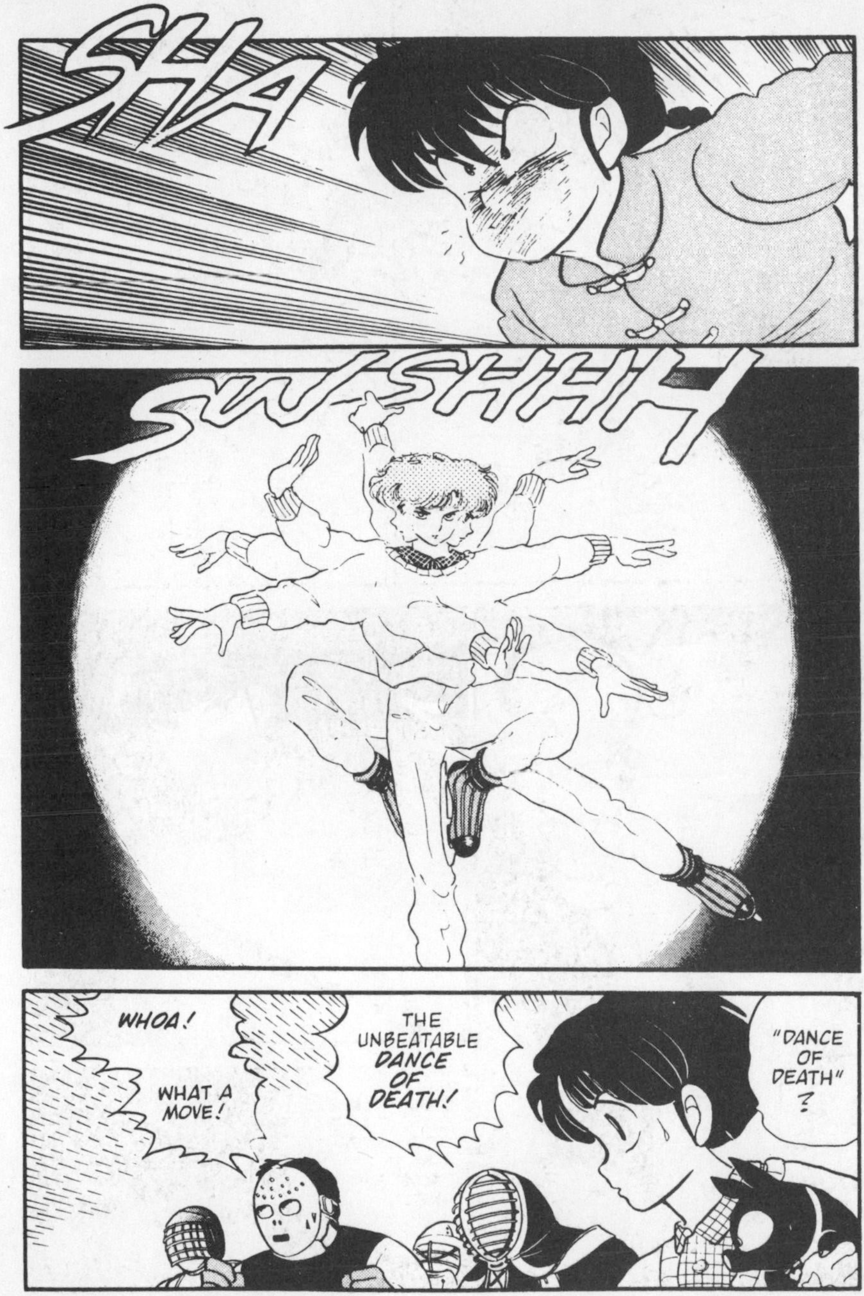
SHA
SWSHHH
WHOA!
WHAT A MOVE!
THE UNBEATABLE DANCE OF DEATH!
"DANCE OF DEATH"?

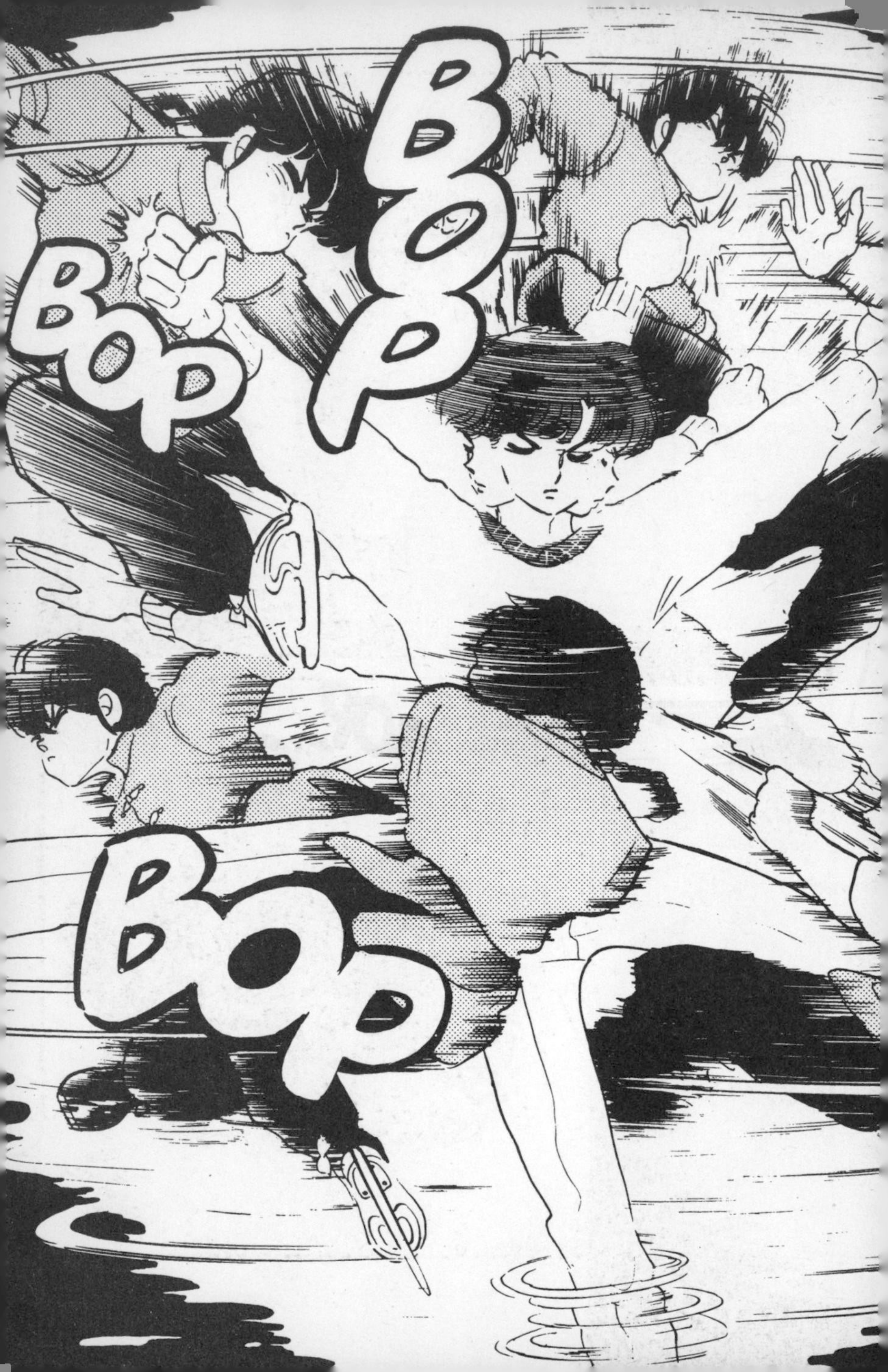
BOP BOP
BOOP
BOP

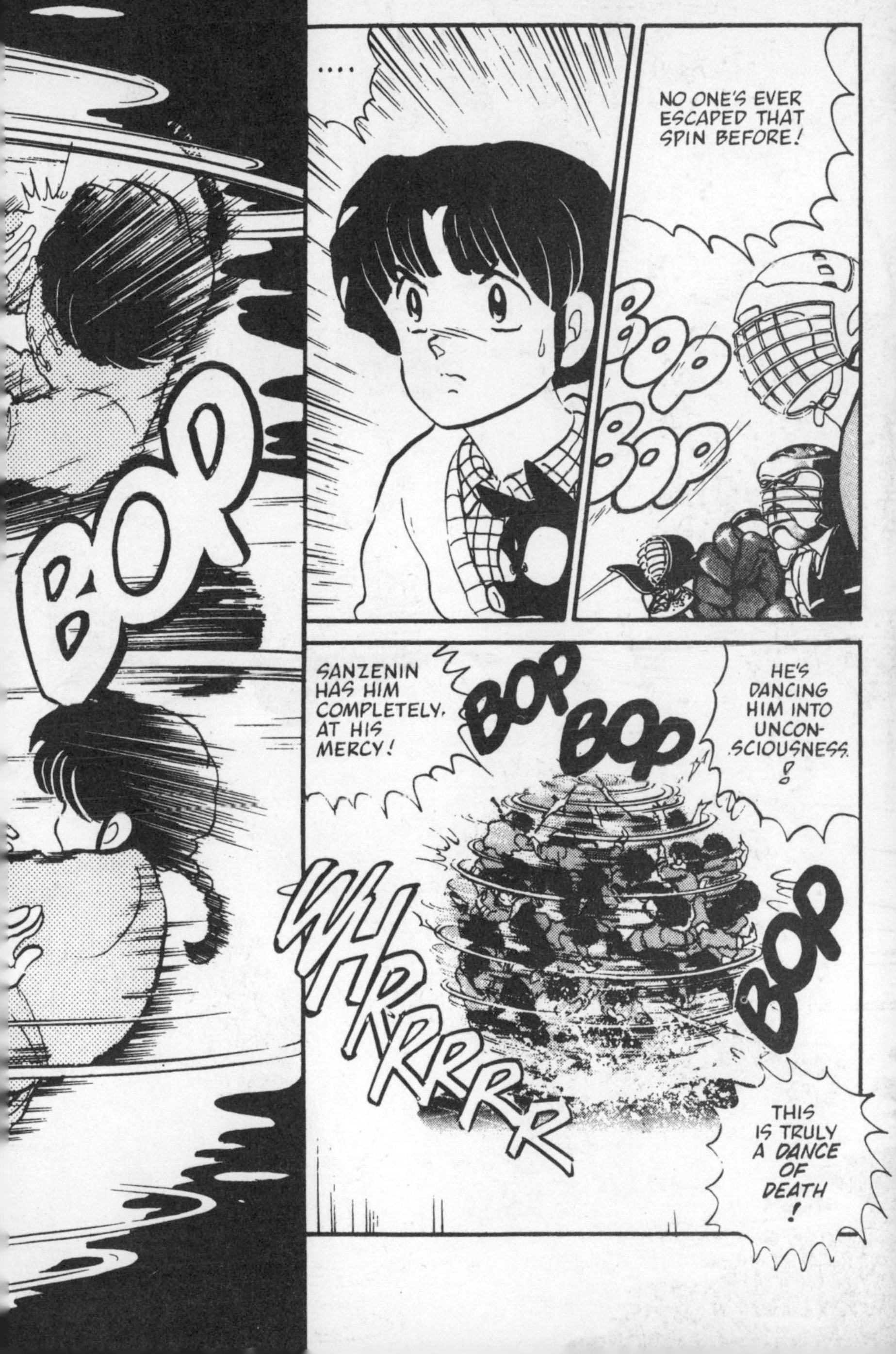
BOP
....
NO ONE'S EVER ESCAPED THAT SPIN BEFORE!
BOP
BOP
SANZENIN HAS HIM COMPLETELY, AT HIS MERCY!
BOP
BOP
HE'S DANCING HIM INTO UNCONSCIOUSNESS!
WHRRRRR
BOP
THIS IS TRULY A DANCE OF DEATH!

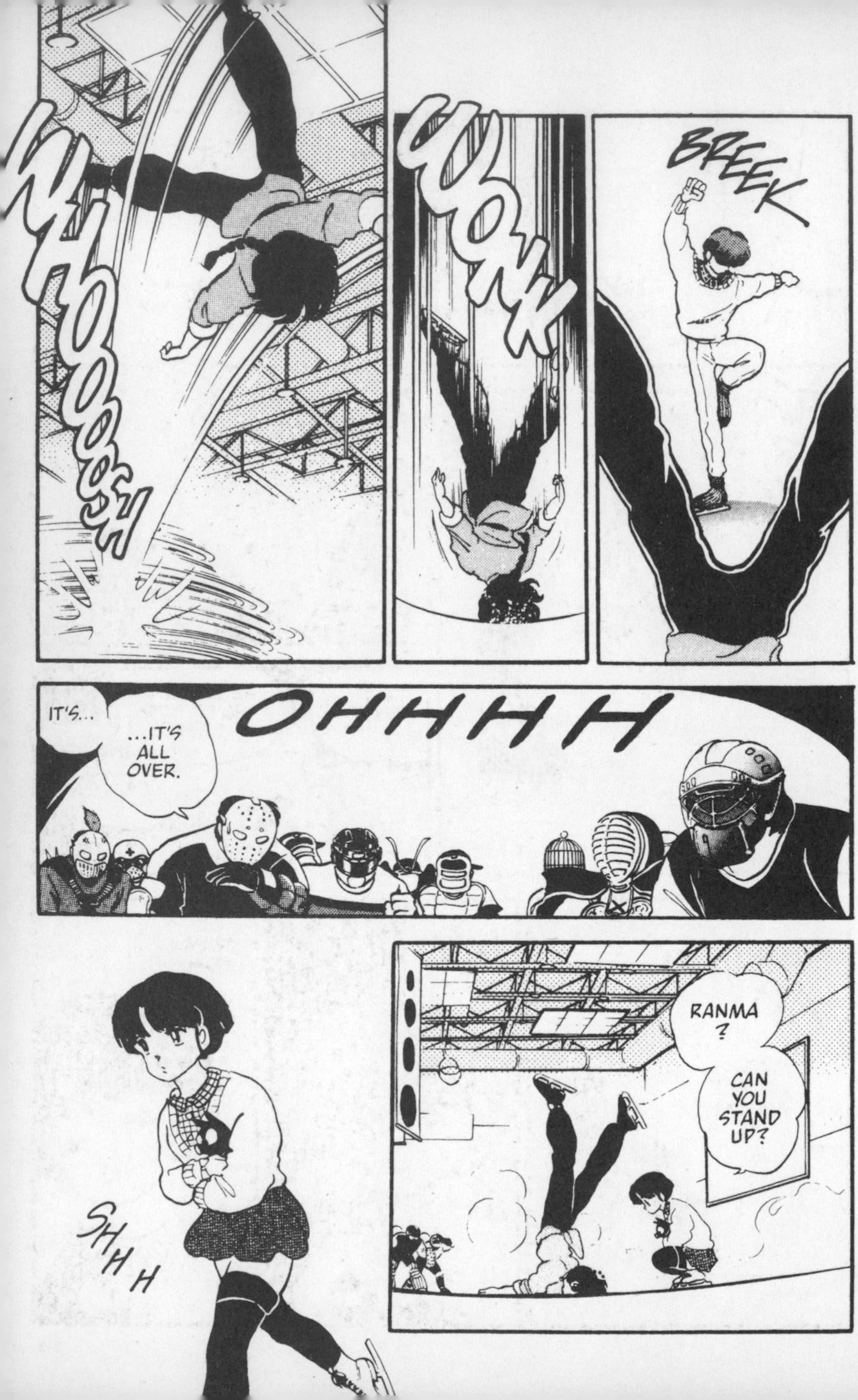
WHOOOOOSH
WONK
BREEK
IT'S...
...IT'S ALL OVER.
OHHHH
SHHH
RANMA?
CAN YOU STAND UP?

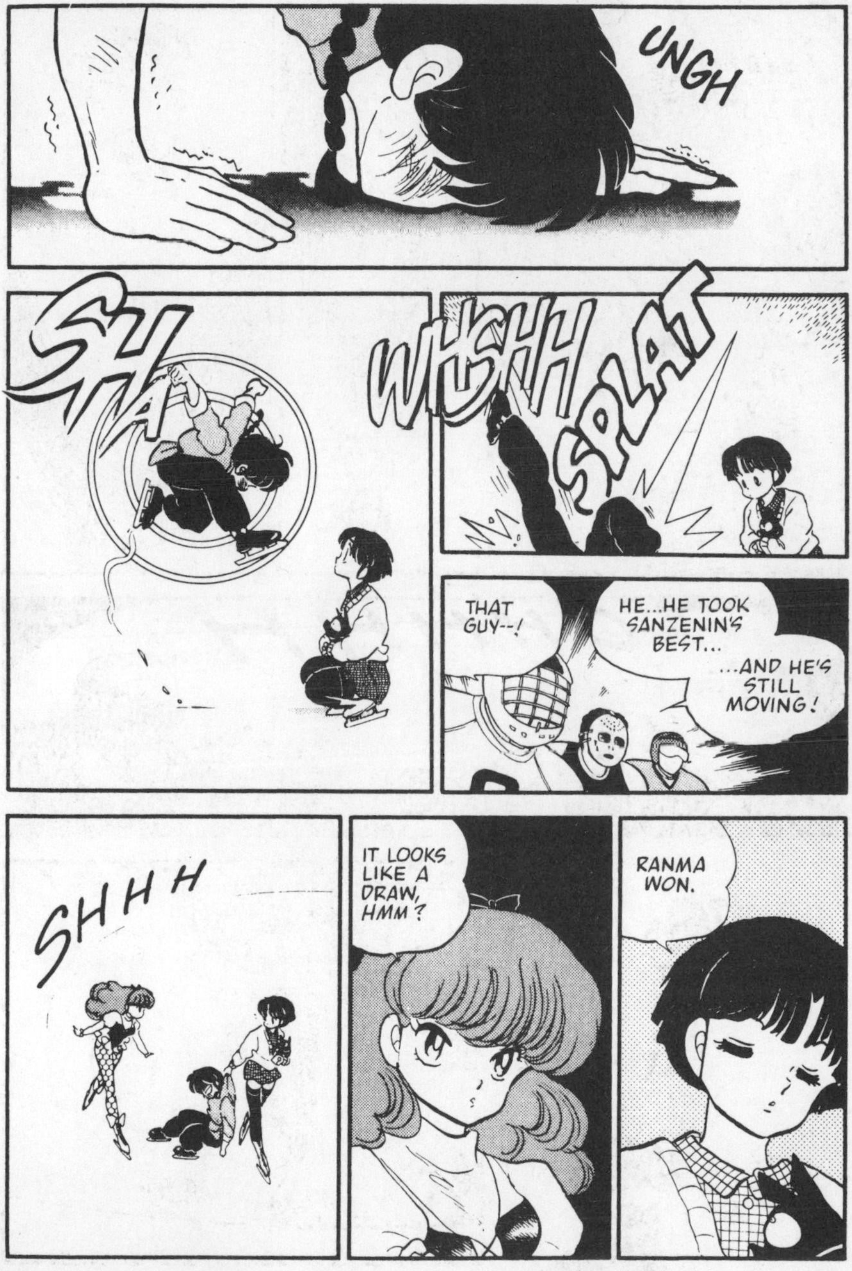
UNGH
SHA
WHSHH
SPLAT
THAT GUY--!
HE...HE TOOK SANZENIN'S BEST...
...AND HE'S STILL MOVING!
SHHH
IT LOOKS LIKE A DRAW, HMM?
RANMA WON.

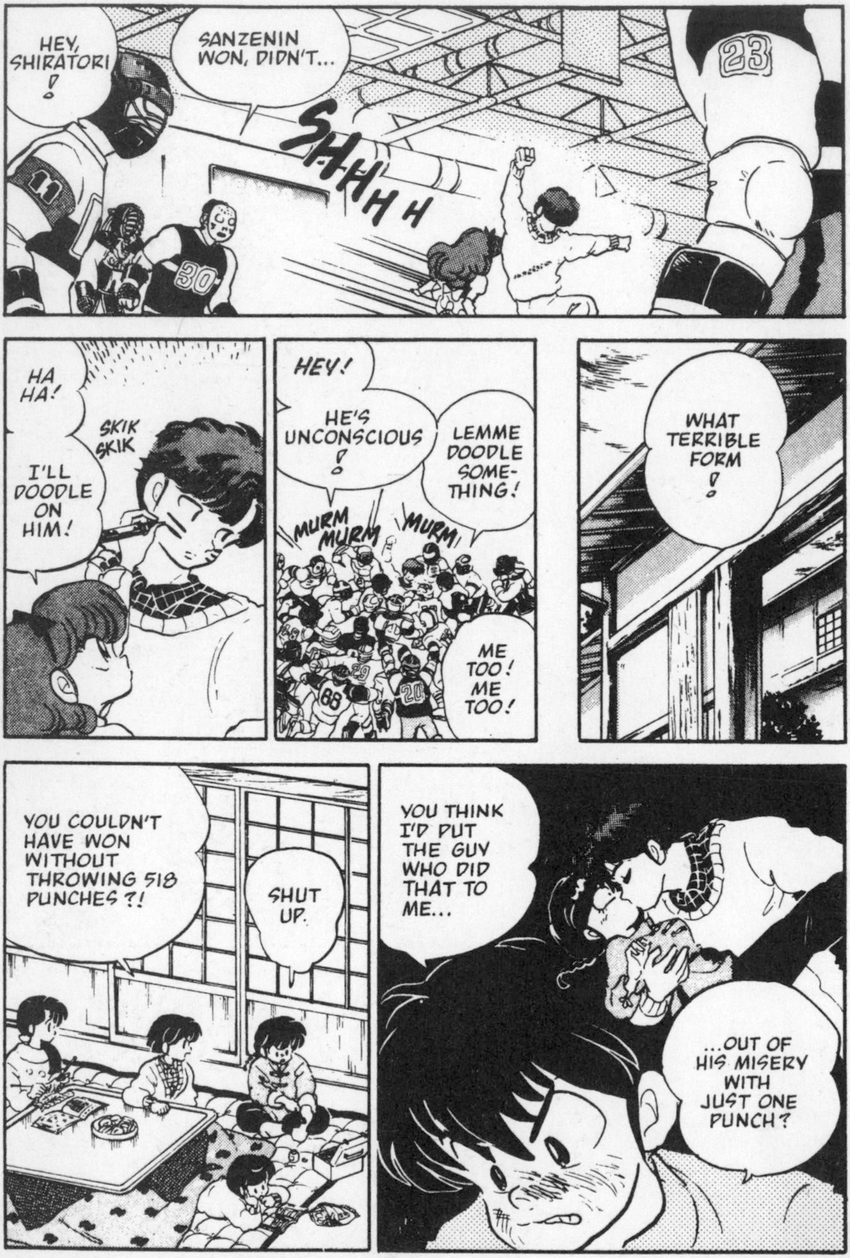
HEY, SHIRATORI!
SANZENIN WON, DIDN'T...
SHHHHHH
HA HA!
SKIK SKIK
I'LL DOODLE ON HIM!
HEY!
HE'S UNCONSCIOUS!
LEMME DOODLE SOME-THING!
MURM MURM
MURM
ME TOO! ME TOO!
WHAT TERRIBLE FORM!
YOU COULDN'T HAVE WON WITHOUT THROWING 518 PUNCHES?!
SHUT UP.
YOU THINK I'D PUT THE GUY WHO DID THAT TO ME...
...OUT OF HIS MISERY WITH JUST ONE PUNCH?

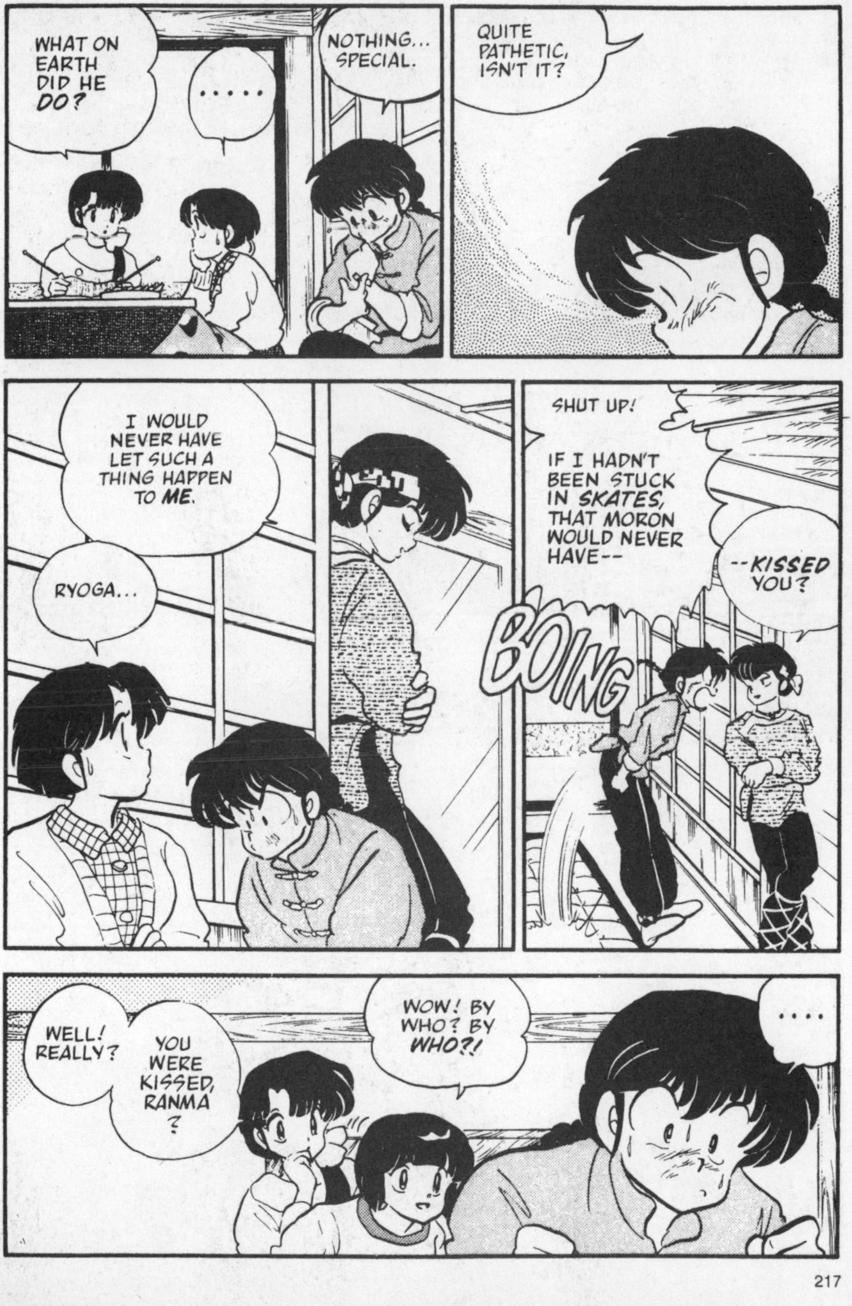
WHAT ON EARTH DID HE DO?
.....
NOTHING... SPECIAL.
QUITE PATHETIC, ISN'T IT?
I WOULD NEVER HAVE LET SUCH A THING HAPPEN TO ME.
RYOGA...
SHUT UP!
IF I HADN'T BEEN STUCK IN SKATES, THAT MORON WOULD NEVER HAVE--
--KISSED YOU?
BOING
WELL! REALLY?
YOU WERE KISSED, RANMA?
WOW! BY WHO? BY WHO?!
....

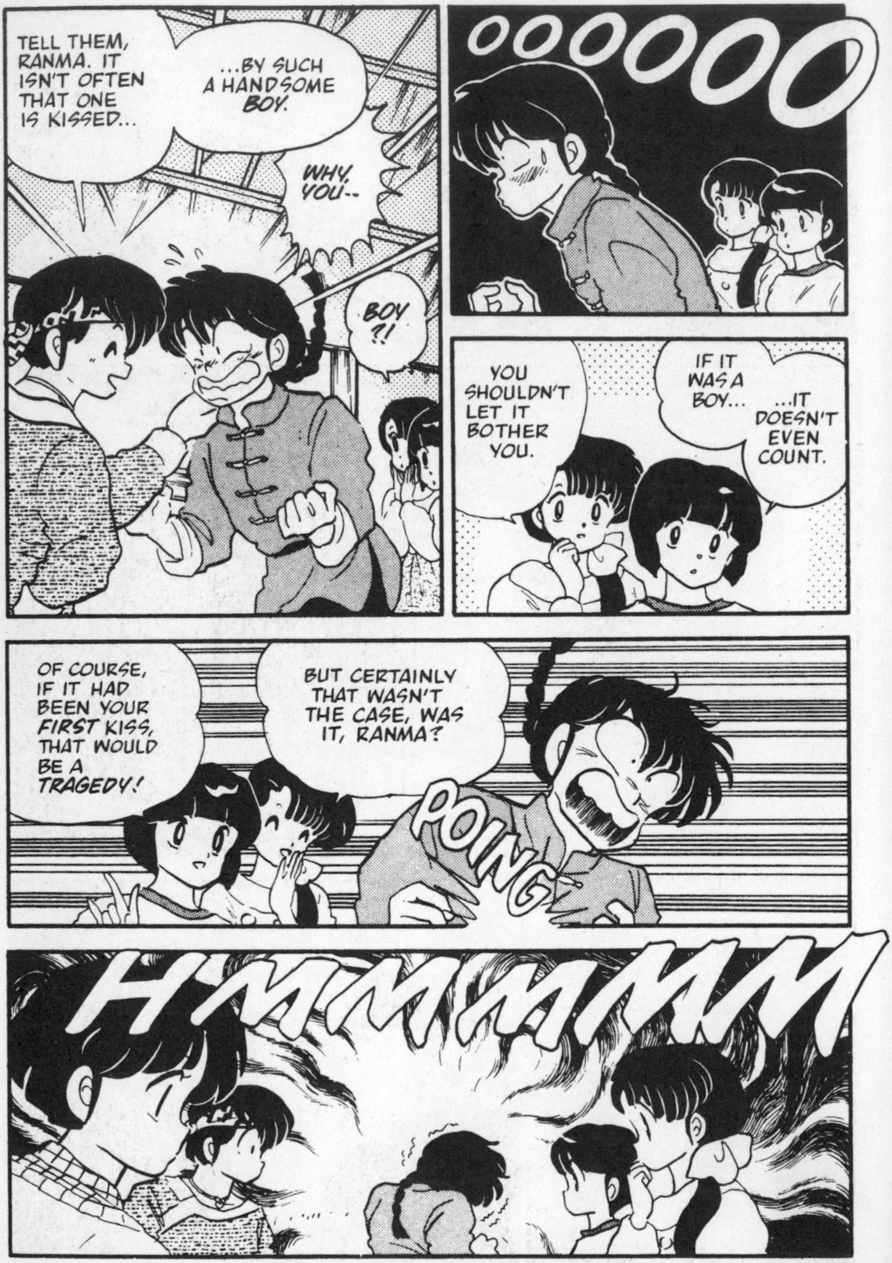
TELL THEM, RANMA. IT ISN'T OFTEN THAT ONE IS KISSED...
...BY SUCH A HANDSOME BOY.
WHY, YOU--
BOY ?!
OOOOOOO
YOU SHOULDN'T LET IT BOTHER YOU.
IF IT WAS A BOY...
...IT DOESN'T EVEN COUNT.
OF COURSE, IF IT HAD BEEN YOUR FIRST KISS, THAT WOULD BE A TRAGEDY!
BUT CERTAINLY THAT WASN'T THE CASE, WAS IT, RANMA?
POING
HMMMMMM

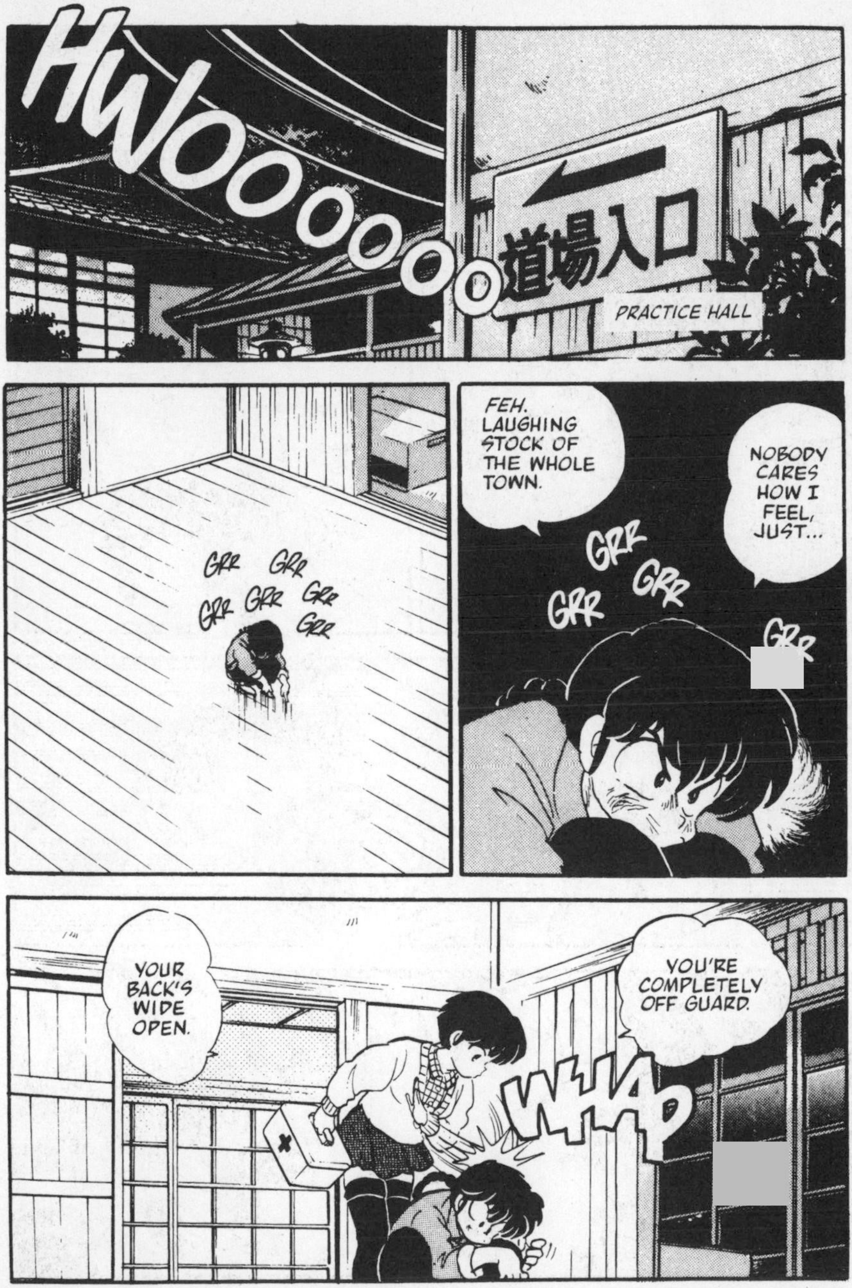
HWOOOOOOO
道場入口
PRACTICE HALL
GRR GRR
GRR GRR GRR
GRR
FEH. LAUGHING STOCK OF THE WHOLE TOWN.
NOBODY CARES HOW I FEEL, JUST...
GRR
GRR
GRR
GRR
YOUR BACK'S WIDE OPEN.
YOU'RE COMPLETELY OFF GUARD.
WHAP

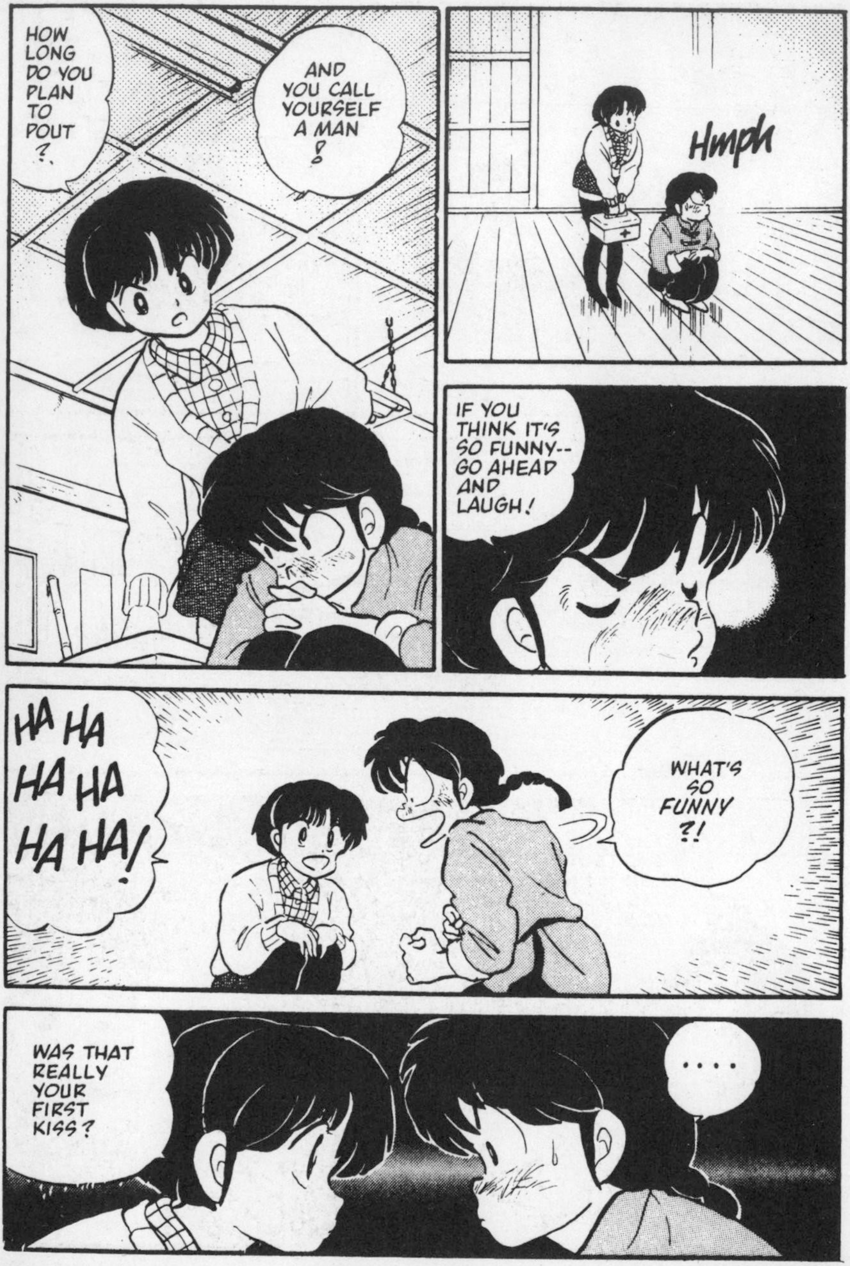
HOW LONG DO YOU PLAN TO POUT ?.
AND YOU CALL YOURSELF A MAN !
Hmph
IF YOU THINK IT'S SO FUNNY-- GO AHEAD AND LAUGH!
HA HA HA HA HA HA!
WHAT'S SO FUNNY ?!
WAS THAT REALLY YOUR FIRST KISS?
....

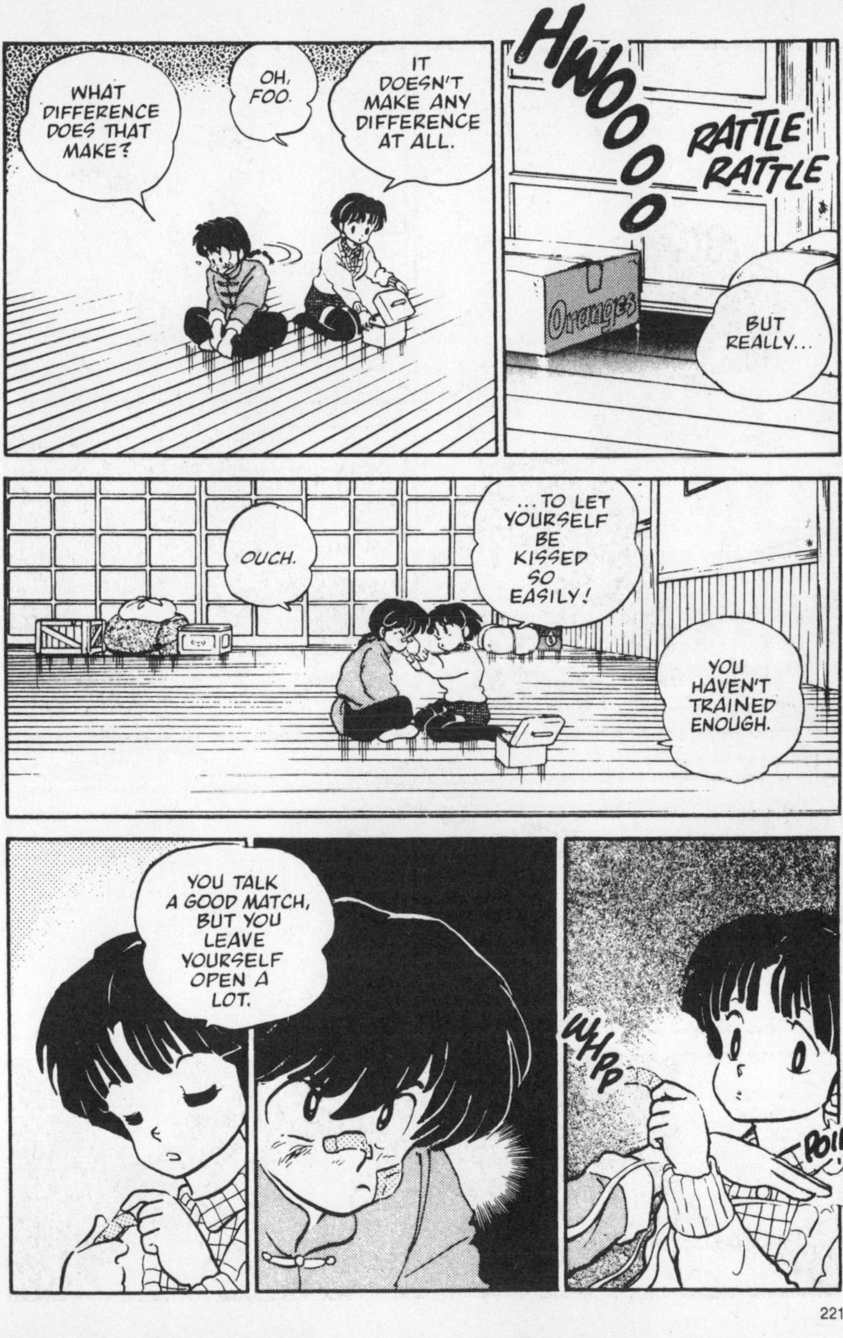
WHAT DIFFERENCE DOES THAT MAKE?
OH, FOO.
IT DOESN'T MAKE ANY DIFFERENCE AT ALL.
HWOOOO
RATTLE RATTLE
BUT REALLY...
OUCH.
...TO LET YOURSELF BE KISSED SO EASILY!
YOU HAVEN'T TRAINED ENOUGH.
YOU TALK A GOOD MATCH, BUT YOU LEAVE YOURSELF OPEN A LOT.
WHPP
POIK

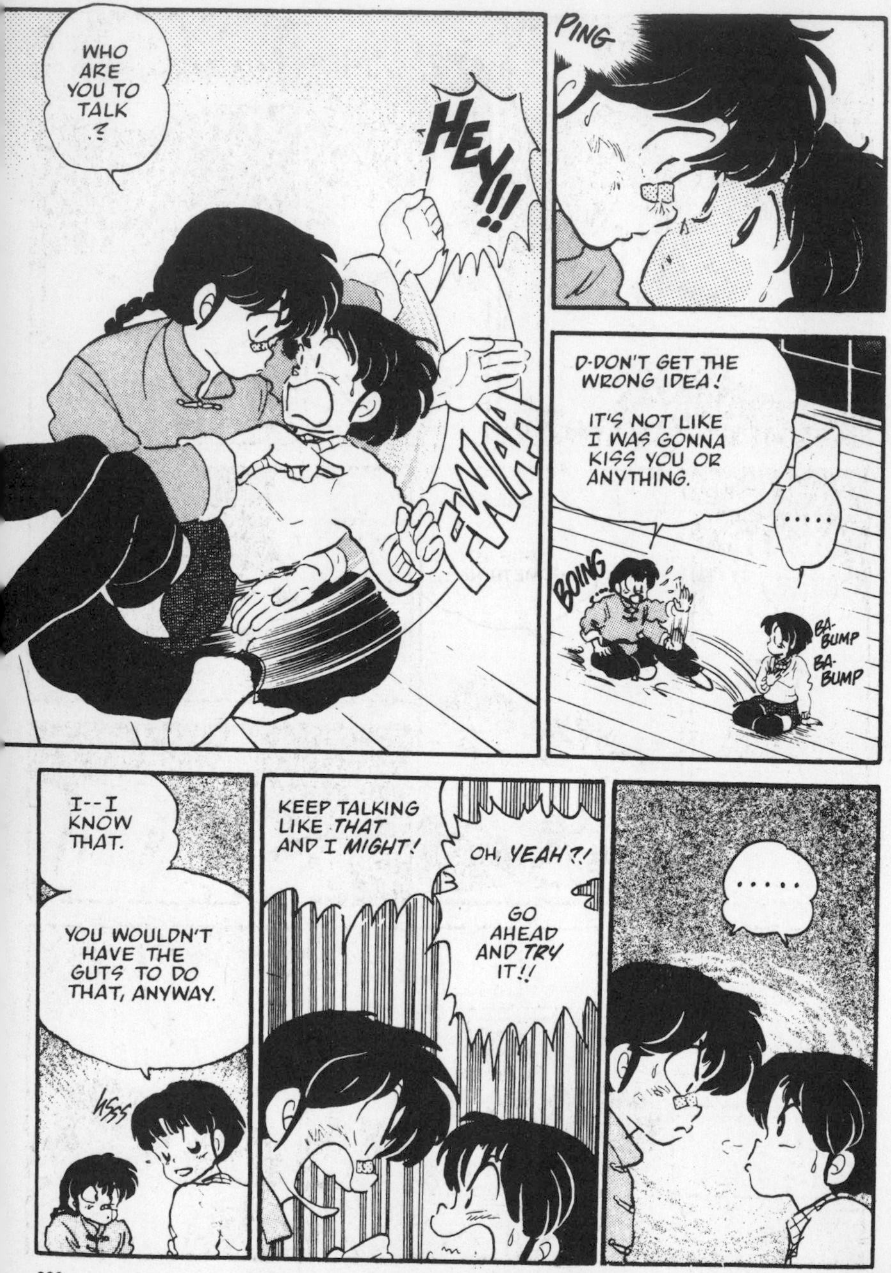
WHO ARE YOU TO TALK ?
HEY!!
FWAP
PING
D-DON'T GET THE WRONG IDEA!
IT'S NOT LIKE I WAS GONNA KISS YOU OR ANYTHING.
.....
BOING
BA-BUMP BA-BUMP
I--I KNOW THAT.
YOU WOULDN'T HAVE THE GUTS TO DO THAT, ANYWAY.
HSSS
KEEP TALKING LIKE THAT AND I MIGHT!
OH, YEAH?!
GO AHEAD AND TRY IT!!
.....

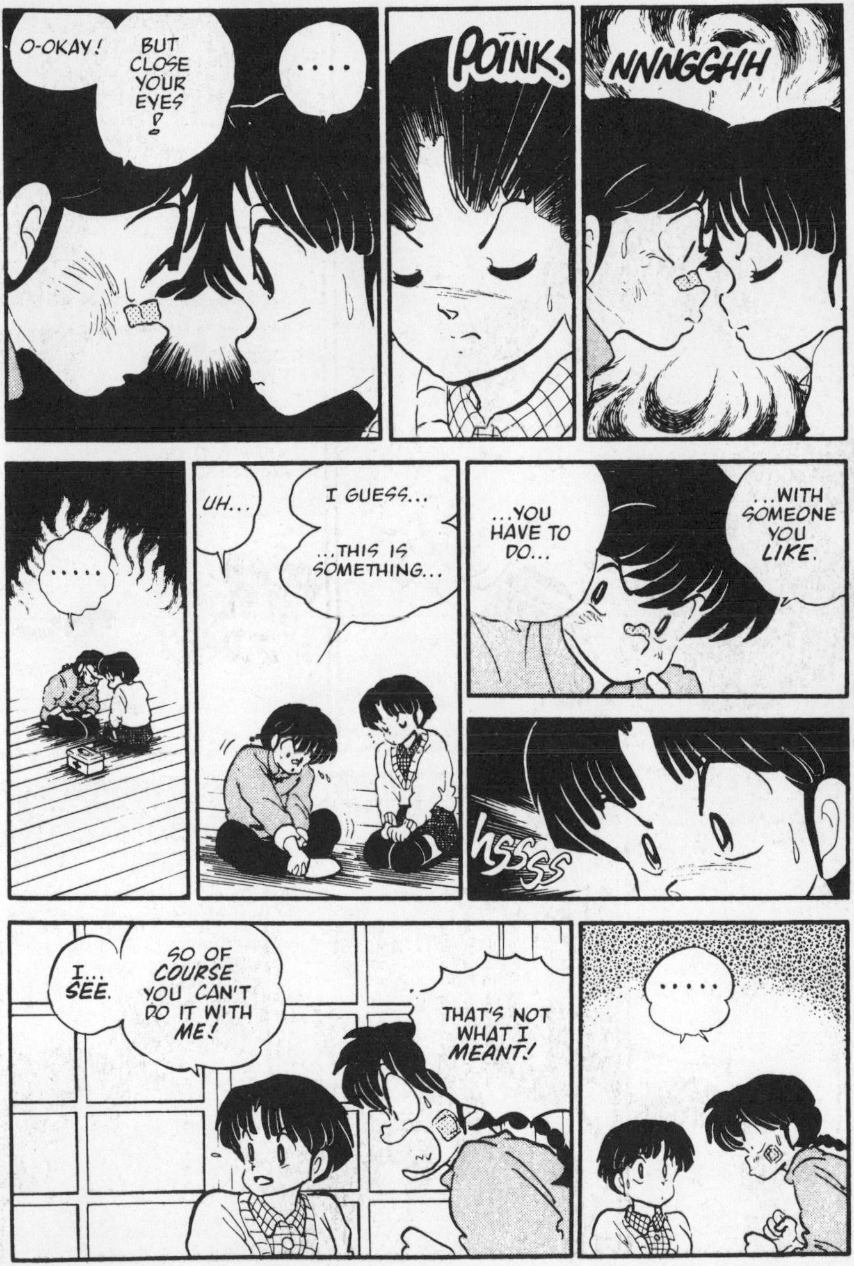
O-OKAY!
BUT CLOSE YOUR EYES!
....
POINK.
NNNGGHH
.....
UH...
I GUESS...
...THIS IS SOMETHING...
...YOU HAVE TO DO...
...WITH SOMEONE YOU LIKE.
hssss
I... SEE.
SO OF COURSE YOU CAN'T DO IT WITH ME!
THAT'S NOT WHAT I MEANT!
.....

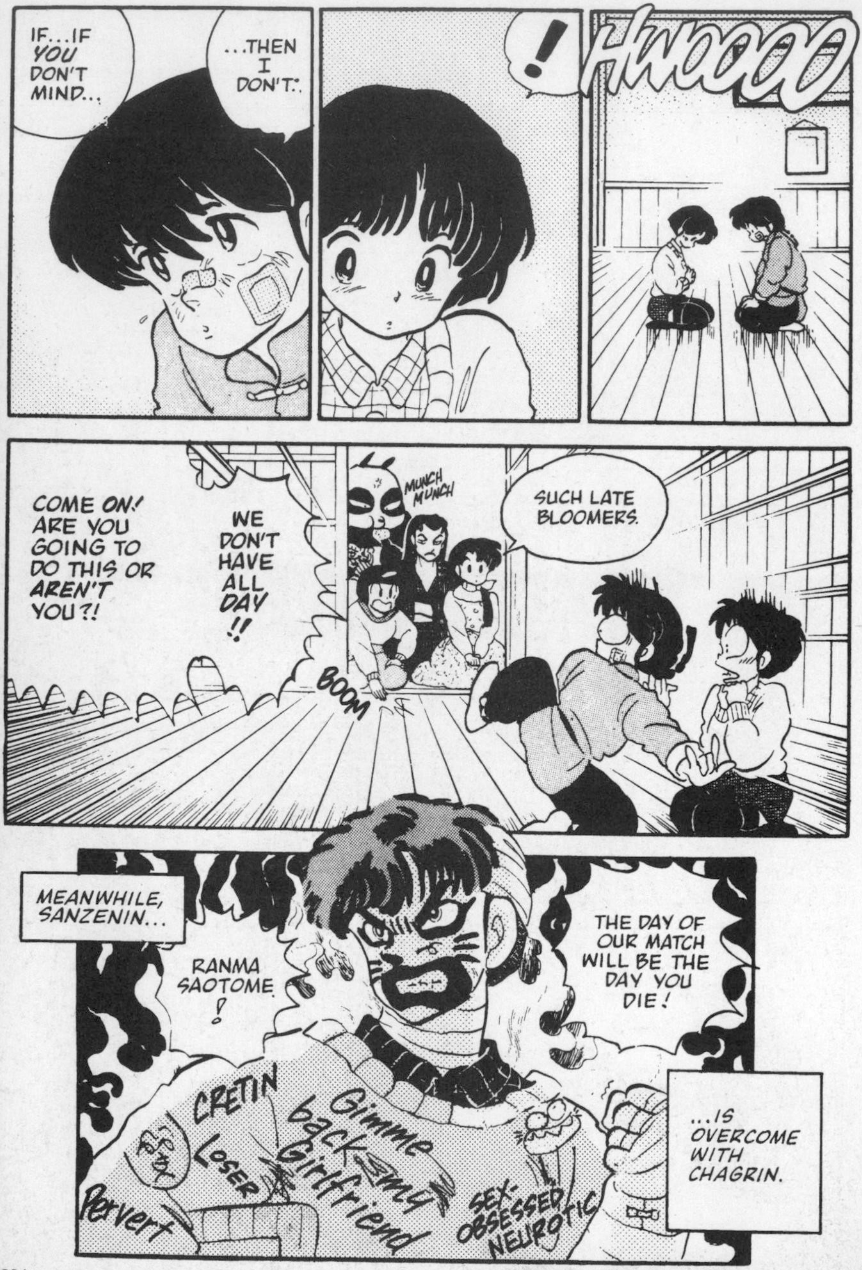

IF...IF YOU DON'T MIND...
...THEN I DON'T...
!
HWOOOO
COME ON! ARE YOU GOING TO DO THIS OR AREN'T YOU?!
WE DON'T HAVE ALL DAY!!
MUNCH MUNCH
SUCH LATE BLOOMERS.
BOOM
MEANWHILE, SANZENIN...
RANMA SAOTOME!
THE DAY OF OUR MATCH WILL BE THE DAY YOU DIE!
CRETIN
Gimme back my Girlfriend
Loser
Pervert
SEX-OBSESSED NEUROTIC
...IS OVERCOME WITH CHAGRIN.

TO BE CONTINUED

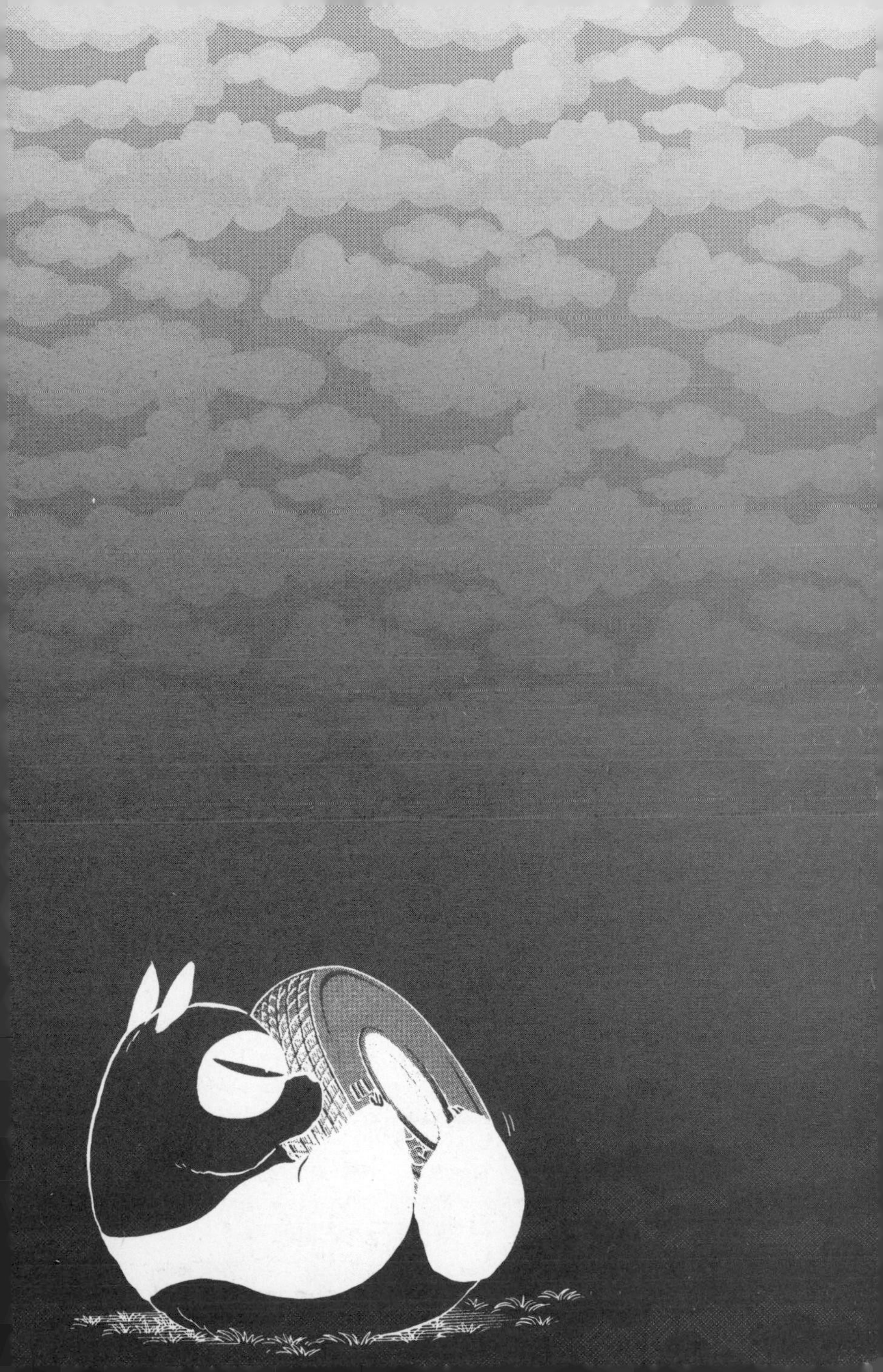

About Rumiko Takahashi

Born in 1957 in Niigata, Japan, Rumiko Takahashi attended women's college in Tokyo, where she began studying comics with Kazuo Koike, author of *CRYING FREEMAN*. She later became an assistant to horror-manga artist Kazuo Umezu (*OROCHI*). In 1978, she won a prize in Shogakukan's annual "New Comic Artist Contest," and in that same year her boy-meets-alien comedy series *URUSEI YATSURA* began appearing in the weekly manga magazine *SHÔNEN SUNDAY*. This phenomenally successful series ran for nine years and sold over 22 million copies. Takahashi's later *RANMA 1/2* series enjoyed even greater popularity.

Takahashi is considered by many to be one of the world's most popular manga artists. With the publication of Volume 34 of her *RANMA 1/2* series in Japan, Takahashi's total sales passed *one hundred million* copies of her compiled works.

Takahashi's serial titles include *URUSEI YATSURA, RANMA 1/2, ONE-POUND GOSPEL, MAISON IKKOKU* and *INUYASHA*. Additionally, Takahashi has drawn many short stories which have been published in America under the title "Rumic Theater," and several installments of a saga known as her "Mermaid" series. Most of Takahashi's major stories have also been animated, and are widely available in translation worldwide. *INUYASHA* is her most recent serial story, first published in *SHÔNEN SUNDAY* in 1996.

INUYASHA

Half Human, Half Demon—All Action!

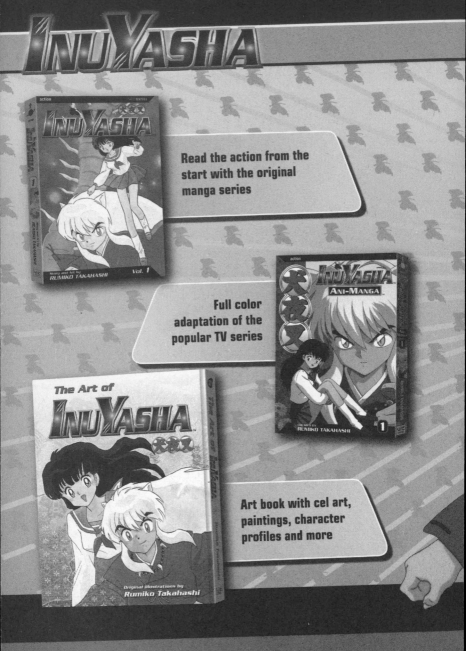

InuYasha

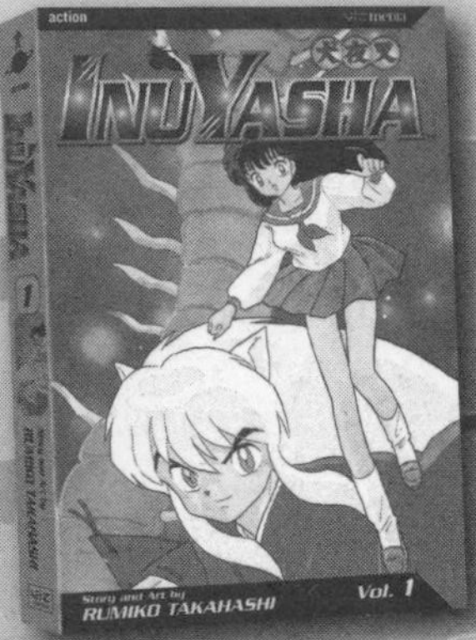
action
InuYasha
Story and Art by
RUMIKO TAKAHASHI
Vol. 1

Read the action from the start with the original manga series

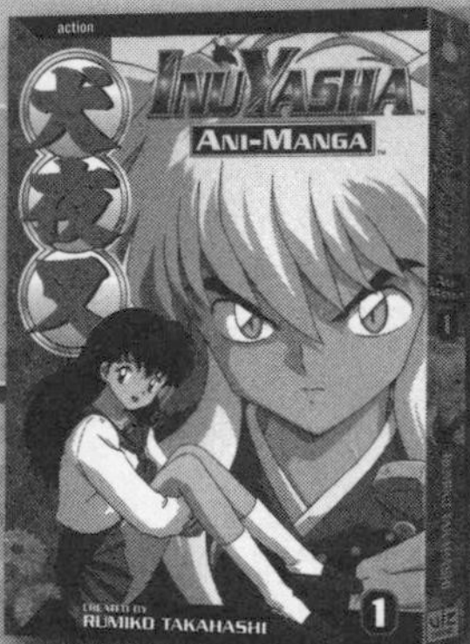
action
InuYasha
Ani-Manga
CREATED BY
RUMIKO TAKAHASHI
1

Full color adaptation of the popular TV series

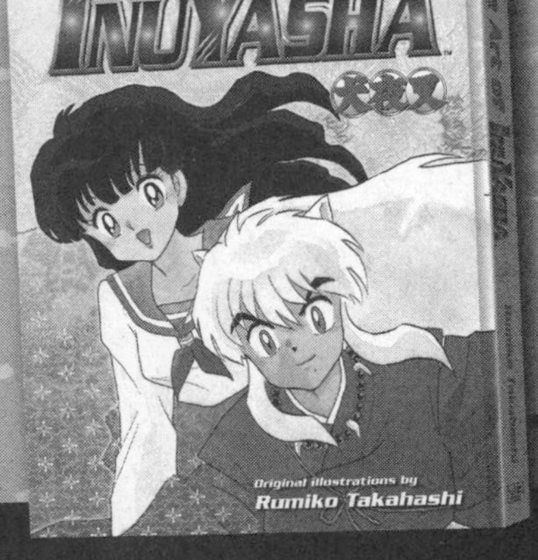
The Art of
InuYasha
Original illustrations by
Rumiko Takahashi

Art book with cel art, paintings, character profiles and more

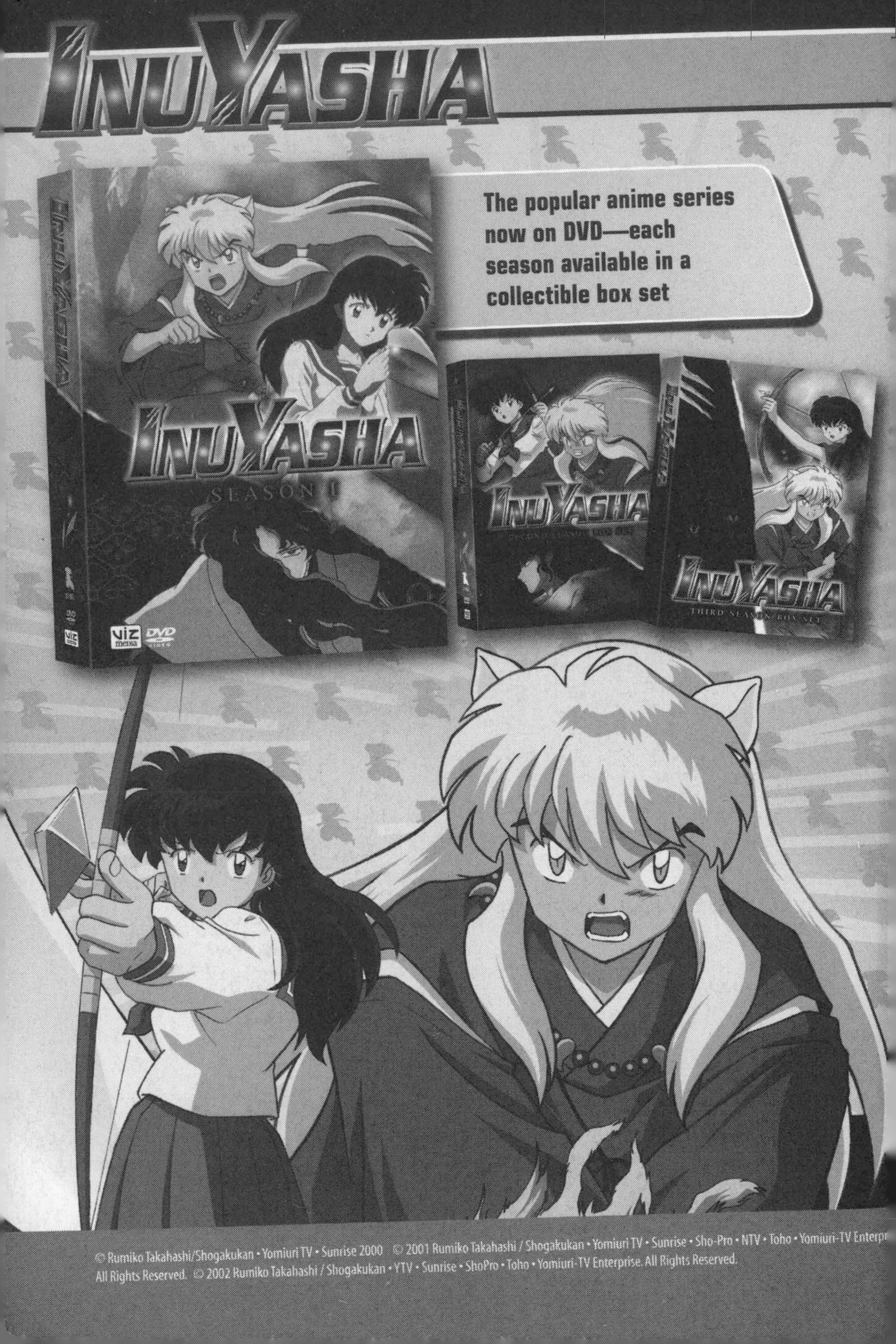
InuYasha
The popular anime series now on DVD—each season available in a collectible box set
InuYasha
Season I
InuYasha
InuYasha
Third Season Box Set

TV SERIES & MOVIES ON DVD!

See more of the action in Inuyasha full-length movies

www.viz.com
inuyasha.viz.com

LOVE MANGA?
LET US KNOW WHAT YOU THINK!

OUR MANGA SURVEY IS NOW
AVAILABLE ONLINE. PLEASE VISIT:
VIZ.COM/MANGASURVEY

HELP US MAKE THE MANGA
YOU LOVE BETTER!